Grandmother's Footsteps

Imogen Lycett Green was born in 1966 and read Ancient History and Archaeology at Birmingham University. She worked on the *Telegraph Weekend Magazine* for two years before taking up a Winston Churchill Travelling Fellowship to research this book. She writes for many publications including the *Daily Telegraph*, the *Daily Mail*, the *Evening Standard* and the *Oldie*, and is now working on her next book in Tanzania.

IMOGEN LYCETT GREEN

GRANDMOTHER'S FOOTSTEPS

A Journey in Search of Penelope Betjeman

PAN BOOKS

First published 1994 by Macmillan

This edition published 1995 by Pan Books
an imprint of Macmillan General Books
Cavaye Place London SW10 9PG
and Basingstoke

Associated companies throughout the world

ISBN 0 330 34394 7

1 3 5 7 9 8 6 4 2

A CIP catalogue record for this book is available from
the British Library

Typeset by CentraCet Limited, Cambridge
Printed and and bound in Great Britain by
Cox & Wyman Ltd, Reading, Berkshire

FOR MY MOTHER AND FATHER

Contents

CONTENTS

Acknowledgements

Firstly, I am indebted to all those friends of my grandmother in India who made me feel that I was their friend too: Alfred Wuerfel in Delhi; Paddy and Nita Singh in Manali; Panchok and Manbadur up the mountains; Christina Noble (though she was in London at the time) for letting me stay in her beautiful house in the Kulu valley; Boura Sing for looking after me there; David Sumsion, the architect, for being calm and making all the trek complications look simple. In Simla I thank especially Reggie and Mrs Singh, Mr N. K. Sharma, Mr B. R. Sharma, Sister Mary Margaret Lane at the Chelsea School for Girls, Mr O. C. Sud of Maria Brothers, the most interesting book shop in the world, Dr Laxman Thakur and Sri Goverdan Singh. I thank the Sharmas, especially Asha and Surinda, for having me to stay and for being so open-hearted about my grandmother.

In the south, half my thanks go to Dr Livingstone Soans, the pineapple farmer who made me feel like one of his family; the other half go to the last John, John Foster from Kettering, who welcomed me with open arms into his Christian haven in the Palni Hills, where I gathered strength for my journey home.

Back in England I owe an enormous amount to John Nankivell, whose teas are incomparable, and to Elizabeth Chatwin, who suffered my questions over several cups of coffee. I wish to acknowledge Ronnie and Judith Watson, who travelled with my grandmother on her final trip and without whose help and emotional support I could never have written the final chapter of this book. There are many others whose memories I have poached for my purpose – Ann Tomkin, Audrey Morris, Stuart Piggott, the late Johnnie Spencer Churchill to name but a few and I thank them all. Billa Harrod, saviour of Norfolk churches and best friend to my grandmother for over fifty years, pulverized local cod's roe in her pestle and mortar to make me homemade East Anglian taramasalata and while we ate it on toast she told me about Aldershot and afterwards; I thank her for her time and for her wonderful snowdrops as well.

I owe an enormous amount to Paul Betjeman, my uncle, who has given me permission to use my grandmother's letters and extracts from her writing.

I would never have got around to writing this book without the encouragement of Alison Nadel (now Nagle) and Hildegarde Serle, with whom I sat every lunchtime in the *Daily Telegraph* canteen, talking it through until, eventually, I left the Docklands to go to Delhi.

I never would have got to Delhi, however, without the Winston Churchill Memorial Trust, the incredible institution which enables one hundred people each year to go abroad to realize their ambitions. There are not words to describe the industry or the kindness of the Trust's staff – Anne Knocker, Rosamund Conner and Sir Richard Vickers, chiefly – who back each Fellow 100 per cent of the way and take a real interest in all the projects conducted under their auspices.

Without Gillon Aitken believing in this book, and in my ability to write it, it would never have been published and without Tanya Stobbs and Roland Philipps, my editors, I could not have managed to complete it.

Finally, personally, I owe the world to Kate and Caroline Valentine, who have both been driving forces behind me all the way, and to Sam Weinberg, who has been pacing me neck and neck while writing her own first book, and without whose keen sense of competition and good friendship I could not have got through all those thousands of words. My greatest love and thanks go to Gus Christie, who lost me to India for six months, then suffered a year of my batey temperament while I tried to write, and even after all that, asked me to be his wife.

AUTHOR'S NOTE: The quotations at the beginning of each chapter were extracted from a notebook of my grandmother's I found among her papers, in which she had written down, in no particular order, what she called her 'Random Thoughts'.

Introduction

PENELOPE BETJEMAN was often begged to write an autobiography, but she was humble enough never to begin. 'But Lady Betjeman,' publishers flattered her. 'Lady Betjeman, you lead such an interesting and varied life . . .' Even her friends encouraged her to write it, but she said no to all of them. She could not see the use of writing down the details of her past and handing them over for public scrutiny and, also, she couldn't think who would want to read about her past anyway for she assumed (on account of her own personal predilection) that most people would prefer to read about horses or India.

At the time of her death she had begun a book about her life with horses, which was to be a semi-autobiographical work with educational overtones (strong equestrian ones). She had written about five chapters. She also planned to write about her time in India from 1928 to 1933, before she married John Betjeman.

But my grandmother died on a Himalayan mountain in North India without completing either project. None of her family were with her, nor had they ever been to the place where she died. My mother says that she felt a huge force of strength flood into her, and that from the moment she heard of her mother's death she felt not so much a huge sadness as an extraordinary inner warmth, as though her mother had become part of her.

I just felt bereft. I had travelled around India with my grandmother in the previous year, when she was pushing seventy-five and I was just eighteen. We had set off in January more than a little wary of each other's close company, yet we returned in April partners to the core – in sickness and in health, for better for worse, in laughter and in tears. She had taught me not only the Devanagiri script, all the manifestations of Vishnu, the sculptural incarnations of the Hindu deities, all about Indian architecture, religion and society, but also about how to deal with my lot. I had been floundering on the far side of a sulky adolescence and she pulled me together.

So when she died I grieved quietly, wondering how on earth I was going to manage without her guiding presence in my life. I thought the gap would close but it didn't – it sat there gaping. Just as I had begun to value her she had gone, and I felt I needed just a bit more of her; I felt I hadn't had quite enough of her.

So I decided to go to India. I thought if I retraced our joint expedition I would capture her once again; I thought I might be able to absorb her from the people she knew and the places she loved. Also it seemed to me that I should let other people know about her too. Her brave and indomitable spirit was worthy of more than being forgotten on a mountain. I wanted to write about her so that other people could be inspired by her as I had been (and hear her jokes). With this dual purpose in mind I planned my journey.

I would visit the Buddhist *gompa* in Rampur before staying with the Panchayat's family in Nirmand; I would settle in Simla and find Mr Sud and Mr Singh who had exchanged temple theories with my grandmother and bargained with her over books; I would dine with the octogenarian German ex-cultural attaché in Delhi and lunch with the Sisters of Charity at their mission; I would take the train past the mosaic-filled palaces of Datia and Gwalior; I would look in on the Maharajah of Orccha in his mock Victorian bungalow where I had come down with fever before; I would take the southern express to Bangalore and go to the zoo; I would watch the buffalo racing in Kanara and converse with the Jain Swamiji in his monastery at Sravana Belgola; I would witness a Hindu festival at Udupi and take a rickshaw to Moodbidri for family life with Dr Livingstone Soans on his pineapple farm. Finally, I would go to the Palni Hills above Madurai in southern-most Tamil Nadu where I would find peace at Goodwill Children's Village. I would absorb my grandmother from all these things and then I would write about her. It was not going to be a biography (for she would have hated that) but a summoning up of her spirit. At least that was the aim in mind.

It was my mother who suggested that I make a detour to Khanag, where Penelope had died, to place an engraved stone there in her memory. My mother had commissioned the stone to be made in India, under the auspices of Sir Robert and Lady Wade-Gery (the then British High Commissioners in Delhi who had been friends with my grandmother). She had composed the words to be inscribed on the stone together with Billa Harrod, my grandmother's oldest friend, and the late Bruce Chatwin, the writer who was also her friend.

Once the stone was finished in Delhi a date was set for it to be conveyed to Khanag, but as can be the Indian way, it never got there. For six years the proposed pilgrimage to Khanag had been unavoidably delayed or postponed each time due to monsoon outbursts or earthquakes or diplomatic problems or warring factions or rioting in the regions. Once the Commissioner's party came within twenty miles of the place with the stone on board but a landslide forced them to turn back.

When I reached the mountains the stone was lodged in a friend's house in Manali (it had made it as far as 6,000 feet up) and it seemed as if it was waiting for me to put it in place on behalf of our whole family. Waiting also were a number of people who had been devoted to my grandmother. In fact Manali was full of former friends of my grandmother's. They too thought it was about time her stone reached the spot where she had died and they thought it only fitting that I had come all the way from England to do the job.

It was a tricky thing to muster the transport, the mason, the porters, the rations and the organization to get that stone to Khanag, and it took ten days or so of negotiating in Manali to bring it about. Nothing would have been possible without Captain Padum Singh, who put my plans in motion, and his plans may easily have fallen apart without the clear mind of his wife Nita. Together we pulled it off.

We wrapped the stone in straw and bound it with hessian rope and we held it in the back of the jeep which dropped us off in Banjar. I walked for three days up and over the Jalori Pass which leads out of the Kulu valley and southwards to the Sutlej Gorge, with Panchok, a Zanskari, and Manbadur from Nepal, who acted as my porters and guides.

On the third day Paddy Singh brought a mason up the mountain with the stone and Panchok, Manbadur and I walked for four hours to meet his entourage (for it was impossible to reach Khanag by road). Manbadur carried the stone on his shoulders to the shaded site we had chosen, and the mason from Banjar began mixing cement.

All the villagers from Khanag came to watch and helped to gather stones for the plinth on which we would set the stone. Most of them remembered Lady Penelope, the Englishwoman who used to ride through their village. Those who remembered her, recalled her death in the village and were proud that she had died with them. They brought stones to the pile just as they had gathered wood for her funeral pyre six years before.

It took all day to build the plinth to the right height and it was dusk by the time the mason from Banjar set the stone on top (at a 45° angle, so that one reads the writing as if standing before a lectern). Paddy, Panchok, Manbadur, the mason, Mensingh, the villagers and I stood back in hushed awe. We said some prayers and then moved away. The inscription reads:

In memory of Penelope Valentine Hester Betjeman, writer and traveller, born 14th February 1910, wife of John Betjeman Poet Laureate, and daughter of Field Marshal Lord Chetwode, Commander-in-Chief of the Indian Army 1930–35 and of Lady Chetwode. On 11th April 1986 she died in these hills she had loved so long.

CHAPTER I
Earlier on:
The C.-in-C.'s Daughter

'When I went out to Delhi, my first impressions were of tan tracks and topis; the tan tracks were used by horsemen and the topis were worn by them.'

MY GRANDMOTHER sailed to India for the first time in 1928 under sufferance. Ordered by her mother to board ship, the precocious eighteen-year-old was a sulky passenger who knew nothing of Asia. She thought India would be a barren, philistine continent with no place for culture on its map. For culture to her then, as an impassioned student of history of art, meant Michelangelo and Giotto, Roma, Firenze, Paris, the Renaissance and the eclectic treasures of civilized Europe. She turned her retroussé nose up at the East.

Penelope Valentine Hester Chetwode was born on St Valentine's Day, 1910, in the Cavalry Barracks at Aldershot. 'How could I help but have horses in my blood?' she said.

Her father, Philip Chetwode, was a soldier who went straight from school into the 3rd Militia Battalion of the Oxfordshire and Buckinghamshire Light Infantry, before he was gazetted to the 19th Hussars in 1889 (and assumed command of the regiment nineteen years later). In 1916 he took over the Desert Column based in Egypt and he was instrumental in preventing the Turks reaching the Suez Canal. They say his greatest achievement in that war was his Palestinian plan of campaign which was put into action by Lord Allenby.

When the Great War broke out, the 19th Hussars were stationed in York. 'I remember a young officer coming into the garden when we were having tea and announcing that war had been declared,' Penelope told me. The regiment was soon sent to the front and Penelope, her mother, Hester (who was known as Star) and her elder brother Roger moved to London. One year later Roger was sent to Summerfields prep school at St Leonards-on-Sea and afterwards Penelope only saw him in brief moments during his holidays.

Following in her heroic father's footsteps, Penelope longed to learn to ride, but her mother said it was too expensive to ride in London and so her only chance came when she went to stay at Wilton House, near Salisbury, with her cousins, the Herberts. There she was strapped into a basket chair on top of a pony and led about by a groom, but that did not suit her at all and she was relieved when her Chetwode grandmother (a horse-lover as well) treated the determined six-year-old Penelope to lessons at Smith's famous riding-school in Cadogan Mews. At last she was learning to ride properly, like her father.

The First World War interrupted the lessons, however, for Star dispatched her precious daughter, together with Zellie, her French governess, to Anglesey to stay with her maternal grandparents, to avoid the Zeppelins. Her grandfather, Colonel Robert Stapleton-Cotton, who had been struck by lightning when trekking in South Africa – and raced about, paralysed, in a wheel chair, knitting and ordering his two gardeners about – had an Egyptian donkey, which Penelope was allowed to drive in a green coster-cart. Progress was slow with the donkey, though, and Penelope was provoked into extreme jealousy by a pair of sisters who lived near by and would drive over in their governess cart pulled by a fast-trotting Shetland. She determined to own her own turn-out one day.

When Penelope was eleven years old and the war was over, her father was appointed Commander-in-Chief at Aldershot, and the family went to live in the barracks in Hampshire in an ugly red-brick building called Government House. Home from the war, her father was overjoyed to find his young daughter so keen to get into the saddle and he bought her a grey pony which Penelope was allowed to ride alongside him. When he came riding, they were accompanied always by at least one aide-de-camp (ADC) and by a trouper corporal carrying a lance; her father rode a handsome dapple grey charger called Brington about which the head groom, who always put his aitches in the wrong place, used to say, 'The hold grey's very hartful.' So artful was Brington, that he opened his field gate with his teeth one wet summer evening, and led all the ponies on to the two grass tennis courts that Lord Chetwode manicured with an obsessive pride. The C in C claimed his courts were second in perfection only to Wimbledon and he examined them regularly and personally removed any weed with a special tool. His rage knew no bounds when he discovered the hoof marks in the morning and the courts took a year to recover and were never quite the same again.

When her father was busy Penelope often went out driving with Moonbeam, a pony which belonged to her best friend Willhemina ('Billa') Creswell. Billa's stepfather, General Strickland, was also stationed at Aldershot, which meant that she and Penelope grew up in the barracks together, and they forged a loyal friendship then which was to last for the whole of their lives. After her best friend's death, Billa (now Lady Harrod, widow of the great economist, Sir Roy Harrod) wrote in *The Daily Telegraph*, 'When she tired of her own pony, she used to "borrow" ours; she attached this poor animal to a hand-cart in which she placed her unfortunate schoolfriend, Catherine Inge – daughter of the Gloomy Dean of St Paul's – who was very promptly thrown out and the pony galloped away. We wondered why Moonbeam was so tired the next day.'

In term time, Penelope and Catherine Inge were educated together at St Margaret's, Bushey, Hertfordshire, a £40-a-term establishment founded originally for clergy orphans by Sir Reynold and Lady Rod.

'Penelope arrived one term after me, and I was asked to be nice to her,' recalled Sylvia Coke (now Sylvia Combe), a fellow pupil at St Margaret's. 'But she was a leader from the first day. She was a great innovator of games and entertainments; six of us started a garden, and planted miniature trees, and I think we won the garden cup. She used to come and stay at home where there was a pond and we'd pretend to be explorers in the boat – her imagination was very strong.'

Sylvia remembered Penelope being better dressed than the rest of the girls – in a felt hat and silk stockings – and she used to get mouth-watering parcels from her mother full of chicken and jellies and mutton pies.

'She was much cleverer than me,' continued Sylvia. 'She always used to say I was a late developer. But then she was quite advanced. Later she talked about "getting the urge". For those days, I suppose she was quite a naughty girl.' In between the gardening hours and the midnight feasts, all the Bushey girls managed to get their school certificates, and the luckier ones were sent to Europe, to 'be finished'.

Penelope and Audrey Talbot, her favourite cousin and daughter of Lord Ingestre (now Audrey Morris), were sent to Mademoiselle Hennequin's Academy for Young Ladies, a finishing school outside Tours in France, where they learnt to fence. Later they moved on to Italy, where they stayed with a Mrs L'Estrange, who had flaming red hair and a temper to go with it.

Their teacher was Irish and called herself Mrs, though the whereabouts of her husband were unknown – if, indeed, she had had one at all. She had been employed by a family called the Christie-Millers (who were friends of the Chetwodes) as a governess, and when her charges were grown, she had an idea to start a select school in Italy at which she would teach Italian and History of Art. The idea was put forward to the mothers of eight girls 'of good family', of whom Penelope was one, and in the autumn of 1927, the mysterious Mrs L'Estrange escorted her chosen charges across the continent and installed them in the Villa Malatesta, a house she had rented outside Florence.

'Mrs L'Estrange liked Penelope a lot,' recalled Anne Tomkin, formerly Anne Glossop, who was another of the eight girls. 'She was a wonderful teacher if you wanted to learn, although she had strong likes and dislikes and she could be cruel if you didn't come up to scratch.' Anne Tomkin says that Penelope was enthusiastic about the art and obviously intelligent. She learnt Italian much faster than the rest of the group, and quite often annoyed the other girls in class with her quick wit; she called Savonarola 'Old Soapy Boy' and invented a nickname for all the other characters in history of art about whom they were supposed to be learning.

Penelope was also full of practical jokes: on a visit to Assisi, home of St Francis where many a miracle, mirage and vision has taken place, the seventeen-year-old Penelope suddenly halted the rest of the girls on their guided tour. 'Stop!' she said. 'I can hear voices! Wait! Wait! I think I'm going to be visited!' And with great drama she closed her eyes and began murmuring as if in a trance. She sat on a bench and leant back her head and spread her arms: 'I can *see the Lord!*' she exclaimed, and a beatific smile spread across her face. The other seven girls stood stunned and frozen in their footsteps, until, a good few visionary minutes later, Penelope opened one of her eyes, and then the other, and then leapt up from the bench with glee. 'Ha! Fooled you!' she chortled and danced off to examine the sculptures, leaving the other seven young ladies of good family bemused and far behind her.

Jokes aside, Penelope was profoundly affected by her sojourn in Italy under the tutelage of Mrs L'Estrange. 'She knew a tremendous lot about the Renaissance,' Penelope said a long time afterwards. 'It was through her that I learnt there were other things in life besides horses.' Penelope developed what she called a mania for the Renaissance and she thought she would write a book on Giotto. 'But it wouldn't have been very interesting,' she later said, 'for all that's known about him can be written on a postcard.' And though at Assisi she had larked about and invented her own visitation, she there encountered the mystic side of Roman Catholicism for the first time – a religious experience which set her thinking, quite seriously, about God.

Meanwhile, her father had left Aldershot when he was made ADC General to the King in 1927, and he had moved his family to

London, into a house that used to belong to the painter, Sir Lawrence Alma-Tadema, in Grove End Road, St John's Wood. Here Penelope returned in her holidays from Italy, sometimes bringing Anne Glossop or her cousin Audrey along with her.

The house was what Anne described as 'lavish'. There was already a swimming pool there when the Chetwodes moved in and they built a tennis court. Lady Chetwode was hospitable, recalled Anne, and gave endless parties. She also kept holy Ganges water about the house in saucers and had a bowl of the stuff on the drawing-room mantelpiece to encourage 'good feeling'. Penelope had her own sitting-room decked out boldly with clashing coloured cushions and bright blue curtains, where she would lie about with her girlfriends.

By the time she returned from Italy in the summer of 1928, Penelope's brother Roger had left Eton and was already up at Oxford, and her father had accepted a prestigious Indian posting, as Chief-of-Staff to Lord Birdwood. Penelope remained in London with her mother, obliged as she was – though it was against her already unconventional nature – to go through the motions of 'The Season'.

'She was terribly naughty and very sexy,' recalled a contemporary, Johnnie Spencer Churchill. Though he later married four times this nephew of Sir Winston Churchill fell in love with Penelope at first sight, when they met a dance in 1928, and wrote about her in his autobiography, *A Crowded Canvas*, (though he disguised her identity with a pseudonym):

My most important distraction at Oxford, however, was my first big romance, [he wrote]. 'The young lady in question became an extremely important person in my life. We met at Lord Wimborne's home, Wimborne House, behind the Ritz. It was a lavish, fabulous dance, the entire house lit by candles. And there, most delectably, with very dark eyes and an intelligent snub nose, was Sophie – the name I shall give her to spare her blushes.

The chapter goes on:

> I fell for her at once. Her mother did not like the look of me at all, and as much as said so. But Sophie and I started to go around together. We frequently went to the opera at Covent Garden. Then we would have dinner. I would sketch her in idealistic poses [he was an exhibited artist and muralist] and talk about Art with a capital A. It was all great fun and terribly high brow, though I sensed danger in that she was much more mature than I. My humble talents were really no match for hers.

After Oxford, Johnnie Churchill worked at Steinways, where Penelope went to watch him play the organ. 'I played a Bach overture for her and she was terribly impressed,' he said. Keen to impress her further he hired the Albert Hall for £5, and played more Bach for her there. Johnnie said, 'The hall was empty and I made a terrific noise, and I think she was even more impressed by that. By 1929 we were deeply in love and I proposed to her several times, but she wasn't sure. She said she would think things over.'

They were carefully chaperoned by order of Lady Chetwode, and had difficulty in ever meeting alone, but, said Johnnie, 'We went as far as we could go.' He was allowed to visit her in her sitting-room at Grove End Road at teatime. 'Oh, she was tremendously attractive. She could be bossy and she was quite serious about her art history. She was stubborn and she was wilful. She got what she wanted. I don't think she wanted to marry anyone at that point, but that didn't put me off.'

Penelope was taken on a cultural tour of Europe by a chaperone and the desperate young Johnnie took off after her with his friend, James Lees-Milne. They followed Penelope through the continental cities incognito. 'She knew, of course,' he says. 'But her chaperone never found out. She'd arrive in Rome or Venice or Florence and we would book into the same *pensione*. She'd give her chaperone the slip outside the Uffizi and we would wander through Florence alone.

'She led me through the riches of Europe. Jim and I would have a table on the other side of the restaurant and meet her eyes behind the back of her chaperone. We made secret assignations. It was intensely exciting. I'd sit three rows behind her in a concert and she'd know I was there but we would not be able to acknowledge each other. I was crazy about her.'

Sylvia Combe, who accompanied Penelope to Europe, told a slightly different story: 'We were with Nanny, you see, because in those days one simply didn't go about with young men. We introduced Johnnie to Nanny pretending that we'd just met him and what a coincidence it was that we should find so presentable a gentleman at our pensione. But Nanny wasn't taken in for a minute. In fact she was very upset, because she hated to think what Lady Chetwode might think if she found out. She said she would only continue to chaperone us if Penelope wrote home saying that Johnnie was there too. When we returned, we were quite nervous of meeting Lady Chetwode. She was a formidable mother and she could be quite frightening. But all she said was:

"Penelope, you are deceitful."

"Oh Bim," (she called her mother Bim), "Oh, Bim," she said, "I thought I was jolly nice to write and tell you!"

And what could Lady Chetwode say to that? Penelope had her mother wrapped around her little finger.'

Back in London, Johnnie stepped up his urgency and called regularly on Penelope at Grove End Road. 'I'd walk across the park from Kensington to St John's Wood, and the porter would always open the door when I tapped twice. I came so often we had a code, so I didn't have to be announced every time. Penelope could come down the stairs to meet me alone.'

Penelope's mother began to fear for her daughter's chastity. She liked the impetuous Johnnie well enough, but she did not want her daughter to rush into marriage with the first young man she met. With her husband now Chief of Staff to a field marshal in India, Star thought it undesirable that the distinguished soldier's daughter should be dallying with a dilettante (by his own admission) in Kensington Gardens. Arrangements were made to ship their wilful daughter to 'Injer', far away from Johnnie Churchill's amorous intentions; Johnnie was devastated and Penelope was furious.

THE EARNEST young art historian had loathed the repetitive rounds of deb dances and tea parties in London, the niceties and chatter about frocks or prospective beaux, and Anglo-Indian society in the late twenties promised to offer similar entertainments. As the only daughter of General Lord Chetwode, Chief of Staff, who was soon to be made Commander-in-Chief of the whole Army in India (a post he accepted in 1930, after which he was gazetted Field Marshal in 1933), Penelope was placed on a pedestal before she had even disembarked ship.

When she actually stepped out on to the Apollo Bunder at Bombay and walked through the Gateway of India, the grand triumphal arch erected to commemorate the landing of King George V and Queen Mary in 1911, battalions of her father's willing aides vied for her attention.

'My first impressions were of tan tracks and topis,' she said. 'The tan tracks were used by horsemen and the topis were worn by them.'

Neither the horsemen's gallant manners nor their handsome smooth-cheeked faces pleased Penelope. 'I went out to India as an incurable highbrow,' she said. 'I never was really social; I loathed coming out in London. At dinners I always used to get subalterns. Subalterns' conversation was frightfully dull, because I only liked people who talked about Giotto, and none of them had ever heard of Giotto.' Penelope refused to look at any Indian art for three months.

By the time Miss Chetwode arrived in India, the British had moved their centre of Government from Calcutta, in the East, to Delhi, the site of seven ancient cities on the northern Indian plain. The architects Sir Edward Lutyens and Sir Herbert Baker had built their 'conspicuous example of town planning': at the Delhi

9

Durbar in 1911, the King-Emperor, George V, had said: 'It is my desire that the planning and designing of the public buildings to be erected be considered with the greatest deliberation and care so that the new creation may be in every way worthy of this ancient and beautiful city.' The building of the 'new creation' was held up, however, by the First World War, and the sparkling new city was not inaugurated until 15 February 1931. Penelope was at her parents' side for the inauguration.

During the winter season, the Chetwodes resided at the spanking new Teen Murti House, designed by Lutyens. The building later became the residence of Nehru, the first Prime Minister of India after 1947, and is now the Nehru Memorial Museum. The C.-in-C. kept a punctilious schedule, a printed copy of which was handed to the members of the household each morning.

A normal day began with an early morning ride, and after a full breakfast, it progressed with various inspections, official luncheons, audiences and diplomatic dinners. 'His Excellency' was required to travel about across the country (which he did in some style by private railway carriage) to fulfil official engagements in other cities. In December and January 1932-33, His Excellency was in residence at Government House in Calcutta. His timetable for 30 December 1932 went like this:

8.00 A.M......Rehearsal for the Proclamation Parade (Military Secretary and Captains Maynard and Battiscombe will attend – Khaki Drill Order)

10.30 A.M.....His Excellency the Commander-in-Chief will inspect 15th Lancers (at Stables)

11.45 A.M.....His Excellency, accompanied by the ADC in Waiting, leaves to be present at the opening of the All-India Institute of Hygiene by His Excellency the Viceroy.

1.30 P.M......Mr. A. Yusuf Ali, CBE, ICS (Retired), has been asked to Lunch.

3.40 P.M......His Excellency, accompanied by the ADC in Waiting,

leaves to attend the Final of the Indian Polo Association
Championship and will present the cup to the Winners.

8.22 P.M......His Excellency, accompanied by Miss Mackenzie, Miss
Anderson and two Aides-de-Camp in Waiting, leaves to dine with
Their Excellencies at 'Belvedere' and will afterwards attend a
Dance at the Unceremonials Club.

When dinner was not at 'Belvedere', His Excellency and Lady
Chetwode took Miss Chetwode to dine with the Maharani of Cooch
Behar at Woodlands, or otherwise they entertained at home. The
Chetwodes were famous for the quality of their kitchen, and they
took their chef and his assistants with them wherever they went.

The menu was expected to feature European dishes, for
otherwise visiting Indian dignitaries would have been offended. To
speak the English language was to show how sophisticated you
were; to appreciate the English food reaffirmed the level of your
sophistication. Yet, however Westernized a potential guest may
have been, Indian rituals and feast days, religious observances and
ceremonies often upset dinner party plans: 'My friend, Thank you
for kind invitation to enjoy an At Home to be given by their
Excellencies the Commander-in-Chief and Lady Chetwode on 5th
October,' wrote the Rani of Koti State, 'but as I and the Tika
Saheb [her husband] both will be keeping fast that day in
connection with Durga Puja I am very sorry that none of us shall
be able to avail of the happy aforesaid party.'

But the Chetwodes' purpose in India was not purely social.
During his appointment as C.-in-C., my great-grandfather set in
motion what was called the Indianization of the Indian Army. Up
until 1932, the army had been run entirely by British officers,
trained at Sandhurst and shipped out to take command over battalions of Indian sepoys. Yet the coming of Indian independence
from British rule meant that changes had to be made in the system;
a nationwide force of Indian officers needed to be trained up to lead
their own men, and it was with this aim in mind that the Field

Marshal founded the Indian Military Academy at Dehra Dun in 1932. His successful officer training establishment, the equivalent of the officer academy at Sandhurst, still takes in cadets today.

While her devoted husband was engaged in his work, Star took every opportunity to explore the unknown East which lay about her. Not for her were the dainty tea parties and ladies' lunches which satisfied most British wives. Whenever there were ADCs to spare, and her presence was not needed at Teen Murti, or at Government House in Calcutta or to play hostess at their official summer residence, Snowdon, in the Simla Hills, Lady Chetwode was organizing expeditions.

There was a certain freedom in her position, so high at the top of the British Indian hierarchy, which allowed her to take leave from station, in a way that other army wives, duty bound to stand by their husbands, were unable to do. Also, without a doubt, she had an adventurer's spirit in her which exceeded most of the women of her day. Born in another time it is likely she would have climbed mountains and swum seas and written brilliant books about her travels. Instead, she took her daughter on some spirited adventures.

On their way out to India, in August 1928, Star had taken Penelope to Poland for a month. They stayed with Star's friend Joy Markham, who had married Count Raczinski (who later became Polish Ambassador in London). Penelope wrote: 'It was paradise after the boredom of deb dances as everyone had horses galore, farming was completely unmechanized, and the country people drove chestnut ponies in pairs to light four-wheeled wagons. The Raczinskis' house had been burnt down in the war, but we stayed in a roomy cottage on the estate and rode for hours in the foothills of the Carpathians.' But it was not merely horses that led Penelope into her enthusiastic eulogy of the Polish expedition.

Miss Chetwode and her mother were invited to stay at a country house called Krasyczyn, in north-west Poland, where there was a house party of over twenty people and enough horses in the stables to mount any of the guests who wanted to ride. But

Penelope's attentions were lured in another direction. In the evenings after dinner, the girls were all taken into the drawing-room by their mothers and grandmothers and aunts to play Halva, while the young men played bridge with the older guests in another room. 'I was thought terribly fast because I sat flirting on the stairs with Andrzej Zamoyski,' wrote Penelope. 'He was devastatingly attractive and all the young ladies of the party, including myself, were hopelessly in love with him.'

The male members of the Zamoyski family were said to possess mesmeric powers and were sometimes sent for by the doctors in the local hospital to calm patients before operations, or even sometimes to hypnotize the patient in place of an anaesthetic. Penelope fell easily under his spell: 'Certainly when we played ping-pong together – and I fancied myself as rather a good player – Andryej mesmerized me to hit the little balls up to the ceiling and sideways onto the walls instead of onto the table.'

Polish princes lingered on in her mind even after Penelope had spent several months in India. In an attempt to distract her daughter Star took her to Burma, and at another time, she spent two months touring the Dutch East Indies. Lady Chetwode and Miss Chetwode would be accompanied by members of her husband's household, and the party was always welcome at official residences in capitals of every nation. At Singapore they stayed at Government House; a night was spent at the British Consulate in Medan. They hopped about in KLM aeroplanes when they toured Java and Bali, and for a South Indian foray to Trivandrum and Cochin they seconded her husband's private railway carriage. Star was no stay-at-home.

Penelope thought she was still in love with Europe, however. She had left her heart with Johnnie Churchill, and cultured Counts in Poland appeared to be more her style than Nawabs or Maharajahs of Mysore. She had arrived determined to hate it all, and she hated herself for growing to love it so quickly.

The first agreeable aspect of life in India to appeal to Penelope was the regular appearance of the horse in her daily agenda. In the early morning she could ride with her father across the Delhi Plains. They would linger in the Lodi Gardens, bewitched by the tombs, or circle the Qutub Minar. 'Father' bought Penelope an Arabian horse of her own to ride. He was a wiry little horse only 14.2 hands high and originally imported from Mosul in Arabia, to race in Bombay. He was so snowy white (though among horsey folk one must say grey) that she called him Moti, which means Pearl in Hindi.

There was a myth about Arabian horses then, that because they were indigenous to the desert where there are neither fences nor hedges, they could not jump. Penelope put paid to all that and entered Moti into many a hunter trial competition where he sailed over upright fences on the hard ground. She also hunted for two seasons with the Delhi foxhounds.

The field consisted of soldiers and civil servants who had to get to their offices at a reasonable time, so the meets were held at 5.30 a.m. most mornings. Also, the foxhounds from England went sick if they were kept out in the heat of the day, and the scent was only good and strong in the early morning, so no one baulked at the dawn reveille – least of all Penelope, who had been a keen huntress ever since her début with the Anglesey Harriers in 1920.

There was the Ladies Hack Class in the Delhi Horse Show too, in which Penelope would ride one of Father's classier horses. Though she liked to ride and hunt astride (despite her father's remonstrations) she would don her smart navy blue habit for the show, and ride side-saddle. Her habit was made by the famous hunting tailors, Collard of Swindon, for £11, and in fact they continued to make all her riding clothes and grey flannel and tweed coats and skirts into the late 1950s. (Her special friend there was Mr Adams who measured her figure as it widened over thirty years and talked to her of downland botany while he worked.) Nevertheless, however smart the habit, she never won the Ladies Hack Class at the Delhi Show.

There were the Regimental Sports to watch and the Indian Polo Association Championships. There was racing in Delhi and

Calcutta too. But Penelope was happiest just riding out. She once said about riding:

> In those days there were no pony clubs or gymkhanas but we were terribly happy just riding and driving around and sometimes we dressed up as Arab sheikhs and damsels and organised mounted displays for our parents to watch. There was no competitiveness of any kind yet and we were never bored like so many children today who are definitely uninterested in riding just for the pure pleasure of it but need a competition in the offing to practise for and eventually ride in.

She did not just love riding for the sport of it, but like her father, she loved horses.

However, she was never so keen on the young men she was obliged to keep company with. The smooth aides-de-camp, who had eagerly anticipated the arrival of Miss Chetwode at the Commander-in-Chief's household, now flustered about the young lady like drones around the queen bee. It must have been immensely flattering, but Penelope, who was unsure of her looks and unskilled at small talk, was never certain of the reasons behind her perennially full dance card at parties. Was it because she herself had attracted a cluster of beaux, or was her card always full simply because she was the Commander-in-Chief's daughter?

If Penelope was to get anything from India, it was going to have to be from the country itself rather than from the young British men who occupied its territory. So it was with great relief that she avoided the social tumble and whirl by disappearing with her energetic mother on the adventurous expeditions. A pattern was set, for Penelope and Star to spend their 'cold weathers' (that is what the British in the East called winter – September through until March) in India, either touring or in residence at Delhi or Calcutta, and to divide their 'hot weather' between Simla and London. Resigned to a good dose of India, Penelope turned her hand to liking it.

From the eighteenth-century engravings of Thomas Daniell and his like Penelope had conjured up an image of India which was dry and brownish and definitely dull; there were no shafts of light on dappled flesh or the rich robes of Renaissance art. She thought that the rivers ran dry and that the valleys were barren. Her memories of the hills around Florence in springtime and the chalky North Downs or the wooded foothills and the pine forests of the Carpathian mountains in autumn blinded her ability to find colour or richness in the Indian landscape.

By 1931, however, with two 'cold weathers' behind her she had altogether changed her mind. In September of that year she and her mother had ridden on ponies from Simla to Kulu in the foothills of the Himalayan mountains in northern India, to the west of Nepal. They rode through the pine forests and across alpine meadows. They breathed in the fresh breath of the mighty Beas river and stood at the Jalori Pass, which is 10,500 feet high. When Penelope looked along the length of the rich and green and jagged and interesting Kulu Valley she was mesmerized. In that moment she formed an attachment to India that outlasted every other love she encountered in the rest of her life.

There was, though, another influence upon her mind at the time which must be acknowledged for its part in switching her on to (rather than off) India. It was one of those 'every other loves' and was in fact a 'he' – Sir John Marshall, the second in what was to become a series of Johns.

When Penelope arrived in India she was an eager student of history of art. Yet, to her, history of art meant only the history of Western Art. Indian art was not Art, she thought, with all the grand arrogance of youth. If anything, it could be best described as craft. The sculpture was base and rough, she thought, the architecture was ludicrous and not worthy of her notice, Indian miniatures were naïve and she wanted nothing to do with Indian 'art' at all. Until she met Sir John Marshall.

Sir John Hubert Marshall was an archaeologist born in 1876, which made him thirty-four years Penelope's senior. After a spell at the British School in Athens, where he took part in the excavations of Crete, Marshall was appointed to the director-generalship of archaeology in India, a post which had just been revived by Lord Curzon in 1902.

Eight years before Penelope was born, Marshall resurrected the Archaeological Survey of India. When she was three, he inaugurated the exploration of ancient Taxila, near Rawalpindi. He defined the Indus Valley civilization when she was just fourteen and in that same year he was knighted. Sir John resigned from the director-generalship when she was eighteen, to take up special duties on specific projects, and in 1931 he found himself dining at Teen Murti Marg, where he sat next to the twenty-one-year-old daughter of the Commander-in-Chief of the British Forces in India.

He was captivated by her enthusiastic nature and flattered by her interest in archaeology. She was thankful at last to have found someone in the whole of British India to talk to about art, and she fell madly in love (he also happened to be very good-looking and, as she later described him, 'one for the girls'). Sir John (who had married a girl named Florence – the daughter of Sir Henry Longhurst, a dentist – in 1902, and had two children) extended his stay with the Chetwodes, for all intents and purposes to educate their daughter about Indian art. Her parents approved; Marshall seemed to be a decent sort of chap.

They say that if Marshall failed at any point during his career, it was in the training of his colleagues and juniors in administration and technical practice, so that on his retirement from the director-generalship of archaeology in India, there was a sharp decline in standards. In recognition of this fault, Sir Mortimer Wheeler, the eminent prehistorian who was later to jump off a cliff in Australia, said of Marshall: 'It has been said of him, with some truth, that he was "a tree under which nothing grew".' Sir Mortimer added, 'But there are no two opinions about the splendour of the tree.' While Marshall may have failed to nurture anyone in his professional wake, under his experienced branches, Penelope blossomed.

She had been unwittingly seduced by the mesmeric mountains

of the Great Himalaya, and now Marshall became her mentor concerning all things artistic. They were chaperoned, of course, when visiting ancient sites, but Marshall was considered a fatherly enough figure (he was fifty-five by then, after all) to ride out with Penelope alone at six o'clock in the morning before breakfast.

My grandmother was never able afterwards to look at the Qutub Minar without recalling the urgent thrill of those romantic dawn rides. Now those ruins are approached through concrete housing enclaves and there are busloads of Indian tourists deposited hourly to swarm all over the ancient stones. Then, one could gallop in a straight line over nothing but grassy plains from Teen Murti to the Moghul tombs and the mausoleums which lay to the south of Delhi.

And it wasn't only grassy plains they crossed in aid of their passion. Years later, when my grandmother was showing some friends around her old house, Teen Murti, she was able to remember the silent route along the top corridor from her own former bedroom to Sir John's. Aged twenty-one, she had worked out a way of creeping along the landing avoiding the floorboards which creaked; aged seventy-three, she hopped back down the passage in a re-enactment of the secret midnight dash triumphantly, without emitting so much as a squeak from the planks beneath her feet. Yet, that Penelope still called her mentor 'Sir John' when they were *au lit*, as she wrote to her friend Billa Harrod in confidence, is a measure of the respect and awe she felt for the great archaeologist even in their most intimate of moments.

The first John, Johnnie Spencer Churchill said to me, 'I think when she came back to England her life had changed. She came back with that Marshall fellow. He wasn't her lover, I'm sure. But he had introduced her to Eastern Art. I thought she would come back from India to me, but when she came back, we just didn't click. I think she found me frivolous. I had written her countless letters. She returned them all without a word. The curtain came down. She had fallen in love with India. End of story.'

CHAPTER II
GrandmamaElope

'Every moment of recreation off a horse's back I have always considered wasted.'

IN HER BROWN gaberdine jodhpurs [jodhpurs with a long O as she always pronounced them correctly because they came from Jodhpur in India] and an Aertex short-sleeved shirt under her mauve and white cotton apron, my grandmother stood at the end of her garden at The Mead, in Wantage, when I first took her in properly.

It is likely she was feeding her ducks or perhaps she was about to wring the necks of some of her chickens. Once, an old school friend took her husband to meet Penelope: 'Come and see my fowl!' commanded my grandmother as she led the timid couple down the garden. 'Oh!' she said when she got to the hen-house. 'Oh!' she said, 'they don't seem to be laying well at all!' And she promptly began to kill the chickens, one by one, cracking their necks as she carried on talking, until there were ten hens lined up at the feet of her visitors, ready for the pot. Without reference to the slaughter, she then led them on to see her horses.

She had big squashy shoes in brown leather which were misshapen by her bunions, and calves like strong trunks which grew from her shoes without the help of ankles. When she walked she appeared to rock from squashy shoe to squashy shoe, and the shoes seemed to squelch as if she was always stepping in mud (which she was quite often anyway).

She must have been sixty or thereabouts when I saw her at the end of the garden, and her hair was a silver grey helmet, fringed and bobbed around her wrinkly face. It seemed wrinkly at the time, although later I found out that it was smoother than other people's – which may have had something to do with her smearing

Pond's cold cream on her face each night (her only concession to a beauty regime). Also, she never smoked cigarettes. The silver hair was cut in a straight line at least an inch above her dark currant eyes, and before she went out she would comb it firmly down.

Her voice was loud and high-pitched and slightly nasal and she said words that I had not heard before, like 'gawn' for gone and 'gel' for girl, but she had this laugh which came with a resonant boom from right deep inside her, and when she really roared, the laughter would send her rocking backwards, silver-helmet head in the air. She had an authentic giggle as well, and often she got so carried away that tears used to run down her cheeks, and then she'd plead, 'Stop! Stop, I can't *bear* it!'

Her bosom came down to her waist and when I first saw her in the bath, I though her skin was like an elephant's, except softer and paler. But her hands were smooth and shiny and brown and speckled with freckles. Her fingers spanned out like flattened sausages, and you noticed them especially, because she held them up a lot. She used to flick her fourth finger nail or her little finger nail from underneath with her thumb nail, which was fairly annoying. Her only other annoying physical habit was her ele-phant's trumpet-call nose blowing, which she did quite often into the handkerchief which she kept either up her left sleeve or in her bloomers if she was wearing a skirt (which was rare).

Actually, the foghorn nose blowing wasn't her fault; apparently it was due to the shape of her nose. With it uncomfortably blocked and painful in the early thirties, my grandmother had gone to an ENT man who said that her nose was not properly developed. 'He says it stopped developing after some disease I had in childhood (that's why it's such a funny shape!),' wrote my grandmother to Star, after the Harley Street appointment. 'He says nearly all nose trouble originates in childhood, but does not develop until ten or twelve years later. He says India hastens such things although it is not the original cause.'

The doctor had told her that most of his patients' troubles dated from the flu epidemic of 1919, and he wanted to know whether she had had flu then. 'Can you remember?' she asked her mother. 'I can't. The only disease I remember clearly is mumps when I was six. He says was I mental (i.e. did I go slightly dotty for a few days) during or after mumps. Did I? Please reply by return.'

She said she would not have an operation as she did not believe in nose operations but that she would have her nose syringed. In her next letter to her mother she wrote: 'Darlingest Mummy, Thank-you no end for 6 guineas. It is very nice of you & Pop to pay for my nose. I don't think it is your fault at all as you couldn't have known I had a germ. . . .'

Later, perhaps my grandmother never smelt as keenly as we did the antiseptic smell of mothballs in the upstairs bedrooms of her house, or the fruity smell of Cochaline (the red, oily leather polish which comes in a tin and softens tack better than glycerine saddle soap) which came from the bridles and girths and martingales, nosebands, breast-plates and reins – all the tack which was most often strewn about the kitchen, hanging from a lamp or the dresser, waiting to be cleaned.

This was a task which often fell to us. My grandmother taught us (that is myself, my elder sister Lucy, my younger sister Endellion and later, my two brothers, David and John) how to take a bridle apart and clean it and put it back together again, just as she taught us to ride. Lucy had a 12-hands bay pony called Tiny Tara and I had a chestnut Welsh Mountain pony called Trigger, and we would take our steeds to stay with Grandmama-Elope, who smelt slightly of mothballs, like her upstairs bedrooms, but mostly of saddles.

We called her first GrandmamaElope, and then GramElope, a shortened version which was shortened even further to GramElps by my brothers, and finally GrElope. She taught us to sit on a horse and how to jump fences, and then she took us hunting and on long-distance rides through forests. She taught us how to make brandy snaps and lemonade, and how to cook sausages over a fire when we camped in a tent in her garden. She read us the ancient

Hindu epic, *The Ramayana*, before we went to bed and she taught us how to say Hail Marys and the Lord's Prayer.

Often she got cross. It was more likely to be a form of exasperation than true anger, though, and she would throw her bunch of sausage hands in the air when we had let a pony loose on the road by mistake and cry, 'Oh, what am I to do?'

She was bossy too, by all accounts, and sent my mother letters about how to bring us up:

> you MUST NOT feed the kiddiwinks with those coloured biscuits with icing . . . How will they ever grow if you fill them WITH RUBBISH??? They MUST have wholemeal bread, preferably homemade. . . .

Another of her letters to my mother (and my father) begins with:

> THE GREATEST SINGLE FACTOR IN THE ACQUISI-TION AND MAINTENANCE OF GOOD HEALTH IS PER-FECTLY CONSTITUTED FOOD. I did enjoy my BIRTHDAY TREAT SO MUCH. Thank-you both a lot for taking me to Carmen. I thought it was a very good production (except that the donkey should have had a pink Spanish burro bridle instead of an English one) and it was great fun hearing all the old tunes again made so familiar by our music box. I also loved going to the Boulestin again after thirty years or more and thought the sole was excellent.

She continued:

> NATURAL FOOD DOESN'T FATTEN. PINK AND OTHER MIXED BISCUITS ARE NOT NATURAL FOOD. EAT OATS FOR ENERGY. Thank you Rupert also very much indeed for making me a carriage coat. I do not intend to take advantage of having a fashionable tailor for a son-in-law but

could not resist the offer of that lovely light corduroy. BAKED BEANS AND FISH FINGERS ARE NOT PROPERLY CON-STITUTED FOOD . . .

And so it went on.

Her appallingly typed letters were rendered twice as forceful by her liberal use of capitals and repetitive exclamations, and it was not just her family on the receiving end of such terrifying missives. To a poor researcher at Thames Television who was trying to persuade Penelope to talk about the Himalayas on a travel programme, my grandmother began her reply:

Dear Alexandra,

There are TWO errors in your letter: 1) the Laureate's name is spelt as follows: B E T J E M A N and not Betjamin as your Sec has written. 2) The word ORGANIZE is spelt with a Z and not an S. I have checked this in my old Webster's Collegiate Dictionary. But possibly in these degenerate days an S is permissible????

She wrote in a letter to a friend to whom she had lent Golly, her hunting cob:

I HATE having rows but I do think you have been INCRE-DIBLY MEAN over Golly's SHOES......If you return a horse to a friend after being lent same together with saddle and bridle for three years or more surely the least you can do is pay for the final SHOEING????? [She goes on to instruct her friend about land management]: . . I know you were willing to keep him but you must see that it would be an ABSURD expense now that Jess has two animals to look after and ride/train, also with FIVE horses on six acres your land is going to get really HORSE SICK in no time and the animals will be riddled with red worm – strongyle – and if you had kept Golly as well that would be SIX

23

HORSES ON SIX ACRES! Thank you very much for giving Golly a happy home but now he had much better go to another family where he will get REGULAR WORK. . . .'

When she took us out hunting and we cried because we fell off and it was freezing and we wanted to go home, my grandmother often went into cavalry mode and was unsympathetic. If we ever dreamt of seeing to our own comfort – shedding sopping wet clothes and defrosting our fingers under a warm tap – before we had boiled up a bran mash for the ponies and rubbed them down, we were chastised.

We were ticked off about our manners, our cleanliness (she taught us how to wash our 'smalls' by hand) and about waste. Penelope was a recycler of paper and string and bottles and tins by instinct long before she had heard of global warming. If we let the tap run while we brushed our teeth we were reminded of little children in Africa who had to walk five miles to collect their water every day. She always made sure we used the toothmug.

Nevertheless, going to stay with GrandmamaElope was always an adventure. At first we went together, we three girls, then latterly she would have us separately or in twos, so that she could concentrate on each one of us in turn. Later on, when she had moved in to New House, near Hay-on-Wye, in the foothills of the Black Mountains, there would be treats like carting over the Brecon Beacons and playing witches in the 500-acre Forestry Commission forest behind her house, and camping and trekking. We would ride for a day over the ridge of Hay Bluff into Wales and have a cheese sandwich and a bottle of ginger beer at the pub. Then we would trot home in the dusk, avoiding the bogs on the mountain and singing hymns to keep our own spirits up and ghosts away. We would camp on her private common, the gorse-covered scrubland over a bridge from her garden, where a 'hip' (as she called him) from Hay – Mike the Meadow – was allowed to camp in the summer with his mule and his donkey.

Mike the Meadow would bring his own tipi, but we would

erect an orange tent and build a fire in front of the entrance. She would come and eat bacon and toast, cooked by us on the fire, and then she would pretend to go to bed. Sometime later, when we were still awake and had talked ourselves into a terrified state, she would return to the campsite (unbeknownst to us) and run her nails across the outer lining of the tent, emitting a blood-curdling whine. We would quiver and wait, petrified with fright and then burst into screams and bolt back to the house; she would be waiting on the doorstep, smiling knowingly.

She pretended there were Rakshashis (demons from the *Ramayana*) in the woods behind the house, where she took us, with a pony and the trolley cart, to collect logs. In the middle of the wood, she would hide behind a tree and after a while we would notice that she had disappeared and call and call for her, horrified to be left alone with the demons. Then she would leap from behind the tree with her arms in the air and her face all screwed up in a monstrous expression, roaring like a very demon herself.

She wasn't always so noisy, though. Every so often, when I was watching her doing something manual like stirring a béchamel sauce or darning a stocking, her hands would stop, mid-stitch or stir, and I would catch her gazing, with her eyes half-closed, through the window, beyond the kitchen. Then the sauce would begin to bubble, or she'd prick her finger, and all of a sudden she would jolt back into reality and the wooden spoon would begin to stir again, or the needle would begin to stitch again, as if she had never stopped.

Then, I don't suppose I stopped to wonder what she was thinking about in those stolen moments. I didn't know then that she had met my grandfather in 1931 and that she had married him in a Register Office in Edmonton, Herts, in August, 1933 without telling her parents. I didn't know that six months later, the young Betjemans had rented Garrard's Farm, in Uffington, below the Downs in Berkshire for £36 per annum. Four mornings a week she drove my grandfather in their maroon-coloured Ford to Challow station in time to catch the 9.15 to London where he had to watch several films a day. He earned £900 p/a as Film Critic on the London *Evening Standard*, while she stayed in Uffington and turned her hand to running a household.

I DID NOT KNOW that there was a time in her life when she had not even polished so much as a sideboard and could not cook at all, so that she employed a German 'cook-general', called Paula Steinbrecher, to help and also teach her. When her white grey Arabian, Moti, arrived from India, she was faced with the problems of stable management, about which, again, she knew virtually nothing. She later said that it had never entered her head, although she had no children and left all the housework and the cooking to Paula, that she could look after one horse all by herself. So she engaged Jackie Goodenough, a school-leaver aged fourteen, whom she paid ten shillings a week. She fitted him out in black breeches and gaiters – the traditional groom's uniform in those days – and taught him to ride so that he could exercise Moti when required. And then she set about learning to groom and feed her horse from a book.

I knew that my uncle Paul was born just before the Second World War, and my mother, Candida, told me that she was born during the war in the Rotunda in Dublin. My grandfather had been sent to Ireland as Press Attaché to the British Consulate, and the Betjemans (a family now) only returned to England in 1943. Later, Penelope's father, Philip Chetwode, bought them The Old Rectory, a red brick house in Farnborough, another village in Berkshire, nearer Lambourn than Wantage.

They remained at Farnborough for not very long before selling it to buy The Mead, a Victorian 'villa' in the middle of Wantage, where they settled, pretty well, for over fifteen years. By the time the Betjemans reached The Mead, my grandmother had learnt to cook excellently, and to keep horses efficiently; my mother boarded at St Mary's, Wantage, and my uncle Paul went to Eton. So there

26

was time (and she had plenty of inclination) to try out other ventures.

At first, her experiments were of a more domestic nature – she branched out into waterfowl farming, selling ducks for the table. Later, she tried her hand at catering, when she opened King Alfred's Kitchen, a café cum library in the town square. For six years she also wrote a weekly cookery column in the *Sunday Express*, under a pseudonym made up from her second and third Christian names, Hester Valentine. She did all these things and lots of other things as well, and drove her carts and had picnics and people to stay, but towards the end of the fifties it appeared her life was still not full enough.

She had converted to Catholicism in 1948, and in 1961 she made up her mind to ride on a horse through the deep-rooted Catholic province of Andalusia in southern Spain. Her trip turned out to be a kind of pilgrimage, and she wrote an account of her uncomfortable equestrian journey in a candid and funny book (her first) called *Two Middle-Aged Ladies in Andalusia* (the other middle-aged lady being her twelve-year-old horse). The book was published by her husband's publisher, John Murray, but even adding 'author' to her roll of accomplishments appeared not to have brought her the satisfaction she sought, for as soon as Candida had been safely dispatched with a ring on her finger into the arms of my handsome father in 1963, my grandmother found herself on another journey, back to India.

As I WATCHED my grandmother pause as she stirred the béchamel sauce, to stare into another world outside the window, I didn't know all those things about her life. I just knew that she wore a Tibetan jumper most of the time and that she knew all about the Rakshashis in the *Ramayana*. I knew that often she was away for part of the year in India and that she came back laden with hand-dyed writing paper and Gujerati folk-art. I knew she was a flavoursome cook and a strict teacher, and that she was funny and that she loved her horses and her grandchildren, though I was not totally sure whether she liked me.

Lucy (the eldest grandchild) was Darling Luce who was just as brilliant at riding as she was at making brandy snaps, béchamel sauce and wild flower arrangements. Delli (the youngest, before the boys) was Dellikins who was musical and funny and who loved to drive the pony carts. I often felt I annoyed her. I could be lazy and insolent and devious. For some reason, I found it difficult to show overt keenness. I might like something, but I found it hard to be outwardly enthusiastic. It felt silly to gush, and I imagined she found me a disappointing pupil.

I went to stay with her in Herefordshire in the Easter holidays to revise for my A levels. We kept to a rigorous routine: breakfast, work, lunch, walk/ride, work, tea, reading, supper, bed. She said she found my studies (I was revising for Greek and Latin and history) 'edifying', but I cannot have been much company that spring. I was moody and messy and podgy and sulky. I came away moodier, cross with myself, and not much enlightened by my 'edifying' revision.

Our 'non-relationship' was entirely imagined by a cross and adolescent me, of course. The next term, she wrote:

Darling Imo,

Here are some PISTACHIO nuts to help you with your 'A' Levels. I think of you daily and I pray that the questions are nice.

Pistachios are grown all over Turkey and Iran and when I twice drove overland to India (1963 & 1970) I ate them all the time – we all did – and spat the shells out of the window so there was a trail for about 3000 miles which the police could have easily followed had we committed a crime.

I am going to Oxford to get a possible dress and shoes for the memorial service [of J.B.]. I ordered one in London and they couldn't get the stuff oh dear! As you can imagine I would prefer to go in JODHPURS, but they wouldn't look quite right in the front pew of W.A. [Westminster Abbey].

Much love and I HOPE the exams are not too dreadful, from Gr Elope.

Nearer the exams she sent me a bar of Cadbury's Dairy Milk. She wrote in a note: 'Very best luck for exams next week. KEEP COOL! [A phrase she had picked up from my brothers] I think you might allow yourself just one bar of choc???' Over the 'edifying revision' period we both forbade ourselves chocolate for the purpose of reducing our figures. 'NO REPLY REQUIRED. Much love and I am still saying a daily decade of the Rosary for the successful outcome of your 'A' Levels – Gr Elope.' However, neither cheering letter nor the rosary could lift my spirits in that gloomy year: I did badly in my A Levels, failed to gain a university place and failed my driving test four times.

It had been our grandmother's intention to take all of us, individually, to India, for what she called an 'educational tour'. She had taken Lucy when she left school, and in the spring of 1985 it was my turn. I did want to go, but I was nervous of travelling alone with my grandmother. I thought it was fairly uncool to travel around India with a seventy-five-year-old, when all my friends were joining up together to go 'travelling'. Secondly, I was still sulky, podgy and perhaps even slothful, and I was terrified that I would disappoint her and that we would not get on together at all.

She sent me a packing list which included 'petticoat (if required?)', something I had never owned nor was likely to, 'bosom busters', 'inflatable cushion', 'linen sun hat' and 'two rolls W.C. paper'. I packed up my rucksack ('It is CORRECT to say ROOKsack, because it comes from the German RUCK,' she would say) and set off with her on an aeroplane to Bombay. I was eighteen, at the same age as she had been when she first arrived in India in 1928.

Three months later I had decided that my grandmother was definitely cool. The education I had received was richer than a whole MA's worth of learning; the people I had met had opened my eyes to their culture, their forms of worship, their ideas of family life; we had ridden, taken trains, gone on buses, bicycled, walked, in fact, we had positively danced around India, covering the length from the Himalayas to the southern city of Madurai, and I, for one, had been dazzled.

It was a relief to return to England, though, for after three months in India, one is often overwhelmed and certainly in need of a breather. I didn't say I'd never go back on my return, but I think I said that it would be a while before I hit Bombay again.

After that, what you might call a slow sinking-in of the experience took place – the dual experience of India and my grandmother. About a month after we got back, I began to feel completely recharged, changed even. I retook an A Level, passed my driving test, got into university and became possessed with energy. My father sent me my first pair of Reeboks (pink and white) and I started running. I even began to ride again more frequently (I had forsaken horses for parties when I was about sixteen).

I started to write to my grandmother regularly and I found I wanted to tell her things and that I wanted her advice. She used to come on a bus from Hereford to Birmingham to visit me at university. We walked round the Pre-Raphaelites in the City Gallery, and I found myself able, at last, to be openly enthusiastic (if I liked the picture, that is). We always ate quiche for lunch in the top-floor restaurant of Rackham's Department Store, and I would tell her all about my archaeology lectures, about which, to my surprise, I really was keen. We talked about God quite a lot, and by my second term she had become so important to me that I could not imagine life without her. There were so many things I wanted to ask her.

But then she died. Worst of all, she died in India, far away from all of us on a mountain in the Himalayas, and she was only seventy-six. Everyone said how wonderful it was that she had died 'in harness' as someone put it, that she would have wanted to go in the way that she did. But we were all distraught.

We had a memorial service for her in Blackfriars on St Giles' in Oxford, and there was a huge tea afterwards for which we had made mountains of chocolate éclairs and flapjacks and walnut cake. As they sipped on their ginger beer, people talked about how marvellous she was, and what an eccentric she was. I knew they were right about some things, but wrong about others.

Gavin Stamp, the architectural writer who was her friend and correspondent, for example, wrote in *The Spectator* that she hadn't cared a jot about her appearance. So I wrote back saying that she always, always made sure her nose wasn't shiny and that her hair was combed. After all, he had never been to an Indian Military Barracks with her, so he couldn't have known. And then we all went back to our lives.

Except that missing her got worse, not easier and constantly I would be thinking, oh, I must tell GrandmamaElope that, and then I'd remember that somehow, the healthiest, fittest, most vivacious, funny and energetic seventy-six-year-old I'd ever known had actually died. It was most awful for my mother, I know, and for everyone else as well, but your own grief is a private thing and this was the first person I had known and loved who had died, so I thought about her a lot.

I thought about her more and more, and I decided that I just had not had enough of her. So I made up my mind to return to India – thinking that India had to be where to look, because I did not seem to be able to get hold of her in England – and I went back to India to get some more.

MY GRANDMOTHER never liked aeroplanes. She said she thought it was rude to God to go up into the region where he hangs out: 'I never think He approves of it,' she said. 'I'd rather drive fifty wild horses in a dog-cart!' But wild horses wouldn't carry you across

Europe and the Middle East to Asia, even if you did manage to control them and keep them going in the right direction, because you cannot travel overland through what used to be Persia any more, so you have to fly.

I flew on Air India flight 126 on a glowing September Sunday afternoon. There could not have been a worse day to leave England, looking so wholesome and golden as it did, and I felt quite drenched in misery. It didn't take long for me to make my first friends, though.

A motherly Hindu lady – mid-fifties – in an aquamarine blue sari and gold sandals was sitting on my left. She worked for the Post Office and lived in Slough. She was travelling to Delhi to visit her brother and niece-in-law who were both in a comatose state after a car crash which killed the brother's wife and her nephew. She told me the tale of the tragedy and munched coated almonds and picked her teeth and slurped her orange juice all at the same time. While she told the tale of the tragedy she was also smiling. The Hindu mentality is a fatalistic one, and if the Gods choose to let a lorry ride over the top of your brother's car just after your nephew's wedding with the bride and bridegroom in it, then those Gods know best. It is a sensible way of coping with the death of the people you love.

On my right sat a small man with an oily nose and a tight brown jacket. Throughout the tale of the post-nuptial car accident from the lady on my left, he had been sipping whisky and ginger and throwing handfuls of honey-coated almonds to the back of his mouth with quick thrusts. He was also a Hindu and he could not resist spinning his own tragic tale. He told us he was going to Calcutta to see his uncle who was in hospital because a motor car hit him and he broke his leg last week and the poor man, who was evidently nearly ninety at the time of the accident, appeared to have suffered a stroke as well.

My tale was not going to impress those two veterans of suspense in the intensive care unit. They were not interested in the already dead. If I had been travelling to visit my dying grandmother we might have compared notes. As it was, my excitement about trekking through India in search of her spirit held no mystery for them. They clucked and tutted and clicked their nails and munched their almonds, and their eyes glistened with sorrow for their own tragedies, but my sorrow meant nothing to them. So we talked about *Dynasty* and *Dallas* and *EastEnders* and *Neighbours* and other soaps, because, as the lady from Slough said, you must have a soap in your life.

We met our dinner trays with moistened lips. 'Lamb in vegetable decoction' was complemented with 'caramelized sponge cake with lemon foam'. Mrs P.O. Slough on my left was moved to tears again by the lemon foam, for while her brother used to relish her homemade lemon sponge cake, she suddenly remembered that now he was being fed by a drip.

'You see, Imagine,' (her penchant for soap opera caused her to mould my name into something glossier) 'we are so close, we Indian families. We think nothing of travelling for many days for our uncle's birthday. If one family member is sick, then the others must always throw up everything else to come and take care. We can use all our savings to make these journeys. Our family members may not fear to die lonely.'

The water in the glass bottle in the top right hand depression of our plastic trays stated on its label that it came fresh from the Radnor Hills. I drank the water bottled on the Herefordshire borders, where I had ridden with my grandmother and I wondered whether she had died lonely. After dinner we all slept, and, as if by a miracle, when we woke up, we were about to arrive at Delhi.

The fetid Indian smell – a mixture of coriander, sweat and excrement – envelops every traveller as he descends on to the tarmac runway, like a warm blanket, tangible and suffocating. After a week or so the smell seems to evaporate but that is merely the moment when one has got used to it, for actually it is ubiquitous and it never fades. I thought I would have forgotten the smell of the air, but when I disembarked, flanked on each side by the lady from Slough and the slim man in the brown leather jacket, the smell seemed quite surprisingly familiar. We arrived in the early morning, just when the eighty million Hindus of India are 'cleansing' themselves by squeezing waste from their bowels on to the peripheral areas – railway tracks and derelict houses and river banks and beaches.

I must have stored that smell in my nasal memory, if there is such a thing. I did not remember India being so crowded, though, nor so wet. For Delhi was awash with the late monsoon rains and I found the pavement exploding in front of me as underground wires everywhere short-circuited when I walked through the floods in the streets; there was rubbish steeped up against the pavement and it was depressing.

I managed that day to book my seat on a bus into the hills. I would return to Delhi later and meanwhile make for the mountains. The magic lay in the mountains. The Himalayan Mountains that had lured my grandmother back to India thirty years after she left it in 1933:

> Certain landscapes imprint themselves upon the mind's eye and for me the most persistent picture throughout the years has been that of the Upper Beas valley of Kulu in the Western Himalaya, with the great snow ridge above the Solang 'nala' and the twin Gyephang peaks at its far end. Ever since I left India in 1933, the vision of this valley has repeatedly come before me during the day as well as during the night . . .

Thus she introduces her book, *Kulu, The End of the Habitable World*, which was published in 1972. She continued:

> In September 1931 my mother and I trekked from Simla to Kulu on hill ponies, and rode in short stages some hundred and forty miles as far as the base of the Rohtang Pass . . . In 1963 I returned to India after an interval of thirty years and the following summer I was able to indulge my whim of riding once again to Kulu by the same route.

I was indulging my whim now. In 1985, my grandmother and I had not gone together to the Kulu valley itself, but to the adjacent Sutlej valley which is a deeper, more barren gorge. This time I wanted to see the Kulu valley and the landscape that had commanded her devotion. She had returned by pony in 1963. Nearly thirty years on, I returned by bus.

It was dark at five o'clock in the morning and the rain came down in a warm haze as I sleepwalked out of the YWCA to hail an auto-rickshaw. The rickshaw leapt from uneven stone to pothole like a grasshopper while my suitcase and I ricocheted inside from one side to the other like dice inside a cup. I fell out at my destination and haggled to be free of my maniacal driver. It proved a novel way of waking up.

The HPTDC (Himachal Pradesh Tourist Development Corporation) bus was 'deluxe', they said. 'Deluxe' it was, with spongy brown seats and fans if you wanted them. I sat at the front with a fine view through the driver's cabin on to the open road, but the September sun did not venture out for another two hours, so I was saved the gloomy scenes of the Delhi suburbs and the industrial sites.

By the time it was light we were flying along the great straight eucalyptus-lined Grand Trunk Road. At least that was what it was called in Kipling's time. He called it the 'Great Road which is the backbone of all Hind'. Says a soldier to Kim and the lama just as they are to embark on their journey to find the Holy River: 'All castes and all kinds of men move here. Look! Brahmins and chumars, bankers and tinkers, barbers and bunnias, pilgrims and potters – all the world going and coming . . .'

The pace is quicker now, for the bulk of the traffic is motorized. Gaudy orange and yellow toy-like lorries laden with apples tear from north to south, tinsel flying and neon gods held high for protection. Minibuses sway, so stuffed are they with huge extended families on holiday and heading to the hills.

The bullock carts still haul the 'grain and cotton and timber, fodder, lime and hides' that Kim so marvelled at, but they are pushed almost off the road by larger, faster vehicles. Skinny men still bicycle, umbrellas balanced aloft, and neat parties of school children march in crocodile along the road's edge. The boys wear blue shirts and brown shorts and the girls wear pink and white 'salwar kameez' – a long shirt over baggy pantaloons. Their hair is parted and oiled and smooth and their satchels are strapped to their backs. No parent guides them as lorries flash by at 60 m.p.h. – they must learn to step sideways on the Grand Trunk Road before they learn to write and read. The plains of Uttar Pradesh lie flat on either side of the way, sown with paddy. Egrets stalk across the crops, followed by women bent double under brushwood loads, their saris tucked up into their waistbands to reveal baggy, sagging knees.

Along the road were eating-houses where lorry drivers gathered to eat from the steaming brass pots of dahl and rice and potato curry. Others smoked and drank their *chai*, some talking, others gazing, blinded by the activity. We did not stop until we were past Umballa: this is the great market town of the northern plains, a historical crossroads which also happens to be the Newmarket of north India where horse traders meet to do their business. The Grand Trunk Road continues from there on to Ludhiana and Lahore which is now in Pakistan, but we bore right and directly northwards towards the foothills of the Great Himalaya.

We stopped at a 'service station', a recently developed tourist complex with signs saying 'IN' and 'OUT'. These *dhabas* are an upmarket version of the traditional Indian roadside eating stop, where travellers rest and mingle to swap traffic stories and exchange news of roadworks. They are the equivalent of our motorway service stations with Trust House Forte 'Granary restaurants', and Happy Eater diners. In India now, with a growing number of private car owners, the *dhabas* are becoming more popular and proprietors are beginning to compete, installing STD telephone booths and fridges and televisions, to attract the passing trucker trader as well. Yet a meal will still cost you no more than ten rupees. I passed on butter chicken and channa masala and bought some boiled sweets instead. My grandmother would never travel sweetless, and always sucked her favourite lemon flavoured bon-bons noisily. I did the same and offered my booty around the bus.

We forded a river and watched helpless as a crowd attempted to push their lorry out before it tipped up, and then the road started to climb upwards into the mountains. It was green, for the monsoon was not yet over, and I wished I knew what all the trees we passed were called – I know my grandmother would have recited them off pat.

We stopped again for biryani and then again for bindi curry and chapatties. It became clear that we would not reach Manali before ten o'clock, and the driver's cabin began to fill with raucous young men whom we seemed just to pick up along the way. The day turned into night again when at last we entered the Kulu valley, but it was too thrilling for sleep. I breathed in the breathtaking sharp alpine air through my window and watched the moon play shadows across the snowcapped peaks. From the de luxe bus, with the sky star-studded, Kulu looked like an enchanted fairyland, until we entered Kulu town.

The main road is not built for two-way traffic and the wooden houses almost overhang the narrow passage of a single track road which has to bear the burden of thundering lorries daily. It was midnight and we came to a halt with a jolt. A fruit-laden lorry was wedged alongside a minibus between two houses. All the women come to their verandas to watch the scene: there was much discussion taking place and not much action as is the Indian way. Likewise in the Indian way, we were patient, played dice and smoked before the bus lurched on its way, two hours later.

Our next hurdle was a five-hundred-yard long snaking column of a flock of black-and-white sheep and goats. These were the Gaddi sheep. The Gaddies are nomadic shepherds who wear a length of rope coiled round their waist, partly to keep their stomachs warm when they are crossing snowbound mountain passes which may be up to 18,000 feet high, and partly to use as a noose if one of their flock were to fall down a mountain ravine, or as a lifeline if one of their family suffered the same fate.

In early summer the Gaddis herd their sheep and goats northwards through the Kulu valley, and up over the Rhotang pass, which separates the green and fertile Kulu valley from those barren lands beyond: the rocky moonscape where the rains never reach. They graze their flocks there, on the slopes of the mountains of the Great Himalaya in the nether regions of Lahul and Spiti all through the summer months. In the autumn, when the grass is all gone, they bring their charges back over the pass, herding them southwards to more hospitable climes for their winter camps in Kangra.

In September, therefore, great white streams of sheep, that look like bands of seething maggots from afar, make their passage down the forty-mile length of the Kulu valley floor. Once they might have travelled unhindered, but now they must compete for road space with wretched smoking vehicles. Some herds travel southwards at night, to avoid the heavier traffic, and we met such a herd just beyond Kulu. The white tweed coats of the shepherds stood out bright like their sheep in the moonlight as they filtered round our patient, stationary bus.

We could hear the crashing Beas river now, down below to the right of the road and the gorge narrowed as we approached Manali. As we entered the town at precisely four o'clock, thunder roared and flashes of lightning tore across the sky and the gods sent down penny-sized pellets of hard and heavy rain. Our journey had taken twenty-two hours instead of sixteen, but instead of being exhausted I was exhilarated. I felt as though I had finally arrived where I was supposed to be. I had not found much evidence of my grandmother in Delhi, but I hoped to find her in the Kulu valley.

CHAPTER III
Apple Country

'The Broadwoods are my two legs. My husband has always called them that because of their resemblance to the legs of the grand pianos of that name. Some wives might be insulted, indeed it might have broken their marriage, but I have always found that the secret of happiness is to realize your limitations and it has always been perfectly clear to me that among the manifold blessings that God has showered upon me, the gift of good legs is not among them.'

'PENELOPE's favourite thing was to climb on to my Cox's Orange Pippin tree, which is just outside the dining room, after lunch. She would tell any other guests here – "DO NOT PICK, this is NOT a good apple, it is very sour." The Indians would be curious then as to why she is picking this apple and eating it and they would pick one too, but they would spit it out then, and they would say who IS this possessed English lady who is eating sour apples, but she loved it and warned everyone not to eat them, and she would sit munching high up in the tree and eat as many as five for dessert.'

A dark olive-skinned middle-aged man with the unlikely name of John Banon sat on his white-painted, wooden veranda at sundown a few days after my journey up and told me about the history of the Kulu valley (and where my grandmother came into it).

John Banon's grandfather had been an Irish captain (also called John Banon) in the British army who had become known as 'the white Raja', or the uncrowned king of the Upper Beas valley when he retired in the 1860s to Manali (which was then nothing more than a trading post). He had been so enraptured by the beauty of the Lower Himalayan hill region where he had hunted once while on leave from his barracks in Garwhal, that he decided to return to make his life there. A wholehearted Indophile, the Captain had not only been a co-founder of the Indian National Congress but also he had married a local Pahari girl, with whom he had four sons. However, he could not have given his boys more British names than Henry, Herbert, Harold and Hugh, nor could he have introduced a more foreign crop to Kulu than apples.

Captain John Banon planted the first apple trees in Asia in his orchard at Manali in the 1870s, initiating a trend which spread the length of the valley. The climate was found to be perfect for fruit, and apples in particular, and Kulu is now planted with apples and pears from end to end and the people have grown rich on the crops. However, though the Captain began with Cox's and Blenheim Orange and other traditional varieties from England, which he sold to the British in India who were missing their orchards, the Indians have long since expressed a dislike of their sour taste and bitterness; they prefer the fluffiness and sweetness and the colour of the Red Delicious apple which, in answer to demand, is today the most common apple on the terraces in Kulu – the valley which has grown famous the world over, since Captain Banon's initiative, for its apples.

Manali looks quite different now from the paradisical picture the Captain must have seen in 1860. It sits fifty miles by road (and about 7,000 feet below) the great Rhotang Pass which, at 13,300 feet is the gateway from the fertile Kulu valley to the nether regions of Lahul and Spiti. Thus Manali is the first stop on an important trade route, connecting the Great Himalaya with the southern foothills, and it has suffered as a result. An itinerant population swells in the summer months from about 2,000 to 8,000 as Lahulis and Zanskaris and Tibetans come over the pass searching for work. Others, merchants, come to swap yak's milk and potatoes for apples and jewels. From further afield have come Westerners, often drawn by the complementary attractions of abundant *Canna-*

bis indica (the commonest weed in Himachal Pradesh), coupled with an idyllic landscape in which to smoke it. Westerners need accommodation and hoteliers need labourers; the more hotels, the more labourers and the more hotels, the more Westerners which all results in overcrowding and, ultimately, more refuse than a mountain town can cope with.

'There's dysentery rife in the bazaar ... don't eat the potato pakoras ready cooked,' they whispered in the street on the morning after I arrived at Manali. There was a groaning man or two lying in the road and several mange-ridden dogs picking over piles of waste food at the backs of restaurants. When it rained the streets weren't cleansed by the downpour and left glistening and fresh, rather were they sodden by it and made murkier. There was mud mixed with excrement in the gutter and children played in it.

With the monsoon so late, the mountain streams had dried up that year, or managed just to trickle, so that much of the drinking water there had been polluted. With the recent rains, however, the Beas river had swelled and was raging and on my first morning two of the pitiful force of twelve police officers in Manali had pulled out of the water the naked and defiled body of a Dutch girl. She and her friend, both only eighteen years old, were trekking through the Himalayas together, and had stopped to stay in a Manali hotel. The girl slipped out of the hotel one night at 11 p.m. to post a letter before going to bed. The other girl waited for her friend to return from the post office just two minutes' walk away. She never came back. She disappeared and for a week there was no sign of her until she was found belly up four miles downstream.

Buses sit at the bus station and backfire and apple lorries tear down the mountain roads now, but it wasn't always like this. For at the end of the nineteenth century, when Manali grew from a traders' encampment into a couple of shops and a post office, it was already earning its reputation as an unspoilt holiday retreat. In 1910 a Public Works Department rest-house was built for British officers on tour who wished to take advantage of the opportunity to hunt or fish; for red and black bear were once common there, and ibex, *burrhel*, *thar* and *ghoral* as well as leopards, and the Kulu streams were stocked with trout.

If the rest-house was full, the only other place to stay in 1910 was Captain Banon's guest-house. Now there are all manner of places to stay in Manali, but Captain Banon's grandson John still runs the family guest-house, a short walk up from the bazaar. The veranda we sat on at sundown was built by Herbert, John's father, in 1934, on the site of the original house in the middle of the original orchard.

I had imagined meeting a blue-eyed white-haired Irishman, but of course John is three-quarters Pahari (for his father Herbert married a local girl too) and in fact, he had a dark olive skin and black hair and hooded dark eyes. He spoke English fluently (with a slight Indian accent), but he also speaks fluent Hindi and Kului – the local dialect.

I bumped into John on my first morning in the bazaar and he said to me in that sing-song Indian way, come to see me any time – Wednesday, Thursday, today, tomorrow. When I did arrive unexpectedly it put him into a fluster and he ushered me up the stairs past varnished deodar beams into Room No. 11, where my grandmother used to stay, which opened out on to a white balcony with white wicker chairs. He behaved in a strange, shirty way: 'I have no dinner now,' he said crossly. 'I'll see you in the morning.' He left me in the ghostly room with its crooked mirror and half-used candles and tall mahogany wardrobe swinging with empty hangers, and shuffled off down the stairs.

The next morning he still seemed to be avoiding me and I was taken to the dining-room alone. Dark brown eyes watched me eat chapattis and jam in a gloomy corner, and the boy who brought me coffee smirked and the cook stared through the window and the other boys gathered at the far end of the dining-room, busying themselves with napkins but intent on stealing glances at me. Later on in the morning John found me reading in the garden, munching a Cox's Orange Pippin, and he was ready to talk.

John Banon was baptized a Protestant in Manali and he went to Bishop Cotton School, the smart English-run college in Simla, founded originally for British boys. He served in the army and for a time was based at Selby in Yorkshire and then in Norwich, after which he moved back to the Kulu Valley for ever. He married a Pahari girl from Goshal, a village not three miles up the valley, and his son Thomas ran a perfume factory. But John's other son, Arthur, a photographer, was killed in 1978 when he was only twenty-five: he accepted a lift from a truck on the mountain road, which then plunged over the edge into the *khud*.

John could not talk about his loss. He was silent and moody, and his Pahari wife, who used to be charming and vital and beautiful, sat alone, rocking on her haunches, wizened with age and crazed with grief. She passed by us while I was talking to John, and he failed even to introduce me. She fixed a smile upon me for a moment: 'Have you brothers and sisters?' she asked and walked away muttering before I could answer.

'Penelope wrote to me in 1963 and asked if she could stay here,' John told me, munching quietly on stale cream crackers. He was diagnosed diabetic two years before and follows a complicated diet. 'We became good friends then and every year almost she would come to stay. She was writing her book about Kulu that first time, and after she went back to England, she wrote a long letter saying if I could answer some of her queries about the temples, she would appreciate it. It was a command, really. But then you see I could not answer all of these questions – there were so many! Not less than three or four foolscap pages! Some of the answers I knew – the names and dates, but mostly I had to leave the questionnaire blank.'

AFTER MY grandmother had returned from Spain in 1961, and after the success of her first book, *Two Middle-Aged Ladies in Andalusia*, she drew up a plan with her publisher to write a book about India. It would be a then and now book, comparing life in the Raj with modern India. She would spend the summer of 1963 doing historical research in the Indian Institute section of the Bodleian Library, and fly out to Delhi in September. It would be her first time back to India for thirty years, but it was something she had been thinking about for as long. She said she felt compelled to return to the Kulu valley where she had trekked with her mother in 1931. The mountain landscape had imprinted itself on her mind and she burned to see it again. So she made arrangements to fly to Delhi (although she abhorred aeroplanes) but before the arrangements were complete, a young doctor called Dick Squires offered her an alternative.

Dick Squires was the six-foot-six tall and capable son of the local GP in Wantage who was also my uncle Paul's friend. Dick was a groupie of my grandmother's, who called him Dickoi or just Dear Boy. He would feed her ponies with carrots for her and load the eggs from her waterfowl venture on to the back of her 1958 Vespa scooter. The Mead was just a short bicycle ride down the garden from his house, The Priory, over the bridge that straddled the stream.

Dick had three ambitions which he had dreamt about for as long as he could remember – to go logging in Canada, to go to the outback of Australia and to see Mount Everest, in Nepal. With the spirit of adventure in him, he decided that he would drive overland to India and Nepal, thereby fulfilling No. 3 with the added bonus of the outward journey.

The moment he told Penelope of his plans, she abandoned thoughts of intruding into God's place in a beastly aeroplane and threw in her lot with Dick. She offered her historical knowledge and her culinary expertise as assets to the expedition. Dick was (and is) good with machines, and thus took charge of the mechanical side of things, as well as the planning of the route. Chris, a fellow youthful medic, came along with medicine and was put in charge of campsites, and Elizabeth Simpson, who was a young art school teacher and friend of Dick's sister, came with her expert eye to interpret the art they might come across.

In addition to these four, was a twenty-one-year-old minx of a girl called Isabel, who was keen to visit an old flame in Delhi, she said. En route, however, she became rather enamoured of Dick, a feeling soon reciprocated by him. Penelope never entirely approved of Isabel because the girl appeared quite uninterested in 'culture'; Elizabeth, on the other hand, showed knowledgeable enthusiasm and got on so well with Penelope that they became firm friends for the rest of their lives and travelled together again to India.

The five set off in a Volkswagen van (converted by Dick into an expedition–mobile with varnished maps of Persia and Asia stuck on the insides) on 25 September and arrived in India eight weeks later. Penelope said that their main source of bickering was over blue airmail paper and Biros but that otherwise they had got on remarkably well. She managed to produce porridge, bacon, eggs and tomatoes and coffee, cooked on the Primus stove, almost every single morning of the trip, being of the firm opinion that one needed a hearty breakfast when travelling. She also managed to cook some premium risottos in the pressure cooker.

After crossing the border at Amritsar, however, her talents were truly tested. They lost their way in the outskirts of the city, and Dick asked a Sikh the way to Delhi. But his accent was too English for the Indians, so Penelope, who felt herself to be an expert in communicating with the Indians (although this was to be the first time in thirty years) asked in a high-pitched accent for the 'Delly Rood'. They were directed on and got lost again. Once more Penelope tried, only to be asked if they wanted the Delhi Road or the road to Delhi, which were, apparently, in opposite directions. They made it, though, and on arrival, split off into their various directions. Elizabeth went to Hyderabad, Isabel went into the arms of her Indian lover, the boys drove the Volkswagen on to Nepal, and my grandmother travelled by train to Simla and the foothills of the Himalayas.

Penelope's plan was to follow the same route she had taken with her mother in 1931, finishing up in Manali. She would research her book and then fly home. However, she had reckoned without an unstoppable curiosity about the Kulu valley and its temples, which welled up inside her, kept her in Manali until late in 1964, drew her back again in 1965, and continued to draw her back for the rest of her life.

For in the Secretariat library in Simla she discovered a list of 119 Pahari Hindu temples compiled by a Mr H. Lee Shuttleworth, ICS (Indian Civil Service), who had been Assistant Commissioner in Kulu from 1917 and 1919 and again from 1923 to 1924. My grandmother fell in love with the Kulu valley as he had, and she made it her mission to visit all the temples on his list – to photograph them and measure them and to document their histories – a challenge she set about with increasing passion and determination.

She used Manali as her research base in the Kulu valley that first summer in 1964, and quite naturally she gravitated towards Captain Banon's guest-house, which she must have remembered from the old days.

'SHE WOULD stay five days or three days to organize her treks into the hills and then she would stay on her way down again,' John Banon told me as we sat on his veranda in Manali. 'This house was built by my father in 1934 and she stayed because she liked the balcony. She always wrote and said please book up Room 11 for me please. It is in the old English style and now you don't get these balconies and bay windows and those things, but she liked them. Wood was cheap then and my father employed an Italian architect.

'She was very nice to have to stay for she would be talking to everybody in the dining-room. She had all the people interested in her topics' – this sounded familiar – 'and she told me so much about the temples. She played a trick upon me with Parashar Rishi. She showed me photographs of this pagoda temple and she said, "Where is this, John?" and I thought it was somewhere in Switzerland. She said, "You're a fool, John, because it is right in front of your nose," and so I made the effort to walk up there, and I discovered this beautiful temple in our valley which she opened my eyes to.'

John never accompanied her on her treks. 'She was not slim, but she was very active,' he smiled, remembering. 'She could run up these hills where I could barely walk up. Then she had that pony called Ugli. She said every time she was going to take him up into the hills, he got a gloomy look on his face, and he dug his toes in the dirt. She was a daredevil that lady.'

In 1965, at the time of the trouble in Pakistan, Penelope had been staying with John when all the British were summoned back to Delhi by radio. 'She was taking the bus, and you come to a bridge at Pando on the road from Mandi, where a man is employed to walk along in front of the vehicle so that it does not exceed a certain speed. It was 5 m.p.h., I think. Well, she thought this was very funny and she stepped out of the bus quietly and she took a photograph of this man walking with the bus on the bridge, and a policeman caught her.'

She was then escorted all the way back to Manali, where she was asked to hand over the film. So she secretly put a new one in and hid the used one in her vest. On her return to the rest-house, she said to John: 'Your policemen are very good,' and he asked why and she said, 'The chief gave me a cup of tea in the police station and then they took my camera and removed the blank film and said it's OK now, you can go.'

They had thought that she was a spy during the Indo-Pakistan war, because that bridge was the gateway to the whole valley and they did not want the plans of the bridge to get into the hands of the Pakistanis. 'I thought it was very funny,' said John, 'and she thought it was very funny. She did many of these things you see. She would be defying the police always to get her photographs.'

As soon as she had visited more than once, Penelope became a recognizable figure in Manali. 'Soon everybody knew she was the daughter of Chetwode, who was the Commander-in-Chief, and the people were anxious to find out about her and she talked to everyone and she did not avoid the subject. She had the whole dining-room in laughter, she was such a good talker.'

There were ten rooms at the guest house, but John lived and slept and ate in just one. He stays in Manali in winter, when the snows come to cover the ground and block the Rohtang Pass, but Penelope never came in winter, because it was impossible to reach her beloved temples then.

Just up from Banon's guest-house, in the dark shade of a glade of ancient cedars stands the strange Dunghri temple, dedicted to the demon goddess Hadimba, who has controlled the forest there for two thousand years. She took charge of the trees after the holy rock, around which the four-tiered pagoda-style temple is built, saved her from being washed away by the great flood which the Hindus, like Christians, say ravaged the universe. According to the Hindu epic poem, the *Mahabharata*, (sister to the *Ramayana* in the same way that Homer's *Odyssey* and *Iliad* come as a pair), Hadimba was later married to Bhim, the most powerful of the heroic Pandava brothers, but only after Bhim had killed Hadimba's brother Hadimb, who was trying to protect his sister's honour. That the murder of her brother and the rape of herself endeared Hadimba no less to Bhim, her future husband, is typical of Hindu mythology. The gods and goddesses are always engaging in the most violent of rows, but they appear to be able to forget death and kiss and make up with enviable ease.

It is not so much the domestic complications of the Hindu pantheon which attracts Westerners seeking solace and escape from their material world, however, as the eternal spiritualism that is inherent in Indian culture. There is a regular population in Manali of Westerners who have adopted what they see as an Eastern way of life. There is an ashram up the hill a little from the Dunghri forest, in Vashist, where 'drop-outs' congregate. Yet the mellow ideal of a simple life led close to nature has palled for most, for dreams of heavenly flower-power and peaceful salvation are often brought down to earth by drugs.

Take a walk down the Manali bazaar and you see beggar boys selling saffron and Tibetan monks in maroon habits. You see stick-thin Kuluis with bent backs, neatly attired in grey tweed Kulu coats. There is a dirty fellow with a monkey on his shoulder who walks up and down, up and down the same three hundred yards over and over again, and there is a fat Tibetan with several chins who picks over gemstones with chubby fingers, stringing necklaces and sucking his teeth. Toothless Kului women in checked *pattus* and taxi drivers in Delhi-bought anoraks stand side by side, and there are brown Mongolian-shaped eyes flashing alongside the green eyes of the Kashmiri.

Then there are stoned Westerners in tie-dye clothing with pallid and spotty faces and glazed eyes. A French girl may have hair dyed yellow with peroxide, but her countenance is colourless. In all the myriad faces and shapes and colours of the mixed Manali population, hopeless Westerners, hooked on drugs and debilitated by an inadequate diet stand out, ridiculous and sad.

John Banon, Manali born and bred, was sick of them all. 'Marijuana grows everywhere,' he says. 'It is growing at the back of the kitchen, have you seen it? Here you pay about 50 rupees for 10 grammes. You can pick the leaf and rub it yourself to make resin. Then you scrape it off and dry it into small balls and then you mix it with tobacco and about three cigarettes are equivalent to a peg of whisky. If you are happy it will make you keep on laughing and if you are sad you become sadder. You start weeping.

'You can make it yourself – that is why you have all these hippies here.' John's son Thomas, who is in the perfume business, was approached by 'this very interesting person' who wanted to use the perfume oil plant to distil resin, to make the hashish oil. 'We said, 'No, sorry,' to him. He was a smuggler, you see. This is how they survive, by making these oils and balls and they sell them. The thing is, this hash is not so bad. It is that they become not satisfied with this simple drug from our weed, and then they are wanting the hard drugs. The heroin and LSD and they are bringing them here to Manali, to have "trips" in the mountains, and now our local people are buying these hard drugs from these Westerners.'

John met a girl who was tripping once: 'Some years back I was having this party and we were running out of drinks so I borrowed this important man's jeep to go into the town to get some more, but as I was driving down, by the circuit house gate, I saw in front of me a stark naked Western woman. I thought, My God. In the olden days there were stories that this place was haunted and I thought it was a ghost. But I braked as I came up to her, and then she sat down on the bonnet, naked. She wouldn't get off. I knew it was a human being, but she wouldn't get off. So I pushed her off but she picked up a huge stone; I thought, My God, this is an important jeep and if she throws the stone in the windscreen I will not be able to replace it, so I backed all the way home.' John talked to friends of hers some weeks later and heard that she was taken to Delhi for treatment, but that she had died in hospital. 'There are now many local boys on smack,' said John. 'They are slightly tilted, and they will not get work again.'

Penelope became interested as well in finding out what trip the 'hips', as she called them, were on. While she was staying with John, she conducted a series of interviews with 'irredeemables' like Michael Martin, an Australian farmer's son, who had thick curly chestnut hair, crawling with lice. He smoked *bhang* (marijuana) all the time and took LSD about once a week.

My grandmother wondered who paid for his LSD and Michael told her that money didn't exist for him any more. He begged for pennies to buy his drugs and he hadn't worked for years. 'But don't you get bored having nothing to do and no object in life?' wondered my grandmother. 'I'm very happy in this beautiful forest,' said Michael. 'And it's even more beautiful when I'm on a trip; then I feel one with it.' My grandmother said that she thought going on trips was like trying to gatecrash Heaven, but Michael just turned round and said, 'But lady, it is Heaven!' Her final word was: 'Sorry, but I don't believe it. God is not so cheap. Now all of you get ill incessantly and go down to the hospital to get help: what would you do if everyone went hippie and dropped out and there were no doctors and nurses to help you any more?' To which Michael replied: 'Oh I know the world couldn't go round if everyone dropped out, but it can take a certain percentage of us OK.'

Penelope wrote down her observations in a notebook and called the body of research her Hippie Treatise. After Michael in the book she observes Susan, 'a very pretty but rather stupid blonde American girl' who left New York when she was twenty to come to India and experience LIFE. She had been raped in the forest by five youths simultaneously, and wanted more than anything else to be a Lady. She was interested to know whether my grandmother had been born a Lady, or whether it was possible just to become one. Steve, 'a hopeless case of opium addiction', and Vicky, who had infective hepatitis, were observed after Hans, a Dutchman, who knew nothing about Indian art. 'I find it quite strange that 99 per cent of the drop-outs I have met know nothing about Indian Art,' wrote my grandmother. 'Vicki and Hans came to see us twice, and were very agreeable, but not very interesting.'

John Banon reproved an American 'hip' once, who was up his cherry tree, stealing cherries. The 'hip' shouted down from the top branch: 'They're not yours, they're God's!' Later that day he was asked for the price of a packet of biscuits by another American 'hip', and he said: 'I'll give you biscuits if you'll come and work for me.' 'What kind of work?' 'In my orchard.' 'That's not my kind of work.' So he got no biscuits. Richard, another American, rented a village house above Manali at the time when my grandmother was conducting her investigations. He had filled it with eight 'hips' for six months who were to learn to live together, do a bit of meditation, and plan their reform for society. 'They dress in dotty clothes with Hindu mantras printed on them but they can none of them read the Devanagri script,' she despaired.

She sat one afternoon on Richard's veranda, eating apple pie:

'A huge fat cigarette was passed round, but I said, "I don't smoke thank you," and only later did I realize that it was POT! However, as I have no idea of how to inhale, I should only have blown it out and not had a trip. I am PERFECTLY happy without it thank you. I agree that alcohol is just as bad for health when taken in excess, that is to say spirits, though wine I am sure is good for people. But speaking personally I prefer ginger beer . . .'

It is whisky that these Indians with Irish forebears have grown to love, however, and it was for just such a welcome beverage that I was invited to Jimmy Johnson's house. Jimmy's father (who was also an Irishman who married a Pahari girl) came to Kulu in 1920, and built a wooden house just along from Herbert Banon's in 1934. We walked over beautiful parquet floors made of plum wood, and admired the stylish 1930s fireplaces. Jimmy was quite frank about Penelope's physique, but admiring of her scholarship on Himachal temples. Like John Banon, though, he had avoided accompanying her on trek. 'The only time I ever sat on a horse it bolted from under me and I've never ridden since,' confessed Jimmy, who is rounded and jovial. 'We did look after her pony, Ugli, here,' he said. 'It was almond coloured and blind in one eye – a sturdy little thing and the children used to ride it. One day it just ate too many apples and died. I think Penelope was quite cross with us at that time. She was a well-built sort of woman, stout, you might say. I think she was big boned. For her size she used to move around quite a bit. I thought she was an extraordinary lady. I've got signed copies of both her books.'

His wife, Bala, a serene beauty with a knowing smile wafted on to the veranda from the kitchen where she had been instructing her cook in the art of making kedgeree: 'You take the skins of sheep and boil them up with kidney beans and onions and spices, (especially turmeric, because we have that with everything) and then you add rice and lentils.' She was less than complimentary about my grandmother. 'Personally I found her book about Kulu very dull,' she said. 'Just on and on it went with this boring trek. There was no real plot. I read her Spanish book too, but I think even the Kulu one was better than that.' We downed our whisky sodas in silent reflection.

For research purposes, my grandmother had needed a more knowledgeable pundit on temple matters than the recalcitrant John, who had failed to complete her demanding questionnaire, or the jocular Jimmy who knew much about farming but little about architecture. So John had introduced her to Pandit Balak Ram Gaur, a local landowner of some stature. Pandit Balak Ram was over eighty by now and lived on his orchards at Katrain, down the valley, with his son, the imposing Raj Krishan Gaur, and his daughter-in-law.

So I went to see the knowledgeable Pandit in his orchards, following instructions from John about taking the bus. Probably, I should have walked, however, for the bus conductors at Manali bus stand were noticeably lacklustre. There was a great deal of smoking going on, and sitting, and chatting, and not a great deal of driving, or information giving. I approached the inspector behind his grille and said, simply, 'Katrain?' he looked at me with contempt and said '695 number' before placing another peanut on his tongue. I sat on the stationary 695 for one hour and twelve minutes and ate my way through a brown paper bag of tangerines.

You have to learn to love this inevitable delay, and if you cannot love it, then you must learn to live with it. In India, patience is the virtue you need most. You must believe that the stationary bus on which you are sitting is going to leave eventually and convey you to the correct destination. You must resign yourself to the wait and enjoy watching the chattering Kulu girls with their parcels and their babies; however, it is nigh on impossible to quell the sneaking feeling that you may be on the wrong bus after all, and you end up watching every other bus wondering whether you ought not to get off this one and run after that one, like swapping queues in the bank.

My bus did leave though, although it took an hour to go the

fifteen kilometres to Katrain. But after my twenty-two-hour marathon from Delhi, this was a simple stretch, and I sat, compliant,
and watched the stoneworkers who were chipping bricks all along
the side of the road from great lumps of rock. I walked up the track
opposite the bus stop (where I had been instructed to walk in order
to find the house), but I did not know whether it was the right
track, and so I tried my grandmother's method of speaking in what
I hoped was the local vernacular to a particularly dotty-looking
cowhand: 'Pundeetbollockrum?' I ventured to ask. He pointed up
the lane as if he did it every day and I walked on, reassured.

The only thing I knew about Pandit Balak Ram was that he
was an octogenarian who had had a stroke two years before.
Penelope had often stayed with him, forsaking Room No. 11 at
John Banon's for a room at either one of the Pandit's three
residences: at Duff Dunbar, his house in Manali, or at Katrain or
at his house further down the valley in Kulu town, because after
she had discovered how much he knew about Hindu temples in
the area, she could not leave him alone. She revelled in quizzing
him for information, and he loved her passionate curiosity.
Through their mutual interest, they became the best of friends.
His son, Raj Krishan Gaur, was fifty years old and had been a
politician in Simla, a Minister for Tourism at one point (about
which his father, a modest and unassuming gentleman, said: 'I
don't know why he doesn't give it up and come home to farm. He's
had a flag on his car – what more does he want?').

I found the drive off the track, and strolled up it ambling more
confidently than I felt inside. I came to the two-storeyed tall house
round the first corner. It was made of wood and stone and painted
brown, and it was big and oblong and quite ugly, with a grand
circular set of steps leading up on to the stone veranda, and on the
veranda there sat a small man. Pandit Balak Ram Gaur was sitting
in a wicker and cane chair. He wore a stiffly starched white shirt,
open at the neck, with a pocket handkerchief and a pair of smart
pale blue creased woollen trousers which, magically, seemed to
hold fast around his huge protruding belly without the aid of

braces to keep them up. He wore smart shiny brown laced shoes and when he stood up to greet me, he only came to my shoulder. He said he had been waiting for me.

His head emerged from his shirt like a tortoise from its shell, and his skin lay in folds, soft, translucent and dappled with liver spots, even up over his shiny balding head. He had watery pale blue eyes that matched his trousers, but he was firm in his welcome. 'How good to meet you,' he said. 'Penelope's grand-daughter is here at last. How we miss our dear friend Penelope.' His stroke had impeded his speech somewhat, and he spoke as if he was trying to get his tongue around several cotton wool balls in his mouth, and he beckoned me to follow him into a high-ceilinged sitting-room, where wicker chairs were arranged around a coffee table.

'We are the third generation living here,' he said in muffled tones. 'She would stay here, your grandmother. She liked the apples.' The Pandit's family are hereditary *pujaris* (priests) of the Hadimba temple at Manali: 'There are a set of different *devtas* [local deities] in every village, or every group of villages,' explained Raj Krishan Gaur, the son, 'and these *devtas*, during the previous days, when the Rajas ruled the place, were given land and the land was sufficient food source for the people who worked the temples. In lieu of the land given to them, they were supposed to render some service to the temple. So they became *pujaris*. That is how our family have become *pujaris* at the Hadimba temple.'

As well as holding the responsibility for the Hadimba *puja*, father and son are farmers. 'We grow paddy, maize, wheat and chestnuts. And apples of course, as well,' said the old man. 'In the old days we used to grow all the British varieties – the pippins and the Cox – but now we must cater for the market and grow only Red Delicious. We never used to send the apples to market before. We gave an advertisement in the paper instead, and sent boxes to individuals by post on request. Then we had many different sorts and the English would buy all the different ones.'

Pandit Balak Ram used to take Penelope to the Dusshera

Festival in Kulu town. Dusshera takes place all over India in October, to celebrate the victory of Ram, the hero of the epic *Ramayana*, over Ravana, the demon king of Ceylon. In the Kulu dialect, '*dushet hera*' means 'the demon killed'. Peculiar to Kulu is the practice of bringing all the local *devtas* from their village on *raths* down from the mountains to attend the ten-day *mela*. *Rath* is Sanskrit for chariot, but these mountain *raths* are more like palanquins on which metal or wooden masks of the local gods and goddesses are fixed. Each processional journey is led by the temple band, their drums beating, and the whole village will come and camp with their deity on the banks of the Beas near the open *mela* ground. The *devtas* are washed in the river and offerings are made by the villagers and the *rath* bearers and the priests to Durga, who slayed the buffalo demon, because she is Goddess of Victory. There is much merriment and dancing too.

'Penelope was INDEFATIGABLE,' pronounced the Pandit carefully and with awe. 'Twice and thrice I have seen her there at the Dusshera in the evening to see the lights and the fires and she will be dancing too. She would ask me to go with her so that I could tell her things about the *devtas*.' Pandit Balak Ram always keeps an open house over the festival period, as his home is a popular starting point from which to view the proceedings. One can hear the festivities going on all through the night from his veranda and my grandmother loved it, especially the drums; for she always said there was nothing more haunting than the tribal beat of a temple band.

Raj Krishan's wife interrupted then, and silently poured milky hot coffee into delicate bone china cups. She handed round a tin of coffee creams and shortbread biscuits, and then withdrew as noiselessly as she had entered. I made an attempt in vain to introduce myself to her, but her husband acknowledged her only with a nod before she disappeared.

'You would tell her about such-and-such a temple and she will make a point to reach it,' her father-in-law continued, ignoring the cup before him. 'The more difficult, the more eager she is to pursue it. I remember I told her once, there was a temple over at a place called Bagpon. For four and a half years she continually made approaches to that temple, but the *pujari* there was old and traditional thinking and he would not allow her to enter the temple – not even the premises. "Why am I not allowed?" she asked me. I said, "Penelope, even I am not allowed because I am not of that village." But she would not desist and next time she took one of the officers from the army station and she was allowed in the place. She would do anything to get into a temple. She was quite persistent and dogmatic in her approach. Nothing would come in her way.' He fell silent and took up his coffee, spilling a little as he brought the cup to his mouth.

'As a matter of fact, I think people who have the same interests will always get on well,' said his son, with solemn profundity. 'She was good company for my father.' He went on: 'She was a good soul. She had a human approach. She liked the entire humanity – and especially the downtrodden. She had a great liking for them, for the poor people, and a great understanding of them also. Many people remember her, right from the humblest porter to the highest notary.'

I was getting a bit hot, what with the coffee and the dark intensity of the room and Raj Krishan's jet black eyes. His father seemed to have slipped into a nostalgic reverie all of his own, and Raj Krishan went to stand by the mantelpiece, on which there was a picture of himself and Rajiv Gandhi arm in arm. 'Ah yes, you see I was in politics,' he said grandly as he caught my eyes wandering to the photograph. 'But what about religion?' I said, getting back on track. 'Some people seem to think Penelope believed in reincarnation and wanted to be reborn a Hindu. Did you talk to her about God?' 'As a matter of fact we are Hindus,' he said. 'But in common with Penelope, we never believed from a narrow sectarian point of view. She was a devout Catholic, but she had respect and tolerance for all other religions as well. We wanted to see religion from a wider point of view also. She was the same type as us and that is why we were rather close. Our main topic was always the deities, though. She did not talk to us about her family or her husband.

'As a matter of fact, she found satisfaction in this valley, I think. She felt at home here. We Kulu people, we never forget our place. We are attracted to our surroundings. There are very few who leave the valley after they are born here.' The atmosphere in the quiet room was suffocating now, as Krishan Gaur moved into the more general sphere of the way of Kulu, which led quickly into the way of India and then into the way of the world and I did not seem to be able to get him to be more specific about Penelope. His polemic continued, and I tried to think of getting us outside. He was wise but I was claustrophobic.

Thankfully, his father appeared to start awake and turn his mind back to our conversation. 'I do miss Penelope. She was a good lady, and amusing too,' he said. I missed her terribly then and as the sweat prickled on my brow, I could feel tears of frustration rising. I wanted her to be there to walk out into the orchard with, and to sit next to on the bus ride home.

But the Pandit saved the moment by rising neatly to his feet with surprising energy. 'I must be off to see the doctor,' he pronounced carefully, with no explanation, and marched out on to the clover lawn. He stood under the spreading walnut tree with his felt hat on and his suit jacket over one arm, waiting for his driver to bring his car round, then he slipped into the cream Morris Ambassador, on to a smooth brown leather seat, and with a wave of his walking stick, he disappeared down the lane. The imposing Raj Krishan Gaur slipped back inside the brown and cream house and I walked down the drive alone, reeling from the two-hour ordeal and revelling in the mountain air.

CHAPTER IV

Boura Singh at Prini Ropa

'It is of course inevitable that what we are pleased to call civilization must come to these hills – but I do hope it will come with discretion and not destruction as has happened so often in the West.'

PANDIT BALAK RAM's estate rests on more than just his orchards at Katrain: he owns a house above the Dungri forest as well. Perched a mile above Manali, near to the Hadimba temple, the wide, wooden Pahari-style house sits in its own apple field which is untended and overgrown now. The house is called Duff Dunbar, after the Scotsman who built it in the 1870s.

Duff Dunbar was a Conservator of the Kulu forests who became so devoted to the Kulu valley that he decided to build a house there, in which he might live for ever. Alas, as the story goes, just as he was sipping his first cup of tea on the veranda (which was so new at the time, you could have smelt the wood shavings), he received a telegram from Caithness. An uncle had died and it was his duty to return to Sutherland; Duff Dunbar of Manali was obliged to slip home and become Laird of Hempriggs.

So he sold this brand new house to a Mr Mackay, and through Mackay's childless Pahari wife, Bhagti Mackay, the house was left to an aunt of Pandit Balak Ram's and thence to Pandit Balak Ram himself. Lucky landowner that he was, the Panditji already had his hands full with his house in Katrain and another house in Kulu, and so he began to let out Duff Dunbar to visitors. In the summer of 1971, he leased it to my grandmother who had become his friend. She settled in Manali from April till September, grounded by the task of correcting the proofs of her Kulu book. The book, which had been conceived originally as a 'then and now' tirade, had turned into a comprehensive historical, architectural and cultural guide to the Kulu valley. She had intended to compare modern travelling with visits to Maharajas in the old days; she was supposed to have given equal page space to the eccentricities of the Raj as to her own experiences in 1963 and 1964, but what began as a personal memoir turned into a tribute to the Indian valley, lovingly penned by a Kulu devotee.

At the beginning of the book (which was published in 1972, eight years after its original deadline) she held the Indian Institute in Oxford responsible for the delay: 'I have spent so many fascinating hours there,' she wrote, 'following up one reference after another in the most obscure periodicals, so that it has needed a superhuman effort to get down to writing at all, as everyone will understand who has worked in great libraries.'

My grandmother was so busy with research after 1965, that she waited until 1970 before returning to India. She decided to stay for at least a year this time, so she had no reservations about taking the long route out: she would drive overland through Europe, Turkey, Persia, Afghanistan and Pakistan for the second time.

Another motley crew was assembled for the expedition. Joining my grandmother again was Elizabeth Simpson, who had been on the 1963 trip. Then there was Bess Cuthbert, a 'nice young gel' who had spent a year previously teaching in Hyderabad, and the third Elizabeth was Elizabeth Chatwin (Chatters), the American wife of the British writer, Bruce.

Elizabeth and Bruce Chatwin had met Penelope in the 1960s at a dinner party given by 'rich' Ron Gurney's uncle, near Wantage. Bruce, who was working for the *Sunday Times* at the time and had not yet written a book, sat next to Penelope, and within three minutes of them lifting their forks they were engaged in deep discussion about India. My grandfather, John Betjeman, said later: 'They were talking nineteen to the dozen, just like little Indian love birds.'

The newly married Chatwins would visit The Mead; that Elizabeth was not only mad about horses but also a Catholic pleased my grandmother no end, while Bruce she simply adored for being Bruce. When she saw 'the golden-haired boy' walking up the path through the garden she would burst out laughing, she was so happy to see him. My grandfather was impressed with him too: once when they were staying a whole weekend with the Betjemans, Bruce took John his tea in bed. 'Imagine being given tea by Chatwin,' he said afterwards.

After Penelope had moved to the Welsh Mountains, Bruce went to stay with her there. While a *Sunday Times* journalist, he had written *In Patagonia*, which had been lauded by both critics and the public, and now he was trying to write some more. He wanted to do a short story on these two brothers, farmers in their seventies who had never married and lived together in a house not far from my grandmother's. He would call it *The Young Men*, he said. He stayed with Penelope and collected wood in the forest and ate her soda bread and every day he would go to see the brothers.

When he made the brothers into twins and began writing in earnest, his wife Elizabeth says she knew that the work was going to turn into something else altogether. My grandmother introduced him to other local Welsh farmers and butchers and parson's daughters, and bakers and blacksmiths and clerks, and he began to hear muddled tales of incest, and murder and old vengeances, and he listened and he learnt and he bound the tales together into what became his acclaimed masterpiece, *On The Black Hill*.

However, all that was after Elizabeth's trip to India in 1970 with Penelope. 'Chatters' was encouraged by Penelope to join the overland expedition after she was commissioned to write for the *Pelican Guide to Indian Art*. She had had some trouble in getting started on the task and Penelope wisely advised her to go to India for a fresh look at what she was supposed to be writing about.

The fifth member of the crew was a talented young artist who had met the Betjemans in Wantage. John Nankivell had been teaching art at a girls' school in the Berkshire town when he dared to walk up the Betjemans' garden path on a Sunday morning to show my grandfather his drawings of Victorian buildings. He caught the poet ambling, alone, back from church, and lost nothing by foisting the roll of paper upon him. For John Betjeman liked what he saw and invited the young draughtsman back for breakfast the following day. He could see what Penelope made of him.

John Nankivell found my grandmother terrifying and knew that she thought he was an impertinent interloper. But much later, she said to him: 'I spend my life protecting J.B. from people like you, but you slipped through the net, thank God.'

Young John (whom my grandmother christened the G.B. – The Growing Boy) became my grandfather's unofficial chauffeur, driving him to visit churches and to Pusey House and to Bateman Brown's (who said the G.B.'s drawings were like young Augustus Johns). Old John (my grandfather) became the G.B.'s unofficial patron, encouraging him to draw and teaching him more (although he already knew an enormous amount) about architecture. 'I think John knew where I was coming from,' says the G.B. 'I was socially insecure and a bit chippy, you could say.'

Later, after the G.B. had moved to Longleat to commune with Lord Weymouth and his 'art group' it was Penelope whom he returned to Wantage to visit. She would feed him up and tell him about India, and one day she said, 'There are these Indian pagoda temples and I'm making plans to go on an expedition. Would you come with me and draw them?'

It was a year later before Lord Weymouth's art group fell by the wayside ('He was far too extravagant with the paint,' says John. 'We'd squeeze £150 worth of Windsor & Newton tubes into a bucket and then we'd flick it all on to a wall in one afternoon.') and John telephoned Penelope: 'I can come to India with you,' he said.

'So I ended up being eunuch to four dotty women,' says John. Chatters says that John was terrified of them all at first. He was responsible for the tyre pressure on the two vans they drove, and in return for his mechanic capabilities he was getting a free ride. The others, the three Elizabeths, had sent Penelope into Oxford with enough money to buy two Volkswagen vans. She was charmed, however, by a handsome young salesman and ended up buying two J4 vans instead. The others were furious with her, because J4s have their engines in between the two front seats, making the interiors particularly hot and noisy. But Dr Dick Squires (the 'Captain' of the 1963 expedition who practised in Wantage) was employed to render the vehicles fit for travelling, and by the time they left, everyone had simmered down.

Penelope and John drove one van, while Chatters drove the other. Simpson and Bess swapped about a bit, for various reasons. Bess was, in actual fact, about to fall for the G.B. (as he was about to fall for her). Elizabeth Simpson was fascinated by my grandmother. She found that although she had an extrovert side, Penelope was incredibly private, and did not show her feelings often. Elizabeth had been worried that she disappointed Penelope, as she was not especially conversant with religion; she did not realize that my grandmother fed off enthusiasm, and that Elizabeth's love of the art they came across was enough for Penelope to hold her in high esteem. As Elizabeth Chatwin has said, my grandmother was so good at making people out to be 100 per cent better than they thought themselves to be. She made jolly sure everyone knew that Elizabeth Simpson was a champion at tennis and Elizabeth (Simpson that is) says: 'Penelope made the most amazing difference to my life.'

Penelope inspired all the Elizabeths, but Simpson especially, and at one point, when they were crossing the border into Turkey, she probably saved her life as well. Penelope had sent the others on to meet her and Simpson at a campsite near a garage further up the road, as she and Simpson were deep into an artistic discussion and preferred to sit in the stationary van for a while before moving on.

All of a sudden, a big, dark man appeared out of the night and tapped on the window of the van. In one strong, brisk movement, he opened the door and got hold of Elizabeth and started to pull her out on to the ground. He had her by the legs and she held on to the wheel, and Penelope held on to her neck (and nearly strangled her); meanwhile he was trying to get the key out of the ignition (he was drunk, they thought). He struggled for a bit and then it appeared he suddenly decided that he'd have Penelope instead. 'Penelope stroked his neck and forehead,' recalls Elizabeth. 'She said, "Mama, Mama." I thought she was trying to tell him that she was my mother and that she was looking after me, but in actual fact, she meant that if he raped me I'd have a baby, but that if he raped Penelope there would be no baby, so he'd do much better to rape Penelope.' (My grandmother had had a hysterectomy after her children were born and in any case, she was pushing sixty.)

Penelope told Elizabeth to go and get help, but Elizabeth wouldn't go. 'Penelope really was going to allow herself to be raped,' says Elizabeth. 'She was going to be passive and grin and bear it, which she thought was the least dangerous way of getting out of the situation.' In the next instant he seized my grandmother and yanked her out of the van. Her bloomers were revealed, Elizabeth's jaw dropped, and Penelope shouted: 'GO AND GET HELP!' And with that she broke loose from the astounded assailant and started to run off into the field by the road, hoping that he would be distracted by her and leave Elizabeth to drive off. She planned to hide in the corn if he started chasing her. Indeed he didn't know which way to look and in the minute's space that gave her, Elizabeth started the van into reverse. But, on the brink of escape, the attacker grabbed hold of the wheel. There might have been a ghastly end to the tale had not some headlights come beaming round the corner at that moment; in a split second the rapist vanished and a van load of Americans leapt out of their vehicle to the rescue.

'There was this heap of potatoes at the side of the road,' says Elizabeth. 'And the next minute the heap got up, roaring with laughter, and Penelope said that she'd learnt from the Girl Guides always to hide her face from the moonlight, so that the glint of her eyes did not attract attention! She didn't appear at all frightened although it had been very frightening. She said, "Elizabeth, LUST is a very TERRIBLE thing," and then we drove on to the campsite beside the garage to tell the others.'

When they all arrived safely in Istanbul, Bruce Chatwin was there to meet them – he was due to see his wife and her companions off on their final leg. Bruce was in Santa Sophia when they found him and Penelope walked up to him in the middle of the cathedral: 'Oh my dear, we've been raped!' she said to him, and for quite a number of years afterwards she lectured about the incident on the convent circuit.

Penelope was forever turning into convents which was fine for the girls, but it meant that the poor G.B. had to sleep outside the gates. More often they camped. On one occasion, when they got to the Khyber Pass too late to cross into Pakistan, they had to spend the night in their vans in the car park in Afghanistan, alongside six or seven other vans parked there, which were filled with 'hips' on their way from India.

In the morning, Penelope got up incredibly early, as usual, to see the sunrise. There was a luminous sunrise, pink and glowing, and she couldn't bear for the hips not to see it. So she went round banging on the windows of all the vans, shouting: 'C'mawn, c'mawn, up you get!' (to the mortification of her travelling fellows who had been woken already) and slowly these filthy, raggedy-haired youths began to appear, stumbling out of their vehicles, wrapped in blankets. They could not believe this woman. The dawn was truly beautiful though, and the hippies were grateful to Penelope for having woken them, although they all went straight back to bed as soon as the sun had fully risen.

These and other incidents (like being stoned by nomads in Iraq, throughout which Penelope roared with laughter) as well as Penelope's insistence on stopping for at least two days at a time to photograph monuments in both morning and evening light, meant that the cavalcade moved slowly, and they were late arriving in Delhi. It was too late for John and Penelope to make their way into the mountains, so the five split up and travelled off in various directions. Penelope remained in Delhi to learn some Hindi ('which she promptly forgot,' says John), and then she and John embarked on a southern tour, while they waited for the snow to melt on the Himalayas.

Penelope had not been to the south of India since the 1930s when she had visited Madras and stayed with the Maharajah of Mysore in Karnataka. This time, she was captivated by the easy going Dravidians and enchanted by the rural areas; also, she discovered that she liked the ornately carved stone Hoysala Hindu temples (which she had previously dismissed, with youthful disdain, as being too 'folksy') and that she was, this time, interested in the Jain temples; there was also joy in the fact that all the temple sites were much less visited than sites in the north. She tied a knot in her handkerchief (her way of remembering things) to remind her to come back to them.

For Kulu already was becoming overrun with 'hips' and tourists and, worst of all, what she called 'Progress', which meant roads and televisions and telephones and cars. Her beloved Kulu valley was being 'opened up' and it was beginning to upset her, for even since 1963 there had been vast changes. Her torrent of anger always targeted the poor electricians: 'It is extraordinary', she once wrote, 'how in every country without exception the electricians (the most unaesthetic class of technicians known to "civilization") have gone out of their way to spoil the best buildings by attaching cat's cradles of wires to them, and choosing a really photogenic piece of architecture beside which to erect a transformer pole.' She continued: 'Electricians have an aesthetic all of their own; so proud are they of their contraptions that they set them before great works of art.'

The temples on Shuttleworth's list, however, were for the most part too far away up side valleys to be attached to electricity yet, and she had not driven overland from England on a perilous journey to India to give up on her long-anticipated temple-seeking agenda. Therefore, after wintering in the south, Penelope and John Nankivell arrived in Manali in the spring of 1971.

They based themselves at Duff Dunbar where they planned their various treks in search of temples. Penelope spent five weeks searching for an adequate riding pony (she hated to walk, of course) and eventually got hold of a Bashahri horse-dealer who took her to see his herd which had been wintering in Mandi (the town at the gateway of the Kulu valley, which you pass through if you come by road from Simla to Kulu). Among the herd, she found a stocky thirteen-hand palomino which she called Thakur (which means chieftain in a medieval baron sense as opposed to a king of a country), and a dun with a dorsal stripe, a Roman nose, a ewe neck, a long back, a low-set tail, which on account of his many physical disappointments, she called Ugli.

Between mid-April and the end of June, Penelope rode and the G.B. walked to more than seventy temples on Shuttleworth's list, and photographed and drew and measured them all. When the monsoon broke (and it was the worst monsoon since 1901 which lasted four months instead of the usual two and a half), the odd couple nested at Duff Dunbar to make sense of their notes, and for Penelope to correct the proofs of her book (and add still further research) which John Murray had sent out from England.

There were hundreds of rats already resident at Duff Dunbar. John stuffed all the holes which led into his bedroom, but Penelope refused to sleep inside on account of the heat, and always slept on the veranda. In the middle of the night, John would hear screams – HELP! HELP! – as the rats ran over her middle and down her legs and then they would both get up and spend half the night rat-bashing. They left all their food in tins piled up on top of one another in the middle of the kitchen floor like a tower, and sometimes in the night they would hear a terrible crash and all the tins would be spread about and ransacked. 'It was horrible,' says John

The next most virulent pests that wet summer were the sandflies. John, being naturally dark-skinned, was not susceptible, but Penelope was badly attacked. And then she would pick her bites until they turned into lesions and then she would go riding and rub them and those on her leg would turn into ulcers. On one temple trek, to Sainj, a tiny village miles up a side valley, one of her ulcers became so infected that she became delirious, and John had to despatch the guide and the two ponies back down to Manali to bring up a nurse with antibiotics. Three days later, the aid arrived and John says it was like seeing Joan of Arc – a saviour riding on a white horse, when the nurse finally appeared over the brow of the hill riding Thakur, the palomino pony.

Penelope survived the septic period and continued correcting the galley proofs of her book. Her hectic correspondence with Jane Murray (John's wife), which had to survive from Albemarle Street in Piccadilly to Manali, via the worst monsoon since 1901, kept her in some contact with the world outside Kulu, but for the most part she lived a Pahari life.

That summer, she met Christina Noble, a brave and intrepid Scotswoman from Argyll. Christina (who has since written two books – *Over the High Passes* and *At Home in the Himalayas*) had walked through the Himalayas from Simla to Kashmir in 1970 and had fallen in love with the mountains. To enable herself to keep returning, she decided to set up a business organizing trekking holidays, and she based herself at Manali. She had been introduced to my grandmother when she was doing research in the India Office Library in London in 1969, and had quizzed Penelope for information about the Kulu district; they were to meet for the second time in the Manali bazaar – it was a small town and they were both such odd residents, so it was unlikely they would miss each other – and my grandmother did everything she could to encourage Christina's resourceful venture. She divulged all the local knowledge she had accumulated about the area since 1964, and introduced Christina to her Pahari friends. She also agreed to act as guide on several treks which were planned along temple-lined routes.

Out of this simple meeting of like minds came the beginning of my grandmother's tour-leading career, which was to be her regular 'job' (though for a variety of employers) during the next sixteen years. She always said that she should have been a schoolmarm and that she loved showing people beautiful things they might never have seen before. But the most compelling reason for doing the tours was that the free return flight and fee paid for the two- or three-week-long expeditions would bring her back to the mountains every spring or autumn, and provide ample resources for a good eight-week or three-month exploratory trip of her own afterwards.

Christina Noble's company, West Himalayan Holidays, grew hand in hand with the Kuluis' increasing respect for its founder, and she added more treks to her list annually, keeping a hand-picked and loyal band of porters and guides on retainer. She stayed in Manali from April until November every year and soon enough she met Kranti, her late husband, who was formerly an English lecturer at Simla University. Kranti, who was an intelligent and kind Brahmin, resigned from his job to come to Manali and help her run the trekking business, and in 1977 she produced Rahul, her son (who became Penelope's godson) and, a few years later, Tara, a daughter.

The simultaneous growth of the children and the trekking business stretched Christina so far that she advertised for someone to help. It seemed that Boura Singh (the man she employed as houseman-cum-cook) appeared out of the blue but in actual fact he came from a farming community in Garwhal; he joined the household, fell in love with the children and ended up not only cook and nurseman but also as head porter on some of the treks, and on several he went along as my grandmother's right-hand man.

Boura Singh was still working for Christina when I got to the Kulu valley. As all the family were back in England, he had been left in sole charge of their Manali home, Prini Ropa. Christina had entreated me to go and see him and she kindly said that I should use Prini Ropa, the Pahari-style house designed by Christina and Kranti and built by local masons a mile from Manali, as my base in the Kulu valley.

What with one thing and another – endless glasses of whisky with jolly Jimmy Johnson; a trip in an Indian tourist bus to see the Rhotang Pass which took six hours up the fifty-mile road, and five hours down again, with just half an hour squeezed in between the two journeys to look at the overwhelming view from the 13,300 foot pass; and many hours' work of bargaining over shawls in the Tibetan market – what with all these things, I had hardly set foot out of Manali.

So when I set off along the road to Prini (a single-track tarmac lane is how it would be described in England) with my white cotton cricketing hat on my head, my black umbrella swinging in my right hand and my smart pink and purple rucksack on my back, I felt for the first time that I might be about to see the kind of Kulu valley landscape my grandmother had fallen in love with. Manali in the rain is not a pretty town, and it is thick with diesel fumes from the fruit lorries.

Along the road away from the town the air became clearer immediately, and though I had to walk through a depressing shanty town for a hundred yards or so, the roadside after that was marked only by the odd small, family-run hotel. Less than half a mile on, all buildings disappeared and the road was flanked by acres and acres of orchards and paddy fields, green as you like.

All the apples were ripe on the trees, and it wasn't long before I had picked and eaten about fifteen of the shiny Red Delicious crunchy fruits. My grandmother once wrote:

Florally speaking, the Himalayas are pleasantly suburban – I mean in the face of such awe-inspiring heights. With everything on such a colossal scale, it is refreshing to be surrounded with the familiar flora of a suburban Surrey garden: every kind of conifer, rhododendrons, a profusion of rambler roses, berberis, irises, marigolds, indigofera, jasmine, spiraea, cotoneaster and, high up, sunspurge. Potentilla, delphinium, columbine and Himalaya creepers are a study in themselves.

To my shame, I would not have been able to identify such a floral feast had I come across it, but I knew that most of those flowers were over now anyway, for it was autumn. Instead, round the apple trees grew a huge variety of grasses which would have needed a botanist to differentiate them, and in place of flower-filled meadows I was treated to the lush, moist, vivid green paddy fields. The cultivations gave way, up the sides of the valley, to pine forests, and the whiff of the pine needles was splendid. The alpine freshness of the atmosphere made you feel high as a kite.

I was going to use Prini Ropa as a base from which to organize my trek. I planned to walk up and out of the Kulu valley over the Jalori Pass, via the hill villages of Banjar, Gaggi, Shoja, Khanag and Ani, to Rampur, the summer capital of the Rampur Rajas, which sits deep in the gorge of the Sutlej river valley. It was a route riddled with temples, and one along which my grandmother had led many a breathless tourist. In fact, her treks over that way had become so established in the West Himalayan Holiday brochure, that they had become well known as 'Lady Betjeman's Temple Tours'.

But I was not walking only to retrace her steps, for along that route lies Khanag, a tiny Pahari village sitting high on the other side of the Jalori Pass, looking away from Kulu and over towards the next great valley, the Sutlej. And at Khanag my grandmother had died. My task was somehow to carry a memorial stone there, and set it in cement.

I reached the house after walking for an hour. It was set to the left of the road, one paddy-field's width back. It had been built in the indigenous timber-bonded style of the Western Himalaya, with alternate courses of stone and deodar beams, like Duff Dunbar. The old Pahari houses which were built in this way with dry stone, are said to be earthquake proof because the absence of mortar is supposed to give the house a chance to quiver with the quake instead of fighting it, but Christina and Kranti's house was stuck well together with plaster, a concession to modern building methods.

Like the village houses, it had a wide wooden veranda round its upper storey – with a balustrade decorated with carved friezes chosen by Christina – on which you could sit all morning or all afternoon or even all day. From one side you gazed southwards, right down the length of the Kulu valley towards Simla, and from the other side, you gazed right up the Kulu valley, northwards to the 13,300-foot-high Rhotang Pass and the snowcapped peaks of Lahul and Spiti beyond. East and west you looked up the Hampta mountain behind the house or out across the paddy-fields and the apple orchards lining the breadth of the valley.

Prini Ropa would have been the most beautifully situated house in the world had not some developer planned his red tin-roofed concrete monstrosity of a hundred-room hotel just below it (a development which Christina had not bargained for). When I was there, they were still building the hotel, and in the early morning of every day the stoneworkers would begin their relentless chipping of the blocks, a chimeless, monotonous sound which was infuriating. A film-music channel from the radio blared up the valley sides too, so that the natural silence was broken. This was the 'progress' which my grandmother had been against so vehemently.

Still, after Delhi and the everlasting long bus ride and Manati and John Banon's strange moods, and the Pandit and his severe-looking son, Prini Ropa was paradise to me. When I arrived, there were two dark little men sitting smoking on the paving round the base of the house. Their expressions were somewhat friendly but still seemed a bit wary of me and indicated that I should go upstairs. I went up the wooden stairs and out on to the wooden veranda, to inhale the view.

On the north side I found a pale, weak-looking Englishman who just managed to lift his head from his charpoy to utter the warning: 'Don't drink the water. Don't even brush your teeth in it,' before flopping lifelessly back down again. He had a migraine and a terrible stomach from indulging in his favourite snack of *pakoras* from the bazaar and he was sick as a stoned cat. 'Boura Singh's back later,' he mumbled. 'Shopping . . .'

I trod quietly away along the veranda and back inside, remembering that this must be Christina's nephew, David Sumsion, the architect who was staying in Kulu for a year to do measured drawings of all the pagoda temples in the valley. I supposed I would meet him properly when he was better. I tiptoed down the stairs and outside, and there I bumped into Boura Singh. He eyed me with suspicion as I introduced myself. 'No Lucy?' he asked. (My sister Lucy had met Boura Singh with my grandmother several years before.)

He was fifty years old and bendy-looking in shape; he had deep, intelligent velvety-brown eyes which glistened and you could tell he was sharp as lightning; but he was also kind and I knew from Christina that he was a first-rate cook as well.

He seemed to recover from his disappointment quite quickly and he took me to sit – or rather he was squatting on his haunches and only I was sitting (on a wooden stool) because at that point I wasn't able to squat without leaning up against a wall – we were settled anyway in front of the stove inside his smoky kitchen. His kitchen is a corrugated iron hut separate from the house – what they call in India, a 'go-down' – with murky corners. There was one bulb hanging from the ceiling but the frequency of power cuts in the vicinity was such that for most of the time we sat in candlelight. He called me Imomemsahib and he chuckled as he worked his tongue round the new word.

'Ah Penelopememsahib,' – that word was much more familiar to him – 'She was always sitting on a pony.' His words danced round the memory of her. He had found her antics on trek hilarious. Mischievously, he had loved her having to walk (when the path was too precipitous for riding or the pony was too tired) because he knew she hated walking. 'She walked slowly, slowly, crying "Aste, (slow down) Aste" all the time, and she would pretend to cry, woo hoo hoo woo hoo.'

Boura Singh doubled up with laughter at the memory of her flailing on the mountainside and then I gave him a photograph of Penelope that I'd brought, taken of her in the hills behind Prini. 'This is truly a beautiful Penelope picture,' he said, mirth dispelled. He looked a touch wistful and sucked long and hard on his *bidi*, the local Indian tobacco cigarette. He always had a box of matches tucked into his smoking hand, because his *bidi* would keep on going out. He smoked No. 10, which are quite strong but all right once you get used to them, and he always offered me one; but I never became a confirmed *bidi*-phile. Mainly, because I couldn't cope with them always going out.

'You know, Imomemsahib,' he said, holding the picture up beside my face. 'Mmmmm,' he murmured. 'You look like Penelopememsahib, but I think you don't eat like her.'

He told me how she always had big pockets full of biscuits on trek. 'And for breakfast she is having four pieces of toast hot with *ghi* [clarified butter] and apricot jam. And her favourite thing is banana *lassi*.' I loved him talking about her in the present tense.

His was probably the tenth confirmation of Penelope's sweet tooth that I had had since coming to India. My diary of our trip together has a cream bun reference on every page. Whenever we reached a new town, it seemed that our first imperative was not, in fact, to seek accommodation, but to find the coffee shop which provided the most superior pastries and ice-cream milk shakes. My grandmother would attempt to justify the imminent consumption with: 'Well, we have just walked up that steep hill,' or 'We spent three hours in the museum this morning, we deserve a reward,' or 'We'll be needing energy for tomorrow's trek,' or, better still, 'I think we're both looking tired and peaky, we need sustenance.' It was not my natural instinct to refuse her suggestion.

Though she could make a delicious chicken curry with poppa-dums at home in England, Penelope always preferred European food to Indian, which was probably a habit she formed when she was a girl in India during the Raj, when she ate French and

English food at her mother's table. A habit many of the Indian restaurants in India have inherited from the days of the Raj is their pudding selection. In a roadside eating-house in a tiny town in Uttar Pradesh you could find *crème caramel* and rice pudding and treacle toffee. Penelope would hire a bicycle and ride for an hour on it if she thought she might find a lemon meringue pie at the end of it, or failing that, 'tostbudder' at least. Indian toast is made from white bread as white, light and tasteless as polystyrene, and the jam it comes with is red and glutinous, but it was manna to my grandmother if she had been curry-bound for a week or two.

There has not been another trekker in the Western Himalaya, apart from my grandmother, who has tried to cook macaroni cheese followed by banana custard from a Bird's packet over a *chula* (the ubiquitous open clay oven). She undertook this daunting challenge in a candlelit rest-house seven and half thousand feet up a mountain, and produced the delights on day three of our trek together up the Sutlej valley. We devoured both courses outside on a table in the moonlit rest-house garden, with a panorama of the Great Himalaya before us, and a scornful *chowkidar* (caretaker) looking on (who had sulkily vacated his godown for the evening).

Boura Singh had never allowed Penelopememsahib to bring the threat of white sauce into his kitchen, however. Boura Singh cooked chapattis famous for their thinness, and weightless pakoras which melted in the mouth. Since David (the ailing architect on the upper veranda) could not address so much as a poached egg for the first three days of my visit, Boura Singh rolled his chapattis for me alone, and fried up delicious potatoes with fresh herbs and light tomato curries with peas and rice. David had told me that Boura Singh loved having someone to talk to and cook for and that he had felt a bit morose while David had been off games (and breakfast, lunch and dinner), and he said that I was to make a fuss of him and to try to be always hungry.

So in between breakfast, lunch and dinner, I spent a lot of time charging up and down the valley, up through the pine forests to Hampta, through the apple orchards, and past the village children running after me and screaming: 'Hello, hello, hello, lady, lady, lady.' I explored the *nalas* (ravines) with a black woolly dog who attached himself to me one day, and I was having such a lovely time, that I forgot it was my birthday.

When I remembered (in the afternoon of the day – I was writing a letter and had asked David the date) Boura Singh whipped up some of his melt-in-the-mouth pakoras, and we decided to have a party. David disappeared off into town, and I telephoned Paddy Singh.

It is confusing when so many people are called by the same name, but if you knew Paddy and Boura and had known Kranti, you would certainly find them different makes of men. Captain Padum (Paddy) Singh was the tallest Indian I had ever met. He must have been six foot three at least. He was lean and good-looking and wore faded denim shirts and jeans.

He comes from a family of Rajas who brought him up in Simla with a British governess, and then sent him to the Bishop Cotton School (India's equivalent to Harrow.) His education completed, he joined the army, got into quite serious trouble by marrying a tribal girl when he was stationed in Ayodyar, and then left the army and joined the tourism trade in the Kulu valley.

He had met my grandmother for the first time at a party Kranti and Christina gave at the Sunshine Inn for some of their trekkers (everyone knows everyone in Manali, and if there's one party, everyone will go). Paddy had talked to my grandmother for some time and had been amazed at her continuous consumption of pistachio nuts during their conversation. Paddy and his second wife Nita were working for a hotel called Span Resorts at the time, but soon afterwards Nita went to work for West Himalayan Holidays (Christina and Kranti's company) and Paddy set up on his own, running Paddy's Treks from his and Nita's cottage in Vashist, above Manali. In the absence of both Christina and Kranti, to whom I would have gone first, I asked Paddy and Nita to help me organize my trek.

Paddy arrived for my birthday with a bottle of whisky and a

beautiful dark grey Kulu shawl. David came back from town with some madly coloured hand-knitted Kulu socks, and Boura Singh provided the pakoras (which we dipped into tomato ketchup). We sat on the veranda and watched the valley cool towards night and then we went in to the living-room, which was lined with striped cushions and warmed by a wood-burning stove.

Paddy was wonderfully evasive about trekking plans. 'Anything you want I can arrange,' he had said. But when I showed him the map and said I would like to walk from here to there and stay here and spend a night there and then walk over that bit, he said but you can't stay there, and why don't you stay here and you can take a bus up that bit, and here is much nicer than there. And when I said I would like to leave on Tuesday, in the morning, he said but you might as well leave on Wednesday in the afternoon. And when I said I would be happy with one guide and that I could carry my own bag, he said but you must have two and don't you want a pony?

We hustled over the arrangements for a good hour or two, gently depleting the whisky in the bottle at the same time, and by the time he left we had not especially sorted anything out at all, except that Panchok, who was one of the trusted porters retained by Christina, would come with me, and that he would bring his Nepali friend Manbadur along too. I said I would telephone Paddy tomorrow, and I knew he would sort everything out in the end. It would just take a few days.

The next morning I was woken by Boura Singh bringing my 'bed tea' – a British Indian custom which Christina instilled on her treks and then extended to her home life. The caffeine and sugar in the tea kick-start you into the day. Over our breakfast of *dahi* (curds) and bananas and fried eggs, taken in the morning sunshine at the slate table outside in the paved garden between the house and Boura Singh's godown, David (who was much better) suggested we walk to Paddy and Nita's house at Vashist for our morning's excursion, because Nita had been caught there by a landslide. We set off after breakfast; with his umbrella and his collarless white shirt, his tweed Kulu waistcoat and his balding brow, David looked so like an Englishman walking in the Indian hills. But he seemed to fit, because the Indian hills were so like England sometimes, with the apple trees and the stinging nettles and the clover fields.

The rest of the day, however, was Indian without a doubt. First we set off, then along the road we met a messenger who had run from Nita's to tell us that she would be coming to Prini at ten o'clock (it was already eleven o'clock at the time). So we kept walking – hoping to meet her on the road. We got to the junction where there is one road to Manali and another to Vashist. Worrying that she might have gone to the bazaar on her way to Prini, we waited at the junction for half an hour. Then we walked up the hill (and climbed over the landspill which was blocking the road) to Nita's house; but she had gone and the *chowkidar* didn't know where she was except that she might have gone to see us at Prini. So we had a glass of lemonade on the green-painted veranda and waited half an hour and then we walked all the way back to Prini, none the wiser. We sat down at the marble table where we had had breakfast and Boura Singh suggested lunch.

The following day at three o'clock, without explanation, Nita appeared at Prini Ropa. She was petite and beautiful and highly organized. 'You want to do this and this,' she said. 'Right, that's organized.' And we had a cup of tea and arranged to go over the final plans – provisions, timing, chits for the rest-houses along the route – the next day. We would meet at the Tourist Café in Manali at 1 p.m.

The next morning a note arrived via a messenger from Nita: It was long and complicated and littered with apologies and sentences beginning 'I have spoken with Paddy in Delhi . . .' (for Paddy had flown to Delhi on business suddenly) and after Boura Singh and David and I had deciphered it, we realized it said that the trek would not commence on the following Wednesday as arranged. There was to be no lunch at the Tourist Café, and would I come to Manali the day after?

In between assignations with the Singhs for 'preparation discussions', I mucked about at Prini. David and I rode on the roof-rack of the bus down the valley one day to Nagar where there is a huge four-storey pagoda temple and an old castle. On another day, I walked 2,000 feet up the hill behind the house and watched the apple harvesters carting crates of Red Delicious down the mountain on their heads, springing from rock to rock like mountain cats.

On rainy days (the monsoon was just trailing off) we would sit in the living-room and David would draw and I would do 'homework' which consisted of writing out the Hindu pantheon and the history periods and the temple types and trying to learn a bit of Hindi. David was properly applying himself to Hindi and could almost have a conversation with Boura Singh.

Boura Singh said my grandmother's Hindi had been hopeless, and Christina always said that in the beginning my grandmother's Hindi had been the typical Hindi of a memsahib with a vocabulary limited to the command form. The trouble was, that by the time she started coming out to India regularly she was already sixty and though she tried and tried to learn a wider vocabulary, the words she learnt went in one ear and out the other. She understood quite well, though.

Every day I went to talk to Boura Singh in his smoky kitchen. He would smoke while I ate, because while Boura Singh is from the Kshatriya caste, I am, as a non-Hindu, casteless and not fit to share a table with him.

He explained the caste system to me, in simple terms: the highest Hindus are the Brahmins, who are by tradition the priestly ones whose wisdom makes them leaders and arbitrators. Next are the Kshatriyas who are soldiers and administrators. The Vaisyas are the merchants and artisans, and the Sudras are farmers, or agricultural workers and labourers. The four castes are said to have come from parts of the body of Brahma, the Creator in the Hindu triumvirate to which Vishnu (the Preserver) and Shiva (the Destroyer) also belong. The Brahmins are supposed to have come from Brahma's mouth, the Kshatriyas from his arms, the Vaisyas from his thighs and the Sundras from his feet.

Today, of course, a Sudra can become a politician and a Kshatriya a writer. Some Brahmins are businessmen, others farm land. There are also many thousands of sub-castes which separate different craftsmen, like blacksmiths from carpenters, for example – Hindus who may not be craftsmen at all any more, but whose ancestors were. In the rural areas though, the hierarchy is still recognizable, and a good Hindu will not soil himself by eating with heathen types like Christians. So Boura Singh smoked and talked to me, while I had the pleasure of savouring his food.

'Penelopemensahib, ah yes, she had a good intellect,' he often said. Boura Singh was a mild intellectual snob, in that he was worldly and well-versed in politics and religious philosophy himself, and appreciated a good mind when he came across one. That is not say that he would condescend towards the other men who worked for Christina and Kranti – the porters and guides – but he was aware that it was likely that he knew a bit more than them about most things.

He thought my grandmother's knowledge of his own religion and her appreciation of the temples was astounding. In the tin-roofed godown through a haze of *bidi* smoke, he conjured up the image of her – in her jodhpurs and Mackintosh with the pockets bulging with films and snacks, and her camera-case strapped round her middle (so that the camera was always there, handy and right in front of her whether she was on a horse or not) with her white cotton cricket umpire's hat and her sunglasses, which Boura Singh called her 'goggles'. He rocked on his haunches and and nearly fell over backwards laughing as he remembered her slipping over a lot of the time and lying laughing in the grass, crying, 'Help! Help! I SIMPLY can't get up!' He imitated her high-pitched cries so evocatively that we really thought that at any minute, she might walk right into the godown with her yellow sou'-wester hanging on its knicker elastic round her neck.

Boura Singh thought that I should take her place and lead

treks through the hills, because I was young and could walk fast. I said I'd have to do a lot more 'homework' first. He was fed up with leading old people, he said. Not my grandmother, he said, because she was never old, if I knew what he meant.

There was a television at Prini Ropa, which flickered and twitched and went out with the power cuts, but we watched a film or two and then dug out of Christina's video collection a copy of the BBC documentary made about my grandmother in 1974. It is a funny film, mostly made so by Penelope's antics as she leads the unassuming tourist officer, Mr N. K. Sharma and a camera crew over the mountains in search of Hindu temples. Boura Singh's heartfelt emotions fluctuated from glee at the sight of her on screen, to sadness at the nostalgia the film brings, and he sat on his haunches right close up to the screen, to get a better view of her.

She seemed a bit impatient with the crew, I thought, as if the whole idea of five people with tripods and cables and lights following her about on the goat tracks was absolutely ludicrous (which it was). Also, by 1974, she was fairly disillusioned with the development advancing its way up the Kulu valley. The electricity cables in Kulu town (which is halfway down the Kulu valley) depressed her. As did the ever-increasing number of tourists who now swept up the Manali road by the bus-load. She said: 'The inner Himalaya is beginning to resemble the Welsh mountains in August – there are hikers everywhere and more and more mule tracks are becoming jeepable. Those of you who would see these mountains still unspoiled in their remote tracks must hurry therefore, or soon there will be a jeepable road up Everest.'

She conceded to N. K. Sharma that the hill people wanted television and light, and she allowed for her part in bringing tourists to the area, but she began almost to wish she had never publicized the valley by writing her book and other articles and lecturing on it. She also wished she had never accepted to go on television.

She wrote to her friend Billa Harrod: 'Re TV, I have seen the RED LIGHT. The last thing I want to become is a "television personality"! I want to concentrate on my Himalayan temples; cataloguing my unique slide collection of same & lecturing and writing about them. I love lecturing but I honestly don't enjoy acting.' Boura Singh, however, thought she was marvellous. Lady Penelope was a better movie star than any of the girls in the regular Hindi films, he said, and he watched the film all over again.

By which time I had been invited to meet the Singhs in Manali again. I hitched a lift into town in the back of a truck loaded with Zanskari apple-pickers, who were beaming with smiles, and I met Paddy and Nita in an open-air café which served pizzas and continental food. We drank hot milky coffee, and I sat back and watched Nita and Paddy contradict each other on every point, because Paddy was determined to keep plans open, while his wife was determined to pinpoint every detail. It was very funny and I wondered if their completely opposite attitudes were what had kept them married so long.

We needed to arrange to get the slate – two feet by three and weighing about fifty pounds – up to 10,000 feet, then find a mason to set it in stone. Finally, we reached a compromise. Paddy said that he would drive me and Panchok and Manbadur (who were still coming with me) to Banjar, the village from where we would start towards the Jalori Pass. Confirmed. Then Paddy said that he had a friend in Banjar, Mensingh, a local Thakur, who might be able to help us employ a local mason – we would see when we got there. He said we would definitely leave on Saturday morning. Done, I said.

CHAPTER V

The Stone goes over the Mountain

'I love the companionship of animals. My idea of heaven is trekking alone on a pony through beautiful country; I feel I really get in touch with God.'

PADDY ARRIVED in his jeep to pick us up at 7.30 a.m. on Saturday morning (we had not expected him to be on time at all and were still enjoying a breakfast of bananas and *dahi* when he arrived). Panchok, a small, wiry Tibetan, was ready and squatting beside my rucksack, smoking a *bidi* and guarding the stone.

With serene reverence the night before, Boura Singh had wrapped the stone in newspaper, straw and hessian, and tied it up with string. He was morose in the morning. He wanted to come with us, he said, in fact he didn't think we could possibly manage the trek without him. Watch those clouds, he said, as he gloomily stirred the tea in his godown.

Like a concerned parent, he instructed Panchok to look after me. And don't put too much chilli in the *dahl*, he told him. Then he waved us off furiously, until our jeep had rounded the corner along the road back into Manali.

The bazaar in Manali was just beginning to show the first signs of waking. Wisps of grey smoke were rising from the Tibetan huts clustered round their Buddhist *gompa*, and the stallholders in the main street were sweeping the steps in front of their stores. Buses sat purring in the bus stand, and against a bill-covered wall beside the bus stand squatted Manbadur, our second man.

Panchok, the Tibetan, was short (he barely came to my shoulder) but Manbadur, a Nepali, was shorter. He looked like a leprechaun, with pointed ears and bandy legs. His smooth, tough, brown face folded into even creases when he smiled, and he leapt nimbly into the back of the jeep. He was shy and couldn't quite meet my eye.

The drive to Banjar, which is only twenty miles down the Kulu valley, took a good two and a half hours, as Paddy found it necessary to wave at every passing notable. Several times he stopped to conduct a shouted conversation with two engines' worth of clamour, after which he would accelerate off violently (so that Manbadur and Panchok and I lurched backwards), slapping his horn jovially in salute.

We also stopped halfway for provisions at a bustling market town called Bajaura. Panchok and Manbadur had a whispered conference and then disappeared into the market. I could not see them for apples and mounds of lentils and the dust raised by laden carts and straw in the packing boxes. Their tiny lithe fingers were lost between huge-bottomed housewives in lurid purple saris.

Not that that made them any the less skilled at efficient shopping. The pair of them returned half an hour later and handed me a list of thirty-four 'items', neatly drafted in Hindi on a piece of cardboard. I was baffled by the number of different things, as I knew that Panchok only cooked rice and *dahl* and sometimes cauliflower. I added tea to that and sugar, powdered milk, coffee, flour for chapattis and oil and still I counted only nine 'items' at the most. He began to go through the list in Hindi, but I was flummoxed after four names and could only hope that he had brought a whole spice rack with which to flavour his *dahl*. I anticipated a wide variety of mountain-top culinary delights.

My grandmother always complained about what she called DDD (damned dull dahl), the thick and nourishing lentil soup which provides the only protein in most Pahari diets. She used to stock her own supply of tinned sardines and chocolate bars and pistachio nuts. Rice and lentils are the staple diet of all the hill people, because vegetables are hard to grow high on the hills, and eggs are rare and precious. Rice and lentils are also the cheapest commodities available. You can dine out in a roadside eating-house on such a menu for 5 rupees a head, which is about 14p, and the restaurateur will go on filling your plate until you are sated – a case of 'have as much as you can eat'.

I bought simply a bag of dried apricots in Bajaura for emergencies and trusted the rest to Panchok. I thought he ought to be able to conjure up something tasty from thirty-four different ingredients.

We trundled on down the main valley and then turned off left into a side valley up beside the Tirthan river (a tributary of the Beas). We halted for toilets at the rest-house at Larji where my grandmother had had a memorable egg curry in 1964 (so she wrote in her book). I doubt if the same *chowkidar* was still in residence, but whoever it was he gave us a strong *chai* (tea) each and told us that he had a party of Indian civil servants arriving that day for a weekend fishing trip – there's a good stock of trout on the river.

All over the lower Himalaya is a series of Public Works Department (PWD) rest-houses built by the British in the last century to accommodate the commissioners and engineers who walked all over those mountains inspecting their appointed regions. The Victorian bungalows crop up at ten-mile stages on all the old routes in and out of the valleys, and are now meant for use by Indian government officials. Each rest-house has a *chowkidar* who protects his particular property fiercely. A *ferhingi* (foreigner) is only permitted to stay after a certain amount of persuasion and on one condition – that if an Indian dignitary arrives in the middle of the night, that *ferhingi* will disappear quickly. It's a risk you have to take. Panchok seemed on speaking terms with all the *chowkidars* we encountered, and it became his job to negotiate the deal at each rest-house. I doled out packets of *bidis* where and when it was required.

The deal usually meant that we could use the kitchen (always a smoke-filled clay-built outhouse with an open wood fire or *chula*) and that when Panchok cooked our supper, it was understood that he'd cook enough for the *chowkidar* as well. I began to see why we needed thirty-four items on our shopping list when the *chowkidar* so often produced a friend or a son and his son's friend too.

We didn't stay to fish with the civil servants but climbed up a thousand feet to Banjar, where we all hoped Paddy's plan of operation would come into effect. Our first task was to raise Mensingh, the local Thakur, out of bed. Which might not have been difficult had not the Thakur built his farmhouse five hundred feet up a precipitous slope on the outskirts of the village. It was raining hard now, and Paddy and I stood under a black umbrella shouting up the mountain, while poor Panchok was detailed to race up the zigzagging goat track leading to the house to see where Mensingh had got to. Paddy had written to tell him we were coming, but it was impossible to tell whether he had received the missive or not.

He hadn't, it transpired, and he was most surprised to see us. He came bounding down the mountain after Panchok, in his pyjamas of all things and his eyes were stuck together and puffy. He had the pale skin and brown hair of a Kashmiri, and an air of relaxed confidence about him (which Paddy said came of his having been to Europe). Paddy gave him a cigarette to wake him up – which seemed to do the trick – and then we got down to business. However, at every suggestion Paddy made – to find a mason, to buy two bags of cement – Mensingh shook his head vigorously. I despaired.

Mensingh spoke English and he had been to France, but he was still an Indian, and for an Indian a shake of the head does not always mean no. It sometimes means no, but more often it signals assent. It it easy to forget this common Indian habit, and as Mensingh shook his head at every turn, I thought that we would never reach Khanag and lay the stone, for it seemed that he thought it was impossible to go to Khanag, impossible to get cement, impossible to carry the stone and impossible to find a mason. I was furious with Paddy for having built up our hopes for nothing.

In fact, of course, as Paddy explained to me after I had simmered down, it was possible to do all these things. We arranged that while Panchok, Manbadur and I would walk up and over the Jalori Pass to Khanag, reaching the rest-house there in three days' time, Mensingh would see to the mason. Then, somehow, Paddy would get the mason, the stone, Mensingh and himself to Khanag in time to build a plinth for the stone.

The rest-house at Bajaura was lavish. A blue and white Victorian bungalow, it stood in its own lawns, terraced especially for it on the side of the mountain. Running along the front of the house there was a great glass enclosed veranda which was furnished with a three-piece suite in black leather. You could hear the water rushing in the river below. Paddy left me there and wished me luck.

Dinner was delicious. Panchok appeared at 6.30 p.m. looking flushed and pleased with a huge tray heavy with potato curry and fried cabbage and chapattis and rice and *dahl* and lime pickle and set it down before me. I had never been cooked for alone and I felt silly and spoiled when the monumental meal materialized, but I learnt that first night that my porters were eating the same food at the same time and that Panchok actually liked to cook and took pride in what he produced. If I left so much as a chapatti on my plate he would be disappointed. So I tucked in nightly to a series of varied vegetarian feasts and had no more say on the subject.

It rained hard in the night on to the corrugated iron roof over my head and the mosquitoes were persistent and aggressive, so I was up and out of that room at six sharp. I'd bought a smart black umbrella in the Banjar bazaar and I used that as my early morning walking stick. On my way down to the Tirthan river I came upon a smiley Sadhu, who was shrouded in the morning mist and swathes of orange cloth, and swung an umbrella, just like mine, on his arm.

Sadhus are Hindus who have rejected the material world for a nomadic life of prayer and pilgrimage. But there are many Sadhus in India who are not really Sadhus at all and Mytannion was one of those. He let down his tied-up dreadlocks especially for me and they tumbled, thick and dark and matted, to the back of his knees. He spoke perfect English.

'Will you come and see my ashram beside this heavenly river?' he asked. I followed him down the goat path, and with energetic swings of his dreadlocks, he turned his head to tell me about his German girlfriend.

'She has gone back to Germany, you see. We have two sons who are called Rama and Krishna but only in her homeland will they get the schooling they need.' He went on: 'And now I am so lonely.'

Then he showed me his beehives.

'You would enjoy to stay here at the ashram? It would be no more than 300 rupees for one night,' he said. 'I will teach you how to make honey and also to meditate.' Persuasive though he was, I explained I had my own mission to accomplish.

'I am leaving today for Khanag,' I said.

'And I must meditate all day and tend to my cabbages,' he said, dolefully. 'Would you come to the *chaikhana* [teahouse] for a glass of tea?'

I imagined him sitting there all day, gossiping and accepting hand-outs and tempting every passing stranger with lures of honey and heaven at his well-appointed ashram, and I declined. I hurried back up hill to gobble down a chapatti with a banana rolled up inside it before Panchok, Manbadur and I put our packs on our backs to walk to the bus stop.

I like walking, and I wanted to walk all the way over the mountain, but Panchok and Manbadur and all Indians as well (sensibly, I suppose), think you are potty to walk when you might take a bus instead. I could not persuade Panchok that I would prefer to walk the whole way. There was a bus at 8.30 to Gaggi, five miles higher than Banjar, and we three were going to be on it. We were at the bus stop well in time, but the bus didn't come.

We made a place for ourselves on the sloping forecourt of the bus stand, which seemed to double as the market square and the town's meeting place. We waited there while a pan-wallah with red teeth set up his stall. He took some popcorn out of a dirty tin box and pushed it in fresh plastic bags to sell.

As we waited a madman asked me for a cup of tea. He wore a khaki uniform and a coloured pillbox Kulu cap into which he'd stuck a bunch of wild flowers as he marched up and down the market-place shouting military commands to the village at large. Nobody took any notice of him except me.

We waited as I listened to a woman vomiting in an upstairs room above a vegetable shop and I hoped it was a pregnant mother with nothing but morning sickness as three stubby (and grubby) children then came down the stairs. They stood giggling and shy and dared each other to cross the street to say hello to me, but then their attention was taken by three little boys in matching stiff prickly shirts and brown dungarees. The little boys marched in unison up the hill with their hair parted in the middle and oiled down each side, and their mother, trussed up in yellow chiffon, walked with mincing steps behind them, treading carefully through the market-place in her pink plastic sandals, as if she could not bear to touch such filthy ground. She glanced down with disdain at my three grubby friends as she passed. My stubby three with the vomiting mother followed the glowing family unit, all dressed in their Sunday best, and stared after them with wistful longing in their eyes.

We waited while a wiry man with a jeep, and a twitch on the left side of his face, told us the bus was cancelled and offered us a taxi service at an inflated price. But Panchok knew best and we waited on, for one and a half hours until our bus arrived. Perhaps the timetable was changed on Sundays.

When we got down at Gaggi, we had left densely populated bazaars worlds away. Gaggi was one short street with five or ten one-storey wooden houses on the left and five or ten one-storey wooden houses on the right. The track up which the bus had hauled us ended here. The bus turned round and went back down again and then the valley was quiet.

Panchok decided it was time for a cup of tea and a smoke, so I bent my head to enter one of the wooden houses on the right and we all sat down in line on a warped wooden bench. Tea is *chai* in India and this was a *chaikhana* or teahouse. But *chai* is not tea as you know it. It is brewed in a special way and you have to grow to like it because that is the only way it comes. There was no coffee up there in the hills.

Tea powder and milk powder and sugar and water are boiled up all at the same time in a saucepan on an open clay *chula* until the liquid is of syrupy consistency. It is poured from a height into small glasses and then poured from one glass to another for cooling purposes before it is set before you. It is warm and sugary and comforting.

So we had a cup of tea and a smoke. Panchok and Manbadur spoke the same language as each other which was slightly different from what the Paharis spoke, but they could all understand one another. Though I could not understand their tongue, we established a vague sign language and we always knew what each of us was on about. We sat together and walked alongside each other mostly in true companionable silence.

My two tiny pixies of protectors would not let me carry a thing. I sensed that Boura Singh must have had a word with them about that. I pleaded to be allowed, at least, to carry my rucksack with all its special straps and buckles that I loved to adjust so much, but Manbadur was firm. And then he ignored all my orthopaedically correct backstraps and strapped my pack instead to his shoulders with rope which he also wound round his head.

It would take three or four hours to walk up through the deodar forests to Shoja, our next stop, with a rest-house perched on a promontory just a mile below the pass. Now, after the bus rides were over, and the crowds were left in the valleys below, our trek would properly begin. We expected not to come across a single soul except for the odd herdsman with his flock of mountain goats or a woman gathering brushwood for her fire.

We expected too much. Not five minutes after our departure from Gaggi, a young man ran to catch up with us from behind, and introduced himself as Anul Kumar Arora. He was the only doctor in this wild region and he was walking that day to the civil dispensary at Kothi.

'Would it be of any inconvenience to you if I accompany your party for part of the way?' he asked, hopefully. We were so jolly and buoyed up with the mountain air that we didn't mind if he walked with us at all, but as the climb progressed through the thick ferns and the iris leaves of the forest floor, the magic of the woods enveloped us all and the doctor's remarks and comments and jokes began to pop up and irritate like uninvited guests at our private reverie. Our murky, dripping woodland atmosphere was crowded with his inane conversation. And I suffered most because he spoke English and directed his remarks at me.

'Actually, I do not like my mountain posting but it is necessary for a young doctor to do service in a remote area first of all . . . Actually I am bored by nature and I do not have any persons of interest to converse with . . . Actually, it is good to talk with you . . . Actually, I am perspiring because I come originally from the plains.'

Panchok was leading a fast march at this point up a steep and narrow goat track. He'd taken a short cut through the woods, and when Panchok veers off you follow, up however steep a goat path he happens to lead you.

Dr Arora continued: 'Actually, most of the diseases I attend to are respiratory and gastronomic. There are few casualties here . . . Actually I do not believe in these Gods . . . Actually with some bribery I may be able to take a better posting in the city.'

Uncharitably, I expect, I wished he'd bribed his official already for a distant posting. He was just the sort of handsome, charming young Indian that my grandmother tended to adore, and the sort of man she would have considered just right for me. One of her hobbies was fixing up her granddaughter with the right sort of

Indian husband. Of course high-caste Indians would rarely take a Christian bride from abroad so we were usually quite safe, but that didn't stop her from making the preliminary arrangements.

This time, I wasn't in the mood. I had anticipated with relish our peaceful climb with not a word uttered in the still air, and with that prospect dashed I was even more distraught when the doctor came all the way to the rest-house and stayed for another two hours to talk incessantly and share my lunch. A proper monsoon thunderstorm then erupted across the skies and as he didn't have a coat or an umbrella it would have been mean to send the doctor off, so we had another discordant couple of hours together before I feigned exhaustion and sloped off 'for a rest'. He went then.

I sat on the yellow sofa in candlelight wrapped up in my Kulu shawl with a cold nose and cold toes. Panchok surpassed himself and arrived from the outside kitchen bearing delicious *dahl* and fried cabbage and rice and while I ate I read the myth about the Hindu demon goddess Durga killing the buffalo demon, to make myself brave and fearless.

Then I read the passage in my grandmother's book *Kūlu* which describes her preparations for bed on the night she spent there at Shoja rest-house in 1964:

> Went to bed in my pink silk and wool combinations, nightdress and jersey, with a tepid hot water bottle and my heavy hunting mac over the blanket which covered my sleeping bag. Even then I was cold and had to keep moving about to keep warm so I slept very little.

I went to bed in my thermal underwear, three shirts, pyjama trousers and slipper socks. I draped my Kulu shawl over my mountain sleeping bag, but still I fared little better than she had. There was deathly quiet that night in the Victorian rest-house, but it was not a companionable kind of silence.

The first thing I did in the morning was to wash my 'smalls' like my grandmother had always taught us. Then I climbed out of my various layers and had a cold bucket bath. Penelope had loved chucking jugs of cold water from a bucket over her body, so I steeled myself to perform this ritual daily. There was not exactly any alternative. After chapattis and *chai* with Panchok I felt washed and nourished and bold enough to venture out.

The grassy bank on which the rest-house sits in its commanding position at the head of the valley is covered in the leaves of irises. In May and June, the grassy bank is blue. But I just had to imagine that. I walked down on sheep paths to the village which hugs the steep side of the valley supported by terraces of crops. There were wild roses and horse chestnuts growing between the houses. There was meadow sweet and meadow crane's bill, ragwort, mint and sweet pea. There were whole fields of white sweet peas. I longed to try the fresh wild apricots that my grandmother had written about, but I didn't find any. And the apple trees and pears were fruitless too. There had been no rain that summer and the monsoons were only coming now, late, in September, so most of the high crops (unlike the valley crops) had failed.

The houses in the village and all the true Pahari villages in those hills are built in alternate courses of dry stone and deodar (Himalayan cedar) beams. On the ground floor the animals are often kept – a few cows or sheep and goats – and above them hay and corn may be stored. Round the top storey there is usually a veranda where the old men will sit and the toddlers will play and covering them is a chalet-style roof made with huge grey slates. There is no plumbing inside the house, and the villagers will wash their pots and themselves at the well or pump in the middle of the village. They go to the loo wherever they think is best.

Up and down the vertical village, the farmers who lived there stared briefly at me as I passed and then ignored me and went back to their work. In a flash of forwardness I showed a picture of my grandmother riding a pony up one of the mountain roads, to a man who was smoking a hookah on his veranda. He shook his head knowingly and said in his best English, 'Yes, I have seen her.' I supposed he meant five years ago, but I hoped he meant he had seen her spirit riding about more recently.

I poached a lot of peas and took great trouble shelling them and making sure there were enough for three and then I found some good strong mint, because I thought peas and fresh mint would be a welcome vegetable on the supper menu. When I showed my gatherings to Panchok he smiled in a sympathetic way.

'Good food,' I said and offered the mint for him to smell but he just looked knowledgeable and took it from me and threw it away.

'Not good food,' he scoffed. 'Not food.' He did the same with my preciously picked peas, threw them away and we had *dahl* and rice and fried cabbage for supper as usual.

The track which climbs the last stretch to the Jalori Pass is at first banked by irises, then ferns and lichen and then, near the top, lone tall fir trees and scraggy grass. There is no snow there in September but each time we climbed a few feet higher, our panorama of the far-off snows of the Great Himalaya grew wider. Every twenty minutes, Panchok would look round at me:

'*Bidi?*' he would say. 'Mmm, *bidi*,' I would answer, and we three would squat there on our haunches and smoke a *bidi* and survey the wondrous scene before us.

'Bot sunda! Bot sunda!' I could not help exclaming at every turn. Panchok taught me this phrase which means 'very beautiful', and each time I said it he would nod in solemn agreement.

Then after a while spent gazing in silence he would turn and nudge us, '*Chelo?*' (Let's go), and on we marched.

We took tea in one of the three wooden shacks that are eating-houses at the 10,570 foot Jalori Pass, and huddled close in the biting wind. The cooks in their godowns were stirring lentil stew in anticipation of the needs of hungry travellers. The familiar smell of frying onions was a strange one to encounter at the top of a mountain pass. We ate only a stale and crumbly Marie biscuit or two with our tea and we did not linger.

Panchok led the way through the woods eastward along the top of the ridge to the holy Lake Saryalsar. The original route from Kulu to Saraj passed not where the rough motor road now crosses Jalori, where we had stopped for tea, but to the east at Lake Saryalsar. When my grandmother first entered the Kulu valley on horseback in 1931 with her mother, she must have come by the lake. She would have seen the view that we now saw, and she would, most probably, have been overcome by the magnitude of the mountains, as we were overcome.

She had probably slipped about in the mud as I was now slipping about. Panchok and Manbadur made a sandwich of me along the path to prevent me from falling but without fail I fell again and again on to my bottom, which they thought was very funny.

So we stumbled and I tumbled for those three high miles and we were in need of more hot beverages on arrival at the lakeside. Beside the small lake, which is fifty yards across and said to be full of live worms, is a shrine to Kali, the demon goddess, and wrapped in a blanket by the door was a very gloomy *pujari* (temple priest). His expression grew gloomier as I approached to have a look. Fog had descended and the outlook was grim, so in sympathy with his gloom, and to appease the goddess Kali and allow us smooth passage, I gave him eleven rupees. He looked gloomier still.

But there was a smiling *chai* wallah who cheered our hearts a little. He sat in a warm cave and he seemed glad to see us, and brewed up a saucepan of tea in our honour. He and the *pujari*, the only inhabitants of this spooky, raven-watched place, apparently were not on speaking terms.

Panchok found the atmosphere oppressive too and shortly uttered our moving off signal – '*Chelo?*' It was more of a command than a question, so Manbadur and I slipped in line for the last leg to Khanag. The euphorious morning's climb to the pass was overshadowed now, by the swirling mists of Lake Saryalsar, and we trudged down the sheep track, deep in thought. I was thinking about my grandmother, but I have absolutely no idea what they were thinking about.

We passed a Pahari woman who was watching her herd of cows with one eye and sewing a pair of *pulis* (string shoes) with a big needle. She had nine earrings in one ear and three black teeth. The Kului women wear a large, often checked, tweed shawl (a *pattu*) wrapped round them in such a way that it makes a long warm dress to the ground which is fastened on one shoulder by a sort of kilt pin. They tie a cotton scarf round their head like a gypsy. Since we had now come over the pass and out of the actual Kulu valley and into Inner Saraj, I could not call this woman a Kului, but her dress was still the same as we had seen on the other side. She beckoned us on past her and down to Khanag.

We could see the village now and the whole valley lay green and deep before us. We reached the village – a rough, ramshackle huddle of wooden and stone houses – and a group of perhaps ten boys and men were washing and fooling about by the pump. They wore skimpy trousers and their bodies were wet and glistening with soapy lather. The women on their verandas were knitting and the old men in the open-fronted tea shop abandoned their card game to follow us with their beady dark eyes as we pressed on down the main street. The rest-house sits alone, below the village, and it seemed we dragged our feet along the final last few hundred yards.

The rest-house itself is a brick-built bungalow with a corrugated iron roof and a wooden gabled open veranda which looks away from the mountainside over a round stage of a lawn. The lawn was edged with a tall and blooming border of mauve and white cosmos flowers. They were just the mauve and white of the checked shirts Penelope always wore and of her pinafores. Mauve was her favourite colour and I was absolutely sure that she must have seen to it that they grew there.

I collapsed on the veranda steps and I read what she had written about her arrival there in 1964:

A more wonderful situation could hardly be imagined. In the foreground lay a little ledge of clover lawn with sweet-scented carmine, cabbage roses growing close to the bungalow veranda and beyond the lawn the *khud* fell steeply down the valley where you could see the torrent a long way below dashing in and out among the spurs of the mountain, while to the North West there was a great amphitheatre of deodars going round to the Jalori Pass, which was hidden by a fold in the hills.

It was heaven there, on the edge of the world. It was not India or Switzerland or England but a sort of magic land suspended between nations which might just as well have been Heaven. I minded so badly that my grandmother was not there in person but I was glad that she had died in the most wonderful situation she could imagine. I had no doubt that she was riding about there, still inspecting temples.

Just as I was feeling like the last person in the world, a short man with swept back hair, horn-rimmed glasses, a Kulu cap full of flowers and a long, smart, brown tweed coat appeared, leaping about like a dotty professor and gesticulating in a jerky way to his companion. His companion was a smiling, spacy looking young Sadhu in nothing but an orange sarong, slung so loosely around his narrow hips it seemed about to fall. The Sadhu kept kissing his mad master's knees. I thought, for a minute, that I was having an apparition.

The man in the brown tweed coat told me that he was the roads engineer of the district and that he lived in the cottage behind the rest-house with his personal Sadhu. The villagers later told me that he attended more to the Sadhu than to the roads and that he had a perfectly nice wife and ten children whom he kept in another village.

I invited the engineer to lunch, but it appeared he was fasting on some religious account, so it was just Panchok, Manbadur and I who sat down to sweet fried potatoes. (They would eat with me at lunchtime, but never at 'dinner'.) The plan had been for Paddy Singh and Mensingh to arrive here at Khanag with the mason and the memorial stone the next day. We would build a plinth and set the stone in plaster strong enough to weather the monsoon rains. Of course, the plan had now changed.

The communication system in the mountains was extraordinary. Panchok told me over lunch that now we were to walk back up to the Jalori Pass the next day by the motor road to meet Paddy at ten o'clock, because the jeep would be unable to manage the road any further down to Khanag, devastated as it was by landslides and as yet unrepaired by the recalcitrant engineer.

The *chowkidar*, whom we had met on our arrival at Khanag, had given this message to Panchok. How Paddy knew in advance from forty miles away up the Kulu valley at Manali that the last three miles of the mountain road had fallen into the *khud*, and how he had relayed his instructions to the *chowkidar* at Khanag so that we might be told of the new arrangements when we arrived, I had no way of knowing.

I was so excited about laying the stone at last that I woke very early and went to sit on the lawn. The mauve and white flowers were a firm reminder of Penelope. Vaguely, I had hoped that her ghost would visit me in the night, but I was never so lucky and I did not even dream of her. We walked back up the shoulder of the mountain, round the amphitheatre of deodars to the Jalori Pass in a couple of hours and met Mensingh and Paddy Singh and a very neatly dressed and precisely mustachioed mason whom they had hired for the day. It felt like a proper pilgrimage as the six of us struggled back to the rest-house carrying 40 lb of cement and the heavy slate that Boura Singh had wrapped in straw and hessian and bound with twine a week ago.

We chose a site at the entrance to the rest-house so that the stone might be seen by travellers passing – a flat plateau of ground where we could plant a garden of irises and more mauve and white cosmos. We all began to gather stones.

Manbadur was selected as cement mixer and with gentle care

and almost reverence he mixed the sand with the dry cement. A gleaming brass pail of water was brought by the *chowkidar* and a hole made in the round mound. For half an hour we all watched mesmerized as little by little the water was poured into the hole and allowed to seep right through from the middle to the outside, and Manbadur's delicate spadework held the soaking mound together. Our skilled mason did not touch it – he gave orders as to how it should be done, and was treated with respect by the other men. For now a small crowd had gathered.

Men who had gathered wood for my grandmother's funeral pyre five years before, now gathered stones for a monument in her memory. Mensingh told them all that I was the *putri* (daughter's daughter) of Lady Penelope, the lady who used to ride on a pony there. Mensingh told me they all had known her for many years and loved her and that they all remembered the night she died. We gathered more stones.

The mason began to build a plinth and the afternoon came and the children were out of school. We'd heard them repeat their lessons in the open barn behind the rest-house, and now they delayed their separate journeys home to watch our proceedings. They stood clutching their slates to their chests in awed rows, and watched in wonder at the skill of the mason from Banjar. The mason knocked each stone we brought into shape, making corner stones and bricks to fit. He always knew exactly what shape was required and with extreme dexterity he manoeuvred his manicured hands about the rocks, feeling for just the right one. Every slick but careful movement of his trowel bewitched us all.

It was dusk in an instant it seemed and I worried that we wouldn't finish by dark. But the mason began to quicken and we handed him stones to fit the gaps and then each man would place his own stone on the plinth himself, so that though the mason was the architect of the building it seemed we had all helped it grow. And the chatter ceased and we worked silently and then, just before dark, the mason fitted the wide flat engraved stone on top and smoothed the cement round its corners and the job was done before night came. The crowd dispersed and Mensingh took the mason and Manbadur home, and I stood there in the heavenly place on top of the world and said as many Hail Marys as I could and fumbled my way through the Lord's Prayer and we all hoped that my grandmother might have been pleased with what we had done.

CHAPTER VI

God in the Ani Valley

'It is something indescribable in the air of India which gave me my religious sense; India helped me to find my religious feet.'

The Hindu idea is: I hope one day to be God. My reaction is: I don't want to be God. I don't want to be worshipped. The idea fills me with horror. My whole instinct is to WORSHIP and this is what I want to do for ever and ever because it satisfies an instinct in me and I feel I was created to do it.

MY GRANDMOTHER wrote these feelings down in a green notebook she carried with her, under the heading, Random Thoughts. This thought was hardly random, however, more likely it was the central force in all her doings. It became a visible force in her life after she had converted to the Church of Rome in 1948, when she was thirty-seven; but actually her religious instincts were roused long before then, by India.

'I know I owe my first real experience of the Reality of God to India,' was another Random Thought. 'India made me God conscious,' she continued. 'The two countries where the air is electric with God are India and Spain.' Her Christian beliefs were always inextricably entwined with the pantheist spirituality to be found in India.

'When I was a girl I became passionately interested in Indian religion,' she said in the *Observer* in 1983. 'I think it's interesting the way the young today go out to India and return thinking how square their parents are. We've all [the elder generation] been interested in Indian religion for generations; there were lots of books written in my young day about Yoga and so on.'

Penelope's first introduction to spiritual religion (as opposed to the ceremonial Anglican church-going she experienced as a child) came when she arrived in India. The eastern mysticism of Asia reminded her of the Christian mystics – St John of the Cross and St Ignatius, for example – who had titillated her fancy during the time she spent in Europe.

My grandmother always had an enormous capacity for believing. If she could summon up faith she could believe anything. The visions and miracles and the powers of healing of the Christian mystics were a real arm of the Church to her. Her Catholicism was never an entirely religious and rigid regime of guilt and confession, repetitive murmurings and daily Mass. Hers was an all encompassing religion, adapted to her surroundings: it was a mixture of East and West.

She told her grandchildren (in a letter): 'I regard religion as a prop. I need a spiritual walking stick. I mean I couldn't depend on myself.'

My grandmother taught us our prayers. From the earliest days when we went to stay at The Mead in Wantage we knelt beside our beds at night and said the Lord's Prayer, the Hail Mary and blessed our family' and our friends and all the ill people in the world and the unhappy ones and the Queen. Later, after she had moved to New House, her hill cottage in the Black Mountains near Hay-on-Wye, we would sometimes be spruced up for a Sabbath visit to the Roman Catholic church in Hay – a huge, hideous and soulless chapel it seemed, with no stained-glass windows to look at during the sermon. But she never expected more from us than prayers and she never once tried to convert us to her way of thinking. She simply explained to us how she felt, so that we could understand why she went to Mass at the hideous Roman Catholic church.

Only later, in India, was she able to begin to demonstrate the spiritual depth and mixture of her beliefs. She sometimes talked of going to heaven: 'I think this is a much nicer thing to believe in than reincarnation, which is what everyone believes in India, don't you?' she told the *Observer*. 'You could come back as a crocodile.'

But later in her life, she had changed her tune somewhat; not only was she keen on crocodiles (since she had visited the Crocodile Farm at Madras, and had digested some information about the toothsome reptiles) but also she had become more receptive to the idea of reincarnation, so that though she was loath to undertake the fundamental Hindu belief of wanting to become God, her own worship of God was not so far removed from other aspects of the Hindu religion.

For example, a Hindu will pray to a particular God for a particular service: to Ganesh for wealth, or Durga for victory, just as the Romans prayed to Mars for their victories or the Greeks to Aphrodite for beauty and to Zeus for success in battle; and so Penelope would pray to her saints: St Anthony of Padua, patron saint of lost causes and things, would be fervently called upon when even so small a thing as her Biro had gone missing. St Christopher would bear us safely across rivers or over rickety bridges. In 1985, when we were trekking up the Sutlej Valley, my grandmother, myself, our guide and two ponies had to cross the 2,000-foot-deep Manglad *nala* by a narrow swinging string and wooden bridge. Before we crossed, we dismounted, knelt and prayed in earnest to St Christopher. After we had safely crossed, we threw up our hands into the air and thanked him profusely. Surinder Sharma, our guide and a high caste Hindu did not think we were dotty at all, because belief in the supernatural is just as inherent in Hinduism.

Childless Hindu women from all over India will make a pilgrimage to the tomb of Shaikh Salim Christi at Fatehpur Sikri, to tie a piece of cotton to the marble lattice screens in the hope of a son. Just as Akbar, the greatest and wisest of the Moghul rulers, came to the saint four centuries ago looking for a son, Penelope went there and tied a knot for my mother, who subsequently produced two sons, my brothers. Knots in marble screens held as much truck for her as the knot she would always tie in her handkerchief in order to remember things.

Just as she adopted Hindu customs when she was travelling in India, she adapted her Catholicism to fit into her journeys.

Penelope once trekked in the Siwaliks in the Western Himalaya with Father Joachim, OFM, a priest from a Mysore parish in Karnataka, as her chaplain. She wrote one day:

> The Holy Sacrifice was offered up on the large dining-room table with the two wax candles Father had brought with him stuck onto two tin lids. Although the rest-house is wired for electricity and there is all the power in the world a quarter of a mile away in the confluence of the Parbatti and Beas rivers, the current hasn't arrived as yet which was a great trial to poor Father as his sight is very poor and he had to struggle on with the aid of his torch.
>
> By this time the *chowkidar* had long since gone to bed so poor Father, after saying mass in such difficult circumstances and after a seven-mile walk from Kulu town carrying 40 lb of baggage, had to be content with a miserable supper of bread and butter and jam washed down with Beas water which has to be carried from the river 10 minutes walk away.

The next day, 8 May:

> Mass at 7 a.m. During the offertory the *chowkidar* walked in to fetch the teapot. He didn't seem a bit surprised to see Father in vestments. I said '*puja*' (worship), pushed him out and locked two of the doors leading into the dining-room and the third was warped and wouldn't shut at all . . .

Sunday, 9 May:

> Father said Mass – undisturbed by the *chowkidar* – at 6.30 a.m. I always read the introit and the Epistle. We have considerable difficulty over the English versions: I have the Bombay diocesan one (also used in Delhi) and he has the South Indian text and many of the responses differ slightly and the *gloria* and the creed

differ considerably. Both have incorporated a new Our Father which I don't like at all.

Despite her dislike of the Lord's Prayer, Penelope enjoyed two and a half weeks of daily Mass with Father Joachim as they trekked through the Western Himalaya. Father was such a fantastically good walker that he only rode (on a pony) twice, just for the fun of it. At one stage, the Father walked eighteen miles in one day:

> . . . Father insisted on walking all the day. As he bicycles 30 or 40 miles a day in his own parish in Mysore state and all along dusty, uneven bullock-cart tracks, he is remarkably fit and leaves us all standing when it comes to climbing.

As Penelope adapted her prayers to suit the mountains, so she adapted her principles:

> Father and I took the ponies down to the forest reserve on the banks of the Beas to graze. This is against the rules and I have always deprecated the fact that the peasants often cut down the barbed wire fence and let their animals in to graze when the forest guard isn't about. They also have what I used to think is a dreadfully destructive habit of lopping branches off certain kinds of trees (notably FICUS POMMATUS and BAUHINIA and holly oak) and using them as fodder. Now I am living the life of a peasant and having to fend for my poor ponies I think very differently. I slip them into the forest reserves whenever I can and had I a billhook in my baggage I would gladly lop off some leafy branches for their supper; as it is I sometimes break some off when no one's looking.

Panchok and I were ponyless alas, when we took to the road again, to continue our journey from Khanag. But whereas my grandmother never liked walking, I love it. (In the same way that Indians think it mad to forsake a bus when it's on offer, my grandmother thought it potty to walk when you could ride.) Before we left the rest-house, the Junior Engineer appeared suddenly round the corner of the veranda to inspect us, without his worshipping Sadhu this time. I asked him where he kept his legendary ten children.

'Ah, they are working with their mother at my homeland,' he said.

'Ah, and when do you see your family?'

'In the winter months of course, when the snows come and the passes are closed . . .'

By which time, of course, no one else can see whether the roads have been repaired or not. Paddy Singh had told me that in India one hardly ever qualifies for a government job now – instead, one buys it. Everybody wants a 'job' because a 'job' means you sit idle all day, so it is a different thing altogether from 'work'. You pay someone higher up for the privilege of your office and then you sit back and receive your salary. You cannot be sacked now either, because of the unions.

You may pay a lot – say 5,000 rupees to be a Junior Engineer – but for that initial outlay, you buy the right not to have to lift a finger for the rest of your life. Nothing can be done about the situation because it goes on right up the scale to the ministers; everybody gets a pay-off somewhere down the line. So the hopeless father of ten can reside contentedly at Khanag with his Sadhu for nine months of the year, lazy and happy in his 'job'.

Away from the rest-house towards the village, it could be seen how life was for those who did work (as opposed to just having a 'job'). The fields were full of women bent double scything hay; sound travels so well in the valleys, that they just raised their voices a little to talk to their sisters or mothers or daughters working on another terrace up to eight hundred yards away. 'Time for tea!' they whispered through the grasses before they loaded upon their backs bundles far bigger than themselves to bear homeward. There were children of five and six and seven who herded the cattle home and collected hay loads themselves on the way back from school, while their fathers and elder brothers idled the day away playing cards in the tea stall.

Before we left I walked up to the small shrine on a hill top to the east of the rest-house, the only abode of the *nag* or snake *devta* of Khanag. To get to the shrine a stream must be crossed, at the exact spot where my grandmother was placed upon a funeral pyre in April 1986 and burned in the early morning. It was a private, almost secret spot beside the trickling water.

As I stood there, three huge golden eagles circled above, swooping down so close they could have snatched me up like a lamb. Three times they came almost to my shoulder and I wondered whether my grandmother had, after all, been reincarnated. Perhaps she was now soaring the skies in the form of a golden eagle. I thought it was a form quite worthy of her. And for the rest of my journey after we walked away from Khanag I felt her there, at my shoulder. Perhaps ridiculously, I imagined I saw her sometimes manifested in a local form.

Mindful of her watchful eye, therefore (and knowing her to be a keen educator), I went to visit the school behind the rest-house before we left. I had thought I might have a talk with the teacher, but he could not speak English at all. In spite of this shortcoming, he instructed his charges daily in the art of speaking and reading English with the aid of a text book – *English Text Exercises* – which had sentences inside such as: 'And tomorrow the man who lives on the farm will go to market.'

Now that Kulu district forms part of the Himalayan state known as Himachal Pradesh (until 1968 it was included in the Punjab state), the Punjabi language is no longer taught. All the state schools of northern India use Hindi as the medium of teaching and in Himachal Pradesh English and Urdu are taught as second and third languages respectively.

The poor pupil's task is made more difficult than it sounds, for each of these languages uses a different script: Hindi the Devanagri, the script of classical Sanskrit; English the Latin script and

Urdu the extremely difficult and beautiful Persian. I was disappointed that the master has mastered even less English than his pupils, and that consequently my hopes for a discussion about the modern education system were dashed. In fact he regarded me with some suspicion and I was soon shown the door. Perhaps he thought I might have reported his lack of command of the English language to his superiors.

WITH FATHER JOACHIM, the Mysore parish priest, my grandmother had been more gratefully received at a Pahari school. She wrote in her diary:

> The young headmaster . . . invited Father to give an English lesson!
>
> This consisted of reading a story out of the textbook sentence by sentence and getting the pupils to repeat them after him. Afterwards we were entertained to cups of sweet tea and invited to return tomorrow morning and to bring our ponies to graze in the school back yard.

Grazing time was seized upon as a religious opportunity.

> It cleared towards evening so we took the ponies to graze in the forest glades while Father and I strolled up and down reciting fifteen decades of the rosary followed by the Litany of our Lady. This gave the animals a good forty minutes in which to guzzle grass after which we picked up sticks and fir cones and drove our herd 'home', to our little kitchen-cum-stable-house where I cooked 'oeufs à la tripe' for supper while Father recited his office in the tiny oratory leading out of our smoky little kitchen.

*

MY GRANDMOTHER went to Assisi – the Italian home of St Francis and the artist Giotto – when she was seventeen, with Mrs Le Strange, her 'marvellous teacher – my God, what a lot all of us owe to certain teachers.' She continued: 'I just knew that I would one day come back there as a Catholic and exactly twenty years later I did. Many people have been started off on their religious pilgrimage through St Francis of Assisi. I didn't do anything about it for a long time . . .'

On 7 March 1948, Evelyn Waugh, the famous writer and himself a Catholic convert, wrote to my grandmother:

Dearest Penelope,

Laura and I will be thinking about you very joyfully on Tuesday. May you live happily ever after. I am sure you will. You are coming into the Church with vastly more knowledge than most converts but what you cannot know until Tuesday is the delight of membership of the Household, of having your chair at the table, a place laid, the bed turned down, of the love & trust, whatever their family bickerings, of all Christendom. It is this family unity which makes the weakest Catholic nearer the angels & saints, than the most earnest outsider.

It is a particular joy for me to be able to welcome you home, who have known you in so many phases. Your prayers will be especially powerful at the moment, so please pray for me.

Yours most affectionately

Evelyn

I had always been told that Evelyn Waugh converted my grand-mother to Catholicism, not without a great deal of accusation pointed at him by her Anglican friends. Actually, it was St Francis who had planted the seed in her young mind in 1927, and not Evelyn Waugh at all, whom she only met several years later. Naturally she let Evelyn know she was under instruction with the Dominicans in Oxford, as he was one of her few Catholic friends.

She first heard his name mentioned in 1928, when her mother and her brother Roger were discussing 'a very risqué book' at the far end of the drawing-room in their London house in Grove End Road. The book was called *Decline and Fall* and she later said they shut up like clams when she approached to join in their discussion.

She first met Evelyn Waugh four years later when she was engaged to my grandfather, John Betjeman, and he took her to stay with his great friends Christine and Edward Longford at Pakenham Hall in Co. Westmeath. She accompanied the young author on a memorable woodland ride during which he fell off his horse.

By 1948, Waugh had long since married Laura Herbert and settled into country life. But in the intervening years he had often stayed with my grandparents at Uffington, particularly often while he was writing his life of St Edmund Campion, in the thirties. Penelope used to motor him over to nearby Lyford Grange, where Campion gave his last Mass and sermon, and where he was squashed into a hiding-hole with two other priests before his final discovery and arrest.

Evelyn Waugh and my grandmother knew each other well by the time of her conversion, but he had not been the reason for her going over to Rome. He was delighted to hear of her decision, of course, though she thought he would have preferred her to have been instructed by Jesuits, as he thought all Dominicans (by whom she had been instructed in Oxford) were communists.

My grandmother went about her conversion in a much more serious and dogged manner than Waugh ever did. On 'Shrovers 10 February 1948', he wrote in a letter to her from Piers Court, his country house at Stinchcombe:

> I am greatly impressed & edified by the depth of your studies. I just talked half a dozen times to Father d'Arcy about T. S. Eliot & Havelock Ellis, then popped into Farm Street on the way to dinner one evening & sat up with Driberg in the gallery of the Café de Paris to see a new negress singer. It took me years to

begin to glimpse what the church was like. I was constantly
travelling in those days and it was chiefly missionaries who
taught me. Of course I was a bit younger than you but not
much – 27, how old are you, I suppose 35? Well I shall
constantly come to you for advice and instruction.

My grandmother was received into the Roman Catholic Church
on 9 March 1948, at St Aloysius, Oxford. She was in fact thirty-
eight. It was typical of her determined mind to have undertaken
such a project and to have thrown herself into laborious study so
avidly, even pedantically as she did. Just as she later determined
to research completely thoroughly all aspects of Himalayan architecture, until she became an expert, so she read every mystic and
learnt every creed and fully understood the Roman Catholic
Church (if one ever can) before she entered it in 1948.

There had been a certain amount of religion abundant in the
Betjeman household already. My grandfather was High Anglican,
and a regular worshipper in Wantage, and he, particularly, found
it hard to understand why his wife saw it necessary to 'go over' to
Rome. In some way, he felt betrayed by her decisive action.

For then, among the people they saw in and around Oxford, a
conversion meant, to a certain extent, that the converted person
was going over to the 'other side'. It meant a different set of friends
discussing a different set of philosophies. More immediately, it
meant walking in the opposite direction on Sunday morning (which
was hurtful enough); more fundamentally, it meant walking in
opposite directions for life.

But my grandmother always enjoyed being contrary; she liked
to take the opposite line. She held a perverse delight in shocking
people which may have been a contributory factor behind her late
conversion. Yet the greatest reason for her decision stemmed from
her dissatisfaction with the rational dogma of the Church she had
been born into. She found the Anglican Church lacking in spirituality; in India she discovered that spiritualism did exist and was
all-pervasive and could still lead to God; and thus, following her

twin yearnings for religion with structure as well as mysticism, she found her place in the Roman Catholic Church.

IF IT WASN'T my grandmother at my shoulder, then it was a saint who led Panchok and me from Khanag to Ani, the next village down the mountain, where we met the Reverend Adolphus Solomon, a saint himself who was also Priest in Charge at the All Saints Christian Missionary Society Anglican Church.

We had reached the small mountain town of Ani at midday and located the rest-house. It was crawling with men however, and a sweaty crowd of teachers were sitting out at the gates, striking for higher pay, and waving their placards menacingly at us as we staggered past. Panchok had gone ahead to strike a deal with the surly *chowkidar*, but returned a few minutes later shaking his head ominously.

'Kerosene no,' he said. 'No dinner.' He shook his head vehemently. '*Chowkidar* bad man, bad man.'

We were exhausted. Ani is tiny and there was no alternative, so we took a room and then escaped from the grim atmosphere to the bus stand where the 'Sunny Hotel' – a shack with four wooden tables, sticky and fly ridden – offered rice and *dahl*. A fat woman in pink sat wedged between the wall and a table and fed greying chicken into her betel stained mouth with betel stained fingers and slurped her hot tea as she watched us. She sucked her bones and then licked her plate and then smiled, showing a wide gap between her two front teeth, belched long and low, and squeezed herself out of her place. She waddled past us and smiled encouragingly at the two bus conductors lounging to our left, who had long since licked the *dahl* from their tin plates and remained only to watch the lady in pink.

I could not finish my watery lunch, so excused myself and slipped out of the 'Sunny Hotel'. My grandmother has written about Ani and how she went to call on the Rani of Shangri who offered her walnuts and popcorn and polite conversation, and I thought that was just the sort of company I needed right then. The young Rani, daughter of the former one, was supposedly still living in Ani in purdah, alone up the mountainside, but at her house I found instead one R. K. Goushal, an accountant who was too busy with his paperwork to explain to me what had happened to the Rani.

I wandered on, anyhow, and up, as if drawn by a magnet to the highest point of the village, clinging to the valley wall, where there was a two-storey Pahari house with a veranda and walls painted with vegetable dye in turquoise, blue and green. There was an old, old, thin man sitting there on the veranda and upon seeing me, he bade me come up. This was the Reverend A. Solomon, who had not spoken with an English person in twenty years, though he knew the language as a boy, he said.

The first time my grandmother came to Ani, she arrived with a train of ADCs and bearers wearing the same double 'terais' hat as her mother, and sitting on a pony. The village temple band was playing and celebrations went on long into the night. That was September 1931, and Lady Chetwode asked the Salvation Army couple who were living in the village to dinner at the rest-house.

The second time she came to Ani, my grandmother arrived on a pony in 1963, accompanied by two young students whom she had requisitioned as temporary pretend ADCs, carrying a black umbrella to keep off the sun. The villagers thought she was a missionary and asked her to speak at a special memorial service to be held for Jawaharlal Nehru. When I arrived in 1991, I came unmounted with Panchok as my partner, and no one noticed us much at all. Until the Reverend Adolphus Solomon beckoned me up on to his balcony.

Long before my friend Adolphus, there had been a Reverend Marcus Carleton, who sailed from America in 1854 and worked unstintingly in the mission field in India for forty-four years until he died in 1898. The last eleven years of his life were spent at Ani, where he established a self-sufficient Christian farming community, in a not altogether orthodox way. He was against 'compound

Christians' in India, who were settled on to missionary land as soon as they were baptized, and hoped that the converts he made would become independent proprietors. His wife, however, was not able to hold out in the remote outpost for much longer than a year after her husband's death and she returned to America in 1900. Subsequently, in 1907, the village was taken over by the Salvation Army, though their number depleted soon after my grandmother and her mother had visited Ani in 1931. After them came the Church Missionary Society, in whose service Adolphus Solomon remained.

But Adolphus Solomon no longer had a congregation. There was a sign up at the gate reading:

'CMA Anglican Church (INDEPANDENT) Morning Prayer 7.30 am, Evening Prayer 7.30 pm, Sunday Prayer 11am.'

But no one ever came to a service except the Reverend's family – his grandchildren Kanath, Evaline and Samuel Solomon and his mentally deficient daughter Shunila, who was happy and smiled a lot.

The Reverend was so excited to see an English person, and a Christian at that, that he promptly asked me to stay the night. And to dinner. And to breakfast if I would too. He spoke shyly in halting English and his grandchildren watched me warily.

He showed me the church where nobody comes, which must be the 'stone chapel up a side valley' which my grandmother wrote about in *Kulu*:

Mr and Mrs Carleton had come up from the plains during a terrible famine with several convert Punjabi boys who had married local Pahari girls and settled down to farm on land bought for them by the missionary. The chapel had originally been one of the outbuildings attached to the house, but since selling it to the Rai of Shangri, the Christians had built themselves a stone chapel up a side valley. They were upset because some Seventh Day Adventists from Simla had recently estab-

lished their own mission at Ani and had built a stone church
nearer the village!

The Reverend introduced me to Mungo Dass, retired priest of
those selfsame Seventh Day Adventists 'nearer the village', and he
seemed to be on the best of terms with his neighbouring vicar.
Mungo, who was stocky and short like a jockey, spoke English
better than his friend and he told me he had learnt it at the Kurga
Missionary School; then he went into the military and fought for
the British in Burma from 1939 to 1945. After the War he was sent
into these hills. Nobody came to his church any more either, so he
had retired himself and he lived up the hill from Ani with a few
cattle and his wife (who was sick with lumbago), while all his
children had gone to live in Bangalore.

I excused myself to run down the hill to the rest-house to
explain to Panchok that I wished to stay the night with this strange
man on the hill.

'Good man?' asked Panchok, suspicious.

'Good man, so very good man,' wishing I could say ninety-
year-old priest in Hindi.

Panchok, neither Christian nor Hindu but Buddhist, nevertheless believed in the power of prayer, and I knew that he would be
happy once he knew that we were to stay in a priest's house. We
packed up and marched out of the rancid smelling rest-house,
which must have lowered its standards immeasurably since 1931,
for no couple from the Salvation Army would be likely to dine
there now.

Within half an hour we were sitting with the Reverend Solomon
on his veranda, drinking tea, and Panchok kept catching my eye
and winking and grinning at his tea-leaves. Then the Reverend
showed me to my room, which I knew was his room, but he would
not hear of me sleeping anywhere else. The room was small and
washed blue and everywhere hanging there were photographs of
his family and crucifixes and signs saying 'God is love' and 'Trust

in the Lord'. There was a mirror, and a round clock ticking on the wall.

All his combs and ornaments were neatly lined up on a brown silk cloth on the mantelpiece, and there was a glass-fronted cupboard shut up with a padlock which had in it sweets and a bottle of apple juice and some glasses and a few small silver pots.

The Reverend Solomon asked me to sing from his English hymn book and when I looked it up and started singing 'Love Divine, all loves excelling . . .', he knew the tune (because the Hindi and Urdu hymns that he has learnt are just direct translations of our words set to the same music) and he hummed along with me and then he started to cry and he kept looking at me and sniffing with watery eyes. He made me want to cry too, him being so courageous and carrying the lead on, when there was no one to follow him.

'We will have Evensong at 7.30,' he said, and I wondered whether anyone else would turn up. I had to say Grace (and recalled the most boring one, the only one I knew: For what we are about to receive, may the Lord make us truly thankful, Amen), and then we ate a special dinner of *dahl*, rice, potatoes and a fried egg; or rather I ate first alone, followed by the others. (For even though they are Christians, these Paharis cannot shake off the customs and traditions of their Hindi forefathers and of all the Hindus who live around them.)

The evening service was conducted, as I suspected, with us as the only worshippers. We said prayers on the veranda. I had to say the Lord's Prayer in English, which was quite embarrassing as I always get stuck on the trespassing bit, but I do not think they noticed. Evaline, who was about eight, read from the Hindi Bible.

Afterwards Adolphus brought out his concertina and began to play tunes from his Urdu hymn book. His eyes grew misty again as we settled into a full rendition of every single Christmas carol – the carols being the easiest for both of us – and we sat on the veranda and sang and played under the moon until midnight, and I think his grandchildren thought we were quite odd. Panchok seemed to sense that we were singing holy songs and he grew sombre too, and we may have even become morose, had he not been compelled to giggle every so often, if only to relieve the tension. Adolphus said I must come back to Ani in 1992, because if I waited until 1993, he may have 'expired'.

My grandmother had sung hymns in the Himalayas before me. On trek in 1971, she regaled the other members of the party with her favourite Anglican hymns, sung in parts. She wrote in her diary: 'I am very grateful for having been brought up Anglican as I have a heritage which cradle Catholics do not; for example the heritage of hymns by the Watts and the Wesleys . . .

> His dying crimson like a robe
> Spreads o'er his body on the tree.
> Then I am dead to all the globe
> And all the globe is dead to me.

I know that "When I survey the wondrous cross" from which this quatrain in taken, is now incorporated into several modern Catholic hymnals together with other Anglican hymns, but it will be a generation before they become popular, except in avant-garde circles. Then there are passages of scripture from the Authorized Version which we were made to memorize at school – I can still quote most of St Paul's speech on the Areopagus to anyone who would care to hear it. And of course the glorious English of the Prayer Book. I can recite most of the Collects which occurred during term-time but none – to my shame – which occurred during the holidays. And whenever one of my favourites comes round I want to scream at the modern vernacular version which is invariably far more complicated and difficult to understand than the seventeenth-century one. What for example, is more simple and direct than the Prayer Book Collect for Trinity VI . . .

> O God who hast prepared them that love thee such good things
> as pass man's understanding; pour into our hearts such love
> towards thee, that we loving thee in all things may obtain thy
> promises which exceed all that we can desire.

No, we converts from Anglicanism are very fortunate in that conversion to the Roman Catholic faith is the fulfilment of everything we hoped for and at the same time we have our own storehouse of prayers and psalms in the old translations and verses of these hymns to use as prayers, which are a part of us.'

My grandmother was a convert to Roman Catholicism and Grandpapa was Anglican. My Uncle Paul was a Mormon for a while, and I have several friends who are Buddhist. Panchok was a Buddhist, and Adolphus had a Hindu's blood, but Christian beliefs. I believe in God, some greater being, although I am unsure of his form as yet; but it doesn't matter how people go about finding God, said my grandmother, just as long as they find a path and get to Him in the end. And only in India are there so many different paths to choose from. In India the air is electric with God.

CHAPTER VII

Going Bazaari in Nirmand

*'If you were accused of "going bazaari" it meant you were
making friends with Indians. I am proud to say I was
continually accused of going bazaari.'*

AN ADC OF MY great-grandfather's who had become a friend of
my grandmother's in the early thirties wrote a poem for her:

SIMLA SCANDAL

or

A Bazaari Ballad

An Aide-de-Camp from Far Bengal
Was sitting in the Snowdon Hall
Consuming with delight a small
But most refreshing Brandy
He said in accents pained and sad
'I say I feel an awful cad
'After the topping time I've had
'With your champagne and shandy
'In raising questions which no doubt
'I hardly am concerned about

'One day before I came up here
'I was startled by a minor peer
'Remarking with a drunken leer
'Miss Chetwode's gone bazaari'

If my grandmother startled minor peers into drunken leers while
she was still Miss Chetwode (on account of her attempts to learn
Hindi and to mix with the people in whose country she was living),
her behaviour as Lady Betjeman might have given the minor peers
apoplexy. She could not help but make friends wherever she went,

be they English, Indian or Martian, youthful, aged or contemporary. She simply had an incurable curiosity which led her to make all manner of acquaintances, and she was never shy.

It was hardly surprising, therefore, that she should introduce herself to a man called Pandit Mela Ram Sharma, as soon as she arrived with her party of trekkers at the village of Nirmand in which he lived. For not only did he live there, but he also happened to be the Sarpanch of Nirmand, that is the head of the Panchayat, or village council. And his was the only Pahari family in the village that could speak English. She wanted to know about the temples and he could tell her about them, so it was quite natural for her to introduce herself.

The minor peers of the Raj might have condoned such an academic introduction, but it is the development of her association which would have caused remark. Pandit Mela Ram Sharma introduced her to his then twenty-year-old daughter Asha, to his eldest son Surinder, to his other son Rajinder and to his wife Sushila, who used to be a teacher. Penelope not only corresponded with them, but she advised them on family affairs; she became their confidante and she went to stay with them every time she was in the neighbourhood; she ate at their table and she helped them in the kitchen. In short, they accepted her as part of their family. She most definitely went bazaari in Nirmand.

The temple-rich village is the biggest village in the Kulu district, sitting 4,000 feet above sea level (which is the same height as Ben Nevis, the highest mountain in Britain) and some 2,000 ft above the River Sutlej, the largest of the five rivers of the Punjab.

It is known as the 'Kashi of the hills', Kashi being the name in classical Sanskrit literature for Varanasi (alias Benares), that holiest of Indian cities. Nirmand resembles Varanasi not only because it is a place of pilgrimage but also because it is a Brahmin stronghold. (For many Himalayan villages are not lived in by Brahmins any longer in which case the temples are served by *pujaris* [priests] drawn from the lower castes.)

I went to Nirmand first when my grandmother took me up the

Sutlej valley on the first leg of our two-week trek along the old Hindustan–Tibet road. My grandmother had been a 'member of the family' for over fifteen years by then, and had visited the Sharmas on as many occasions but we were still ushered into a reception room where we were to eat alone and I never saw one inch of the rest of the house. My grandmother had wanted to give Surinder, the Sarpanch's surly son, a chance to prove himself, and had invited him to guide us on our trek and to take charge of the ponies and other arrangements. He shuffled out from the nether regions of the timber-framed house and beckoned us to follow him for morning *puja* (prayer) at the Ambika temple.

Although only twenty or so, Surinder was overtly religious at the time and superstitious and believed in every god imaginable and saw the shape of a lingum (the phallic symbol of the god, Shiva) on every mountain top. He worshipped the sun as well as Shiva and Jesus Christ, and said the sun had sons. He predicted that the gods would not allow us to travel on the following day until we had made obeisance to all the Sharma relations in Nirmand and he was right, for the next morning monsoon rains swept the mountainside and instead of walking ten miles up the valley as planned we postponed the trek and walked about the same distance round and round the village paying social calls on Surinder's extended family.

Practically everyone in Nirmand is related to everyone else, and all the houses looked the same and we were so full of tea and walnuts by four o'clock that my grandmother had adopted a fixed smile and a knowing nod that did admirably for all social communications. Surinder had trailed us about with notable lack of lustre, and my grandmother said he was being all adolescent because I was a European girl. That night I really did think he was tiresome. The evening ended on a low note with some aged local musicians playing for two hours in a crowded front room.

We had left the next day and apart from a few minor lapses in organization, Surinder managed to lead the trek successfully. But his trek-leading skills were not efficient enough for my grandmother to think of recommending him for employment to West Himalayan Holidays (which had been the object of the exercise) which was all very well in the end for only a few years later Surinder had married and taken over as Sarpanch and head of the household (and attendant land) from his father and would have never had time to lead treks. His wife was a Bilaspur girl called Manjula, who had borne Surinder two boys – Surya (sun) and Himalaya (mountain). Manjula had majored in interior decoration, yoga studies and doll making and I was interested to see what sort of wife Surinder had chosen.

Panchok and I took the bus up the narrow mountain road from Rampur to Nirmand and walked with our packs through the muddled village, collecting a train of children behind us as we searched for Surinder's house. As we came to it, there was a thin, small man hunched over the telephone (a clunking black 1940s model which sits on the veranda and seems to be communal village property) in an olive green kurta and trousers. I tapped him on the shoulder, he turned round and I recognized him as Surinder. His actual face had become blurred in my memory but with one glance it all came back. He seemed quite pleased to see me and Panchok and led us, as before, into the reception room.

'Oh Imogen,' he exclaimed. 'You have arrived on a terribly auspicious week.' This was the Surinder I knew. 'There is a practice you see which the pandits carry out. It is called "*shradh*". There is one week in the year when they will offer meals to Brahmin priests in remembrance of their relatives who have died. You have arrived in this very week.'

I had corresponded with Surinder about my visit, and we had agreed by letter on the rough date of my arrival, but Surinder was convinced that it was the gods who had brought me in that particular week, and he was hugely overexcited about the implications of my auspicious arrival. So overexcited he forgot to introduce me to his wife and instead bore me off to visit his orchards.

There were apples and pears (the Chinese variety), apricots, tomatoes, chilli, bindi, potatoes and newly planted carrots all growing in the orchard. As master of the house now (though only for seven months by then) Surinder was in sole charge of the land his father had handed over to him.

'My grandfather was an orphan with no money who had to go away from Nirmand to work in the lemon farms,' he told me as we walked along the terraced mountainside.

'But then he had a dream in which Durga [the demon goddess] appeared, and she said, "Go home and start a business – your hard times are over." So he came home and started a meagre business selling oil and rope and then one day, as he was washing, he was seen by the wife of the richest man in Nirmand. My grandfather was very tall and handsome, and when this rich lady saw him she thought, "I'll have that man as my daughter's husband", and so it came to be that he married the lucky heiress and his fortune flourished and soon he had land from here to Delhi.'

His exaggeration having perhaps got the better of him, Surinder concluded the tale on a humble note: 'But my grandfather was very holy and never immersed himself in worldly goods, but he gave to the poor and even helped poverty-stricken fathers marry off their daughters by giving them money for dowries.'

We walked on through the lush grass and he kept chucking me ripe pears. Then we sat down 'for a rest' to have a cigarette and for a dreadful moment I thought he was going to get all romantic again (he had proposed to me in an impulsive burst of passion in 1985 under the shade of a wild rhododendron) but instead he got spiritual.

'I had a dream once – me and Asha [his sister] and Penelope were all sitting down and Jesus visited us. I wrote and told Penelope and she was very moved.' He looked across his orchards.

'Penelope used to love to come up here in the moonlight. Sometimes she would get up at two in the morning and go for a moonlit walk. She was an admirable walker and she was heavy too. Even in her seventies she would stride out ahead. Once I brought her up here to a wheatfield and made her carry the wheat down roped to her back like the Paharis. She didn't mind at all.'

He went on: 'When I first met her I felt immediately that she was like a relative. We were always arguing and she used to scold me all the time. She was motherly and full of advice and reassurance.'

So much so that she took it upon herself to advise the Sharma children about their marriage plans. As the elder brother, Surinder was to some extent responsible for vetting any prospective suitors of his sister, and he turned to my grandmother for final approval. Asha is beautiful and headstrong and as the Sarpanch's daughter, she was considered a desirable match. Doctors, lawyers, teachers and landowners courted her keenly, but in her early twenties she was not having any of it. 'There was just not one who was good enough,' she told me later in her office in Simla where she works for the tourist board and lives, still unmarried.

The only one who came close to passing her scrutinous inspection was the brother of a friend whose brother knew a cousin who knew a sister of a friend who was in some way related to Asha's aunt, and he was an enthusiastic young man who was keen enough for a high-caste Brahmin bride to apply for Asha's hand all the way from England.

So it was Penelope to whom fell the task of feeling him out.

My Dear Surinder, [she wrote from Hay-on-Wye in 1978]
    AT LAST I have got hold of ARUN KUMAR BAWA! I wrote to him as soon as I returned from conducting my bus tour of Central India. I invited him to come and stay last week-end OR for the Easter wk-end. He (like me) has no car but he got a friend to drive him over last Sunday, just for the day, but they lost their way and instead of arriving at lunch-time they did not reach my house until 4pm! However, they stayed till 9pm and we spent a very pleasant evening together.

Here is where she gets properly tucked in:

Arun is of medium height (I should think about the same height as Asha), stocky build, with a fair complexion and a black moustache. He is a serious minded young man, very religious, and his GURU is the 'Boy God' Bagheleshwar (from Dehra Dun but he now lives mostly in the U.S.A.). I like him very much: BUT I told him he couldn't ask Asha to come to England and live in Wolverhampton, which is a horrible large industrial town. If I were your mother and father I should insist on him returning to the Punjab (where he comes from) and getting a good job in Chandigarh or Ludhiana before they allow him to marry Asha. And then ONLY IF SHE LIKES HIM! You MUST give an educated Indian girl of today a SAY in the choice of her husband, do you not agree?

At present Arun is working for Marks and Spencer behind the counter, but he says he will get a proper job in his field soon. I showed him slides of Nirmand and Asha and he was very impressed and he is coming again after Easter for more slides.

Her final judgement:

Nice as he is SURELY it would be better to choose Asha a husband from a family in the Punjab hills with whom you are well acquainted?

To Asha at the same time she wrote:

The impression I got was that he is a very nice and serious minded young man, but I still think you should MEET before the marriage is finally settled?

My own view is that it will be a very hard transition for you to leave the lovely Punjab hills and settle in a large ugly industrial town like Wolverhampton where there is a good bit of racialist feeling. For this reason I wish your family could find a young man of the correct caste who has a good job IN INDIA, preferably in the hills, which you know and love so much.

She signs off in an uncharacteristically unfriendly manner – showing her true feelings against the proposed liaison with poor Mr Arun Kumar Bawa, who really did not have much of a chance of a successful suit from the moment he arrived three hours late for lunch:

> However, should you all decide that you are going to marry Mr Bawa in October, I may or may not be able to attend your wedding, as I shall be conducting a party of trekkers and I shall only be staying two nights in Nirmand . . .'

My grandmother had, by then, some measure of experience to offer to a young girl embarking on marriage, for she had been coping with her own for over forty years already.

By the time she met the Sharmas my grandmother had already sold The Mead, the Wantage home where my mother spent most of her childhood, and from where my grandfather commuted to London. But neither her husband nor wild horses could have dragged my grandmother up to the capital city on more than occasional visits; she was irrevocably entrenched in country life.

At The Mead she had run a waterfowl farm for a number of years, selling eggs and ducks for the table, and in the late fifties she had put her legendary culinary expertise to a more public use, by opening King Alfred's Kitchen, a 'library cum caff' in the centre of town. Neither venture was as lasting, however, as her continual horse activity, and as she said, one cannot lunge horses in a London garden.

When Grandpapa was spending more and more time in London and he was beginning to feel the immobilizing effects of Parkinson's disease in the mid-seventies, it seemed that my grandmother was just getting an energetic second wind. Though procrastination was always her worst vice, she said, in 1972 she managed to make the momentous decision to sell the family home and buy herself a smaller, more manageable house where she might devote herself to writing and to horses.

It was after her longest Indian expedition so far – in 1970–71 – that she discovered New House, Cusop, in a dilapidated state at the front of Hay Bluff in the Black Mountains, and made up her mind to go there on her own.

She called where she lived Kulu-on-Wye in the Hereford Himalaya, and she determined to live a life there as near to Pahari-style as she could get away with without actually decamping to the Himalayas themselves. Her water came from a spring in the garden and she got about by pony and cart. She collected her wood in the forest and lived a mile from her nearest neighbours. Her letterhead read, 'No Telephone Thank God' and she made her own Irish soda bread in place of chapattis. She did say she was vegetarian and that oh, it was so much better for you not to eat meat, but then every time she came to stay with us in Wiltshire she could never resist a sausage – or the telephone, or the television.

Surinder says she wanted to be reborn a Pahari girl in Himachal Pradesh, and that you are always reborn what you think about just before you die. He says that as she died in a Pahari village she will have been thinking about the hills and its people and that she will definitely be reborn there.

'She wanted to live here always,' he said. 'She liked to have big lemons in her tea and to eat *dahi* [curd]. She liked to have learned talks about the religion and the people. She liked this simple life better than the English life. She always was so sad to leave here.'

Miffed that my grandmother may have loved her Pahari family more than her English one, I asked Asha whether she also thought Penelope would rather have lived in India than in England.

'She told only me that she was living separately from her husband. No one else here knew that they did not live at one house. It made her so sad, because she loved him so much always. But she did not like always living in England where she was reminded of this love that could not be happy. She had no telephone so people could not ring her up and tell her about him.

'I think when she came here she could leave these troubles behind. She wrapped herself up in the temples and the mountains and she contemplated her life in a quiet way. She hated gossiping and social chit-chat, but she could not leave England for ever because of him and because of you, her blood family. She always loved him though.'

Asha's confirmation of suspicions that were already developing in my own mind made confrontation of my grandmother's emotional life much clearer and easier. My grandmother had not come to India in 1963 wholly to escape from an unsatisfactory marriage – for it was never simply that – but her individualism and her joy in independence had led her back to India and helped drive her spirit on to fill her life to the brim with other attachments – to temple architecture, to the mountains, to her horses, her articles, to her lectures and her photography.

If she had never married, I know she would still have roamed the world on various quests – for knowledge, for ways of life, for religion too – but without a love in her life and without a family she may never have been happy at all.

At one point, it could have gone either way; she nearly gave up John for her studies before she married him and three weeks after they were married, she waltzed off to Munich for six months to study German. He cannot have been much reassured by that.

'The secret of happiness is to know your limitations,' wrote my grandmother in the introduction to a first draft of an article she was writing about horsemanship. In that case she was referring to her riding skills: 'I have tremendous admiration for jockeys, show jumpers and eventers who have got to the top of their chosen field, but I know my limitations . . .' I know she applied the maxim to all her 'fields'. She would never fight shy of trying, but it would not be the end of the world if she did not reach the top. She knew that to strive through life to be something you cannot be leads only to dissatisfaction and unhappiness. She did not live by this rule through fear of failure, however, but through appreciation of efficiency.

She realized that she alone could not alleviate all poverty, so she concentrated on one charity, Goodwill Children's Village, in

South India, of which she was patron. She knew she could never hope to understand the nature and culture and geography of every country in the world, though she wished she could visit them all, so she turned her attention towards India. 'I need five more lifetimes,' she would say, and in that time she meant just to understand India thoroughly.

Penelope's limitations in her wifely capacity need only be known between her and John. But I do know that she knew that she wanted to travel alone to India, and that she loved to bury herself for hours in the Bodleian. She was independent beyond the wildest dreams of most of the women of her generation, and inquisitive and eager to learn beyond the wildest imaginations of most of my generation. She was what you might call outward bound and surely it is hard to expect a marriage just to sit and wait for you while you are forever branching out in your own directions – especially if those directions are diametrically opposite to your husband's.

Surinder wanted to talk to me about marriage, as most inquisitive Indian men do. He wanted to know if all English girls were experienced and how many men I had slept with. It was not from nosiness that he sought such information – it was not my past history that particularly interested him – but curiosity drove him on. Even educated Indian girls will not talk about sex, and there is not much sexy literature on sale in Simla either. A well-brought-up Hindu boy has not a chance of sleeping with a girl before he marries unless he pays for it or he becomes a movie star in Bombay and meets an actress who is looser than most. Yet if he is well educated he knows that people do it before they are married 'in the West', and he wants to know why and how and when. However, I was not particularly keen on amusing Surinder with details and anyway I was more than anxious about his own marriage.

In the morning I sat with Manjula for a while at the foot of the three hundred steps which lead down to the Ambika temple. I had shown her a photograph of my sister Lucy and her husband Al and their daughter Jasmine and she said hopefully, 'Is it a love marriage?'

Manjula is determined to build up the orchard and to have a dairy farm and to reinstate the family shop, selling oil and rope. For her, marriage was less about making a relationship work, than taking on the whole caboodle – the childbearing, the home economy, the providing, and the creation of a rock-solid family base for her husband and children. And not only for them, for her aunt-in-law and cousins of her husband all live in the houses round about and as the head of the family Surinder must constantly keep open house.

When I told her that we all lived separately from our parents and tried to carve out independent lives she was surprised.

'I think the joint-family system is a good thing,' she said, but she later confided that all the busying about of her parents-in-law and their telling her what to do and how to run things made her feel claustrophobic.

'There is not time for my crafts with the children and the cooking,' she despaired.

Surinder would never help in the kitchen or with the babies, and it took some persuasion for Manjula to allow me, a European guest, to help knead the chapatti dough. Slowly we became closer, though, and finally she showed me her wardrobe and we sat for an afternoon on her bed discussing saris. The only other women there were in the village for her to talk to were relations of her husband's, and she was fearful of confiding in them. She missed her sisters in Bihar terribly.

I asked her why she had married Surinder.

'He comes from a good religious family,' she answered. 'When I met him [they met only once before they were married, in the presence of her parents] I was impressed with his seriousness about our religion, and by his devotion to *puja*. There are not so many men left who are so good and devout.'

That afternoon Surinder asked if I would not mind him kissing me. I was trying to talk to him about my grandmother, but he would not stick to the chosen subject.

'Penelope, she invited me on her treks I think mostly for company but I also went because I wanted to learn and she knew so much,' he started. 'She was my friend and there is nobody else who I ever talked to like that who is a foreigner. But she often scolded me – mainly because I liked to stay in bed late. Do you like to stay in bed late?'

'Older people like to get up early,' I said. 'She wanted you to get up early so that you could learn more. What did she teach you?'

'She gave me advice about life,' answered Surinder, juggling a pair of apples in his slim brown hands. 'About sex she said I should have control over it.'

'Quite.'

'One trek once,' he continued, 'we stayed in a yogi's ashram and she slept in the ladies department and there was a yogi here who became possessed and screamed and cried and sweated all night, and Penelope was terrified.' He gave me a flower: 'You are not so girlish now. I think you are more mature.'

'And what about the time you stayed at Nirth,' I said, squashing the flower and dropping it to the ground.

'Ah yes, Nirth,' he said, successfully back on course. 'At Nirth she took three photographs of the sun temple and the locals told her the pictures would not come out, because it is forbidden to photograph by the gods. She did not believe them, of course, and so when the pictures came out blank she was amazed and frightened by that. Have you slept with more than one man?'

I gave up with Surinder and went to talk to his father.

Mela Ram Sharma wore a lack of expression similar to his son's on his face, a little face with a pointed nose and two large ears, while his mouth had some important teeth missing. Although it was warm on the veranda where the sun reached, he hugged a grey blanket around him and when he talked you could hear that his pointed nose was blocked up. He was not particularly forthcoming either and sat and spat and snorted and looked very sorry for himself; he was not used to holding confidential conversations with young foreign women.

Sushila his wife passed on her way to the hospital to get some medicine. She had even fewer teeth than her husband, the gaps all the better displayed for her expansive grin. She looked jolly and laughed a lot, but her English was limited so we did not have much verbal communication. 'Penelope was in our family,' she said to me. 'You are my daughter and Surinder is your brother. Penelope looked so nice in her Pahari skirt that the tailor made in Nirmand.' She cackled at the thought. She and my grandmother used to sit peeling potatoes together chattering in pidgin Hindi, and giggling at their own jokes.

Penelope loved pottering about finishing farmyard tasks, like bringing the cows home and stacking the hay and counting eggs and trussing chickens, as much as she loved climbing thousands of feet up a mule track on the back of a pony and writing articles for *Asia* magazine. Sushila and she would sit, drawn together on the veranda by some domestic task, and they would mumble on to each other about the children and the weather and merits of wholemeal chapattis.

My grandmother loved wholemeal chapattis, and Manjula kindly made a special batch to go in the basket of her favourite foods which would make up our offering to the Brahmin priest in Penelope's name, as we practised the custom '*shradh*'.

'There are ten days in September when you remember people in your family who have died,' Surinder informed me. 'You perform "*Pind dana*" *pujas* beforehand, to call the dead ones and pay them homage. You make small balls of cooked rice and put them in milk water in a pot and take it to a nearby water source. Then you call the Brahmin priests and his relatives and serve them with a meal which you think the dead person likes.'

He suggested a meal: 'Rice, two or three *dahls*, *sabji* [vegetables] and then *bada* [grind pulses into a paste and add coriander and other masalas and then fry it – very tasty] and then *kheer*, which is rice pudding made with milk.'

For Penelope I went to the market with Surinder and purchased corn on the cob, *nimbus* (limes), walnuts, raisins, cauliflower, potatoes, pears and apples and a few sticky strawberry lollies for good measure. Out of all the goods in the market, these were a few of her favourite things.

'Penelope knew *shradh* and she would have liked it,' added Surinder. 'It gives a lot of satisfaction to the departed soul.'

He told me the tale of one Doctor Harivens Rojbashn – mother of the popular Bombay film idol, Amritar Bashn – who died and her husband never did *sradh* for her.

'So she appeared in one of his colleague's dreams,' said Surinder, 'and in the dream she said, "Tell my husband to do *sradh*!" So the husband did as he was told and now she is happily departed.'

We invited in the sober chief priest who took our quite shabby plastic bag of offerings together with twenty-one rupees. Apparently at temples one is always suppose to give one or eleven or twenty-one and it is unlucky to donate money in any other multiple. Surinder told me to give him twenty-one. The priest (who said he was also an accomplished astrologer) blessed the food and murmured some prayers with his eyes shut, and then backing out he bore off the booty to cook up at home and savour in memory of Penelope.

I am certain she would have loved it, because she could never resist a Hindu ritual. The ritual which fascinated her most, however, was the *Bhunda*, the Himalayan rope-sliding ceremony, a Hindu ritual of history and rarity that is supposed to be celebrated every twelve years at Nirmand.

She wrote to Mela Ram Sharma on 4 April 1974 ('ji' being the suffix to his title denoting respect):

Dear Sarpanchji,
    I am longing to hear whether you are going to hold the

BHUNDA CEREMONY at Nirmand this autumn or not? You said it might take place in October or November, but that rising costs may rule this out? IF you hold it I would very much like to come as I have wanted to witness this ceremony for the past forty years or more! I would come about a week before so as to see the HAWA, or purifying of the atmosphere by the burning of corn and oil on that circular stone outside the temple of Parasuram. I think you told me it is called the HAWA (which means wind or air doesn't it?)

I much regret to say that the National Geographic magazine of America is NOT interested in having an article about it. It is extremely foolish of them as it may be the last time in history that it will be performed owing to 1) to rising costs 2) to the loss of faith in the old religions all over the world. This means I cannot get a contribution from them towards your costs.

Over here the prices are SKY HIGH and the cost of living is really frightening. I thank God we have reared our family and both our children are settled in life. I live in a small cottage in the Black Mountains on the Welsh border and my expenses are reasonable, and I save petrol by riding ponies . . .

It was rising costs as well as disasters, earthquakes, landslides, and lack of the right grass for the making of the rope, that in fact led to the postponement of the rope-sliding ceremony until 1981, nineteen years after it was last performed in 1962, instead of the customary twelve.

Every year my grandmother wrote to the Sharmas hoping that the *Bhunda* might be 'on'. Every year it was 'off' until 1981. She wrote to Asha Sharma in March of that year:

I hear you plan to celebrate the Bhunda later this year??? Is it really true and have the astrologers settled the date yet? I believe it lasts for three or four days?? I have been invited on a 3wk tour of China in August so I do hope that Bhunda is not going to take place in that month??? DO PLEASE let me know. If it is CERTAIN this time I would so like to come but it will be terrible to have to decide between the Bhunda and China. But surely it won't be celebrated mid-monsoon??? . . . I have always wanted to see the wonderful Buddhist paintings in the TUN-HUANG caves which we are going to, but I also desperately want to attend Bhunda. Please let me know quickly!!!

After all the set-backs and the arguments among the villagers about the cost of the ceremony, Bhunda was eventually scheduled for the late summer of 1981. Penelope's quandary did not last long, however. She wrote in August of that year to her friend, the historian Hugh Richardson from Simla:

> You will be pleased to hear that once I reached Simla after a VERY trying flight to Delhi and a derailment at Faizabad which made the Kalka mail 3 HOURS late and we had to wait on the hot sticky monsoon platform until 1.30 am, well I suddenly realized I was mad to think of missing the Bhunda after waiting half a century to see it, so I sent a cable to my American friend [the PPM, or Paper Plate Manufacturer, Sheldon Nash, who had been on several of Penelope's South Indian tours and had become a devoted fan and later friend of hers] CANCELLING the China package tour. I was TORN in TWO, as I shall never get the chance to visit the Far East again but there it is: Parasuram [the god, Rama with the Axe, the sixth incarnation of Vishnu, to whom the Bhunda ceremony is devoted] has WON and I shall see the whole of the Bhunda ceremonies from start to finish.

The strange ritual act of rope-sliding had been recorded in Tehri Garwhal in the Sutlej Valley and in various centres in Tibet, particularly in Lhasa, where it used to be performed at the New Year ceremonies. In Himachal Pradesh, a post is erected at the top of a hill and another at the bottom. A rope made of dried *munji* grass is stretched between the two, and a man is made to slide down it on a wooden saddle, narrow but grooved to fit the rope as closely as possible.

Penelope found a description of the ritual in Lhasa by Sir Charles Bell in his book, *The Religion of Tibet*: the rope was stretched 'from one of the lower buildings in the Potala to the obelisk inside the precincts, a distance of some 250 feet with a descent of 100 feet. . . . Formerly the rope was attached to the top of the Red Palace on the summit of the Potala right down to the ground outside the village below, a drop of 300 feet or more. But this was discontinued after one of the performers had been killed, his abdomen ripped open . . .'

Buddhists may have seen the 'sliders' as performers and have considered accidental death abhorrent, but in the Western Himalaya the Hindus definitely regarded the slider as a victim of sacrifice, and the possible death of the *beda* or sacrificial slider made the ritual all the more exciting. The friction of sliding saddle against rope frequently caused smoke to rise and occasionally the rope broke and the man was killed. This happened at Nirmand in 1856 and at the next festival in 1868, the British Government decreed that a goat be substituted for the *beda* at the last minute. So Parasuram now has to make do with a goat.

When Penelope arrived in August at Nirmand with her old friend Elizabeth Simpson, a very good photographer, to, as she put it, 'study' the rituals leading up to the actual 'rope-sliding', she found Asha at home.

Asha told us that the committee organising the Bhunda were all 'hopeless fellows and had no idea how to run it' [she wrote in her journal of the expedition]. The last one took place 19 years ago when Mela Ram Sharma [her and Surinder's father] had run it. The committee wants him to run this Bhunda but he has refused as he does not get on with the Kardar and appears to have no use for the rest of the temple committee either!

My grandmother and Elizabeth stayed in a tent parked in the garden of the PWD rest-house on the edge of Nirmand for the ceremonies, as the Sharma household was full to bursting with relatives. Surinder told them that there had been a shortage of *munji* grass (*saccharam munja*) that year which is used for ropes and mat-making in the area, and

> that the rope was much thinner than usual and only 30 FEET LONG!!! The old accounts refer to the Bhunda rope being between 300–500 yards long. However, Indians are seldom accurate so I HOPE he is wrong, otherwise this Bhunda is going to be a very feeble affair!

All the tailors in Nirmand were fitting and finishing the long printed cotton dresses which the Brahmin ladies had ordered for the festival, and the completed outfits hung in brilliant coloured rows in the open-fronted shack-shops awaiting collection. Penelope wasted not a minute in ordering her own, for any opportunity to go completely bazaari could not be passed up.

While the tailors stitched, the chosen *beda* had spent a busy three months weaving the rope out of what *munji* grass there was available. During the weaving of the rope, the middle-aged *beda* – from a low caste group of entertainers settled locally but happy to perform a little singing and dancing on the side to supplement their income – was obliged to abstain from sex, from eating meat and from shaving. He is regarded with reverence by all Nirmandians and during the final dedication to death in the temple he is worshipped as a God.

> The most fascinating and unique of [the preliminary ceremonies] was the opening of the cave on the night of August 31st, [wrote GE in her journal] But we found to our dismay that we could only learn about it second hand as the time was a 'top secret' and only men of the Brahmin and Sonar (goldsmith) castes were allowed into the courtyard of Parasuram's temple. We could

however sense the great excitement which prevailed in the village . . .

The next morning Penelope and Elizabeth went to pay their respects to the god:

> Outside the entrance stood a handful of young men from the neighbouring village of Koel and Bae, the traditional doorkeepers of the bhunda who must see that pilgrims cover their heads and remove their shoes. We passed the test with flying colours as we were walking bare foot and wearing our long local-style dresses with cotton squares tied around our heads.

For the four days of the festival proper from 9 to 12 September, my grandmother documented every ritual. Not every one went according to plan, though, and she spent most of the 10th asleep in Parasuram's courtyard waiting for the *chhamachhari*, the arrival of the gods and goddesses from various outlying villages along with their retainers:

> . . . 33 had been invited and 26 had accepted and the State Minister of Education, Mr Shivpuri, had come from Simla to receive them. He and members of the Bhunda committee sat expectantly on a dais under the sacred pipal tree at one end of the square which was overhung with a network of blue, green, gold and silver tinsel Christmas tree decorations and a string of balloons. Elizabeth and I climbed onto the first floor of the veranda above Ambika Electronics and waited patiently amid the rows of squatting women for the gods to arrive: but they DIDN'T.

Apparently a dispute over rations was in progress. Each *devata* and his retainers had their allotted camping-ground to which a five-day supply of rice, flour, sugar, tea and onions should have been

138

sent, but two lots of supplies had as yet not been delivered and evidently there was solidarity among the *devatas*, as none of them would enter the square until all of them had received their rations.

The police tried to keep the processional route clear, but the crowds kept closing in on it and one poor god-bearer quickly had to move the *Kalash* from his head as it was on the point of being knocked off, and he clutched it closely to his chest.

> ... at one point in the long proceedings a group of young men started to fight with the police and one was pushed into a deep open drain. We were told later that some of the bloods of Nirmand objected to so many police coming from outside (the District Superintendent from Kulu and twelve constables) maintaining that they themselves could keep order.

On the final day, the actual rope-sliding was scheduled to take place at 1 p.m. At 2 p.m. in 100-degree heat the great rope was carried up with the poor *beda* following. It took an hour to secure the rope, with a lot of discussion among the keepers of the rope as to how best to secure it.

Penelope wrote:

> The next conundrum for the men of Katanda was to fix the saddle to the rope, and having done so, they held two large shawls over it and whipped them suddenly away to reveal the beda sitting astride with his arms in the air. This was his great moment and the crowd shouted loudly and repeatedly 'VIC-TORY to PARASURAM!' Then the shawls were held up again and he jumped off and the poor nanny-goat was tied to the saddle with much bleating and then without warning they let her go and she shot by me and down to the bottom in what seemed like a split second. The lower post was well padded so the animal arrived unhurt in a cloud of sand as the bags which were keeping the saddle upright burst. She was not beheaded on arrival as

nowadays it is considered inauspicious for the victim to die. Two months later when I returned to Nirmand I saw her in the beda's cattle byre unblemished and contented.

Total costs of the ritual worship of Parasuram amounted to just over three lakhs of rupees by the end, which is about £30,000. The Himachal Pradesh Institute of Language and Culture had contributed Rs. 20,000 and there were many individual donations, but nevertheless the brunt of the cost had fallen on the people of Nirmand themselves, and my grandmother was inclined to think that everyone felt it was a terrible anticlimax when the *beda* got off the rope and the goat was sent down instead.

I asked Surinder whether he, as Sarpanch, would be organizing the next *Bhunda*. 'Ah, Imo, it is in the hands of the Gods,' he answered, raising his hands to Heaven. 'I am powerless, you see . . .'

CHAPTER VIII
Rampur Men

'Who would be young again? Always ill, always tired, always crises de cœur. At fifty-four I am far healthier and have twice the energy I had at twenty.'

'I HAVE A diploma in eyes,' said the stocky Doctor Jamwal, who was wide faced, softly fleshed and palely coloured. He wore a purple sports shirt and glasses, and he had a thoroughly modern look about him.

Nirmand is comparatively well equipped for a village in the hills; it can boast 100 per cent literacy and has its own cottage hospital. One afternoon when we were in the mountains together, my grandmother and I had walked down the slope to the surgery (pleading not an illness between us) where we had met and conversed with the resident doctor, or rather pair of doctors, Doctor and Doctor Jamwal, and keen as I was to resurrect the relationship, I had asked Surinder where we might locate the doctors now, six years on.

'In Rampur they are now working,' he told me, and he took me to see them. But Dr Urmila Jamwal was away in Simla, it transpired, so it was on Dr S. S. Jamwal alone that we had called.

'The state of medicine in this area is fairly good now,' he told me. 'Except that the hospital in Rampur has too many patients and no room to expand.' He said there was no surgeon there either and that people had to go to Simla for operations. There are three private practitioners in Rampur, but they come under nobody's control and they can charge as much as they like. Jamwal and his wife were both government doctors and were paid a non-practising allowance.

'I saw Penelope at the *Bhunda*,' he remembered. 'She came a few times for tea, and she was always inquisitive about people in their professions. She had fresh ideas and a sharp and clear mind.'

He was sitting in his Rampur apartment which was a small series of boxrooms in a modern block. Imitation wood chairs and a sofa furnished the sitting-room sparsely. There were a few paintings about the walls – mostly sentimental prints of rosy English cottages – and there was a bunch of purple plastic flowers on the glass-topped table. In comparison with the earthy village dwellings with their matted floors and unadorned wooden walls, this was the very latest in Western-style living. A big white fridge in the kitchen and a stainless steel sink completed the ideal home.

Surinder's wife Manjula, who had come with us – for relief, I expect, from her daily village life up in Nirmand – eyed the furnishings enviously. She fiddled with the magazines on the coffee table, and while the men retired to the kitchen for a man to man discussion and a plate of peanuts, we ladies fell into conversation easily.

'I chose Surinder because his family were good and religious and he looked all right,' she said, repeating her reasons for marriage without much enthusiasm. Her marriage was arranged, but she had viewed a healthy tally of prospects before she was introduced to Surinder Sharma.

'I only met him once,' she revealed, 'just two months before we were married. It is chance whether the marriage will work out or not, but I think things are fine.

'He's a good father,' she added, glancing over at Surya and Himalaya who were tackling a jar of Bombay Mix. 'He has some bad habits, but you can't have everything, eh?'

Dr S. S. Jamwal met his wife Urmila in Srinagar, Kashmir, in 1970, where they were both working. They too had since produced two sons: Rajat, studying for an arts degree at Chandigarh, and Raman who was at the Bishop Cotton School in Simla. For the previous five years between September and March every year, Dr Jamwal (Mr) had trekked around the Himalayas with a family planning unit, giving motivating lectures to villagers, and doling out benefits.

'In Himachal Pradesh the younger generation has started to understand about family planning very fast,' he said. 'But the older ones don't see the point.'

Family planning was high on the Indian government agenda, with a population the second biggest in the world after China, but Jamwal reckoned advice had not made much impact on the Indian people without the imposition of stringent laws. People were more inclined to listen to their forefathers or their priest in India, he said. For example, he said, contraception is forbidden in the Muslim religion (and Muslim men may often marry more than once) and among the Parsees.

'We should impose a tax or some liability if you have more than two children,' he said, impassioned. 'How can someone earning 2,000 rupees a year support five children? They say it's God's wish, but then the daughters are ruined and some try to marry them off for money, aged ten or so, or sometimes they are murdered.'

In those hills, the contraception on offer was commonly a vasectomy after two children, and then the operation could be reversed if the children were to die.

Jamwal told me, 'The person who has the vasectomy signs a legal bond, saying that he has undergone the knife of his own free will, and then he gets benefits and food and travel expenses and some compensation for lost work time.'

The couple can undergo counselling if they wish, and sometimes the woman may be operated upon, but her operation is not so easily reversible.

'I have performed operations with the patient lying in cow dung,' he said. 'I once performed nine operations in one go and the local *padwan* [village councillor] was drunk. Then I trekked twenty kilometres to Kurga that afternoon.'

Manjula, who makes the chapattis and cleans the house and

wants to resurrect the family shop, was still breast-feeding Himalaya, who was already three. 'Motherhood was a wonderful dream
that I looked forward to,' she said. 'But the reality is a different
matter altogether.' I said, inadequately, that perhaps she would
reap her rewards with grandmotherhood, when her sons would be
grown and might look after her. She smiled and sighed and rescued
her sons from the Bombay Mix to take them to get vegetables at
the bazaar.

Dr Jamal was cracking nuts still when I joined him at the
Formica table in his kitchen. 'Yes, I have seen many foreigners,'
he sighed in a world weary way, 'and some don't have instant
appeal. But Penelope's very look made you think she was a nice
woman and a straightforward woman of authority. Her first
appearance was so striking.'

He remembered her staying in a tent near the rest-house at
Bhunda time in Nirmand and how she lost some articles and she
was very surprised, and very angry too. Then she prayed to St
Anthony hard, he said, but they were never recovered.

'Staying in a tent at her age! She was an outdoor lady indeed.
She was very popular and respected by the villagers, even those
who knew no English so she could not even talk to them,' continued
Jamwal.

Surinder had told him about Penelope's death. He was shocked
and surprised. 'She was never ill and always hale and hearty.
Being a doctor, I knew she was a healthy lady, especially for her
age.'

When Manjula had returned loaded with pink plastic bags
rounded with swollen red tomatoes and stretched by courgettes (or
Indian cucumber), we left the sleek, white flat where the Jamwal
doctors lived, and rode back again on that bus to Nirmand.

The Sharmas' house was a split-level timber-framed one with
four storeys at the back and three at the front. It was connected by
a wooden walkway to his aunt's house, built not ten feet away. All
the houses in Nirmand were built in the traditional timber-bonded
style of the hills, with the cattle living in ground-floor byres and

the owners on the first and second floors, with roomy wooden verandas alongside the outer walls of most of them and often a wooden bridge across a 'street' from one house to the other. The street scene was a medieval one.

There were no toilet facilities when my grandmother stayed there.

> When I asked Asha for a chamber pot, she gave me a basin and told me to empty it over the veranda into the street [Penelope wrote in a letter to my mother]. The first morning I was extremely embarrassed but after that I emptied it as if I had been doing it all my life.

A loo seat had been erected over a bucket by the time I returned to Nirmand alone. I do not know whose task it was to empty the bucket, but it was not one of my jobs. In fact I had no jobs at all. I slept downstairs in the 'guest apartment' which was a thin room with a thin bed divided by a curtain from the reception room, and until I gained enough confidence from Manjula to enter the kitchen and help make chapattis, all my meals were brought at appointed times and set on the reception room table. My grandmother may have gained enough of the family's confidence in order to be invited to dine communally, but Surinder hardly deigned to talk to me while I ate – and he was much too grand a Brahmin to let a morsel pass his lips in my presence.

One evening I wrestled with my *bindi* and *dahl* and commented on his wife's cooking.

'My servant made this meal,' he replied, as if even talking about cooking was beneath him. He had toothache, he said, so he could not do much more than sleep that day.

'Personal happiness is the most important aim,' he said suddenly, profoundly. Surinder was keen on yoga and he wrote poetry. He showed me a copy of my grandfather's *Collected Poems* which had been inscribed 'From one poet to another, John Betjeman 1977'. Then he told me what he believed.

He said there were four ages: Satyuga, when all people were pious and good; Duwaper, when corruption starts; Treta, when there is more corruption; and Kalyuga, by which time people are infested with sin, adultery and corruption.

'We are in number four now,' he said. 'It will take thousands of years to change. It is written down in the histories and the holy books.'

He told me that in every age God takes birth as a human, for example Ram Chandra and Krishna, and that in this age he will take his birth as Lord Kalkya.

'Lord Kalkya will form a garden and then the Satyuga age will come again and the cycle will begin over. The scriptures have predicted the village, his parents and what sort of look Lord Kalkya will have. He will be riding a black horse.'

Before this Messiah arrives though, people will do all sorts of polluted things, he said, for Kalyuga is in its extreme form. A knowing look of foreboding spread from brow to smile on his face as he said it.

The next morning we sat, as was becoming usual, on the veranda doing very little. 'There is a man in this vicinity who knew Penelope so well,' Surinder informed me. 'I think it will be necessary for you to talk with him.'

The man, A. D. Sharma, was tourist officer for the Rampur district of the Sutlej valley; he wore a red shirt and a blue blazer with shiny buttons when we met him. He was very tall and slim, with sloping shoulders and a slick and sheeny head of oiled black hair.

'Oh it is a pleasure to meet you,' he greeted me cordially with a white-toothed grin. 'I am Tourist Officer in charge of the district,' he announced proudly. 'I talked with your grandmother many times and I have much to tell you,' he finished confidentially.

With Surya and Himalaya in their best shorts and shirts, Surinder and Manjula had loaded themselves on to the bus with me for our second hair-raising ride down the rough hairpin road to Rampur.

We walked from the busy bazaar town up on the Simla road to the smart rotunda of a Rampur restaurant. It was air-conditioned inside and the management laid on tea and wafer-thin pakoras. When the smooth-walking and willowy tall A. D. Sharma entered the lounge through the swing doors, there was much bowing and scraping among the restaurant staff. The waiters offered refreshments and the chef even emerged from the kitchen for acknowledgement. Here was a fine figure of a man who had earned much respect amongst his department.

He appeared courteous, polite and respectful; I was entranced, and Surinder seemed to be on the best of terms with him. So I didn't think twice when it was suggested that I accompany the gentleman up to Sarahan, the mountain village which is the summer capital of the Rampur Rajas. At the high village of Sarahan there is an impressive temple dedicated to Bhima Kali which my grandmother had praised incessantly. In fact I had visited Sarahan with her in 1985, so it seemed right to go back there, and even more right to return with the Tourist Officer of the district who was keen to show me the brand-new splendid Tourist Hotel.

'Lady Penelope, she brought much tourism to the area, you see,' he said. 'We are all grateful for her keen interest in our area. I would like to show you how grateful we are. It would give me great pleasure to accompany you to Sarahan.'

Surinder waved us off joyfully. 'The bus will take only two three hours,' said A. D. Sharma. 'It is a most pleasant route.'

While the main roads of Himachal Pradesh are mostly, but not uniformly, tarred, the side roads are not, and over both kinds there are frequent landslides, especially during the monsoon months of July and August. A landslide may fall on top of the bus or in front or behind it. If in front, you either have to wait for the road to be cleared by a team of men and women without machines, or you get involved in what my grandmother called 'transhipment', that is, you get out of the bus, climb over the landslide and hopefully get picked up by another bus several hours later on the far side.

If a landslide does not befall you, many other problems will.

The battered buses the brave drivers control are ancient and designed to carry about forty people. However they frequently carry a hundred or more passengers as well as their collective baggage on the roof rack. Any surplus baggage, or live baggage – like goats or chickens – is squeezed inside, and the snake-like conductor must be an acrobat to collect his fares.

My grandmother said the most adventurous bus ride she ever had the nerve to remain on, was a twelve-hour climb from Dharamsala to Chamba across country in May 1980. 'The road was what's known as "khachcha" all the way,' she wrote. 'A dusty unmetalled winding hilly lane, perfect for ponies but difficult for a great long bus.'

At one point the male passengers were made to get out and walk up a short steep hill out of a dry river bed because the bus was so overloaded. A young man sitting next to her who was studying Hindi and English literature and economics at the Dharamsala degree college explained to her: 'His gear does not work properly due to this convex slope.'

An Indian's most often useful virtue is his patience; he takes time-consuming bus travel happily in his stride. Every Saturday this poor student would go home by bus to his father's farm near the village of Chuari and every Sunday he would go by bus back to college – a six-hour ride each way.

My grandmother befriended the young man in her boredom and, she wrote:

He spoke quite good English and had a tape-recorder on which he insisted on playing me an English song which began: 'My heart is beating . . .' but I could not hear the other words properly. Then followed tapes of Indian film songs until we got round to 'My heart is beating . . .' again. Little did he know of my loathing for the playing of tape-recorders and transistors in public places, but eventually I became impervious to the row and managed to doze off.

148

As A. D. Sharma escorted me to the gaudy Rampur bus stand he greeted ever familiar face in the constant throng. My Hindi did not stretch as far as to understand what he might have been saying to all the Toms, Dicks and Harrys whom we passed, but several almost lascivious smiles brought a faint uneasiness to the back of my mind.

At 4.30 p.m. we were squeezed sideways on to the strained bus and manhandled into a window seat on the right-hand side. One of my knees pressed uncomfortably against the steel side of the bus; my left knee pressed uncomfortably against the right thigh of the respectful A. D. Sharma, Tourist Officer of the Rampur district of the Sutlej valley. There was nowhere else for him to lay his snakish long right arm except along the metal bar that ran along the seat behind my back. We lurched off with a spin of the wheels and a flurry of dry brown dust, and my fate, it seemed, was sealed. To Sarahan with Mr Sharma I was irretrievably bound.

By the time our obstinate bus drew to a halt at Jeori I was looking for any which way to abort the hastily planned excursion. I had begun my interview in a determined manner:

'When did you trek with my grandmother then?' I demanded to know. I could not imagine my grandmother enjoying the company of this man much.

'You are still a bachelor then?' he replied.

'This is a beautiful valley,' I said. 'How did you become Tourist Officer?'

'How much fields does your father have?' he answered. 'And how many sheep?'

'A few and fifteen.'

'How much money do you have?'

'None.'

'Is your father rich?'

'He hopes to be, one day.'

'I have two wives, seven children and many many acres . . .'

'Lovely. But how did you know my grandmother?'

'Do you drink alcohol?'

At that stage in the proceedings we stopped at Jeori. It was 8 p.m. and dark already. I disappeared off into a wooden tea shack where the lurid glances from a sweat-soaked team of road workers proved infinitely preferable to the insistent questioning and constant thigh pressure from A. D. Sharma. After tea I went to look at the ugly concrete memorial to the two hundred or so men who had lost their lives in the building of the military road after the Chinese invasion in 1962. From Jeori the road goes straight on to Pooh and the Sino/Tibetan frontier but a branch hairpins round to the right and goes up to Sarahan.

My grandmother's bus had given up round the corner. 'Our bus started,' she wrote in her diary, 'but conked out round the steep bend,' – and so did ours. We met a lorry head-on which refused to back up the hill, so everyone laughed and started smoking and got out of the back to direct our poor driver backwards downhill round a corner on the edge of the precipice. I was sitting in the back bit which hung over the edge, and I didn't dare move.

My grandmother was more fortunate in that her bus actually stayed on the designated road and it was still light, but, she wrote, '. . . most of the passengers got out and I photographed the five or six engineers who crouched in front of the bus and banged bits of it with hammers and miraculously got it going again after half an hour.'

Group instructions for our manoeuvre took an hour or so, by which time Sharma's head was almost resting on my shoulder (he was tired, he said). With cheers of triumph we moved on eventually, and our driver and his two friends made great ceremony of spitting at the amused lorry driver who had seized the opportunity for a cat nap. We did not pull up in Sarahan until 9 o'clock, whereupon A. D. Sharma put his final question to me (I had long since given up trying to ask him about my grandmother): 'Do you want to stay at my place or at the hotel?'

In 1981 my grandmother had carried her rucksack 500 feet

below the village to the PWD rest-house, down a series of rough rock-cut steps alternating with scree. The rest-house turned out now to be 'his place', so I steered well clear of that and marched on into the hotel – at which there was no one else staying at all. As I walked in I was met by a completely drunk receptionist whose alcoholic fumes could be detected from ten feet away.

'It is so cold up here, you see,' said Sharma, 'that everyone must brew their own barley liquor. Would you like some?'

I tilted my head sharply upwards in my best memsahib manner and firmly said no.

'Ah . . .' he said, pouring himself a generous finger or three of the liquid.

Because I was nervous about saying I wanted to go to bed, in case my request was take wrongly, I then had to go through a nightmare of a dinner when Sharma sank lower and lower in his HPTDC chair as his eyes glazed over. He talked of his 'girlfriends' and his two wives and I kept trying to bring the hopeless conversation back to my grandmother to keep things above board.

Every so often the drunken cook poked his shiny face round the door for a hasty leer and all the while the drunken receptionist sat behind his desk, gurgling barley liquor and sinking fast.

When these two reprobates joined the table as well, I got cross, demanded a key to a room and nearly burst into tears. I managed to save the tears until I was, I assumed, safely inside room 101. But then I panicked that the oddity of the room number meant that I had been hustled into a particular room which possessed either a peep hole or a secret entrance or an accessible balcony.

I drew the curtains as well as I could and smoked a cigarette. Then I heard the mincing Sharma's voice. He knocked on the door: 'Room service,' he yelled and then there was a lot of giggling.

'Coffee, madam?' followed by further guffaws. I held tight until I was sure their drunkenness must have borne them off to slumber then I locked myself in the bathroom, wrapped myself fully dressed in a blanket, lay down in the bath and pulled the shower curtain across. Seven thousand five hundred feet up a mountain alone in a hotel with three drunks I was taking no chances.

Luckily, I suffered no untoward intrusions that night and as soon as it was light I bore myself off and away from Sarahan on the first bus at 6 a.m., back to the relative sanctity of Rampur. But the 11.30 from Rampur back to Nirmand was cancelled (a fact I learnt through thought transference rather than direct communication – nobody would tell me why it had not come or whether it was half an hour late or two hours late or whether it would come at all) and I had to wait six hours.

It was Sunday and the shops were shut – a habit left over from British rule – so instead of getting fidgety and cross I did what my grandmother would have done and visited the temples. Firstly to the Ram Chandra temple in the old fort by the bus stand, which has carved ceiling panels depicting Krishna and the gopis adoring cows. I read in her diary, 'NOT in the folk-art style but imitating Parari/Rajput painting.'

In summer, Rampur Bushahr is one of the hottest places in Himachal Pradesh, since it sits at the very bottom of the Sutlej gorge. The heat sent the Rampur Rajas up to Sarahan to build their summer capital (not that there was a chance for me to admire the summer palace, on account of the necessary incipient departure from Sarahan). Their winter palace dominated the small town, and it was into their winter palace garden that I climbed over a wall.

The pseudo-Victorian fairy castle of a palace sits idle now, its trellis-like stone verandas empty and unclimbed by roses and the ornate bandstand in the garden never played in. Raja Padam Singh, ruler of Bushahr, built the palace in 1919 and villagers can still remember him giving *darshan* (which means, literally, 'a glimpse' of himself, but is a common term for when the Raja or Maharaja gives audience to his people).

Rampur is the last Indian town before the Tibetan border, and the Rajah had Tibetan paintings on his walls, as well as a collection of jewels unrivalled in the district. But the Indian princes were stripped of their estates in 1973 by Mrs Indira Gandhi, and most of the former rulers who cannot afford the upkeep of their vast palaces have handed over the regal properties to businesses, relegating their former state rooms to a mundane office life.

So I turned back to the temples. I learnt that the nearby Buddhist gompa was built in 1897 and contained a large bronze prayer-wheel and shelves full of Tibetan books. I did my *puja* and had a *tika* dot pressed on to my forehead by a bent priest with bandy legs and a speech impediment, then sat down for Sunday lunch in a downtown *chaikhana* with blue Formica-topped tables.

A pair of fat, jolly Tibetans (husband and wife – she in a glorious pink shiny frock) came in and sat down opposite me at the same table – though none of the fifteen or so other tables were occupied – and slurped their way messily through two helpings each of dark brown mutton curry. They would chuck lumps of meat to the back of their mouths with chubby fingers and then grin inanely at me as they crunched through the bones. I declined the offer of a mutton curry on them, and instead, when they had finished and burped in appreciation, we all had a Limca together and I liked them very much.

When my bus finally came and then crawled up the hill to Nirmand, I was met by a shirty Surinder.

'You said you would be back this morning,' he said.

Clearly he did not believe a word about the cancelled bus and took it upon himself to conjure up a vision of a lusty night in the hills with A. D. Sharma, a picture which confirmed his views of loose Western women.

Always cover your arms, my grandmother had said, and your legs to the ground. I was following her advice to a T, but clearly the advances I had received were nothing to do with my appearance, but all to do with what I was. An unmarried twenty-five-year-old Western woman was easy game, it seemed – fair game even. If I was wandering about India unaccompanied, I was asking for it. She, being a married woman and a grandmother, was respected. Introducing myself as her grandaughter did not seem to make any difference at all to my status and for the first time in my life I wished I was over forty-five. I understood now to some extent the relief which my grandmother had professed feeling when her youth was over, a relief which I had found inexplicable when I was eighteen and she was seventy-five.

CHAPTER IX
Chapslee and Dehra Dun

'The days of the Empire are over, and by the younger generation in India, quite forgotten. Many English people I have talked to say they would rather remember India as she was in their day. All I can say is that I find it extremely stimulating to visit the new India, in many ways exasperating, certainly, but in other ways deeply worthwhile.'

I TRUSTED SURINDER to wake me the following morning in time for my bus back down to Rampur, but he had never before been noted for his punctuality and, as I should have foreseen, I ended up waking myself. I found him ambling along the veranda in his pyjamas and, fretting. I asked him the time.

'Seven fifteen,' he said calmly.

'But I thought you said you were going to wake me at six.' I shook my head in a state of agitated train-fever.

'But I only always wake at quarter to seven,' he answered by way of explanation.

'But then why did you say you were going to wake me at six when you knew you wouldn't get up until 6.45?'

Surinder shook his head non-committally and slunk off to get dressed. Manjula gave me one of her saris – a cream and brown and green one that she said suited my colouring more than hers – as a going-away present, and I missed my bus. I also missed the one after, so that when I arrived in Rampur I had missed my connection to Simla and had to wait again.

The waves of furious temper subsided though, soon after I had met Jakji, a Pahari bus conductor who gave me something to smoke. We sat in an empty bus, practising patience while we both waited for the 6152 for Simla, and he told me about his English girlfriend who lived in Finchley and how she had never returned to India and he had written to her but she wouldn't answer.

The road from Rampur to Simla weaves in and out of the mountain ridges, and reaches its highest point at Narkanda (which is up and coming as a ski resort for well-heeled Indians). The route covers about a hundred miles and the journey can take five or six hours.

When, finally, the bus rounded the last bend before Simla bus station, Jakji had been talked out of love for the Finchley girl and into the idea of finding a much more accommodating love from home in the hills.

Simla is first mentioned by Captain Alexander Gerard, a British officer whose work it was to survey the Sutlej river valley. In his diary, dated 30 August 1817, he describes Simla as 'Semla, a middling-sized village where a fakir is stationed to give water to travellers.'

Later Simla became a refuge from the heat of the plains for the British, and eventually the Government named it their summer capital. But they had had to fight for it. In 1804, the Gurkhas, who had been defeated by the Sikhs at the battle of Kangra, a fortress about sixty miles from Simla, in their rage began to ravage the states and hills around the 'middling-sized village'. By 1811 these Gurkha invaders had conquered most of the fortresses between the Jumna and Sutlej and had begun to rule with a rod of iron from the capital of Arki, twenty miles west of Simla.

Unable to withstand the Gurkha cruelties, the local people appealed to the British for help. In 1815, aided by local chieftains, the British Forces under the command of Brigadier-General Ochterlony engaged the Gurkhas in fierce battle. On 15 May 1815 the Gurkhas, under the command of Umar Singh Thapa, were induced to surrender and Gurkha opposition in the vicinity of Simla came to an end. Many of the Gurkhas later joined the British forces and did loyal service.

The tract of land on which Simla stands originally belonged jointly to the Maharaja of Patalia and the Rana of Keonthal, but after the British defeat of the Gurkhas, the possibilities of the place as a health resort were realized and Europeans from the plains started establishing themselves in the locality, building houses on sites rent-free and with no other stipulation than that they should refrain from kine-slaughter and the felling of trees.

With a regular influx of the European population, by 1830 the settlement had acquired a permanent feel. M. Victor Jacques, a French traveller who visited Simla in 1831 described the new town as 'the resort of the rich the idle and the invalid . . . now there are upwards of sixty houses scattered on the peaks of the mountains or their declivities: thus a considerable village has risen as if by enchantment.'

In 1832 Lord William Bentinck, the Governor-General, spent the summer there. Other colleagues followed his example, and Simla soon became the recognized hot-weather headquarters of the Supreme Government of India.

Looking at Simla now, you would never have thought it could have been the capital of the Government of all India. Since the Empire days the city – which sits on a series of ridges and looks as though it might slip into the gorges at the slightest tremor (the great earthquake of 1905 in fact only shook the foundations of some houses, though it almost totally destroyed the adjacent areas of Kangra and Dharamsala) – the city of Simla has acquired a seedy tone.

The bazaar into which Rudyard Kipling's Kim could disappear at the turn of a rupee coin has spread itself along the south-facing slope of the main ridge. One street displays its gaudy fabrics – crimson silk and purple cotton, checks and stripes and yellow nylon – for close examination from idling women, waddling in their own lurid cloth and laden already with peppers from the fruit shop and flour from the flour mill.

The ladies turn at the end of the street of material and hairpin back into the grocery road where, stall upon stall, the grocers jostle for space along the cramped slope. Each sells the same *chin*, *channa* and flour. In wooden boxes brown beans and orange lentils and green beans and grey beans are prodded and handled by the knowing customer, while the grocer's son hops from bare foot to bare foot yelling 'Chini, chin, chini!'

A fridge is a rare luxury in a mountain home; each day the cook of the household will make fresh chapattis, fresh *dahl* and fry fresh potatoes. The tomatoes that simmer on the stove are today's tomatoes from the bazaar, for every day between five and six in the evening Simla's womenfolk are arguing with their favourite grocer for a better deal on their daily order of vegetables. Over which, that night, they will sweat and swear, and into which they will dip a finger and sprinkle coriander or cumin or saffron.

There is also a special street for stationery, where you may find a thin man in his white cotton *kurta* proffering 'school pens' (fountain pens) and exercise books, over a counter just two feet wide. He wraps your pile of books in an old newspaper and ties them round and round with string, his stiffly jointed fingers looping and twisting the rope until there is a perfect handle. His blackened fingernails leaf through smudged and limp rupee notes, a feeble sum in recompense for the skill of his string-tying handiwork.

In September the air was fresh and the nights were just beginning to bite. My grandmother once wrote to my mother from Simla:

The climate here is HEAVEN – but too cold for you; I have 3 blankets at night and wear a jersey and skirt in the day. It is very like an English summer: quite unpredictable, some days so sunny and hot that one changes into a cotton frock after breakfast, others, as today, cloudy skies and terrific gale blowing. Last night we had two terrifying thunderstorms; the whole Himalayas seemed to rock and the lightning – fork and sheet simultaneously – so blinding that one couldn't see the landscape lit up as I had hoped but had to screw up one's eyes tight. Several panes of glass fell out of the windows on the enclosed verandah outside my bedroom . . .

My grandmother used Simla as her base in the mountains. She would ride there in the Kalka mail train which winds up from the Delhi plains, and settle at Clarke's Hotel or Woodville or the HPTDC Hotel or the Jesus and Mary Convent for a couple of weeks, 'to acclimatize' she said (for Simla, at the start of the Himalayan foothills, is already over 6000 feet above sea level). Before she rode off further into the Great Himalaya in search of temples, she would rest in Simla for a while and visit the intellectual friends she had cultivated there, and spend hours in the library of the Government Secretariat.

Where she stayed would depend on the level of the grandness of the company she kept. The smart tour parties she led for West Himalayan Holidays needed the glamorous accommodation provided at the Grand Hotel, formerly Bentinck's Castle, which was built for Lord Bentinck, the Viceroy of India, in 1830.

When my grandmother was a girl, her father was handed Snowdon, then the official residence of the Commanders-in-Chief. But with the Empire long finished, and Indians rightly permitted to stroll on The Mall (Simla's main thoroughfare, which was banned to Indians during the Raj), Snowdon is no longer a private house but a Government Hospital. Viceregal Lodge, a green-roofed neo-Jacobean Disneyworld castle built by Lord Dufferin in 1885, where my grandmother danced with subalterns at the Viceregal Ball in 1931, is newly named Rashtrapati Niwas and houses the Institute of Advanced Study. And Woodville Palace, the summer house of the Raja of Jubbal (a Simla hill state), is now run as a guest house by one of his grandsons.

> Very nice flavour of the Old Raj days, [wrote my grandmother to my mother from Woodville, where she was entertaining a tour party.] My tourists arrived yesterday and seem a very nice lot. We have a doctor AND a general surgeon among them so should be O.K. if one of us gets an appendicitis. I have my usual ENT trouble and this morning the surgeon and I went to the Snowdon

hospital (on the site of our old house!) and had our ears syringed! I couldn't hear out of my right ear at all. Then we walked 4 miles down to see Viceregal Lodge with nice terraced gardens fairly well kept up. Then we walked 2 miles back to the State museum where I had to give a lecture at 5pm with an AWFUL projector which finally blew up with a loud bang. It was agony, especially as I have nearly lost my voice and had to keep taking swigs of Benylin expectorant. Then thank God we had taxis to take us back to Woodville but we had to walk nearly a mile to them as cars are not allowed in the centre of Simla . . .

When I eventually reached Simla bus stand in the early evening, I moved like a tortoise with a whole house of a rucksack on my back, up the thousand or so steps from the bus station, over The Mall – which needed traffic control at that hour of dusk, for that is when the strollers horde in jaunty swathes in every direction – along and down the other side of the ridge, through the Lakkar Bazaar, where wooden walking-sticks and toys hang from the stall fronts, to Chapslee, the house which was to be my refuge.

My prospective hosts were Mr and Mrs Reggie Singh of Chapslee. 'Reggie' was the handsome grandson of Raja Charanjit Singh of Kapurthala, who bought Chapslee, a two-storey Victorian villa built on the Elysium ridge, from Sir Arthur Kerr in 1938. The Raja (Reggie's grandfather, that is) filled his new house with modish furniture so that now it had an art deco drawing-room in browns and creams with a suite of 1930s sofas and arm chairs, and a grand piano, made in walnut especially to fit. The parlour, or small sitting-room, was draped dramatically in a deep Victorian red – velvet upholstery and silk and satin curtains – and the glass-topped tables were hidden under crowds of sepia photographs of the extravagant Raja and his family grandly framed in silver.

Reggie and Mrs Singh had come to live at Chapslee when they were first married. Mrs Singh was in fact from Assam, the tea country in the north-east of India, and she met her future husband when she was studying in Calcutta. They had turned their home into a guest-house in 1976.

The Rajas of Kapurthala had been Sikhs originally, but somewhere along the line they had switched and were now Hindu. Mrs Singh did *pujah* every morning before turning to her second business of the day – the Chapslee Garden School, an enterprise she started which takes credit for the education of 600 pupils at a time between the ages of three and nine.

'We take in only enough of the "right sort" of visitor to maintain the place,' she told me. 'In fact, we'd rather have less than more because of the wear and tear.' She started the guest-house with Indians from Bombay and then half the British High Commission in Delhi started arriving by the train load. 'It's all by word of mouth, of course.'

My grandmother had been allowed to bring her smaller touring parties to Chapslee, and she had brought me to stay there for a night. The Kapurthala Singhs had kindly invited me to stay again, but upon my arrival, in the dusk after the aforesaid bus journey from Rampur, I was admitted into the hall and handed a note on a silver salver by a sombre-looking bell boy in khaki suit. The Singhs had, sadly, been detained by unavoidable business in Uttar Pradesh. They apologized for their absence and anticipated meeting me in a couple of days, when their business matters had been solved satisfactorily. I was to make myself at home.

Life at Chapslee could not have been more different from hill-dwelling in Nirmand. I slept in the ground-floor bedroom with the single bed where my grandmother had always slept. My bed had brass knobs and a blue and white counterpane and there were daisies in the blue and white vases. There was writing paper and a mahogany chest of drawers and blue and white curtains and a blue and white rug on the floor.

In my own white-tiled shower room there was a blue and white jug and bowl and a bar of Palmolive soap. The bellboy brought me tea, 'with *nimbu* [lime], how Lady Penelope like it,' on a linen-cloth-covered tray with a bone china plate of silver thin sugared tongue biscuits. There were letters from England waiting for me on another silver salver, engraved with the crest of the Kapurthalas.

The joy was delicious. The food was even more delicious. I sat down, alone at the polished teak dining table (in the dining-room with hand-painted silk wall paper), to eat dinner off a silver plate with silver knives and forks. A waiter in another khaki uniform with a fez lit the candles in the silver candelabra, and proceeded to bring me (under solid silver domes) shepherd's pie accompanied by miniature baby greens, followed by pancakes light as air, with apricot purée and double cream.

While I ate (in as refined a manner as I was able to muster after four weeks of eating with my fingers) he stood a little distance away, his face in profile to me, but his eyes moved silently sideways to watch for my every need.

He brought water in a silver jug to replenish my glass before I had realized it was empty and he brought mashed potato in a silver dish as I put my own last melting forkful to my mouth. I tried to be elegant and not to eat too quickly and to read *Simla Past and Present* by Edward Buck which I had propped up against the silver pepper pot, but being served upon hand and foot can be quite overwhelming and I more often looked at him than at the pages I turned.

Breakfast at my private dining table proved more sumptuous than dinner.

'Tea, coffee, cornflakes, porridge, toast, eggs?' asked the bell boy.

'Yes, please,' I said.

Mrs Singh said that Penelope had told her always to serve Indian food to her tour party, so that they might acclimatize their more than likely choosy palates before they went out on the road.

'But she herself, she particularly loved the bread and butter pudding, and of course our steamed ginger pudding,' said Mrs

Singh at tea in the conservatory after she had returned from Uttar Pradesh.

'And now we always have a bucket in the bathroom – in case they should want a bucket bath and Penelope, she loved the bucket bath, with the cold water best of all, and she would instruct them on how to do it. "Anyway," she used to say, "they had better get used to it because that's what they'll be doing in the villages. They won't be getting showers and hot water then."'

Mrs Singh, her petite yet motherly figure swathed in a chiffon sari, popped a warm morsel of buttered scone into her tiny rosebud mouth neatly, before pressing a linen napkin to her lips. 'I always felt she had a special, deep love for this country,' she said as she spread a little honey on the other half of the scone. 'She was visibly upset when Mrs Gandhi died and she was so worried for Rajiv. I started praying for Rajiv because of her, and now look what has happened.' Rajiv Gandhi had been assassinated earlier that year.

Her husband Reggie, a tall man of upright military bearing sporting a smashing curled moustache, joined us for tea. He slipped three scones quick as a flash down his throat and started on the wafer thin pakoras. 'I have litigations in operation at present in Delhi,' he said as he finished his mouthful. 'And I apologize for my absence but now I must return to Delhi.' He pressed another of the linen napkins to his lips before turning on his heel and departing.

Mrs Singh waved him off and then found her wicker chair again. 'Because of who she was, I think people had enormous respect for Penelope,' she said. 'Perhaps even they were in awe of her. They lapped up her knowledge. She had such a British sense of humour. Oh, she kept us all doubled up with laughter. She would deliver chance remarks with a deadpan face and not realize that she was being funny. Nor did she let her parties waste a moment's time. She was always busy and moving about.'

My grandmother painted a picture of one of her typical days in Simla to my brother Dave (when he was only three):

Every day I walk one mile to a village called Sanjauli, hire a bike
for Rs. 1, bike two miles downhill to the bazaar, then have to
walk two miles down the ridge road to the museum where I
work. At about 4pm I walk two miles up to the pony stand on
the ridge near the Anglican Church and hire a pony to ride
the three miles home, as by then I am too tired to walk any
further.

She added:

One day my pony fell down on his knees in some rough stones
and came over on top of me on his side but neither of us was
hurt. Today I rode a much better 13hh bay pony called
Rustam . . .

Edified by her example I headed out on a walking tour of Simla
the following crisp morning. The Mall was stiff with outsized
Indian families in their starched Sunday best. Little girls wore
frilly pink frocks and begged Mama for a pony ride. Little boys
wore shorts and braces and sucked Kwality ice-creams. More
distanced from their traditionally dressed parents, mustachioed
youths ranged along the handrails on the edge of the ridge in
stone-washed jeans and nylon trainers.

I mingled on until I reached No. 78, The Mall, the location of
Maria Brothers, the world-famous bookshop run by Mr O. C. Sud,
proprietor. Piles and stacks of books reached the ceiling in some
places in the softly lit, dim interior. Bound editions of Shakespeare
met leather volumes of Edward Gibbon's *History of the Roman
Empire* mid-shelf, while pocket handbooks to guide you round
Dorset and Lincolnshire lay on the display table next to books,
falling open seductively, of lavish colour photographs of Indian
Princesses.

Mr O. C. Sud lurked, spotlit by a dusty column of sunlight
stealing in through the back window, behind his paper-strewn
desk.

His face, the colour of coffee ice-cream and just as smooth, was thin and long, but his eyes were merry.

'Oh, the Gods be praised!' he beamed at me. 'Penelope's granddaughter here at last! Come, come, will you have some tea?' He bade his assistant, a smiling young man, bring us *chai*.

He raised his hands to the heavens: 'We are so busy now, what with sending our books to Australia and Canada and as far away as Japan. It will take a day or two to find all the letters from Penelope and to collect my memories. And there is Laxman Thakur whom you must see, and Mr Bansi Ram Sharma, who is now the head of the Institute of Cultural Studies, of course. I will gather all Penelope's colleagues together.'

He said would I come back in a few days' time and he would be ready for me. Perhaps I would return to the shop on Thursday? And then perhaps we might go to the Coffee House for pakoras and conversation? He gave me a signed copy of his interesting guide to Simla and its history and his kind eyes smiled. I promised to return on the appointed day and waded through the books to the door.

'How lovely to see you,' he said at our parting. 'Not many people come to our shop any longer.'

So I took the opportunity of a few days' break to take a bus to Dehra Dun. The town, which now supports almost 400,000 people and is the railhead for the hill station of Mussoorie, is also the gateway to the Garwal Himal. The town itself sits at just over 2,000 feet above sea level, in an intermontane valley in the Siwaliks, the southernmost and lowest of the Himalayan ranges. It is a nine-hour bus ride due east of Simla.

In the earliest Hindu legend, Dehra Dun made up part of a region known as Kedarkhand, the abode of Siva (after whom the Siwaliks are named). Rama and his brother are said to have done penance there, for killing Ravana, and the five Panadavas stopped there on their way to the snowy Himalayas where they immolated themselves.

My grandmother wrote to my mother from there:

D. Dun is very beautiful, a Dun being a wide valley between the Siwalik hills and the foothills of the Hims – c. 120 miles across. The gdns – laid out by the British are fantastic and at present [she was writing in March] full of summer flowers; pansies, holly hocks, lupin, candy tuft, larkspur and tall hedges of marvellous sweet peas. The flame of forest trees are just over but there are masses all around in the jungle which were covered with scarlet flowers the shape of parrots' beaks. This is one of the few places left where there are still quite a lot of wild elephants and tigers – all protected now. But recently three retired officers went poaching without permits and one of them shot a tiger and went up to it whereupon the tiger leapt up and killed him then lay down and died. The other two men ran away terrified and the police later found the dead man and the tiger lying side by side.

The headquarters of the Ordnance Survey of India is also here and the Indian Military Academy, equivalent of Sandhurst, which was founded by your grandpapa with a dreadful portrait of him in Chetwode Hall.

My bus to Dehra Dun was driven by a smouldering-eyed Sikh with a splendid turban and corresponding curled moustache down from Simla, along the Great Trunk Road through Umballah and Sarahanpur – sprawling plains towns with traffic jams of rickshaws and six-seater buses which hold up to twenty crushed passengers – and up again, into the Siwaliks. I went there especially to visit the Indian Military Academy, or IMA, founded by my great-grandfather.

My grandmother had been present in 1932, when her father opened the Academy officially and delivered his inaugural speech:

Indian politicians here today know that there has been a strong and persistent demand for an Indian Military Academy ever since self-government for India emerged from the clouds of pious aspiration on to the firmer ground of an accepted policy, [he addressed the assembled notables].

It is an Indian institution for Indians, open to Indians of all castes and creeds, and paid for by Indians, and I am most anxious that representative Indians should see it themselves and give us the opportunity of showing them, that we, Army authorities, are determined to make it in every way worthy of the Indian Army – and that is a high standard – and in no way inferior to corresponding institutions in India.

My great-grandfather was one of the most decorated men in the British army when he died, aged eighty, in 1950. In addition to twenty-three military medals he held the Order of Merit, the Grand Cross of St Michael and St George and the Order of the Bath.

An obituarist wrote: 'Three outstanding achievements in his service career assured him of an enduring place of honour in British military annals. They were his brilliant leadership of a cavalry charge on 28 August 1914, in the Cambrai-le Cateau fighting line; his part in Allenby's memorable campaign in Palestine, where he was credited with the authorship of the plan for the Gaza-Beersheba offensive that culminated in the capture of Jerusalem, and his five-year term as Commander-in-Chief in India, which was conspicuous for the statesmanlike ability with which he handled difficult problems, political as well as military, in a critical period.'

'A cavalryman at heart' was a phrase often applied to the soldier who, in the words of another soldier, General Sir William Bartholomew, 'was a wonderful man to serve. Though no detail escaped notice, he never worried his man as long as he was his man. He worked hard all day, emitting a flood of brainwaves, always sound. I never saw him leave a responsible officer in trouble without if possible a word of praise, suitable advice and comfort if the man was worth it.'

Bartholomew, writing an appreciation in the *Sunday Times*, ended, 'We soldiers, especially the older generation, mourn a great soldier in the field, probably the best trainer of troops we have had for many years, a statesman of no ordinary calibre, and a kindly English gentleman.'

The 'best trainer of troops' instilled in the newly assigned cadets at the IMA these final words from his 1932 inaugural speech:

> The safety, honour and welfare of your country come first, always and every time.
>
> The honour, welfare and comfort of the men you command come next.
>
> Your own ease, comfort and safety come last, always and every time.

The words he spoke in 1932 were adopted then as the credo of the Academy. Those words are inscribed in gold in Chetwode Hall and are still learnt by heart by every officer in the Indian Army.

When I was escorted into Chetwode Hall, a parquet-floored audience hall with a museum of military artefacts displayed in the wide gallery which runs round the perimeter, by Colonel V. P. Singh, there was a thin team of carpenters working, who were just removing my great-grandfather's gold embossed words written in English on the wall. But they were not removing his credo; they had simply translated his advice into Hindi and were to replace the motto on the wall. Lord Chetwode, looking down from Heaven, must have applauded the swap, which signified the complete Indianization of the army, sixty years on.

My smouldering Sikh had dumped me at Dehra Dun bus station too far into the night for it to be decent for me to call on the Colonel. So I checked into the grim bus stand hotel, spooned up some tepid chicken soup and laid out my white shirt (which I had been saving since Delhi, for just such a military meeting) and my black cotton trousers – the smartest combination of garments to be found in my rucksack – and prayed that the creases might have fallen out in the humid heat by morning.

When I had travelled with my grandmother in India, my dress sense had appalled her enough for her to write home about it:

'Darling Rupert and Candida, this is not for general family reading,' she began to my parents. A catalogue of comments followed, and her final paragraph read:

> She is terribly SLOVENLY and her clothes fill me with embar-rassment; all incidentally borrowed feathers – Boozles' [her nickname for my mother) flowered skirt is completely transparent and you can see her legs and behind thro' it so I have had to lend her my petticoat, hoping my Marks & Spencer cotton frocks are not QUITE so transparent. She has an awful loose sort of tea shirt with a large hole in it and she ties a knot in each shoulder to keep it up.

My grandmother, who wanted me to have some experience of military life in India though we were unable to include Dehra Dun in our schedule that time, had taken me to go riding with some officers at the barracks at Jhansi, on the plains south of Delhi. Her letter continued:

> When we rode the Commandant's horses at Jhansi I had to lend her one of my shirts and buy her a tie. One just CAN'T be slovenly in military circles. She hasn't brought a hairbrush so I have to lend her mine. She assures me her friends like it all in a tangle but her appearance often COVERS me with shame. She CAN look beautiful when she condescends to brush her hair . . .

'One just CAN'T be slovenly in military circles' resounded repeat-edly in my ears all night, but still the creases had not fallen out of my shirt by morning. And, to boot, my right eye had swollen up inexplicably, as if I had been stung by a bee. Resignedly, I saw to my hair with a two-rupee red plastic comb I had bought at the bus stand for the purpose, and slipped my feet into my smartest footwear – the filthy white Reebok trainers that had already walked over several mountain passes.

The sentries at the IMA gate greeted me with suspicion.

'Chetwode,' I countered their glares of disapproval with attack. 'Chetwode's great-granddaughter I am,' I announced. After all, the Academy had been informed of my arrival.

The shorter one softened first and lowered his weapon.

'Mrs Green?'

With initial identification verified, I was admitted passage and much more. I have never been so well treated before. A military escort accompanied me past the nail-scissor neat green lawns, past immaculate rosebeds and into the red-brick military quadrangle (each red brick outlined with white paint and re-delineated every six months, giving a toy town appearance to the one-storey buildings).

First I was 'briefed' by a brigadier, then brought a fresh *nimbupani* on a tray. The camp doctor was called to examine my eye and diagnosed the swelling as heat-related. He applied calamine lotion and dabbed it gently.

After a personal film screening and lecture about the academy, delivered to me alone by the brigadier in the plush and red velvet seated private cinema, I read in my 'Briefing Notes':

> The forested environment and rugged mountains in the vicinity form an ideal training ground for young Gentlemen Cadets . . . The campus is maintained, offering every facility needed for moulding the minds, bodies and character of a growing young man. At the Institution, we have well-equipped laboratories, a well-stocked and maintained library, extensive playing fields and training areas for realistic training.

Then I was introduced to Captain Mahesh Joshi. 'You may be surprised,' he said, 'but we are still attached to Sir Philip Chetwode and his credo is the maxim by which we live and work.' Then he showed me to the officers' mess.

There was my name on a name card slipped into the gold plate on the door of my appointed room, or rather rooms. For there was a proper suite at my disposal, with a fridge stocked full of vodka and beer, a double bedroom, a television and a bathroom too. There were roses in a brass jug on the sideboard and three types of toothpaste beside the sink. I wallowed in the facilities for as much time as there was before my prearranged rendez-vous with Captain Joshi, in the lobby downstairs at 3.15 precisely.

A black and shiny Morris Ambassador awaited us at the front steps, and proceeded to convey us round the compound to visit the gymnasium, the cadets' mess, their sleeping barracks, the golf course (a taxing eighteen holes, I was informed), the stadium, swimming pool and finally the stables. The peace and order of the compound bore no comparison to the mess and the filth and the muddle, common to all Indian towns, that I had left outside the Academy's walls.

'One and a half lakhs [a lakh is an Indian way of saying 100,000] of men try every sixth months to get a commission and to train at the IMA,' Captain Joshi told me. 'But they only take 1,000 after an exam and a rigorous interview.'

A place in the Indian army is respected, comparatively well paid and secure. It often means a home and regular food and clothing for men to whom an alternative would mean scrabbling for a living in the bazaars, and perhaps returning home each night to a shanty town overflowing with his brothers and sisters and their wives and parents and all their children.

'Nobody knows how many Sikhs or Hindus or Christians there are in the army,' says Captain Joshi. 'Religion is pushed to one side as soon as you enter the force and nobody takes any account of it.'

The cadets wear dark green uniforms and shiny boots and belts. They saluted us as we passed. A troop was being drilled in the forecourt by a bellowing CO and another lot rode round a manège on horses with gleaming hides. Even the paddocks were trimmed.

'We have 1500 groundsmen,' said Captain Joshi. 'Though I don't know how many grooms.' There were 124 bay and chestnut horses in the stables, leftover from the cavalry days. The horses are used for training and on parade, but for little else now, and I was promised a ride in the morning.

My grandmother had visited the IMA in an official capacity in 1982, on the occasion of the Golden Anniversary of the Academy. She and Mrs Indira Gandhi (then Prime Minister) were the principal guests and I saw their signatures side by side in the visitors' book in the Officers' Mess.

In her letter of acceptance to the invitation to attend the Golden Anniversary celebrations, Penelope could not help suggesting a replacement for the portrait of Lord Chetwode which hung in Chetwode Hall, to the then Commandant, General Thomas:

> I have always been haunted by the very bad painting of my father which hangs in the Chetwode Hall which I believe was done by an amateur woman artist in Simla, [she wrote without hesitation]. The best painting of my father hangs in the Cavalry Club in Piccadilly and was painted by Sir Oswald Birley . . . I would so much like to have this portrait copied and present it to you on the occasion of the Fiftieth Anniversary Celebrations . . .

Our cousin, the French Academician and talented portraitist Doris Lurot-Betjeman, produced an excellent copy, and my grandmother brought it in her baggage to Dehra Dun.

There she witnessed 'the effect of 500 young cadets in immaculate blue patrols, swinging past in perfect unison to the stirring marches played by four army bands. Under a cerulean sky and with the Himalayas as a backdrop, commands rang out, silver swords flashed. . . .' in the glistening words of the *Times of India*.

The two-day celebrations included sky-diving displays and a *son-et-lumière* and, to my grandmother's probable relief, a polo match and a horse show – attractions, to her, infinitely preferable to soldiers on parade.

The Times noted her vigour, and her enthusiasm for diversion: 'Among the distinguished visitors was Lady Penelope Betjeman, daughter of Field-Marshal Sir Philip Chetwode. Lady Penelope seemed ageless and ready to enjoy everything, including a visit with a young forest ranger to the crocodile breeding sanctuary.'

The crocodiles immediately took precedence, for the while, even over the equestrian displays, and my grandmother's letter home skimmed over the celebrations while elaborating on the reptilian theme.

INDIAN CROCODILES

[ran the heading, precluding any 'Dears' or 'How are you?s]

I met a very enthusiastic young forest officer aged 24. Mr Y. P. Gupta. He told me that he had recently attended a CROCO-DILE COURSE! He talked to me for nearly an hour at the end of which I grew quite fond of crocs. He told me they are now a protected species and there are several farms where they are bred and reared until such a time as they are transferred to their natural habitat.

There are three species of Indian Crocodile:

1) *Garialus gangeticus*, the Gharial of the Ganges which has a long narrow snout with a blob on the end. It is fish-eating and not dangerous to man.

2) *Crocodylus palustris*, the fresh-water croc which lives in the rivers of the Indian plains and also in fresh-water lakes and tanks.

3) *Crocodylus porosus*, the saline water croc which does not actually live in the sea but in tidal estuaries and creeks. It is the most dangerous to man and grows up to 24' in length.

The mating season is Jan. to March and the female croc starts to lay eggs when she is three to four years old in clutches of 12 to

16 eggs. By the time she is mature she can lay up to 70 eggs in five minutes.

Crocs 1) & 2) make nests of brushwood along river banks but 3) makes a hole in the sand about $1\frac{1}{2}'$ deep. No lady croc sits on her eggs but they cover them up and then keep guard from a hideout a short distance away. From here she darts out and drives away (and possibly eats?) any predators which in day time are mostly pariah dogs. Her greatest enemy is the Monitor Lizard (Hindi Goh) which I have seen in Kangra and which can grow up to 6' in length. The Monitors mostly raid the nests in the dark and the poor crocs can't see in the dark so their eggs are often eaten.

At the end of 70 or 80 days the first baby crocs to hatch out start CROAKING whereupon the vigilant mother returns to her nest, removes the brushwood from the clutch and helps her babies out of their shells.

A young croc can store oxygen in its belly and stay under water for an hour, a mature croc for up to two hours.

I asked Mr Gupta if it is possible for a croc to show any AFFECTION for human-beings? He said species 2 & 3 are untameable but the Director of the croc farm had reared a gharial from the day it hatched and it followed him about.

That is all I know about crocs to date.

My grandmother photocopied her 'Croc Treatise' and sent one to each of her grandchildren for reference. She had learned to love the crocs, though they never replaced the horse in her own highest affections.

In a letter from Dehra Dun that Penelope wrote to Elizabeth Chatwin, she began with the horse: 'ཏ is the Tibetan for HORSE, pronounced TA in English. I now know my favourite word in ten languages: – Asb (Persian) अस्वा Sanskrit, घोड़ा Hindi, ἵππος Greek, pferd, cheval, cavallo, caballo.'

She had been to Sarahanpur, where I had passed through, forty miles south of Dehra Dun, on the road to the hills, where there is the Army remount depot (founded in British times), and she continued her letter to Elizabeth:

> There is a marvellous farm there, with paddocks full of specially irrigated GREEN GRASS and fields and fields of alfafa. Each paddock containing horses has a special dungwala who goes round from morning until night picking up the droppings! (An operation I did spasmodically at the Mead but never kept up) . . . There are 3,000 horses at the depot and we drove about 10 miles around the farm lanes to visit various depts in a brake drawn by 4 chestnut horses with a coachman in marvellous livery and two attendantsinditto each carrying a fly wisk. The stallions all have electric fans in their boxes!

Most probably I was riding a horse bought from Sarahanpur when I was mounted the next morning on Rainbow, a narrow chestnut mare, about 15.2 hh. I hadn't a tie, only the white shirt I had tried to keep clean when I wore it the day before. An upright cavalryman was bidden to go with me, and we rode out of the IMA gates like a pair in hand.

We rode straight across the road and into a tea garden – a green carpet as high as our horses' shoulders which was spread in a calm sea before us, the horizon too far lost in the early morning mist to be discernible. Shade-giving birch trees provided a patchy canopy over the tea, and Rainbow dodged them with agile turns, moving any way I fancied with the slightest of indication. The odd white cow lifted its head from grazing and stared as we cantered by, and the baby buffaloes, roaming free in the plantation, shied and kicked. My partner led the way through the tea leaves and never looked back, so I had to gallop after him, urging Rainbow on, faster, so as not to fall behind.

In a clear field on the far side of the plantation he instructed me to ride in a circle around him, sitting tight as I cantered round; first on the right leg, then on the left, trotting, sitting and rising, stirrups off, over a jump. He said I rode well enough, and I was chuffed, but he exhausted me with his instructions and when I could grip stirrupless no longer he halted the lesson.

We turned and walked back along the main road, where bullock carts, auto-rickshaws, cadets on bicycles, mopeds and one heaving bus which seemed to lean sideways with its load, turned not a hair in good, well-trained Rainbow's forelock. I was loath to hand the horse back, in exchange for the rickshaw that would be my transport back to the bus station and the real India again.

When my grandmother had stayed in Dehra Dun for the Golden Anniversary Celebrations, she had slept in the mess, as I did. At other times, when she was passing through Dehra Dun she would stay at the Language School, putting every effort into her lifelong attempt to grasp the Hindi language.

Alas, though she learnt to say *horse* in ten languages, her aptitude did not carry her as far as she would have liked in Hindi, which has its origins in Sanskrit and is the most commonly spoken northern Indian language. She wrote to Elizabeth Chatwin again:

> The language school has excellent Indian teachers who use the latest methods and there is a lab with tapes. But 1) The script slows me down, tho' Bruce must have found NO difficulty as he passed 1st in his year in Sanskrit. 2) There is far more grammar in Hindi than I thought possible. 3) I get a complex about the Explosive aspirated consonants and the tongue flapping 'r's and am much too old even to learn to pronounce them properly. 4) For the same reason my memory is so bad that I cannot acquire a respectable vocabulary. I work diligently for 6–7 hours a day but STILL CANNOT SPEAK.

To my mother at the same time she wrote:

> There is masses of extremely complicated grammar, the pronunciation is impossible with 4 different T's ditto D's, 6 R's and at least six different N's and M's, and I can never hear the difference betwen them! Also the difficult *devanagri* script slows down one's

reading so much. . . . I should really stay at least 3 months instead of five weeks.

However much trouble the Hindi language gave her, however, her unique command of the English language was exemplary; as she displayed at the IMA's Golden Anniversary dinner when she was sitting one place away from Mrs Gandhi.

The Prime Minister was saying to the Commandant that though she most often drank buffalo milk, she liked yak's milk best of all.

'No, no, no,' interrupted Lady Betjeman, across the Commandant. 'You couldn't possibly drink yak's milk!'

'She said she did,' whispered the Commandant to my grandmother.

'It was Dzo's milk, Mrs Gandhi, not yak's milk at all,' said Lady Betjeman, ignoring the Commandant. 'You must know that the female yak is called a DZO!'

CHAPTER X

The Nun, the Receptionist and Five Men in Simla

'India is my University, Western Himalaya my department.'

OF THE FIVE men in Simla who had been fond of my grandmother – Sri Goverdhan Singh, the octogenarian librarian, Mr O. C. Sud, the icon-collecting bookseller, Dr Laxman Thakur, the neat and proper university lecturer, Mr N. K. Sharma, the distinguished-looking former tourist officer and Mr Bansi Ram Sharma, who was jovial head of the Institute of Himlayan Art – only Mr Sud had come to light so far.

Therefore on my return to the hill station from Dehra Dun, I set off to seek out the rest of them. However, before any more of my grandmother's men had surfaced from the mad muddle of Simla society, I was detained by a lady from Co. Galway: an Irish nun called Sister Mary Margaret Lane who was quite probably over eighty.

She lived in the Jesus and Mary Convent in Chota Simla where my grandmother had stayed on several occasions. For while silver service at Chapslee and top-notch military Mess facilities at the Indian Military Academy (transport and driver included) were all very well, Penelope had more often preferred to reside in simpler style in the hill stations; and most often, when she stopped at Simla on her way to and from Kulu, she would stay either at the HPTDC 'Holiday Home', or with the nuns at the Jesus and Mary Convent.

Undecided about the likely constraints of convent life, I had opted for the hotel. A very accommodating Mr Chauhan, area manager, even put me up for free, in acknowledgement of my grandmother's service to the Himachal Pradesh tourist industry

Penelope Chetwode in Berlin in 1933.

Penelope Chetwode in Kashmir in 1931.

Field Marshal Lord Chetwode, Penelope's father, (left) in ceremonial
dress with other dignitaries, Kathmandu, Nepal, 1931.

Drawing by John Nankivell (1973) of the three-storey
pagoda temple at Diyar, a village at 7000 feet, which
sits on a ridge above the Kulu valley.

Penelope Betjeman 'gone bazaari' in her Pahari dress made especially for the Bhunda ceremony in Nirmand in 1982.

Penelope Betjeman in a coracle on the Tungabadra river at Vijayanagar, with (right) Father Joachim at Christmas 1972.

(Clockwise from top left) John Betjeman, Paul Betjeman, Rupert Lycett Green (with David Lycett Green), Penelope Betjeman, Endellion, Candida, Lucy and Imogen Lycett Green (mid seventies).

Penelope Betjeman in the trolley cart driving Bracken to collect wood in the foothills of the Black Mountains, her 'Hereford Himalaya'.

Penelope Betjeman resting on a temple at Badami in Karnataka, South India, in 1985.

Imogen Lycett Green with (left to right) Bihari, Boura Sing and Panchok in the Kulu valley in 1991.

Imogen Lycett Green 'gone bazaari' with friend in front of the pagoda temple at Parashar Rishi, Kulu, in 1991.

Penelope Betjeman in the Kulu valley in April 1986. This photograph was taken on trek by Judith Watson on the day before P.B. died.

Imogen Lycett Green at Khanag with the memorial plaque and some of those who helped put it in place: (left to right) Mensingh, Manbadur, the mason from Banjar, unknown villager from Khanag, Panchok, unknown villager, unknown villager.

through her constant articles about the temples and treasures of the Indian state.

My date with Mr O. C. Sud was not until that afternoon, so it was in the early morning that I walked along Ladies Mile, around Jakko Hill to the Convent of Jesus and Mary, (or rather Chelsea School for Girls, as the convent, once an orphanage and now a school run by the nuns, is now styled), to see if I could find a nun who might have known my grandmother.

Penelope had stayed at the convent for the longest time in 1964. It was when she had completed her trek to Kulu and needed a quiet retreat in which to write her book, that the then Bishop of Simla pointed her in the direction of Chelsea. A letter I had received from one of the nuns, Sister Inez D'Sima described my grandmother's arrival:

'She wanted a peaceful atmosphere and Chelsea was the right place,' the sister remembered. 'I got her room ready in the Cottage, since I was in charge of the Senior Girls. I admired her simplicity, her prayerful life; she tried not to miss Mass if she could help, never went to bed without saying at least one decade of the Rosary . . .'

The first orphanage of Jesus and Mary was opened at Agra in 1842 by Bishop Borghi, chiefly for children of Irish regiments whose parents had died in India. The terrible summer heat, however, took its toll on the young children, whose respiratory systems were bred for wet mist, not dusty dry air, and Bishop Benedick determined to transfer the orphanage to Simla.

The magnanimous bishop bought the Chelsea estate and by the end of 1863 five nuns and forty children had moved into temporary accommodation and a grant-in-aid was promised to the venture by Lord Canning. However, Army Headquarters in Calcutta openly refused to donate money to any Catholic cause, for at the time English official religion in India was intensely evangelical, and Roman Catholic institutions were viewed with stern disfavour. So the orphans and the nuns and the Franciscan Chaplain built the long wooden gabled building – that is now painted green and yellow and has hanging baskets of geraniums all swinging along the front side – all by themselves in 1864.

Later, by military order, the stay of British regiments in India was limited to a few years only, thus reducing the number of orphans, so that Chelsea gradually changed over from a military orphanage to a boarding school for girls. In 1904 the adjoining St Bede's College was founded by Mother St Clare as a teacher-training college (it is now affiliated to the Punjab University) and since Independence in 1947, most of the pupils at Chelsea and St Bede's have been Indian.

All the girls, who were standing about in groups during their mid-morning break in the neatly tended grounds, wore jeans and T-shirts and the latest trainers; I had just bought myself a bargain of a traditional embroidered *salwar kameez* and was rather enjoying wearing it, until they stared after me with bemused grins twitching on their pale brown podgy faces as I crept across the tarmac in search of Mother Superior. Some of girls had cropped hair and most of them clutched personal stereos (one of them was listening to Rod Stewart).

I waited under the yellow veranda, admiring the flowers in the swinging, hanging baskets, until I was approached by the smallest nun I had ever seen, with by far and away the bluest eyes and the whitest hair.

She took my hand with one of those pudgy, cool, pin-cushions of a palm with a smooth glassy surface, and led me to a cream wicker chair on the enclosed veranda, along the Victorian tiled passage.

'Of of course, I remember Lady Penelope, what a lady!' the diminutive sister said in a tickling Irish brogue. Sister Margaret Mary Lane, born in Galway in 1911, kept hold of my hand and leaned her white-crowned head close up to mine as she talked.

'I became a religious in Ireland,' she started. 'I was only a young sister there, just twenty-four, and I'd never been abroad before, when the Mother Superior said, "Would you like to go to the missions?" Well, I said yes. I was obedient then.'

She had a BA in English and French from Galway University and she set sail from England on the 2 January 1936 on a British boat, the *Viceroy of India*.

'I didn't know how to say no at the time,' she giggled.

Sister Mary Margaret kept apologizing for talking so much and touching my knee when a point needed my special attention. She was the archivist of the convent, she told me, and she had written a history of St Bede's and the Jesus and Mary nuns in Simla. There was a report, she remembered, written by my grandmother in 1964, on the occasion of the Centenary celebrations of the convent, in the archives. Let's have some tea, she said, and we settled in for the morning.

There were sixteen 'novices' resident in the convent, who had arrived mostly from Catholic homes in South India, from Kerala and Karnataka, where many of the first missions from Spain and Portugal were successful. Every so often the novices would walk past us – 'Good morning, sister,' they said, and giggled into their hands as they trotted off unnaturally quickly. They did not look remotely holy, but Sister Margaret Mary said they were all terrifically dedicated and that she taught them English.

She herself had met my grandmother only once, in Agra. After her successful sojourn at Chelsea in 1964, my grandmother had slipped into a 'convent circuit', and would stay with nuns while travelling all over India, booking in whenever their choice of domicile clashed happily with her choice of destination.

'I was asked to take her round the Taj Mahal and to the Martyrs' Cemetery where the Italian architect who built the Taj was buried.' The sister recalled the Agra visit. 'I wanted to take a rickshaw, but of course she was for walking. I was in charge of taking the celebrities around, like Lady Betjeman you see, because I knew the history.'

When one of the novices brought tea on a school tray, Sister Margaret Mary rested for a contemplative moment, collecting her memories. In the manner of the ritual of Holy Communion, I dissolved a slightly soggy Marie biscuit on my tongue.

'She had such ingenuity and courage in the face of danger!' said the blue-eyed octogenarian sister suddenly, animated. She settled in her chair again and said, tantalizingly, 'I have one particular incident in my mind.'

Then she told me how Penelope had been travelling by road to India with a party of men and women and a young Irish girl.

'They were in Turkey and it was nightfall and the men went away in their conveyances and Lady Betjeman and the Irish girl said they'd stay in the jeep for the night, but they'd forgotten to lock one of the doors!' Her blue eyes stretched as wide as they could go.

I knew the story – the attempted rape at the Turkish border – but I let her Galway imagination run riot over the tale. It came out somewhat more dramatically than I'd heard before from Elizabeth Simpson, the prospective rapee who had been sitting in the van with my grandmother.

'That story has stuck in my mind,' said Sister Margaret Mary Lane concluded, panting with the exertion of the accurate description of the rape attempt. 'Such courage and initiative she had. Two or three times she was in the danger of her life! It must have been almost spent when she died in the Kulu valley!'

Other qualities that my grandmother impressed upon the nuns were of a more domestic nature. Sister M. Peter Claver, a Jesus and Mary nun, wrote to my mother when my grandmother died: 'We used to enjoy her slide talks, her adventurous experiences . . . but when free she helped in the College kitchen – teaching us some beautiful prayers while slicing vegetables and onions.'

It had not taken my grandmother long to find the kitchen. Writing about the Centenary celebrations of 1964, she quickly admitted where her interest lay:

The preparation which went on for six weeks beforehand (I arrived to stay at the outset) in all departments was terrific. I cannot hope to describe them all, but being, as I am, extremely greedy or passionately fond of cooking, I took most interest in the culinary side. Little Sister Monica may be small in stature, but she possesses the strength of Samson in her right arm, for she beats up egg whites fifteen to twenty at a time, by the antedeluvian method of using two forks, sufficient to make eight hundred meringue cases. She and the other sisters stirred and beat fudge and cake mixtures and made marzipan fruits and hand-dipped chocolates practically by the hundredweight. There were to be four performances of the centenary celebrations, each one preceded by tea for up to two hundred guests. On the fifth day, May 27th, St Bede's feast followed, and for that, according to hallow'd tradition, a three-tiered cake had to be made and iced and put for protection in the empty bath adjoining the store room. When the sisters want to set a mousse for a Bishop's dinner, they put cold water in the bath and stand the mousse in that, lacking a refrigerator.

My grandmother had been astounded by the simplicity of the convent kitchen:

It was an absolute revelation to me what these Indian sisters managed to produce with no modern kitchen equipment bar a mincing machine. They had old-fashioned coal ranges with very erratic ovens, no pudding basins, palette knives, rotary beaters, pressure cookers or cake mixes. In the Chelsea kitchen the nuns had to cater for one hundred and sixty girls and sixteen teachers and fifty-six nuns, and in the St Bede's kitchen for ninety students (twenty of whom are vegetarian), ten lady professors and guests and for the clergy at Eaglemount, the Bishop of Simla's house.

The nuns were similarly astounded by Lady Betjeman's devotion to prayer. 'She was at Mass and Communion unfailingly every morning,' wrote Sister M. Peter Claver to my mother, 'and, indeed, she said her rosary dutifully every night.'

Such a routine was blissful for Penelope, who grew strong on an early night and early rising, and she needed that strength which she derived from an ordered convent life, to give her the energy to carry out the marathon targets of achievement she set herself when 'working' in Simla.

Along the road from the convent was the Government Secretariat, in whose cavernous underground labyrinth there hid a rich and rewarding library.

'I work till 5 p.m. every day in the library,' Penelope had written with pride to Mr O. C. Sud in a letter which went on to thank the bookseller for clarifying a matter of identification of some temple carving and ended with unshy praise and admiration: 'You are the most knowledgeable man in Himachal Pradesh on iconography and I shall certainly consult you about any further problems which may arise . . .'

My grandmother had cultivated a network of intellectuals in Simla with whom she could discuss her temples, her favourite topic. Mr Bansi Ram Sharma at the Institute of Language and Culture gave of his time and knowledge, as did Dr N. K. Sharma, the now retired Director of Tourism. She took on as a protégé, originally, Dr Laxman Thakur, whose letters in answer to hers began 'Dear Madam' or 'Dear Betjeman' or sometimes simply, 'Chetwode'. The most elderly of her 'colleagues' as she called them, was Sri Goverdhan Singh, the octogenarian former librarian at the Government Secretariat.

Sister Margaret Mary Lane had run out of stories by lunchtime, and we were photographed together in front of the chapel by one of her girls. She giggled and glowed beside me in her habit, and all the nuns who passed us smiled the broadest smiles. 'Lady Betjeman was an illustrious and distinguished lady,' were her final words on the subject. 'But then she used to captivate the nuns at mealtimes and spin out story after story and we were all in hysterics!'

It was easy to imagine a tableful of Catholic nuns in hysterical laughter at my grandmother's stories. Never, in my experience, has there ever been a nun who was not of cheery disposition. They are always giggling, and there couldn't be a better advertisement for life with God than such blatant joy. It would have been lovely to stay on at the convent, but I could not keep the punctilious librarian waiting.

You could not see the walls in Sri Goverdhan Singh's house for the books. He was small and slightly hunched, with a round, old face hidden by huge glasses which seemed to magnify his quiet eyes. He lived with his wife in a spartan cottage up on Jakko Hill, above the convent. There were faded cotton carpets on the stone floor, and nothing but bookshelves lining the walls.

The librarian had graduated from Punjab University in 1955 with a BA in Library Service and had served at the Secretariat Library for thirty-eight years before retiring in October 1988. Just after he joined, the library burnt down, so it fell to him to buy new books and build it up again from scratch.

'I have a great passion for books,' he said simply. He spent ten hours a day reading or writing, a passion that had, unfairly, given him a cataract in one eye, but still he was able to find for me the slimmest volumes on his shelves. His smooth brown hands held the books with tenderness. 'Here you see, I have some oddities.' He showed me books with obscure titles like *The Economic Conditions of Simla Rickshaw Men – 1934* and *The Simla Amateur Dramatic Club 1837–1937*.

When he looked up a reference he held the book very close to his face and squinted. He wore a Kulu cap over his bald head and a proper Kulu tweed jacket and he rocked from foot to foot as he walked from shelf to shelf. 'She worked for hours and hours and hours, your granny,' he said, squinting. 'I always say she was *greater than great ladies*.'

His mind read like a human microfiche. I just had to say one word, 'Chetwode' (for I hoped he might be able to help me find out more about my great-grandfather and his exploits), and after a moment's consideration he recited a list of authors, books and page numbers.

And it was not only Penelope who had had the luck of coming across Sri Goverdhan Singh and his library. For Patrick Leigh

Fermor, hero to the Greeks and a marvellous writer, had needed
his help when he came to Kulu to explore the lonely village of
Malana. My grandmother, a friend of Leigh Fermor's, had directed
him towards Goverdhan Singh and the librarian was so helpful,
that Leigh Fermor had dedicated a copy of the paper – 'Paradox
in the Himalaya', published in the *London Magazine* – personally to
the erstwhile book lover.

'To Sri Goverdhan Singh,' the dedication read. 'With very
many warm thanks for his kindly help in the Secretariat library
three winters ago and for his guidance to right sources – and many
apologies for any wrong conclusions, or mistakes! I shall always
remember the many happy and fruitful hours I spent in the
library.'

Goverdhan Singh was proud of his handwritten tribute from
one of the world's greatest writers (he had read all of Leigh
Fermor's books and rated him highly) but he was proudest of all
to have been a close 'associate' of Penelope's, a friend who
described him in an introduction she wrote for a book on Pahari
architecture, as 'the greatest librarian in the world'.

(I found the library the next day, in its closet in the depths of
the Secretariat, but without the learned presence of Sri Goverdhan
Singh or my grandmother, it offered no sanctuary. I browsed, so
as not to appear too lightweight to the new librarian, a lady in
pink, but quickly escaped.)

Goverdhan Singh's wife was a petite and beautiful lady called
Mrs Tikam Devi who brought us tea mid-afternoon, but she had
not known my grandmother. Penelope had been seen by these
Simla folk as equal to the men in her infinite knowledge and her
dedication to study, in a state where often as not, the women had
been taught little more than to read and write.

Asha Sharma, Surinder of Nirmand's sister, proved the exception to the rule, however. Asha was utterly literate and was at
college when my grandmother first turned up at Nirmand; Asha
says my grandmother was surprised and pleased to find a girl in
the family who could speak fluently in English. 'I liked her

immediately,' said Asha over tea at the Meghdoot Hotel, where I met her in a complete contrast of circumstances from Sri Goverdhan Singh's cottage on Jakko Hill. 'She was like my granny – maybe we were related in a former life.'

After college and during the various unsuccessful marriage arrangements that Asha underwent, she worked her way up within the HPTDC from laundry mistress at the cheaper hotel at which I was staying, to House Manager at the impressive Meghdoot, flagship for the tourist corporation. The modern hotel was built on a plateau where formerly Peterhoff, the Viceroy's residence, stood.

While Peterhoff had been a 'cottagey, Tudor affair about which all the Vicereines had complained', Meghdoot possessed notions of grandeur way beyond its station, with a 1930s style sweeping marble staircase in the lobby and suites of rooms with marble fittings. Yet still, as is common in India, it was only half built.

Nevertheless, the hotel was open for business (though nobody was yet staying) and I found Asha behind her neat desk in the foyer. She carried a grave beauty about her, with the pale skin that denotes good breeding in India and thick dark hair which she had hennaed recently, falling below her shoulders. She looked tired, though, and said she had a cold, and I remembered that when I'd met her before she'd had a cold then, and she told me she always seemed to be getting colds.

'I came into the hotel business for the glamour,' she said, snuffling into her handkerchief and glancing about the empty, characterless foyer. Had she found it, I wondered. 'Oh, yes, the life I lead is varied. I am not making chapattis for a family every day, I am dressing for work.'

I went to Asha's lonely box apartment when she was too ill to go to work one day and we sat in the windowless sitting-room and riffled through piles of black and white photographs of Penelope which had been taken at Nirmand. 'All the time she was so energetic,' said Asha. 'She used to work herself to the hilt. I never knew her to be lazy.'

In came Rajender just then, the brother who comes between Asha and Surinder. He worked for a five-star hotel on the plains, where they had recently had a French week, with a French menu in the restaurant. These two Sharmas seemed to be living in a world apart from their landowning brother Surinder, who was head of the Panchayat at Nirmand. While he wore *kurta* pyjamas, Rajender wore nylon slacks and a shirt. Asha would wear *salwar kameez* (to lend a traditional look to the hotel foyer), but only in the latest thoroughly modern design.

We drank rhododendron squash (which Rajender said reminded him of Campari) and Asha cooked turnip *sabji* with curd and chappattis for me and her brother, though she refused to eat on account of her heavy cold.

Asha talked while we ate: 'She liked this sweet thing called *jeera*,' she said. 'It is very heavy but both nutritious and delicious. You soak the wheat for days and when all the water is drained it is grounded to paste and then sun-dried for many days. Then it is soaked in fresh water until it is soft, then you melt butter in a pot and you stir in the paste and add sugar and dried nuts like walnuts and almonds chopped up. Oh, she loved that. She was very fond of sweets and she always brought me chocolates from England.'

Asha was at Nirmand once when my grandmother visited the Sharmas on Janam Ashtami (Lord Krishna's birthday). The family fasted on that day and in the evening *bathoo* (millet roasted and puffed up with butter and gur – like popcorn) was prepared for the meal – a celebration called *prashad*.

'We have this feast at home always in the Indian month Bhado [July/August]. There are many fruits in the orchard then and we distribute them. Since my grandfather's time it has been the tradition to celebrate this festival at our home and all the villagers come and local music is played – *chari* – it is soft music with flutes and drums and Penelope loved to hear that. I think, even she has recorded it. The children dance to it. I don't know how to dance to it, but Penelope danced to it!'

My grandmother had given Asha Bevis Hillier's *Betjeman – A*

Life in Pictures, which we took out on to the grass after lunch. Asha knew it by heart and as she turned the pages she said about Grandpapa, 'He was a very good-looking man, very handsome.' But there was an edge to her tone for she had witnessed my grandmother's unhappiness, and it had prejudiced her against him slightly. 'All these men they are the same,' she said, and I thought of her brother and had to agree.

'Penelope, she was always talking about marrying me off! My father is well known and I used to get offers all the time. Ever since I left college there were many men. We are from a good family, so five or six used to come at a time.' She sighed heavily.

'I got fed up. I even got offers from abroad, from America, Canada, New Zealand. Doctors, one hotel wallah and engineers but there was always some problem and my parents rejected them all.' I reminded her of Mr Kumar from Wolverhampton.

'Ah yes, I saw a picture of him and I thought he was quite handsome, but he had lost his job (he was supposed to be an engineer but he was working in some shop) so there was another problem!'

Asha, who lived in an apartment with a nine-to-five job and a pretty thin social life, likes the joint family system best.

'When there are difficulties all the family can sort it out and peace is restored. It can be intrusive but I think it is good and the old are looked after.' There was a quiet wisdom in her words. 'After all, it will be our turn one day, eh? I like old things and the old ways, old tracks and old temples. Like Penelope, I suppose.

'We were so close. She used to talk about home to me. About how she did not live all the time with her husband. I told her: Your husband is not from a good family, but you are from a good family. I told her: He was not sincere but you are sincere. She said to me: When I go to London to see him, I am happy and when he comes to stay with me I prepare his favourite dishes. She loved him so badly.

'And look, she was always going on about marriage! She even said when you came out – we must find a good Brahmin for Imo, and for Lucy she was looking too. Eighteen is a good marriageable age, she said.'

Rajender ignored our girls' gossip and went to sleep in the sun. We talked and gloated over the Himalayan visual feast spread before us, uniform peaks like snowy meringues lined up, row upon row. Asha sat cross legged on her charpoy.

'She was such a clean-hearted lady, not like other foreigners. She loved the Indian ways and she became quite an Indian type. In her last days she gave up meat and she said, "I feel quite peaceful now." She was in love with these hills.'

If Asha lent my grandmother womanly companionship, companionship of a gentlemanly variety came from Mr O. C. Sud to whose bookshop I returned after lunch.

Mr Sud had graduated from Christian College, Lahore, with an MA in geography in 1946; at that time, Lahore was still part of India, but after partition in 1947, Sud, as a Hindu, came to Simla. He set up Maria Brothers in 1947 when there were precious few jobs going, he said. 'Maria' was a subcaste among the Suds who derive from the mercantile class: 'We people [the Suds] opened up the trade routes with our mule trains and settled here in the 1840s,' he said. 'We had timber contracts with the British Government.'

Sud started by dealing with W. H. Smith, who had monopolized the book trade in India then, buying and selling new books and magazines mostly. But these did not interest him for long, so he began to buy old books, mostly from rajahs and maharajahs. The princes had filled their libraries in the nineteenth century but, 'They didn't open the pages ever, nor knew not what they had!' Mr Sud told me with disbelief. The princes bought books for prestigious reasons, and Mr Sud bought them back again because he loved them. Customers now sent him 'want lists' from every country in the world bar Russia and China. He sold books and maps and hand-coloured lithographs, but he never bought much from the English in Simla, for most of them had left by 1947.

'The last English lady here was Lady Montagu who died alone in 1984,' he told me. 'She ended her days in the Lady Hardinge Home for Distressed Gentlewomen.'

We had pulled up chairs at the back of the bookshop, and Sud burrowed among the papers and notes on his desk for a space to rest our cups of tea. My grandmother had first been directed towards his shop in 1970.

'We discussed the manners and languages of the hills and I offered to show her my huge collection of Pahari bronzes,' he said, recalling the beginning of a life-long friendship.

Besides being a world-class bookseller, Sud was a gemmologist, a botanist, a coin collector, a manuscript collector, and a collector of Tibetan artefacts and Hindu icons (he could also claim to be something of a philatelist).

'I work hard at every hobby,' he said. 'I collect my artefacts when I trek, and I trek whenever I feel like it. I just close the shop and find company to go with. That is what I like best.' It was not long before Penelope suggested she might trek with the learned collector, and in 1973 they set off together in search of the 'lost' temple of Managanee.

In the three years that they had known one another before the trek, Penelope had become familiar enough with her friend to boss him about, as was her natural inclination, but not familiar enough to lose the respectful 'Mr' with which she addressed him always. She was a compulsive note-writer, and Mr O. C. Sud saw as much of her familiar hasty scrawl, littered with exclamation marks and capitals and underlinings, as the rest of us. He has kept even the scrappiest piece of paper she ever wrote him a note upon – a receipt from Mr Lal and Co, the tailor's shop next door.

For my grandmother seconded Mr Lal's shop as a post box for whenever Maria Brothers was shut (which was quite often, because Mr O. C. Sud was always shutting up shop to go off and collect some icon or other), or otherwise stuck her notes into the wooden frame of the door with a drawing pin.

I am IN DESPAIR [started one (dated, incidentally, well after closing hours at 7.15 p.m.)]. You are NEVER open. I came up especially to say goodbye . . . I do HOPE you or your son will be at Maria Bros tomorrow, otherwise could you v. kindly send the article down to the Holiday Home as I leave on FRIDAY. I CAN'T [underlined] come up again tomorrow. I'll be in the library all day.

Another one started with similar exasperation:

11.50 WED Just came up to see you but shop is LOCKED! Am leaving this book with Mr Lal. VERY grateful if you could post it to me in England, and you can read it first if you want to! Am dining out tonight, will try to see you tomorrow evening. Am working in the library till 5 pm every day!

Another:

Dear Mr Sud. Very sorry to hear from tailor next door that you are ill. There are so many things I want to discuss with you! I want to leave my saddle with you! I will call on the morning of the 28th.

Sud remembered that Penelope had always seemed pressed for time. His account of the Managanee trek, which was written with a scholarly emphasis, concentrating more on the temples than on the social aspects of the eccentric party (consisting of Penelope, Mr O. C. Sud and two eighteen-year-old boys from England – David, a photographer and Robin, a caterer – who had driven Penelope's 'sturdy sleeper-diner-all-purpose Morris van BMC J-4 Model' to quote Mr Sud, all the way to India from England), was coloured on every page by a daily reference in passing to 'hurrying our breakfast' or 'bolting our tea'. My grandmother was always racing for the early morning light, or pushing to see one last temple before nightfall.

Mr O. C. Sud himself was inclined to linger, however, particularly when he came across a holy situation. He let his pen loiter over his exceptional command of the English language too. 'The old *pujari* (priest) of the temple who was about 70 years of age, was sitting outside the temple, reading his scriptures on a *tiala* [a kind of round raised stone plinth often built round the trunk of the sacred "peepul" tree], enjoying the cosy warmth of the sun's rays,' he wrote on page No. 4 of his trek report. 'He had come here to offer the morning worship to mahadeva, whose temple it was. The old *pujari*, seated huddled and completely absorbed in his texts, under a giant aged ficus tree in the complete seclusion of the mountain ranges, looked like a midget in the mighty pervasiveness of nature and did not fail to remind me of the place of man in the Zen Buddhist landscape paintings. I bowed to this holy man, and made him an offering of a rupee, which he gladly accepted, conferring on me a reciprocation a "God bless you" along with an apple he had handy on his book. He did not talk to me any further and soon got drowned into the nectar of his holy books as a bee into a flower.'

Mr O. C. Sud was a poet when he talked as well as in his writing. One could not imagine him ever raising his voice or losing his calm hold on life. With his overflowing and multifarious knowledge and his deep understanding, Sud proved a valuable friend for Penelope, though their discussions rarely did more than skirt personal matters, both of them preferring to keep their conversations on a scholarly and professional level.

'We became friends, I suppose, because we have the same interests. I showed her my botanical drawings too,' he said. 'She asked me if I knew of a herbal cure for Parkinson's disease – the tremors. I told her about one of the herbs – *withania somnifera* or *ashwagandha* – and that she might purchase it at an Ayurvedic shop. It must have been for her husband.'

Once, when Mr Sud took Penelope to see a wooden temple in the glen, she suddenly, quietly, declared that it was her sixty-eighth birthday that day. Mr Sud was distressed because he had bought nothing for her. 'I had no gift with which to celebrate the day,' he said. 'If only I had known I would have brought something. Dear Penelope,' he said, 'I had so much respect for her.'

We retired then to the Ashiana for coffee, where we were to meet Laxman S. Thakur, who had been a student when he met Penelope in the Secretariat library, but who now occupied the learned position of Department of History Lecturer at Himachal Pradesh University.

Mr Sud remembered countless trips with Penelope to Davico's, a Raj style restaurant with a 'cool and calm atmosphere', but it had burnt down ('That happens a lot here – it's mostly short circuits in winter that do it') and ever after they would confer over milky coffee and an iced bun in the Ashiana. My grandmother did love her coffee with a bun.

Laxman Thakur was shortish and slight, with crinkled black hair parted neatly in the middle, a large nose on which rested wire-rimmed spectacles, and a thin moustache trimmed exceptionally neatly. He may have been the neatest man with whom I have ever had a cup of coffee.

When he used to begin his letters to my grandmother with 'Dear Chetwode', in nearly every letter back she wrote him a paragraph or two about the complications of being the Hon. Lady Betjeman as well as Miss Penelope Chetwode, and offered advice on how to address her in future ('Just call me Penelope').

'She took great interest in me,' said Laxman, who had met her by chance in the library when he was researching his thesis on a subject after her own heart – 'The Architectural Heritage of Himachal Pradesh.'

'We had an exchange of ideas and she was so encouraging – and critical – and I sent her all my articles. She was so studious herself. She wrote so many notes in the field. Then she would get up so early in the morning and write up the notes of the previous day.'

He told us he had been trekking recently in Kulu Sarahan (a

different Sarahan from the one where I had the unfortunate experience with the drunken tourist officer), and that he had seen her name in the rest-house book there. 'I was happy to see that,' he said. 'I am so happy to see you here, but I only wish she could be here also.'

I left the two learned scholars arguing gently over some temple rite or other and returned to the HPTDC Holiday Home, where I was enjoying free board and lodging courtesy of Mr Chauhan. I watched a silly Hindi movie and ordered egg curry on room service, but it was too rich and made me feel a bit sick. My grandmother used to make the perfect egg curry – neither too eggy, nor too spicy – and serve it up at her house in Hay-on-Wye with her own homemade poppadums on the side.

The following morning I had the great good fortune of sampling some similarly delicious homemade fare, at 'brunch' with Dr N. K. Sharma (no relation, – Sharma is a common surname of Brahmins in these parts), the retired Director of Tourism who had invited me to his house.

I had been seeking him high and low over Simla all week, then suddenly, a couple of days before, when I had been loitering on The Mall without much intent, he had accosted me.

'Green!' he had exclaimed, his bright eyes widening, his strong hand shaking mine vigorously before I even had time to recognize who he was.

'I have heard that you were in station! What luck brings us together!' He had talked at me animatedly amid the confusing crowds, then invited me to a mid-morning meal on Sunday. 'You will find my house,' he said, hopefully. 'No. 2, MIG Housing Colony, Jakko Hill!' And then he was gone again.

'MIG' meant Middle Income Group, a band of housing which perched on the side of Jakko Hill between HIG and LIG, built by the Government. MIG looked much the same as LIG and HIG and monkeys ran all about the identical white concrete blocks, muddling my path and making me an hour late for Dr N. K. Sharma.

If he was getting hungry he showed no signs of it, however, but ushered me cordially into his front room. MIG flats have superior views to those from LIG, and Sharma's looked down over Chota (Lower) Simla and far over the foothills. His wife looked down over the frying pan for most of the morning, while their homely, smiling daughter looked down at her feet.

Mrs Sharma clanged pans about in the kitchenette for a while and then produced a pile of at least fifteen *puris* (fried chappattis) and individual bowls of vegetable curry and curds. The meal was aromatic and tasty. I begged N. K. Sharma to allow the women to come and sit with us, but he just fluttered his hands in the air vaguely and said, 'Oh, you know, on Sundays they are busy with preparing and cleaning and other things,' as if those things were a sort of mystery to him. I smiled conspiratorially with the daughter (who was called Namarta, which means Humility) whenever I caught her eye and commented conspicuously on her mother's cooking and on the prettiness of the house.

In vivid contrast to the primitive Sharma household in Nirmand, this Sharma household was stocked full of 'up-to-date' paraphernalia like dainty doilies and 'objects', elaborate china ashtrays and model horses, lace covers on the settee, model fish and ornamental penholders. Where Sri Goverdhan Singh had had books on the walls, N. K. Sharma had smoked glass clocks.

He even had a television, which all the family were very happy about for every Saturday there was a Hindi movie at 2.50 p.m. and another at ten to eight. 'On Sunday also, we are enjoying these films very much,' said N. K. Sharma.

The retired tourist director was no stranger to the other side of the camera either, for he had performed alongside my grandmother in the documentary film made about her for the BBC, called *A Passion for India*. Jonathan Stedall, a personal friend of both my grandparents, directed the hour-long glimpse into Penelope's escapades abroad, the main feature being a trek with N. K. Sharma into the Kulu hills.

'I have relatives in Slough,' said Navendra keenly (he had

permitted me to use his first name). 'And even they saw this film on the BBC.'

It had been necessary for my grandmother to apply for a liaison officer for the film, and Navendra Sharma, tourist officer, who was based in Kulu at the time, was appointed to go with her.

'There was no script,' he recalled. 'They just made the film around her. She was good with the crew – very accommodating even. Though at times she was a little impatient. At one point she accidentally touched the camera and it fell. Jonathan was a little disturbed, I remember, and she was too. But the crew were calm, and they sent the film to Delhi by air and on to the UK and it came back unharmed after two or three days, to much relief. I sometimes wonder whether she didn't knock the camera over on purpose.'

The crew, director, Navendra, Penelope and the pony wallah, Budhram, all slept in tents or in pilgrim shelters and ate local food cooked by the trek cook. No one was fussy, said Navendra in amazement.

'But there was one night in the Sainj valley when we had come to our last village. There was a pagoda temple above the village which you had to visit by foot. We arrived in the village after dark, and the headman offered us accommodation, but Penelope, she said – No, I must stay on the temple verandah itself! Everyone else was worried for the jungle and the wild animals, but she was adamant. She was such a romantic, she loved the moon and the stars.

'Jonathan said, You go Navendra, and persuade her to come down to the village. So I went at ten o'clock and it was dark, but she would not come back with me. "I'm all comfy, don't worry about me," she said. But there was nobody else there at all. Oh she was a brave lady.'

They also walked and rode on film to Parashar Rishi, a unique pagoda temple 9,000 feet up beside a sacred lake with a floating island on it. There is an unrivalled view from there; you can see mountain upon snowcapped mountain reaching away north and south, as if you are God looking over the world from heaven. My grandmother had always found it to be one of the most beautiful spots in the whole Himalaya.

'We stayed in the temple there also,' said Navendra. 'And Penelope presented the *pujari* with a safety razor and blades, for he was growing a bit of a beard.'

Navendra was presented with a BBC tie and John Betjeman's *English Architecture* as souvenirs of the film-making but his best reward, he says, was a cable from his relations in Slough which said: 'ALL LONDON SAW YOU ON TV. YOU WERE FINE.'

In 1979 Navendra travelled on a fellowship to England to study tourism planning at Bradford University, and Jonathan Stedall arranged a special screening of the film for him in a BBC studio in London. He had not seen the film, in which he was undoubtedly the co-star – the Indian foil to my grandmother's Englishness – until that day.

'London is OK,' confided Navendra. 'But I am preferring the mountains.

'Penelope preferred the country to the city also, I think. She was keen on our ecology and our environment. She even wrote a letter to D. S. Negi, the grand old man of Kinnaur who was speaker at our assembly, when the Sangla valley was being opened up to tourists. "You must take steps to prevent Sangla from disintegrating," she said. "You must preserve it and see that the hippies don't invade." She did not like progress here. She was concerned about the way of life of the Pahari people.

'She said to me once, "Navendra, an entire lifetime is required to see the beauty and the splendour of HP!" She is right, of course.'

His fine-chiselled features set pensively for a moment. 'You know, Green, Indians believe in the migration of the soul, and I believe she must have taken a birth in Himachal Pradesh before this birth.'

Navendra also believed that Himachal Pradesh owed a great debt to Penelope. With her exhibitions and lectures and slide shows she brought attention to the state. 'She told the outside world about our heritage, and we have to thank her for that, for this had brought many visitors.'

On the one hand my grandmother had wanted to demonstrate her love for Himachal Pradesh by writing about it, but on the other hand she had hated to see the 'progress' that an influx of tourists inevitably brought. This dichotomy troubled her constantly.

It may have been naïvety which first led her to believe that appreciation of the art there could exist hand in glove with increased tourism, and that an 'opening up' of the Himalayas would not necessarily mean a Westernization of the Pahari way of life. But she could see Manali changing so much just in the time she knew the town, indeed, so much that eventually she hated to go there; and she knew that even the outlying villages were just beginning to get electric light and television. Why do the Pahari people want money and gadgets when they have such a self-supportive, simple and decent way of life? she asked. In the end it was not naïvety which kept her from admitting the answer, but a conscious decision to ignore it.

Navendra Sharma understood her dichotomy. He concluded our 'brunchtime' conversation with a tribute. 'There will never be another Englishwoman like her,' he said gravely. 'She was born in a high, sophisticated family, but in many ways she was unsophisticated. One of her greatest qualities was that she could adjust herself to any type of person. She was not interested in money or grand things. She wanted no fancy food. She was one of us and she breathed her last breath in this state.'

We mopped up the last of the *dahi* with the last of the fifteen *puris* split between us, and then I left the Sharmas to their movies.

On the morning of my final day in Simla I had words with five people before I was even out of my pyjamas. First came the newspaper, a copy of the *Times of India*, then in trotted a little boy who got himself into the wrong room. The laundryman was next, who insisted on coming properly inside and shutting the door behind him to have a worthwhile look at my personal possessions (which were disarranged in hopeless chaos) before he counted the 'washable items' and left. After him room service arrived with some coffee and ten minutes later a different boy in a green uniform came back to take the coffee pot away.

I then went to the bank, which took not much time at all and turned out, against expectations, to be a relaxing experience as I was passed from hand to hand and placed in chair after chair to fill in form after form to facilitate changing £50, until it seemed I was on an automatic merry-go-round that I could neither speed up nor slow down, moving mesmerized in front of a succession of interchangeable smiling faces, signing where appropriate.

After the bank, I tried to find another Sharma, this one being Bansi Ram Sharma, or 'Dr Bhunda' to my grandmother on account of his all-encompassing knowledge of the Himalayan Bhunda (Rope-Sliding) ceremonies.

A 'department' in India, be it a government department, or a section of a library, or an archaeology department or the ladies' shoes department in a department store, was, unaccountably but inevitably, always impossible to find. Other departments appeared behind doors to mock you, but the one you were searching for proved elusive every time, without exception.

Since I had been informed that the only way to see Mr B. R. Sharma was to find him in his department (for I had failed to reach him by telephone), I allowed a good two hours for the search. Apparently, he was secretary of the Himalayan Academy of Arts, Culture and Languages, a department of the state university which was located the other side of Simla from the rest of the university.

Even with Mr Sud's Simla guide book to hand, I began in thoroughly the wrong direction, mistaking the Indian Institute of Advanced Study for the Himalayan Academy of Arts, Culture and Languages. Then I managed to annoy several sentries guarding the Himachal Pradesh Chief Minister's residence, so convinced was I that the right building lay within the green gates they were protecting.

A nine-year-old schoolgirl in a red-checked shirt and a blue pinafore led me to my target in the end, using as many of her English words as she could possibly fit into a sentence: 'Indeed, the route which it is advisable for you to proceed on, is a particular path which I myself know properly. I will be happy to lead you there, what is your name?'

Several dank staircases and half a dozen dim offices later I stole past four men engrossed in their Remington typewriters and located the Sharma I sought, who was the much-respected secretary of the department. I had to write my name on a piece of paper which was then submitted to his reverence in lieu of a calling card by a subservient employee.

Once inside, I found eight people queuing in his office for an audience with the secretary, each one clutching files tied with red ribbon and chattering noiselessly to the next in line, but I was promoted to the head of the queue, all because he loved my grandmother.

I took a seat beside his desk and he talked to me as he nodded acknowledgement to the various waiting clerks and signed his name lavishly on each appointed dotted line.

'We miss Penelope very much here,' he said. He came across Penelope at the Nirmand Bhunda, where he led a team of documentarians from his department. I asked what his department actually did.

'We initiate activities in fields of arts, culture, literature and languages and publish books, linguistic and cultural surveys, hold seminars and workshops on subjects relevant to our endeavours. We provide pensions to writers and artists in conditions when such persons are not in earning positions, who are indigenous writers. We have training programmes in the visual arts, and we publish three magazines – *Sumsi* in Hindi, *Himbharati* in Pahari and *Shamla* in Sanskrit,' he said all in one breath as he signed more files for several other clerks in white who had crept into the office silently.

B. R. Sharma did his Ph.D. in Tribal Culture in Kinnaur and then became research officer for this department. Afterwards he became Assistant Director of the Department of Language and Culture (a separate department altogether), and later Deputy Director. In 1986 he was invited to join the Academy as Secretary.

He believed, like N. K. Sharma, that perhaps Penelope had been born in Himachal Pradesh in a former incarnation. 'Once I took her to a village called Manan,' he said. 'Frazer had visited it in 1815 and had sketched the temple then. She was keen to look for it so I took her in my jeep. She was so jovial. She told me that she had got a copy of the sketch and that she used to sleep with it under her pillow so that nobody was in a position to steal it!'

B. R. Sharma gave a lecture in tandem with my grandmother once, at the State Museum with the Hon. Chief Justice Mistra presiding, and he was overwhelmed at her knowledge. 'She was always writing, writing in her notebooks.'

They also went together to the Bhunda ceremonies at Sholi, a village smaller and more remote than Nirmand when a man actually slid down the rope, rather than a goat. 'She knew that I am a man for meditation and concentration and one evening I begged pardon and I sat on my cot to concentrate for half an hour. She later sent me her diary of that expedition in which she had written: "Dr Sharma sat on his cot and meditated." And I wrote and told her please don't tell anybody that I sat on my cot, for you are supposed to sit on the ground to meditate!'

The secretary interrupted his flow every so often with an unlikely giggle and his twinkling eyes danced about his office. He answered his shiny red telephone with the same effervescent jollity and managed to continue signing papers with a smile on his face as ever more gloomy scribes crept in, seeking his approval.

When at last the telephone was quiet, the office empty, the last form filled in, the attendants dispersed, Dr Bansi Ram Sharma, in his neat brown tweed suit, turned to me and said: 'You know Penelope, she once said to me, "India is my university, Western Himalaya my department."'

CHAPTER XI
One Old Friend in New Delhi

'What was written on the bath taps never corresponded with what came out of them.'

GRANDMAMA ELOPE hated the cities as much as she loved the hills, but she hated Delhi less than other cities in the world, for at least in Delhi, the seat of government in India, she could get about by rickshaw, wallow in the cool of the State Museum, and, more importantly, she could revel in the familiar company of Alfred Wuerfel.

That is if she caught him at home. For Alfred, who was the octogenarian former cultural attaché to the German Embassy in Delhi, had retired from service but never from life; he spent summer in Stuttgart or Munich and wintered on the Indian plains. He partied like no cultural attaché before him, and more often than not, he was out on the town.

When I had misdirected a taxi driver to the point of impatience before alighting at 13, Barakhamba Road, Alfred was asleep. He had arrived at four o'clock that morning in October from Germany, and was wearing his pyjamas at four o'clock in the afternoon. Though not unusual in India, where men may wear pyjamas at parties, Alfred considered his dress improper, and even as I glimpsed the familiar figure of him, framed by the half-opened doorway into his apartment, he disappeared to change. Waving his slim, soft hands in the air, he said, 'Imo, Imo, hello, hello, I am coming, a moment, I am coming!' And off he went.

So it was Ishrat, Alfred's Muslim servant, cook and protégé, who welcomed me. He settled me into a maroon cotton-covered sofa and brought me *nimbupani* and crisps. He was very well, he said, and he also said that I looked better than I had when he last met me.

For when my grandmother and I had come together on the appointed day, a few years before, to Delhi to visit her friend Alfred, I had been dim with fever.

All I can remember is being restored to life by Ishrat's toast and Alfred's black cherry jam. At that time, Alfred had been living in cramped conditions in the Delhi outskirts, with his Pahari carvings and his awning from Gujurat, his Rajhastani paintings and his South Indian bronzes suffering an undignified crush with his eclectic library of books on subjects ranging from metaphysics and mythology and German philosophy to Indian princesses and food and geography.

When he retired from his diplomatic job, he had lost all the courtesy luxuries – the big house in New Delhi, the chauffeured Mercedes-Benz, the entertaining allowance – that went with it, but instead of returning to Germany, he had wanted to stay on in India, his true spiritual home.

So temporarily he had housed himself and Ishrat and his collections in the cramped house in Madhuvan until he was offered, a couple of years later, the run of a marble-floored first floor apartment, with colonnaded balconies all round, in an early Lutyens building on Barakhamba Road, near Connaught Place in the centre of new Delhi. His carvings and things fitted nicely into these spacious rooms, all the better to display a collection of indigenous art which was testament to his lifetime love of India.

My grandmother had always made friends with people who shared her interests, and in Alfred she found a soulmate. They had been introduced in 1964 by a third Indophile, Stella Kramrisch, the Austrian-born Sanskrit scholar and academic who lived on in her nineties in Philadelphia. They took to each other, in Alfred's words, 'especially because we were both foreigners irresistibly drawn to India by an intangible force'. Tangibly, they were of a similar age and both possessed a formidable talent for storytelling as well as an unusual amount of energy. And the complex web of each of their lives fascinated the other.

Alfred never saw an egg until he was six. He grew up in

Dresden, and his family, too poor to feed him, sent him to cousins in the country where they had chickens. The mother said, 'Now, what would you like, Alfred?' and he said, 'Potatoes, please,' because he thought potatoes were all one could eat, and she said, 'Come on now, won't you have an egg?' and handed him a steaming plate of buttery scrambled eggs. He has loved scrambled eggs ever since.

When the little Dresden boy was eleven, an imaginative German Asian scholar imported to the German town a Sri Lankan village – fully equipped with peasants and potters, silversmiths, cows and even elephants – which had set Alfred's yearning mind alive and made firm in him an ambition to travel to the East.

'When I saw the village, I decided that to India I will go,' he said, and not another day passed without his plotting his route. It was to be a journey which brought him eventually to Benares Hindu University in the thirties, where he enrolled on a Sanskrit course and at the same time earned Rs. 250 a month teaching German to pay for his tuition.

'India is my lodestar – the axis around which my life has revolved,' he said. His imagination has been held by 'Indian culture, which is the only culture that dates back 5,000 years and was contemporaneous with the Greek, the Roman, the Egyptian and Persian cultures, all of which have vanished. But Indian culture is alive even now and that is the proof of its vitality and its wisdom. It is so true that it cannot perish. It is *"amar"*.'

Alfred, or Sri Wuerfel as his Indian friends knew him, immersed himself in Indian culture during the seven years from 1939 until 1947 that he spend behind bars. For in September 1939 the local Superintendent of Police, who was a personal friend of Alfred's, knocked on the door of his lodgings in Benares and gave him just two hours to pack before escorting him to an internment camp. Throughout the Second World War, Alfred lived behind barbed wire at Ahmednagar, Deolali and finally Debra Dun as His Britannic Majesty's guest, detained on account of his nationality. He reserved no bitterness for the British, however, for he abhorred

Hitler as much as the next man, and he said, 'We were treated well. There was no dearth of books.'

Repatriated after the war, Alfred masqueraded on a false passport as an Anglo-Asian with an upset stomach (so that he would have to appear from his berth as little as possible) on a ship from Europe back to India, and he hid in a friend's basement in Bombay, penniless but happy just to be back on Indian soil, until the coast was clear.

He survived for four years doing odd jobs with Indian friends whom he had made at Benares, and then, in 1951, when the Federal Republic of Germany opened its first Consulate-General, he joined its cultural department. In a short time, he moved to the newly opened German Embassy in New Delhi where the first ambassador, Professor Meyers, invited him to bring his knowledge, his wisdom and his mastery of the Hindi language, and he remained in the diplomatic service until 1977.

I had drained the last of my *nimbupani* and was sucking the lime when Alfred emerged from his quarters again, this time neatly attired in one of his 'summer suits', an open-necked shirt and matching trousers in pale blue cotton, with his neatly curling white-grey hair combed smartly backwards and his dark-rimmed spectacles resting on his nose. He was the same height as me – about five feet six inches – and quite pale. His mouth was neat and pursed and bordered by a faint, trimmed moustache.

He walked with equally neat steps and spoke fluent English with the softest trace of a German accent. He mixed up some of his idiomatic English, saying things like 'green thumbs' about another's gardening skills, and he reiterated certain stock phrases, like 'easy of approach' which meant someone was likeable, affable and friendly. Alfred was certainly 'easy of approach', and he looked after me as if I was his granddaughter.

His whole neat appearance led one to believe his emotions might be neater still. Yet, it would be wrong to draw such an impression. For while Alfred would have admitted certainly to being a fastidious man, there was not only a good deal of revelry in him, but also a torrent of compassion.

After ten days, in which we had visited the Arts and Crafts centre, the Qutub minar, Indira Gandhi's mausoleum, the Delhi Gymkhana Club for lunch, an American interior designer called Jan who kept twenty-two antelopes in her garden, Go Go Prakash and her Dalmatian who howls to Pavarotti, the Indian champion of Solar Energy and Teen Murti house; ten days in which we had been through Dusshera, the Hindu Festival celebrating Rama's victory over Ravana, which involves the mass immersion of holy images in water, and had weathered an earthquake which reached 6.1 on the Richter Scale and killed 50,000 people in Garhwal; ten days in which I had met and made true friends with Brinda, Alfred's best friend, and in which we drank whisky and soda at seven o'clock every night and then shared German salami and meatballs and thick 'fortifying' German soups and Swiss cheeses at dinner, Alfred talked and I listened.

After ten rich days of all this, Alfred told me of a German saying which one uses about good friends. 'It goes,' said Alfred, 'it goes: I feel we could steal horses together – which means that you can trust your friend and have fun as well.' He said he could say that to me.

Alfred seemed to inhale his energy from his breakfast yoghurt as well as a daily assortment of homoeopathic remedies (including a brown mixture which turned out to be earth from a notorious German spa town dissolved in water). He did these funny exercises before breakfast, too – one which involved wobbling his stomach in the manner of a Turkish belly-dancer, and another which involved moving his head from side to side while still facing the front (a kind of dislocation of the neck) like an Indian classical dancer. After ten days he was quite happy to show me these movements and for me to see him in his pyjamas.

But truly, his energy came from his passion for life. Though he was eighty, he still burned with the inquisitiveness of a child and he maintained the same level of curiousness that my grandmother had borne until the moment she died on the mountain.

'She died in harness,' said Alfred, speaking never a truer word. He said that Penelope had to have done some wonderful things in her former life because to die so easily and painlessly and happily in the right place was a great honour, which was bestowed only on those who had achieved good things in their former incarnation.

My grandmother had thought pretty highly of her friend Alfred too: 'I must say I do think you are WONDERFUL to your "family", i.e. all your servants and their children and I am sure you will grade up to becoming God-realized and probably won't have to be born into this world again!' she wrote at the end of a letter to Alfred.

In the *Bhagavad Gita* the steps to God-realization have been explained: by living according to the right tenets and doing good works, you achieve a higher birth each time your soul is reincarnated, until you are so good and close to God, that you do not need to be reborn on earth again, as you have reached Heaven.

If Penelope had reckoned Alfred was near to Heaven, she was paying him the highest compliment. She had bestowed the honour upon him for many reasons but chiefly because of his devotion to his 'family'. Alfred had never married, and his only blood relations were his two spinster sisters in Germany. His 'family' were a Muslim family.

He had inherited Ishrat's father (Ishrat was the cook cum housekeeper who had welcomed me in) from a cousin of a friend when he was living in his big grand house in Chanakyapuri (the diplomatic quarter). There he had housed Ishrat's father and his seven children – four daughters and three sons – and since then these Mussulmans had become Alfred's responsibility. Shamshul, his driver, was Ishrat's uncle, and Alfred was not only paying for Ishrat's wedding, but he had also married off two of Ishrat's brothers (who now had five children between them) and had built a two-roomed house for Ishrat and his new wife to move into when they were married. He was also about to buy a wheelchair for Shamshul's sister who was crippled with arthritis.

When Alfred had made it to Hay-on-Wye in 1978, my grandmother had him driving The Shrimp, her strawberry roan Welsh pony, off whom I had fallen ceremoniously in front of a large field, when out hunting for the first time with the Golden Valley Hounds. My grandmother, mounted on Golliwog – whom she renamed Chocolate after being taken to task too many times about the racial implications of his former name – looped her hunting crop through my bridle and led me on to complete the day. She had made Alfred, as she had made all her guests, collect wood in the pony cart for her wood-burning stove, morbidly nicknamed 'The Crem' by my grandfather.

For despite his servants in India (and everyone has servants in India – even the sweeper of the big house will employ a lesser sweeper to sweep his own house) Alfred had shared with my grandmother an ability to eschew all material goods in favour of a simple and more spiritual life.

He had been given a stone mini-place in Rajhastan by a princely Indian friend (my grandmother had called it his schloss). It was far out in the north-west Indian desert, and he escaped there for quieter times than were possible to find in the social whirl that was Delhi.

He had always promised to take Penelope there. They had invented a plan for them both to retire there to write their respective books – he an autobiography, she about horses. They would live frugally on fruit and rice, discussing Hindu philosophy in the evenings. They would take long walks and go to bed early. (As long as they might have imported the odd chocolate éclair for my grandmother and a daily whisky and soda for Alfred, they might have been all right.)

My grandmother had welcomed the 'escape plan', for it seemed that each time she returned to England from India she was overwhelmed with correspondence, and constantly she despaired that she would ever write any of her proposed books. There were other things at home to distract her too. The running of her new household was one of them.

In 1972, my grandmother had decided to sell The Mead, the Betjeman home in Wantage for much of the previous fifteen years. She would give the proceeds to their son Paul, who was then living in New York, teaching music and composing jazz. She had thought that he could do with the money to buy his own house.

There were further reasons behind her decision, though, which she laid out in a letter to her best friend Billa Harrod:

It is very sad selling the Mead, [she began]. It really is looking lovely now as I stuffed it with bulbs last Autumn so it would look its best for 'viewers' in the spring. I know you have always maintained that it is the nicest house we have had and I agree with you. But it is rather a lot to look after in one's old age as there are 5½ acres of paddocks and orchards and I cannot bear nettles and I have to get them cut and it is not so easy to find old men to do odd jobs.

In the writing of her second reason (second in running order though undoubtedly it was uppermost in her thoughts) she summed up succinctly a painful situation:

John is here so little and prefers to travel mid-week so it really won't matter going further afield and he can come down for a week at a time when he wants to and travel on say a Wednesday and avoid the awful week-end rushes.

The Mead took some selling, however. Penelope wrote to Billa Harrod:

It is so sad here as all the lilac is out and the tulips still flourishing and the lilies of the valley at their best and NOBODY WANTS IT! The more I look out of my bedroom window and see the marvellous view to the downs the more determined I am NOT to come down, and the agent agrees with me as the situation is unique, one hears 0 but the hoot of owls at night and no tractors or other typical country noises by day, and the house is in good condition...... I wish I could get everything settled as I have so much writing planned, including two long commissioned articles but I just cannot get down to ANY proper work in such an unsettled state.

Finally the house was sold at public auction and Penelope set about house-hunting with fervour.

I have always adored the Welsh border country and have got to know it quite well thro' staying at Whitfield, [Penelope continued her correspondence to Billa]. I stayed there again last weekend and Mary and I went househunting and the only place I really fell for was a derelict stone pub with no roof and two ash trees growing in the hall. The situation was STUNNING: on the top of a ridge overlooking the little Ochlon valley with the Black Mountains beyond, going up to 2000' so I can fancy myself in Kulu looking up to Tibet. I am writing to see if I can get planning permission to restore and add to it and the farmer's widow it belongs to is very willing to sell.

The following week she wrote:

On Tuesday I go down to Somerset to see a cottage at Pixton, near Dulverton which Auberon Herbert says I can rent. As it is on the edge of Exmoor it is marvellous riding country and I think there is a lot to be said for renting a tiny cottage at my age, rather than buying or building one at a colossal sum so that one won't get much income. Anyway it is worth seeing as I may not get planning permission to rebuilt the derelict pub in West Herefordshire.

Planning permission for the pub never materialized, but my grandmother had swiftly found a better alternative:

This is to let you know I have paid the deposit of £8,000 for a MINUTE cottage on the Herefordshire side of the Black Mountains, 3½ miles above Hay-on-Wye (10 mins by car). It is 1300′ up and faces North, not everyone's cup of tea perhaps but the views are spiffing and it is the most marvellous pony trekking and walking country. At the back there is a Grimm's fairytale forest into which I shall not dare let my grandchildren without whistles round their necks in case they get lost. It is a mature forest, mostly conifers, but quite a lot of beech and wonderful gravel and grass rides in every direction, so PERFECT for pony carts. You walk half a mile through the forest to the Cefn Hill which is 500 acres of common land and down in the valley to the right are the ruins of the Craswall Priory, beside a stream.

She described her abode itself to Billa:

The cottage is stone, 0 architecturally but not unpleasant and next summer I hope to build on another two rooms and bathroom. I hope to get possession on All Saints Day and I shall move in with basic furniture and camp there until I go to India on Jan 20th.

What was to be an accurate prediction of her future way of life followed.

The country around is so dramatically beautiful that I shall want to ride and walk over it all day so I shall WELCOME BAD WEATHER in which I will have time to write!

Early on, Penelope took my grandfather to her cottage to see it. To Billa she wrote:

On the day I took John it was very clear and you could see for miles in all directions and he said 'the air is like wine' to which I replied (tacitly) I hope you will drink it instead of the bottled variety. He also said he thought he would be able to live again up here and it will be a marvellous place to read ghost stories aloud on windy nights and I am sure it is stiff with witches.

She convinced herself that John was going to come and live there too. In her next letter to Billa, she wrote:

We are on a road but such a dim mountain road that very little comes along it and THERE IS NOT A POST OR PYLON IN SIGHT so no mains electricity or telephone bills! We have our own generator and a petrol pump to pump the water from a well so I have got to STUDY ELEMENTARY ENGINEERING IN MY OLD AGE! There are rainwater tanks already which work the radiators AND the WC so we won't waste any water when we pull the chain.

She was filled with excitement and dreams and plans:

There is just the right sized odd shaped garden in front of the cottage at the end of which I hope to build a gazebo facing south, in the shape of a Himalayan temple. There is farmer with 160 acres who is my nearest neighbour and I am sure he will let me graze two horses in his fields. But as he is 80 and stone deaf I have not got this suggestion across to him yet.

She ended her letter:

We really will not need a flower garden because to the east of the garden there is a small stream in a deep gully and beyond that a real wilderness – a former quarry – with every wildflower you can imagine growing in it: masses of willowherb, foxglove, harebell etc. I really LONG for you to see it tho' the cottage is 0 but the address is NEW HOUSE, CUSOP and who is to know it is not as grand as Wilton House, Salisbury??

Her perhaps sometimes too impulsive enthusiasm had not dimmed one year (and several complications) later:

> Owing to the persistent drought most of the springs round here are nearly dry and I realise it would be silly to put in a proper bath we must make do with a shower, and I am not going to connect up my BENDIX as it uses so much water and the Hay Laundrette is only 8 mins drive away and gets everything much cleaner. Also a NEW CHEMICAL LAVATORY HAS BEEN INVENTED IN EIRE COSTING £100 so I have sent for the brochure. We have built a lovely little room for it which I shall paint puce or some other gay colour and install instead of an Elsan which you have to EMPTY, whereas this new one turns everything to PURE WATER which will furnish us with a reliable drinking supply? As there is a universal water shortage I think showers and chemical lavs will become increasingly popular.

Yet she found it difficult to maintain a consistently positive attitude when not everything went according to plan. She had envisaged a dream which was not necessarily going to work out as she imagined. She wrote to Billa when the construction of the additional wing was well under way:

> I am HYSTERICAL over the cost of building here. I do wish John had made it clear that he meant to spend the greater part of his old age away from here BEFORE I STARTED. I would have done something on a far more modest scale. As it is I shall have no money left to invest to provide an additional income so shall have to let the new wing for most of the summer. John has given me a new car but I am paying running costs and shall soon sell it and depend on pony transport. Anyway I seem to be able to get my expenses and return fare to India every winter so I am really quite OK . . .

My grandmother's 'job' at that time, as she saw it, was leading tours in India. She would be paid £100 a week plus fares and expenses, which meant that she could stay on in India after the tour was finished to look for temples under her own steam. For the first few years of her new situation in New House, she returned to India each winter, but in 1975, she decided not to go out in order that she might enjoy a whole eighteen months at home, 'hunting and getting the garden going' as she explained to Billa Harrod. She wrote to her friend on a freezing January day:

> Oh I do want you to see Kulu-on-Wye now that it is finished, I am writing this in a small sitting room in the old part of the cottage beside my newly installed JOTUL STOVE (Norwegian). As I am essentially a MORNING person and useless at night, I now go to bed about 10 pm and get up between 5–6 am and sit by the JOTUL and write but as I am permanently 50 letters in arrears I cannot see how I will ever get down to another book. And [as she had known she would] later in the day I so much prefer riding to writing and a tremendous amount of time is taken up WOODING in the forest, one of my favourite occupations. PS John writes the most endearing letters and is coming to stay in March.

After those eighteen months of uninterrupted stay in England, however, she returned to her former habit of dividing up the year by spending half of it (or at least a third) in India. Her yen to be travelling equalled her desire not to spend longer than was necessary dwelling on a domestic dream which was not materializing. The correct conclusion seemed to be to continue with her tour-leading career.

She began to visit Alfred twice annually again (usually at the beginning and end of each expedition) and when she was back in her own Hereford Himalaya she would write to him regularly (often, as to Billa, in exasperation at her inability to get round to

writing any more books – a problem which she blamed on letters).
She wrote to Alfred:

ONE DAY I very much want to write a book about the old days
of the Raj. But HOW? I seem snowed under with correspondence
and never get down to real writing at all. One has so many
boring letters to answer one never has time to write nice long
ones to one's FRIENDS. So many complete STRANGERS write
and ask me for advice about travelling in India and I just cannot
cope. What I would LOVE to do is P.G. [be a paying guest]
with you in Jodhpur for about six weeks one winter and really
GET DOWN TO WRITING in a congenial atmosphere.

Another letter from New House began:

My dear Alfred,
Thank you for your letter. I am always at least 50 letters in
arrears and having no sec. will obviously go to the grave in this
condition.

The letter went on to describe Black Mountain scenics:

I am writing this in a coffee shop in Hereford awaiting my car
which is having a new exhaust pipe put on because last week I
reversed into a DITCH and had to be towed out. I HATE cars
and when inflation beats me I shall make do without a car and
rely on my three wonderful PONIES.
I cannot tell you HOW LOVELY my cottage is at Kulu-on-
Wye in the Hereford Himalaya – now it is finished at last after a
three years struggle with the builders: a 60 mile view to the north
over the wild Welsh hills and a great forest at the back full of
Rakshashis which provide great thrills for my grandchildren –
and perhaps I shall end up as a forest sage? But it is a bit cold
and damp for that though some of my hippie friends sleep out in

the wildest snow blizzards. Please PLEASE come up and stay if
anything brings you to England . . .

The regular correspondence which grew up between Alfred and
Penelope probably distracted her even more from writing books,
but it fed them both with ideas and energy that sustained their
friendship as well as their interest in life. My grandmother would
comment on exhibitions in London that she had seen and Alfred
kept her informed of India's and cultural developments. She could
not resist criticizing what she knew to be wrong:

I am in London for 2 nights and may have difficulty in returning
home tomorrow as I hear it is SNOWING HARD! [she wrote].
I have come up for a tour promotion meeting of West Himalayan
Holidays and to-night we are all going to HEAT & DUST which
has had RAVE REVIEWS. I actually saw a private view last
Oct. and was bowled over by the beauty of the photography
[James Ivory and Ismail Merchant filmed it in Hyderabad] but
there were TWO ERRORS:

1. British civilians I mean their WIVES (of the local administration DC, Collector etc) would NEVER have been allowed to
curtsey to India Princes at their durbars. ONLY to the Viceroy.

2. They never rode to their offices in Cavalry saddles and bridles,
but used ordinary civilian ones, as did my father in Delhi. He
only used a military saddle on parade when inspecting troops.
Perhaps this is a technical point which few people will notice,
but I think ex ICS [Indian Civil Service] men and cavalry will.

I long to hear what you think of GHANDI I mean GANDHI –
I always spell it the wrong way round. I think it is marvellous
EXCEPT for John Gielgud as Lord Irwin. He is one of our best
actors but in this instance was completely misdirected by Richard
Attenborough and made into an unsympathetic Poona wallah
whereas he was the most sympathetic of all the successive

Viceroys who dealt with Gandhi: they were both deeply religious and got on very well as I am sure you know?

Alfred had met Gandhi himself, when he was studying at Benares. He wrote:

> Perhaps my greatest experience in Benares was my meeting with Mahatma Gandhi when he came here to open the Bharat Mata Mandir. My landlord, Shiv Prasad Gupta, was the editor and publisher of that mouthpiece of freedom, 'The Aaj', and he had donated money for the mandir which had no idols but only a magnificent map of India as the central deity. Gandhiji visited my landlord and I met him then.
>
> I was overwhelmed to see Gandhiji in person. Here he was, so simple and humble and yet I felt I was in the presence of an outstanding human being. He emanated a strangely powerful aura of conviction. From that moment he became the epitome of India. Frail though his body was, he symbolized the inner strength and truth of India. These feelings came to me when I sat beside him on the dais and saw his gentle and smiling face.
>
> None of us knew how far or how close India's freedom was at that time. But I did know that men like Gandhiji came but once in the lifetime of a nation. I have spoken to him and it is a memory that will live with me.

My grandmother summed up Gandhi (whom she had had the honour of meeting in the 1930s): 'Gandhiji,' she wrote. 'Here was a man in whom there was no hatred at all, whose little bespectacled eyes just beamed with love for all living things.'

Alfred had met many of the great Indians of his time – Rabindranath Tagore, Pandit Nehru – but, like Penelope, the Indians he most loved were the many people (and there were eighty million more people swelling the population each year) who made up the patchwork. When he was tired of working all day at the embassy, he used to go out to talk to the jamadars and the chaprasis and the drivers at the office; they talked and cracked jokes and he said the stream of their affection refreshed him.

Penelope too was uplifted by her encounters with 'ordinary' people, who often were not ordinary at all. She wrote to Alfred from Petlad in Gujurat, where she was exploring during one of her winters away from New House. She had become fascinated by the life of an Anglo-Indian nun:

> Marianpura is a Christian village outside Petlad, founded by SPANISH nuns and ditto Jesuits 25 years ago! Now there are no Spanish nuns left (all Indian) and only one Spanish priest . . . The sisters run a hostel for about 80 small farmers' daughters who attend the Govt. High School, also a dispensary.

As was the way of all the tale-rich blue aerogrammes which flew across the world from beneath Penelope's pen, the account customarily began with a few exact explanatory details (brief history, for example, number and type of persons involved in venture/adventure). She continued the narrative:

> As in nearly ALL convents I have stayed in up and down India there is one FASCINATING character: she is Anglo-Indian aged 75 and is called Dadi by everyone. Her father was a Tommy from Dublin in the Irish Fusiliers, married a Persian girl when his regiment was stationed in Iran at the end of the last century. (HOW I cannot think as strict purdah was and IS observed – she may have been a nautch girl?) Then the regt. moved on to India and the Irish Fusilier's wife had 2 sons and then died giving birth to Dadi in Lahore. The baby was brought up in the army orphanage run by Jesus and Mary nuns in Murree. Eventually the father went home, married again, and when Dadi was about 12 years old he returned to India to take her back to Dublin! Dadi saw him in the parlour, but only from afar, whereupon she turned tail and FLED and hid in a walled enclosure which surrounded the convent water supply: she

persuaded the chowkidar to let her in and made him promise to let her out at night after the father had left. The chowk FORGOT! The nuns looked high and low but Dadi did not reappear till breakfast next morning! She told the nuns that O could persuade her to leave India. Her father made one more attempt to get her back to no avail and she entered the order when she was 18 years old and has been happy ever since. She is in charge of the POULTRY here and rears chicks and looks after them and the geese like her own children and produces enough eggs to sell above what the nine nuns consume. She refuses flatly to hand over the poultry to anyone else. She says she will die very soon if she retires from active work.

My grandmother had settled into the convent in Gujurat as readily as she had with the Jesus and Mary nuns at Chelsea in Simla:

They also have buffaloes given by a German organization, Jersey cows given by a British ditto, and masses of soya bean meal from the USA which together with dried egg and fresh meat and veg. is used to feed the boarders. It is encouraging to find foreign aid BEING MADE HONOURABLE USE OF, as one hears so many stories of misuse. A week's stay here is JUST what I want to recollect myself and catch up on my letters and diaries. I go for lovely country walks in this very fertile area (tobacco, cotton and rice) and feel very much at home surrounded by farm animals. There are even very pretty pony carts (a much better design than the Delhi tongas) and I went for a drive in one this morning but the pony was NOT so well fed as the SHRIMP. . . .

Alfred recorded his encounters with the ordinary people of India on film. In 1975 he held his first exhibition of his 'Faces of India', a collection of black-and-white photographs, blown up three times life size, of a selection of faces – a Jaisalmer camel driver, an Andhra peasant, a young girl from Rajhastan, a Mysore Brahmin, a Sadhu and many more – of the myriad of people he had encountered all over the country in his endless travels. It was a beautiful and moving catalogue, but, as Alfred warned me, India must not be romanticized.

'It is a mistake that is especially emphasized in photography,' Alfred told me one morning over our breakfast. 'India gives you an illusion with her colours and contrasts and charm, when in actual fact the stark reality is ever present and there IS poverty and filth and squalor and death and disease.' Living there in Delhi he was reminded constantly of the horrors of everyday life, although he said it was easy to be taken in by the aesthetically pleasing façade.

Alfred talked me through the architecture in Delhi just as my grandmother had done. His energy was astounding as we walked round the Delhi monuments – the tomb of Tughlak (an early Moghul emperor – 1321–1325 AD), his favourite, the Qutub Minar, the Lodi Gardens – and his knowledge riveting.

When I was eighteen I had often been embarrassed when my grandmother had lectured me loudly beside a tomb in front of other people with her spectacles on the end of her snub nose, but with Alfred I did not mind at all. (Even though Alfred was probably more embarrassing than my grandmother had been, for he would always approach people for quick Hindi chats. In fact he could not pass a stranger in the street without engaging them in conversation, and they were always surprised and pleased when they discovered he could speak their own language.)

He also acknowledged every monkey he saw. He saluted the ape with a polite form of Muslim address – bringing the hand up from the elbow, palm upwards – which meant 'O my forefather/ ancestor/elder!'

Just as my grandmother was learning to live alone, to be alone, Alfred had entered her life. Yet, there was never a moment when she seriously considered uprooting to live in Rajhastan with her friend the octogenarian ex-cultural attaché. Alfred Wuerfel was a true friend and mentor and an anchor in India for her. He was an intrinsic link in the chain which bound Kulu-on-Wye in her Hereford Himalaya with the far-off Indian shores.

He made her laugh as well, but never would he have supplanted her husband John in her heart; nor did Alfred's affection ever make up for the infrequency of John's visits to Hay-on-Wye. The way in which Alfred Wuerfel did help was to be there in India. For India, which to some extent was a cause of her predicament, was also Penelope's remedy, and Alfred, for my grandmother, was an integral part of India.

'I am here writing next to the Crem,' wrote my grandmother at New House to Billa in Norfolk once more. 'I WISH I did not have the urge to write and to travel and could just sit back and enjoy my old age and see more of my friends. I fly to India on Oct 8th to conduct a party of 15 trekkers round Kinnaur then I go on up to the Tibetan frontier with the D.C., then on to Dehra Dun. Snow permitting you must come and stay early next year . . .'

In her late sixties, at a time of life when most people are curling up their toes a little at the thought of moving off the tiny plot they call home, Penelope was proving inexhaustible.

CHAPTER XII

Gwalior, Orchha and
the Rani of Jhansi

'A beautiful sari worn by a graceful Indian girl (and show me one that isn't) leaves all the work of the Paris couturiers standing.'

THE MORNING after a Germanic farewell dinner at Barakhamba Road (with plenty of salami and rye bread served), Shamshul (Alfred's driver) drove me to the station in the cream, leather-trimmed Morris Ambassador that Alfred used only for special occasions. Smoothly he hustled me into my reserved seat (No. 56) in an air-conditioned car on the famed Shatabdi Express. The train, India's fastest, was a vital vein running daily southwards from Delhi through the central plains of India.

At 6.18 a.m., the railway station was already lively, although some families still lay side by side under checked blankets on the platforms, snoring or quiet, endeavouring to sleep on through the mayhem which bustled and grew around them. Oblivious, they snoozed while the rest of the station population seethed as if mid-morning had already been and gone.

Porters in their regulation red jackets nipped through the crowds, their skinny legs moving like hockey sticks after a ball through the trunks and parcels, the chai-wallahs and booksellers, the beggars and passengers who congregated alongside the train, chanting, chattering, sighing, crying – all measure of emotions spilling on to the platform.

Whole families would turn out to wave away a weeping mother or a student returning to his college in the south. A tearful grandmother would press sticky *jalebis* wrapped in newspaper into the pocket of the departing youth, and then stand back, unable to speak, covering her face and sobbing into the sodden end of her sari.

Alfred did not believe in aching farewells. I had said goodbye to him ('Not goodbye,' he had said, 'merely *au revoir!*') outside the station. Inside the first-class compartment, calm prevailed. The seats were upholstered in shiny pale blue leather, and the metallic shiny floor was brushed clean. Reservations seemed to materialize and the coach was filled slowly with a selection of middle-class Indians – businessmen in suits with brown briefcases and snappily dressed teenagers with mothers in silk. Single white females were unremarkable in such sophisticated atmospheres, it appeared.

The train moved off and we chugged out into the yellow-brown fug of the city's early morning. We were served vegetable cutlets and tomato ketchup and tea for breakfast, while India's city dwellers completed their morning ablutions alongside the railway line. From the windows we saw neat pairs of children, with their hair plaited up and their pinnies smoothed down, swapping marbles and homework answers and swinging their stuffed satchels from the ends of their little brown arms. Their mothers stoked the smoky fires while their fathers shaved.

From the train we could see right into the lives of the shanty-town dwellers, whose lot could not have been much worse: they were obliged to make home in huts with sewage swilling around their cooking pots and plastic sheeting over their heads. Yet after morning *puja* there were smiles on the faces of the children off to school and laughs over the laundry and games with the mangy pie dogs and teasing among the boys. India's irrepressible faith brings hope and laughter even to the shanty towns.

A first-class railway carriage was a cocoon suspended above reality, though, surrounded by a glass bubble burst only when the train blew its whistle and halted at a station.

The train stopped at Agra first, home of the Taj Mahal, the famous marble-floored tomb which the Moghul Emperor Shah Jahan built for his favourite queen, Mumtaz-i-Mahal (literally

'Elect of the Palace') whom he had married in 1615. She bore thirteen children for her husband before dying in childbirth bearing the fourteenth in 1629. It took Shah Jahan twenty-two years (1630–52) to finish his everlasting marble tribute to her.

No one alighted at Agra from our carriage on the Shatabdi Express, even though the coolies were beseeching us to step down and avail ourselves of the services on offer. 'Chai, chai, chaiaiai!' cried the chai-wallah in his toneless nasal voice; 'Channa, Channa, Channaaaa!' cried the other half of his double act who was urging tin plates of chick-pea curry and rice on the passengers whose heads were poking, tentative, curious, through the window grilles.

The taxidermist gypsies with gold hoops in their sagging ears pulled at your heart and your conscience with their irresistible black-lashed dark brown velvety eyes. They crowded down the aisles of the carriage flashing their eyes this way and that and pushed stuffed chipmunks on to your lap and made the dead rodents dance with bells on their tails. Through the window grille, pot-bellied taxi drivers promised fares each less than the one before and nodded confidentially or winked conspiratorially at a prospective customer.

'Rupee, one rupee,' cried the beggar boys, up and into the carriage and weaving through the compartments before the trains had even eased to its halt. 'Please, pleeeese . . .' they begged, a younger sister on the hip tugging at a passenger's shirtsleeve.

But everyone had seen the Taj Mahal already. Everyone knew that the beggars in this overrun tourist mecca were professionals and that the taxi drivers were crooked and that paying out for a dead chipmunk in a party suit was a rum game and that the Taj Mahal now stands like a pile of white sugar crawling with human ants for most of each day. If you must see this fabled wonder of the world, then you must see it in the rosy-fingered dawn, and at no other time, for all the romance invested in the monument by the once-grieving Shah Jahan is lost with the coming of the day.

My grandmother and I had stayed in a Jesus and Mary convent with high walls around us and metal gates and guard dogs to protect us when we had come to Agra together. She had said that I could not pass by the Taj Mahal on my first visit to India, though she had seen it over thirty times before and she preferred Agra's Red Fort. She could not bear the swarms of ignorant tourists, however, Indian or foreign, so we had stayed only for a brief night and a day.

We had gone together on a bus to Fatehpur Sikri where Shah Jahan had built a tower decorated with stone tusks over the grave of his favourite elephant. I was flashed at (I dropped my sketch-book and ran screaming to my grandmother who laughed when I told her about the trouserless man); my grandmother had a fight with a pregnant Muslim girl in a burka who, far from behaving with the serenity expected of her condition, fought tooth and nail with Penelope in contest over one of the fifty seats on the city bus. One hundred and fifty people wormed their way on to the bus, stepping in old people's laps to gain entrance. I had to climb through a window to get on and had difficulty recognizing my grandmother, so wrapped and smothered was she in other women's burkas and bags.

We made it back to the convent in one piece, however, and at four o'clock the following morning we crawled out of bed and walked to the Taj Mahal. While I had marvelled at Mumtaz's big white mausoleum, Penelope had taken some young Americans to task over their apparel.

'How can you wear those cut-off jeans?' she demanded of them. 'It is simply disrespectful to the Hindus,' she said. 'In their country you simply must abide by their rules!' The bleary-eyed Americans reeled away in shock, flabbergasted at being accosted so early in the day by this sweet, motherly-looking figure. 'OK, lady, OK, OK . . .' they muttered and disappeared into the mist.

We had moved off swiftly too, sensing that the longer we lingered the more difficult it would be to disengage ourselves from guides and touts and taxi drivers. We climbed into a tonga pulled by a fiery bay pony. My grandmother had words with the surprised driver and I took the reins and drove the fiery bay at breakneck speed away from the encroaching crowds in a flurry of dust, and home to the quiet of the convent.

The elections had been in full swing (as they always were, somewhere, in India, it seemed) and some students were beginning to riot in the streets over the unfairness (they considered) of the reservation acts. (These were the acts of Parliament instituted by Mrs Gandhi's government which reserved 25 per cent of university places and jobs and political positions for people from the unscheduled classes – that is, the harijans, the nomads and the gypsies.) The nuns told us it was not safe to be out.

Was it ever safe to be out, my grandmother had despaired, as she instructed me to make ready for moving south. With our rucksacks bobbing on our backs, we had skipped through the streets, dodging trouble, to the bus station. Agra 'done' (as only Agra can be), we were going to Gwalior.

ALONE AND wary of Agra's dangers, I remained in my pale blue leather seat and pressed my nose to the window grille, trying to recall the vision I had had of the Taj Mahal in the dawn six years earlier; the image failed to come to me anything like as strongly as the vision of my grandmother bobbing away from the convent calling 'C'mawn, C'mawn, we're going to miss it,' and then, as I caught up with her, and looked back, panting, hot, at the timid distant row of Jesus and Mary nuns, seeing them squeezed in a wavery line and dwarfed by the huge convent gate, waving hopefully at our departing figures. I remember weighing up the odds and concluding that though it was often touch and go, if I stuck beside my grandmother, there was a likelihood I would survive whatever dangers lay ahead.

Now I had no familiar commanding presence to lead me on, so I passed on Agra, leaving my memory of our former visit intact, and plumped in favour of a straight run on the Shatabdi Express to Gwalior, the next station stop. Gwalior was the capital of the former Gwalior state, one of the largest and most architecturally important of all the princely states. There was a fort there on an oblong-shaped outcrop of rock above the town, from where the ruling Scindia family could view their terrain which stretched in every direction across the dry, flat plains of what became Madyar Pradesh.

In a public garden in the centre of Gwalior town there is an animated equestrian statue of the notorious Rani of Jhansi, with a water tank standing before it engraved with the following inscription in Hindi on one side and in English on the other:

> This monument marks the site of the cremation of the illustrious and heroic Rani of Jhansi who fell in the Bharat of freedom war of 1857–1858.
>
> Born at Benares November 19th 1835
> Died at Gwalior June 18th 1858.

The story of the brave Rani of Jhansi was a favourite subject of my grandmother's, covering several of her special topics, as it did, such as horses and the Indian Mutiny and allowing, as it did, for a mite of female hero worship, a tendency towards which my grandmother had been prone ever since she had embarked upon her first sixth form 'crush' at St Margaret's, Bushey, Herts.

For example, her admiration and respect – bordering on worship – for Lucinda Prior-Palmer, the event rider, on account of the Hampshire girl's courage over fences, her horsemanship and her brisk prettiness, was sustained, without relapse, for the entire time I knew my grandmother. Penelope used to read Lucinda's columns in various horsey publications with religious attention, and rose and fell in sympathy over every fence the lithe Lucinda tackled on television.

The Rani of Jhansi's fearless horsemanship was her only talent comparable to Lucinda Prior-Palmer's, but my grandmother revered the Rani with almost equal diligence, and when we had reached Gwalior from Agra, she told me the tale of her darker heroine.

During the so-called Indian Mutiny in 1857, (when Indian

sepoys all over India, but beginning in Delhi, revolted against their British officers and carried out the massacres of thousands of British troops and families, including the women and children), Maharaja Jayaji Rao Scindia of Gwalior had, besides 10,000 troops of his own, a contingent of two regiments of Irregular Cavalry under British officers. As the Mutiny swept the nation, the Maharaja and his minister, Sir Dinkar Rao, remained staunch, but the contingent mutinied.

It is certain that in May and June 1858 there was much fighting in and around Gwalior between the mutineers commanded by Tantia Topi and the British under Sir Hugh Rose, yet the Rani Lakshmi Bai of Jhansi's part in the Mutiny is shrouded in ambiguity. Some say it was to the British advantage to portray her in an unfavourable light; whereas for the Indian patriot she was among the first few manifestations of proper revolt against British rule in India. She became a cult figure and a source of inspiration to freedom fighters during the struggle for independence.

John Lang, the Englishman who had been the Rani's lawyer, described her:

> She was a woman of middle size – rather stout, but not too stout. Her face must have been very handsome when she was younger, but even now it had many charms – though according to my ideas of beauty it was too round. The expression was also very good, and very intelligent. The eyes were particularly fine and the nose very delicately shaped. She was not very fair, though she was far from black. She had no ornaments, strange to say, upon her person, except a pair of gold earrings. Her dress was a plain white muslin, so fine in texture, and drawn about her in such a way and so tightly, that the outline of her figure was plainly discernible and what a fine figure she had. What spoilt her was her voice.

The tenor tone of her voice has led some to infer that she suffered from a hormonal imbalance. She certainly dressed as a man to lead her troops into battle, though she was most definitely feminine enough, for she sustained quite a reputation for promiscuity.

She had married Gangadhar Rao, Rajah of Jhansi, a scholarly man much older than herself, when she was fourteen. Alas, her only child by him died, prompting the ageing Rajah, shortly before his own death, to adopt a boy. He entreated the British Governor-General to look kindly on this heir, and to allow the Jhansi state (which borders Gwalior) to be ruled by the boy's adoptive mother in the meantime. On the Rajah's death, however, the promise was disregarded and Lord Dalhousie, then Governor-General, decided to annex the state. The Rani, instead of being allowed to rule, was awarded a life pension of 60,000 rupees.

In the following years, though, the Rani did much to impress upon the local political agent, Captain Alexander Skene, her intentions of remaining on friendly terms with her British masters. So when news of the mutiny in the north came through in 1857, she was granted permission to muster an armed bodyguard for her own protection; when the sepoys at Jhansi mutinied, the British were in no doubt that the Rani would do what she could to save Skene and the forty-odd Europeans and Eurasians trapped inside the fort.

My grandmother was moved to tears when she read out the poem to me which was written by Christina Rossetti and inscribed in the Round Tower at Jhansi:

> A hundred, a thousand to one; even so;
> Not a hope in the world remained:
> The swarming howling wretches below
> Gained and gained and gained.
>
> Skene looked at his pale young wife:
> 'Is the time come?' – 'The time is come!' –
> Young, strong and so full of life:
> The agony struck them dumb.

Close his arm about her now,
Close her cheek to his,
Close the pistol to her brow –
God forgive them this!

'Will it hurt much?' – 'No, mine own:
I wish I could bear the pang for both.'
'I wish I could bear the pang alone:
Courage dear I am not loth.'

Kiss and kiss: 'It is not pain
Thus to kiss and die.
One kiss more.' – 'And yet one again.'
'Goodbye' – 'Goodbye'.

Skene saved his wife from a violent death, just before every one of the hostages with their wives and children were taken and brutally massacred. The Rani, noticeably absent from the scene, reported that she had been powerless to help: she wrote that it was . . . 'quite beyond her power to make any arrangements for the safety of the district and the measure would require funds which she did not possess . . .'

In response to this plea, or perhaps to her undeniable charm, the Rani was then bidden by the surviving local Commissioner 'to manage the District for the British Government' until a new official arrived in Jhansi. Central government were less than happy at this arrangement (her protestations of innocence of the Jhansi massacre were not widely believed up north), so that they refused to help the Rani when later in the year neighbouring states took advantage of Jhansi's instability and invaded the fort.

She turned then, not to the British, but to the rebels to quell the invasion from her own countrymen, and the same rebels pressed her to join their fight for independence. However, she still seemed reluctant to commit herself to the mutineers' cause openly, until a formidable British army appeared at the walls of her fort at

Jhansi, intent on revenging the massacre there. Then she determined to fight.

Christopher Hibbert's brilliant account in his book *The Great Mutiny* describes the army manoeuvres which followed: after the merging of the Rani's men with Tantia Tope's army, there was a series of violent encounters with the British at Kalpi, then Kunch and finally at Gwalior where the rebel forces had retreated.

Sir Hugh Rose, leading an exhausted – eighty-four men in a single regiment were incapacitated by heat-stroke – but aggressive band of men, managed to muster the energy to attack again and on 19 June 1858, after a battle lasting five and a half hours, the rebels were defeated at Gwalior. Tantia Tope fled across the Chambal river into Rajputana, but somewhere on the hilly ground between Kota-Ki-Serai and Gwalior, the Rani died fighting.

There were many versions of her death, but Hibbert reckoned the most credible was found among Lord Canning's papers, making out that she was shot in the back by a trooper of the 8th Hussars 'who was never discovered'. She turned and fired back at that man who ran her through with his sword. Canning's note said:

> She used to dress like a man (with a turban) and rode like one . . . Not pretty and marked with smallpox, but beautiful eyes and figure. She used to wear gold anklets, and Scindia's pearl necklace, plundered from Gwalior . . . These when dying she distributed among the soldiery when taken to die under mango clump. . . . The infantry attacked the cavalry for allowing her to be killed. The cavalry said she would ride too far in front. Her tent was very coquettish. Two maids of honour rode with her. One was killed and in her agony stripped off her clothes. Said to have been most beautiful . . .

Another, even more heroic account, told by Sir Hugh Rose, to a friend who later wrote it down in her diary, states that although she was mortally wounded, she was not actually killed on the field.

She was carried off the field, the account goes on, and ordered a funeral pyre to be built which she ascended and fired with her own hand.

In whichever way she came to the abrupt end of her life, she was revered as a cult figure by successive generations of freedom fighters for her valiant efforts, and by my grandmother for her courage on a horse and her unflinching valour on behalf of her countrymen. Politics did not come into it; whether, as an onlooker, you were pro- or anti-British rule, the Rani of Jhansi's bravery at the last was undeniable.

SUCH OUTSTANDING heroism was not to be the imprint I left on Gwalior. I skulked off the train and struggled under my rucksack to the first hotel near the station and moved into a room at a price the equivalent of £1.35 per night. The room was not more than six feet across and the iron bed was not more than two feet wide. The mattress smelt musty. The stained walls had been painted mustard yellow, the light bulb was naked, and mosquitoes sat patiently upside down on the ceiling. I doubt if even Lord Canning could have described it in a favourable light: it was far from coquettish.

Hotel Ambika had not a feature to distinguish it from the hundreds of thousands of similar 'business' hotels cluttering Indian towns which play host to the constant mobile population of Indian businessmen who must always be travelling in their white or greying kurta pyjamas, slim briefcases to hand and plastic comb in their top pocket. I encountered nothing but courtesy from the countless accountants and corn buyers, shoemakers, lawyers and clerks whom I met on the road. Their English was often impeccable, as were their manners. The hotels they occupied while on business were seldom built far from the railway station and one was much like the other. They none of them had a woman within miles of them.

Yet after the first cursory glances and gentle jibing which

always took place when you filled in the registration form, once the room key was yours and the receptionist had accepted you, you felt safe in those hotel vestibules. What happened in town, however, was another matter, for which you were entirely responsible. In the hotel, you were a member of the proprietor's family. In the street, you were anybody's.

I had not liked Gwalior much when I had come there with my grandmother. She only ever visited the town for the architecture – the chain of palaces on top of the fort, especially the sixteenth-century Man Singh Palace, and the Mother-in-Law and Daughter-in-Law Hindu temples – and to offer obeisance to the equestrian statue of the notorious Rani of Jhansi. Together we had hired bicycles and had pedalled about through the stalls along the crowded main street. We had eaten omelettes every day in the Kwality restaurant, and had spent our evenings with the Carmelite nuns and Missionary of Charity sisters who lived together in harmony in a convent down a complicated network of back lanes. We had argued over the state of the nation with a Father Abraham there.

Gwalior had been under *bhand* when we were there, a sort of state curfew which is compulsory when riots are anticipated (or already raging as they were in Gwalior) and most of the shops were shut as well as the museums. There was not much else for us to do in Gwalior but stay inside and talk to the nuns.

Had the convent not proved hospitable to us, my grandmother would rather have stayed in a cockroach-ridden dive where there was at least scope for adventure, than be obliged to check in to a dull middle-rank 'deluxe' hotel which promised all facilities (and almost never came up with them in the end, anyway).

She had been touring central India with Sheldon Nash, her American friend, when she wrote in her diary:

We are staying at the Usa Kiran Palace Hotel [in Jhansi] which, according to the brochure, was converted to a deluxe hotel in

1969. I have presented the following list of complaints to the manager:

1) I judge a good hotel by whether or not there is a WASTE PAPER BASKET in my room. There is NONE.

2) It is very nice having a proper desk in the sitting room, but there is only one central ceiling light with a low watt bulb, and it is nearly impossible to write at the said desk. A TABLE LAMP SHOULD BE PROVIDED.

3) BATHROOM TROUBLES. The WC plug does not function properly and when the handle is pushed the floor all around it becomes flooded. I have to pour a bucket of water down each time I want to flush the lavatory.

4) There should be a tooth mug or glass on the shelf above the handbasin.

5) There is NO BATH MAT. Please provide one.

6) In every well-appointed bathroom there should be a bathroom chair – or at least a stool – preferably with a cork seat.

7) The large bedroom is very badly ventilated and at this time of the year one should not have to use the electric fan. When I opened the only window I found it looked on an extremely dirty confined and stuffy courtyard strewn with rubbish including an old enamel jug. Please have this place cleaned up and at a later date I suggest putting a few pot plants in it to cheer this at present unsavoury place up a bit.

Penelope was not every time such a perfectionist nor so hard on the poor manager, but at that time, in the mid-seventies, her tour-leading career was really taking off, and so it was with prospective tour groups in mind that she vetted various hotels whilst pursuing her individual travels.

After her Himalayan Temple Tours had achieved a certain notoriety, she had been asked by Cox & Kings, the old-established British travel agents for India, to think about tours in central and southern India. She had not spent much time further south than

Agra as a 'gel', apart from the odd trip to Madras with her mother, so when she began venturing further and further south along the ancient central railway, she was delving into uncharted country.

Sheldon Nash had met Penelope on one of her mountain tours in the north and had fallen so completely for her unabashed bravery and mountainous knowledge, delivered with such wit and generosity, that he had asked her to be his guide and mentor on several southern excursions. The pair became good friends, though their habits were not entirely compatible. Penelope would eat anything whilst on tour – unwashed grapes from the fruit seller, lettuce, dodgy looking sugared doughnuts – whereas Nash was a true American in his attitude to the food in India, in that he would eat nothing that was uncooked. He took his fastidiousness to extremes, however, and would often travel for three weeks at a time on a diet of three boiled eggs per meal.

His required standards of cleanliness and hygiene were similarly strict, so Penelope was able to gauge a medium standard between her low choice and Nash's selective choice, which became the measuring stick for reckoning just how low she could expect her tourists to go. With one group she leant a little too far downwards towards her standards however.

Sylvia Combe, from Norfolk, a childhood friend of my grandmother's and often, later, her travelling companion, remembered a bit of an upset on a Cox & Kings tour.

An Indian guide often accompanied the parties led by my grandmother, to facilitate any language problems and to ease the burden of complicated travel arrangements. On this occasion the party had been booked into a particularly unsavoury hotel in Gwalior, especially picked by my grandmother for its standards which were purportedly higher than those at the Usha Kiran Palace Hotel, where she had stayed the year before with the PPM.

But Sylvia Combe and the rest were not impressed. 'A half Irish, half Indian man ran it,' she told me. 'The beds were filthy and one room had a mattress full of bugs. The loos were just holes in the ground!' The Indian guide was particularly upset about his charges having to descend into such squalor and sought to make other arrangements. The trouble was that the only other halfway decent hotel in Gwalior was the Usha Kiran Palace, and Penelope had had such a row the year before with the manager that she refused to go back – and the hotel had refused to have her.

The only other alternative was to cut their sight-seeing short by one day and move on to Agra, where luxury five-star hotels abounded, earlier than planned. But Penelope was not having any of it. Sylvia Combe remembers her saying: 'Oh, you don't know what Agra's like – it's a flea pit.' Meanwhile, as the guide telephoned Agra to see if it was possible for the party to arrive on the Sunday instead of the Monday at the luxury hotel into which they were booked, Sylvia noticed cockroaches crawling under the tables of the dining-room. Still Penelope insisted the party stay.

'I felt so mutinous,' says Sylvia Combe. 'Our guide returned to tell us that the hotel in Agra was willing to take us and how many of us would there be. I'm afraid everyone put their hand up except Penelope and it became a proper Indian Mutiny. We packed our bags and left her there and she joined us the following day. I'm not sure she ever forgave me.' In fact, it was not so much that Penelope wanted her tour group to rough it so much as that she had planned to go to Mass in the Catholic church with an old British governess who still lived in Gwalior and she did not, on any account, want to miss the Mass.

When I returned to Gwalior alone, I searched for the Carmelite convent in which we had stayed, but I never found it. I got so angry with a minibus load of leering louts who crawled the kerb alongside me as I walked towards the fort, that I pelted them with a handful of rocks. I realized what a good strategy I had hit upon when I used the same missiles on two independent motor cyclists and later a cyclist who felt they had an indigenous right to harass me. I saw not another foreigner in the whole town, so I suppose it was natural that I be picked upon but when a group of giggling schoolchildren started pelting me with stones just for fun, I felt quite finished with Gwalior.

The six-wheeler rickshaws loaded high with passengers and belching out black clouds of carbon monoxide made me feel worse, and my burgeoning tears were only quelled once I made it to the Hotel Ambika where, to my intense joy, I heard the comforting and familiar tones of an English cricket commentator.

Six men of varying sizes and ages were craning their necks towards a crackling black and white screen on which Curtly Ambrose was bowling for the West Indies against India. As the game progressed I noticed a further few men, some slumped, others animated, emerging from the darkest corners of the lino-floored reception to refill their misty glasses at the desk cum bar. Some intoxicating local brew was slipping down a treat I feared, and more red-eyed and wobbling viewers confirmed my suspicions.

It was unremarkable really except that in India there are no bars and Hindus, at least, are not allowed to drink. It is all very well walking in on five men and a hookah, but three men and a bottle is distinctly unusual. I stayed watching for a good hour though, and thought how mad it was to be sitting watching a cricket match with an English commentator in a seedy bar below a brothel (for I had realized, after finding the only bulb in my own and all the other rooms along the passage to be red ones and that an inordinate number of men tripped up and down the stairs at regular intervals, that I was most definitely lodging in a house of some repute), down a side street at the back of the railway, sipping Limca in low company.

The scene I was enjoying so had not much to do with my grandmother, however, so I asked the pot-bellied proprietor how I might move on the following morning to Jhansi (where the Rani came from), now a dullish military town with one pleasant hotel and several good bookshops, and from there how to make my way to Orchha, the sixteenth-century forgotten jewel in the crown of

Madyar Pradesh. Of lunar leaning myself (as my grandmother undoubtedly had been) I expected a full moon at Orchha the following evening to provide a more appropriate setting (sixteenth-century Hindu palace and all that) than the one in which I had found myself tonight – however much I was enjoying the cricket coverage.

I did not sleep, as one doesn't in a brothel next to a railway line, but later in the day, once I had arrived by bus (only an hour's ride) in Jhansi, I addressed GREEN PEACE CURRY for lunch, and after a short rest I walked out into Jhansi town.

My grandmother and I had gone to the bookshop there, to swap what we had for further reading. When I travelled with her I was not allowed to read anything that was not connected with India. This was quite right and educational and made sense, but at the time it annoyed me and after I had been restricted (though now I realize that is not quite the right word) for two months to Christopher Hibbert and *The Ramayana*, *the Bhagavad Gita*, V. S. Naipal, Paul Scott, Kipling, Gita Mehta and R. K. Narayan, I made an impassioned plea for the Graham Greene in the window of the Jhansi bookstore. My need was rejected. Narayan's *Tiger of Malgudi* was proffered and I resorted to the underhand purchase of *The End of the Affair* and carefully swapped the cover to avoid detection.

Just after this incident my grandmother wrote to my mother:

> Imo DEVOURS books and I can't afford to buy her any more. In Jhansi she was about to buy 2 Graham Greene novels but I made her put them down and get another R. K. Narayan and the famous S. Rushdie's MIDNIGHT'S CHILDREN which is a really thick 400 plus page book which I thought would last her at least ten days but she finished it in three! She MUST concentrate on Indian books these three months.

A well-worn maxim of my grandmother's was the French expression 'Les voyages forment la jeunesse' which she trotted out a great deal when she felt that I was slipping from her educational clutches. Part of the forming process included mastering the various scripts to be found in the different states in India (there are over a hundred languages in the fifty-five states and thirteen different scripts). Penelope wrote to my mother:

> I don't think she [me] is such a dedicated sight-seer as Lucy and I, but she learns about the history and religions relevant to what we are seeing very easily and had no trouble with Hindu iconography which most people find extremely different to memorize. She also taught herself the devanagiri script (used for writing Hindi and Sanskrit) in ONE MORNING, whereas 20 years ago it took me nearly three weeks sweating BLOOD to learn!

As well as the language from books and the art history from sculpture, Penelope knew that it was essential to understand the culture from the people themselves. To that end we spent quite a lot of time cultivating friends in each town we visited or visiting friends of friends to whom we had introductions.

One of the former was Mr Malhoutra, the proprietor of the cinema in Jhansi. We had met him in the post office queue, where his mastery of English distinguished him from the other stamp buyers, and we three went to the Kwality Ice-Cream Bar for coffee. My grandmother could never resist striking up conversation with an English-speaking local, for it guaranteed immediate access into real life in a town or village as opposed to life as a tourist just passing through. It seemed she had mastered the art of introducing herself, so that not for a minute was she ever embarrassed or lacking in something to say. Perhaps years of experience made it easy for her, for when I travelled alone I found it excruciatingly difficult to start talking to someone I did not know in a bank queue or in a café.

We had several fairly fruitless dates with Mr Malhoutra, who could not stop talking his excellent English once he had started, and only wanted to know about our life in England and stalled all our questions about his life in Jhansi. On our last night he invited us to the cinema. We primped and polished ourselves up in readiness, but he never turned up to collect us. My grandmother muttered something about young men nowadays (Mr Malhoutra being fifty if he was a day) and we stood in the street inhaling armfuls of dust whilst trying to hail a rickshaw.

The cinema in Jhansi was a blot on the landscape if ever one was conceived and built – it was an oblong-shaped purple and apple green edifice, with a huge giant-sized eye cut out of the concrete. There was not a single other woman in the vicinity as we bought our balcony seats, only hordes of adolescent male youths holding hands and smirking with each other, combing back their oiled hair and adjusting their shirt sleeves. However large the group of Hindu youths they would never approach or harass two women. It is when you are alone (for the idea of an Indian girl going to the cinema alone is unheard of) that you are approached and challenged. With my grandmother I felt safe as houses.

Predictably, the Hindi film concerned a fat mustachioed hero who danced in a field and sang and pretended he was a bird. We nearly fell off our seats laughing. Later there were more murders and horse chases and songs and dances until my grandmother nodded off and we left halfway through hoping that Mr Malhoutra might not catch us sneaking out. We never saw him again but we wrote a note to him the next day thanking him for our evening out, and received a cordial one back at the hotel saying his pleasure and come again. That was the end of Mr Malhoutra.

A different kind of friend, one not entirely of our own making, was a friend of a friend, H. H. Madukah Shah, the forty-two-year-old Maharajah of Orchha (a perfect and fitting husband for myself or one of my sisters, my grandmother plotted, until she discovered he had a wife and four children in Delhi). We had met him in his country house near Tikamgarh, directed that way under instruction from Alfred Wuerfel, the friend of both ours and the Maharajah's who introduced us.

My grandmother fretted, as she had become accustomed to, over my skimpy wardrobe, and we scoured Jhansi for garments suitable for a country house weekend. We waited patiently for the Maharajah's car to pick us up (there was no other way of getting to Tikamgarh) but several communication disorders upset each arrangement just after it was made, and we waited two days. Our pressed dresses had gone soft by the time the Maharajah's driver did arrive and it was with relief that we slipped into the leather interior of an old shiny black Morris Oxford and felt the doors go clunk (as they do on old cars) behind us.

Tikamgarh and elegant country house living here we come, we thought, regaining our high spirits and little anticipating the necessity to push the car not only to start it after we had stopped for tea or petrol but also up hills. Little did that matter though, for driving out into the plains and away from the railway lines was getting exciting, and all our waiting worries fled when we stopped for tea at a tiny Muslim mosque beside a clear glassy lake, which used to belong to the Orchha family.

Mirages (fuelled by the romance of the lakeside mosque) of white marble palaces and pink-stoned historical forts sprang up across the shimmering plains during the last part of the journey, occupying all our thoughts until we were told by the mustachioed driver that the government had reclaimed all but a hundred acres of the Maharajah's family estate.

His present Highness's grandfather had been a committed Anglophile and when he moved out of the family fort he built a Victorian country house for himself, with two tiny guest bungalows, one on each side. My grandmother described the interiors in another letter to my mother:

It consists of a central house with a dining room, large library, 2 sitting rooms and bedrooms upstairs, and on either side is a bungalow in one of which we are living with a bedroom on either side of a very dark sitting room full of very heavy carved teak furniture and a bookcase stuffed with dusty bound volumes of Blackwoods Mag, (my father's favourite) Illustrated London News, NGM and the Popular Mechanics Magazine! After lunch I opened the bookcases in the library which contained endless bound copies of Blackwoods and Harper's going back to the 1870s, Punch and a sporting journal called Baily's Magazine.

There was also Henry Irving's *Shakespeare*, the International Library of Famous Literature, novels by Marie Collins, Charles Lever and a copy of *Tom Jones*. Penelope quoted from *Baily's Magazine* in my mother's letter:

> I quote from the 1872 Oct issue: 'Mr Robert Arkwright shot everything from a quail to an elephant and had the good fortune to encounter Dr Livingstone on his travels; the Doctor set a collar-bone which Mr Arkwright had broken by a fall riding down a wounded antelope . . .'

Her letter continues:

> HOW did Dr Livingstone set a COLLAR-BONE? No modern doctor can do it as most of us know to our cost.
>
> The dust in the bookshelves is such that I am suffering from acute dust fever and never stop sneezing and blowing my nose like a foghorn which is very annoying for poor Imo. Imo has been remarkably well up until now, but has had a headache for the past two days. . . .

With an immutable constitution and a determination to eat what I liked with minimum fussiness, I had survived for two months with not a day off sick. Unfairly, just as Oxford marmalade and egg soufflé became the sort of fare we might begin to expect of the table, the headaches turned into nausea and I disappeared vomiting to bed and sank into sweaty delirium for three days and three nights. H. H.'s army of old retainers hovered, thin and bent in white saris at the door of my darkened room, whispering things and wringing their hands. It would have been a terrible misfortune for me, a guest, to have died under their roof, so they prayed and lit candles and swung incense about the room while I tossed and moaned.

Penelope, meanwhile, enjoyed the generous and jolly company of H. H. himself. Of pleasingly round demeanour, Madukah Shah regaled her with stories passed down from his grandfather about hunting on the Orchha estate before the government reclaimed all but a hundred acres of their land. He sent her out with three old men to protect her in the Morris Oxford on a day trip to visit various forts and temples and castles that were scattered round about and laid on a splendid picnic for one, lavish with egg rissoles and carefully cut cucumber sandwiches.

On Holi day, the Hindu festival celebrating spring when everyone goes out in the morning cleanly dressed in white to throw bombs of coloured powder at each other, and returns home spattered with orange and yellow and red looking as if peppered with machine-gun wounds, my grandmother stayed at home reading *Baily's Magazine*. She had seen many a Holi day in her time and did not accompany H. H. to Orchha. He returned in the evening covered in garish splodges from head to toe and then looked in on me. At my most feverish then, when I saw him I assumed I was hallucinating.

When I had recovered fully, we bade farewell to the Maharajah whom I had not got to know (and he was the only Maharajah I met) and set off for Orchha itself, the ancient kingdom built by Madukah Shah's forefathers on a two-mile-long island in the middle of the Betwa river.

Penelope described the journey there thus:

You go along the Khajuraho road for c.5m then turn down a pretty lane to the right and go about 5m along it to Orchha, an enchanting small town with fantastic buildings in a beautiful setting. You cross the main railway line at Orchha station and pass a pond on the right and after 2–3m you go through outer city walls of undressed dry stone – I cannot think how they stay in position. Then you go under a dobachlebas arch and along a very pretty street of low whitewashed 1 storey houses each with a moghul cusped arch around the door. At the crossroads the road to the right leads past a few stops to the Ramji Mandir, whitewashed and enclosing a large courtyard with many shrines . . .

Penelope wrote these instructions to Alfred Wuerfel in Delhi who had lived in India since 1935, yet had never discovered the marvels to be seen at Orchha. Nor had any other tourist, except my grandmother. She soon included the 'romantic jungle-covered ruined city of the sixteenth and seventeenth centuries, once the capital of Orchha state' in her Central Indian Tour for the Intelligent Beginner, bringing small parties of discerning Western-ers to stay in the TDC guest-house within the palace walls. So incensed was she at the Madyar Pradesh government's lack of funding for the conservation of the *chhatris* and palaces at Orchha, that she wrote an article for *Country Life* on the central Indian village, illustrated it with her own photographs and ended the article in an outraged tone, pleading for proper attention to be paid to the masterpieces there.

'Now that the package tour has come to India. . . . the famous sightseeing centres such as Agra, Ajanta and Khajuraho swarm with tourists throughout the winter season. It is therefore reward-ing to go off the beaten track to places like Orchha . . .' her article, entitled 'Orchha: A City left to the Jungle' begins. For though Penelope led tours herself, the itineraries were her own inventions, and mostly she managed to entice friends or friends of friends, on them, ensuring that she had a party of like minds to travel with. The lucky 'intelligent beginners' were treated to an eccentric merry-go-round of her own particular favourite spots.

Her *Country Life* article further described the terrain around Orchha:

> The surrounding countryside is up-and-down – but not undulating – terrain with frequent outcrops of purplish pink rock known to the geologists as Bundelkhand gneiss. There is some cultivation and a lot of scrub jungle of thorny scrubs and small trees such as catechu, mimosa and the lovely flame of the forest (*Butea frondosa*) which grows over most of central India and is covered with orangey-red, parrot-beaked flowers throughout the month of March. A small agricultural community occupies the once great capital city, which is now reduced to village status.

Orchha state was founded in the early sixteenth century by a Rajput chief called Rudra Pratap. He began to build the two huge fortress-like palaces enclosed by a tall crenellated wall and connected to the rest of the deserted city by a twelve-arched bridge but nobody knows how far he got with the building before he was killed by a tiger in 1531. He was succeeded by Bharti Chand, who is said to have completed the Ramji *mandir* (palace) and the city walls. The Raj *mandir* and the Jahangir *mandir* were built by his successors, Madhukar Shah (1554–92) and Bir Singh Deo (1605–27) respectively.

All Hindu states had memorial grounds for the reception of a deceased ruler's ashes in specially built shrines called *chhatris*, and also for those of his wives and near relatives. On the anniversary of a death of a member of the royal family, his descendants, together with the Brahmins attached to the household, went to the shrine to make offerings and recite prayers according to the customary ritual.

Penelope wrote: 'No collection of *chhatris* that I have seen forms a more impressive architectural group than those on the right bank of the Betwa at Orchha.'

We had found a small private sandy beach beside the *chhatris* from where we bathed daily together at Orchha. Not a soul came to spy on us, or so we thought until the dreadful day when, as we sunbathed on a flat rock in the river, about twenty feet from the shore, a slim man in white trousers and a dark blue shirt, moved out from the jungle, hovered over our bags for a second and then, quick as lightning, seized my mini rucksack, turned and bolted back into the jungle.

The spasmodically occupied plains and deserts of Central India are littered with dacoits, but lulled into false security by the peace and privacy we found at Orchha, we had relaxed our normally stringent safety measures.

My grandmother screamed in protest at the robber and we dived inelegantly back into the water and splashed to the shore in hot pursuit. All sense went out of our heads as Penelope led the chase into the wood. He had seized our clothes as well, but we never stopped to think about running through a jungle in a dripping bathing suit barefoot. Rage was our driving force and long after my grandmother had given up, panting and cursing at the thief, I charged on through the undergrowth until I came to a woodman's hut.

Not until I was standing in the woodman's smoky kitchen trying to explain our predicament in garbled English spattered with pidgin Hindi, did I take note of the lascivious expression on the woodman's face, and notice that he had closed the door behind me. Who knows whether he had given asylum to the robber (he may even have been his brother, I suppose) but whatever his relation to our thief, his all-consuming interest now was held by the wet and angry female *ferhingi* in his kitchen. Eyes glistening and with a smile beginning to play about his lips, the greasy-haired woodman lunged towards me just as all became clear in my adrenalized brain and I managed to burst through the back door, into an enclosed yard. With the woodman (and the woodman's two dogs, who obviously enjoyed a chase) in furious pursuit behind me now, I was propelled by some superhuman force of desperate energy over the courtyard wall and, with all thoughts of catching the thief forgotten, I raced back through the jungle to the river bank where my grandmother was pacing about, fearing the worst.

Tear-streaked and filthy, I admitted defeat and after admonishing me for running half-naked into a single man's house, my grandmother collected me up to report the incident to the police. We did return to our rooms in the ruined palace to change before we repaired to the police station.

Anyone who has ever visited a police station in rural India (or even one in a large city, for that matter) will appreciate the frustration we endured while waiting for the four overweight policemen to finish their card game and drink three cups of tea before they would deign to listen to our complaint.

Not trusting me to speak rationally, Penelope relayed the events to the now attentive custodians of the law, and diligently in one corner a bespectacled minion noted down her every word. We were silly to swim in the river, said the chief of police. We were even sillier to leave our belongings unguarded on the shore. How could one expect a poverty-stricken Indian peasant to pass a Western-style rucksack by? We had offered a severe temptation to the boy, and it was not his fault that he was unable to resist. We left the police station feeling stupid, hopeless and quite definitely in the wrong, and I could muster no enthusiasm to write an account of the dramatic robbery for the insurance company. Penelope, an old hand at such notes, enjoyed composing a dramatic yet unemotional version of the unsettling events:

On Monday March 4th we were at Orchha, in Central India for the purposes of sight-seeing and in the heat of the day we bathed in the river Betwa. We were about fifty yards from the sandy bank when a man in white trousers and a blue shirt walked down to the river, washed his hands and then turned on his heel and walked back up the sand and as he did so scooped up – with his left hand – Miss Lycett Green's rucksack containing her camera, wallet and a paperback book by Paul Scott. He ran off into the scrub jungle to the left of the Raja's Chhattris (memorial buildings). My grand-daughter and I swam back to the shore and she rushed after the thief but of course he had completely disappeared into the jungle. . . .

And we got the money back and I bought a nice new camera which means that everyone was happy – the thief who gained some photographic equipment made in Japan, the police who did their duty and we *ferhingis* who lost nothing in the end.

For most of the time, however, Orchha is a haven of peace and romance and tranquillity. My sister Lucy wrote in her diary of her stay: 'Words could never describe the beauty . . . A wide, sparkling river flowed by some of the most incredible temples I have ever seen. They are now out of worship and stand with grass and climbers rambling in and out of every niche and crack. It really is the most romantic place I have ever been to . . .'

Once when my grandmother stayed at Orchha she wrote home to my mother:

I am sitting on a terrace above a VAST sunbathed river in the very heart of Central India. It is so hot from 11am–3pm daily that we have to stay indoors. I am burnt black. How CRUEL to tell you all this when you are sniffling at home in the damp December of wintry London. . . . The stillness is marvellous, broken only by the innumerable birds: cranes, ducks, wild geese and lots of others I cannot name. How I WISH I could press a magic button and get you all here to enjoy the sunshine and peace.

Well I am in a state of almost continuous POTLESS EUPHORIA here in India and am doing exactly what I most like doing without any feeling of guilt. I must be one of the few people in the world who is doing what she really wants to do. I miss my grandchildren quite dreadfully and think of you all

ALOT, but the magic of India has me so completely under its spell that somehow I manage to do without you. I am flattered to think I am missed – as you say I am – but I can't come back yet: got to prove Viking influence on the Western Himalaya first!

CHAPTER XIII
On the Beaten Track
to Bangalore

'In India I first learnt about the omnipresence of God; she taught me that God is the most important thing of the universe.'

PENELOPE NEVER proved there to be any Viking influence on the Western Himalaya, but she spent several years in pursuit of her theory. For quiet scholarly study, she began to go more and more often to settle for weeks at a time in the south of India, where she was not tempted from the schoolroom by mountains quite so often as she was in the north.

Among the Dravidians, the gentle, ancient people indigenous to south India, were many Christian converts who seemed to live in harmony alongside the long-established Buddhist, Jain and Hindu communities, thereby echoing Penelope's own philosophy: that God is there for everyone, along whichever path you seek to find him.

I was not seeking God but a ride in a rickshaw when I walked out and under the portals of the Jahangir palace at Orchha, on the first leg of my own journey south. Without an aeroplane or a car or a swift horse, the most convenient way of moving southwards in India is by train. The worst method of transport to choose (second slowest, least comfortable, possibly least safe) would be the bus and the best (slowest, most comfortable, safest, best view, most interesting) would be a bullock cart, but my grandmother had never had enough time to allow the gentle bullock gait to rock her all the way down through central India, and neither, this time, had I, so it was to go back to Jhansi to catch a train, that I needed a rickshaw.

The moment I hit town I attracted ten drivers. Walking down

Bazaar Street in Orchha is like walking down the aisle to collect a prize at school – everybody watches your progress. Only in Orchha, everybody has a brother or an uncle or a son with a rickshaw, and by the time you reach the stand with your rucksack on your back, you are considered fair game.

Ten minutes of ten men's smiles and entreaties and jokes led me to believe that it would cost 5 rupees to go to Jhansi in the tempo (ten-seater open rickshaw) but that I would have to wait, perhaps all morning, for it to fill up with other passengers. If I took a two-seater rickshaw the same distance would cost me fifty rupees. Or if I wished, I could 'reserve' all the seats in the tempo for fifty rupees and travel immediately. After some deliberation I plumped for the two-seater rickshaw and ended up paying twenty-five rupees, sharing the cost and the journey with an elderly man who did not appear to notice that I could not speak Hindi and apparently explained to me all about his grandson's new job (so the rickshaw driver told me afterwards).

The train was not due to leave until the evening so I went to the Jhansi bookshop with my grandmother's advice foremost in my mind, and bought a second-hand copy of *Freedom at Midnight* and a brand new biography of Rabindranath Tagore. I looked longingly at the Agatha Christie selection.

Jhansi was alive with cricket furore, or rather dead, for the streets had emptied of their usual throng and everyone was inside their local tea shop crowded round the television set. I watched Imran Khan score to make nine in an electrical shop and then moved on to the newsagent's to see him caught and bowled with only thirteen off twenty-two balls. I installed myself for a period in a dried fruit stall with a colour television and a charming owner who refreshed me with a pomegranate juice, then spectated further in the company of a baker who handed me a kulfi-pistachio ice-cream.

By the time I had reached the maroon velvet-padded television lounge of the faded Jhansi Hotel, Pakistan were all out and Mohammed Azharuddin was coming to the crease to face Waqar

Younus. I felt quite part of it as I sat down and ordered a banana
lassi without taking my eyes from the wicket. It was annoying to
find, however, that the Indian cameramen were far more interested
in the Middle Eastern oil magnates' wives and daughters sitting in
the Sharjah stadium boxes than in the bat, and that several of
Sachin Tendulkar's finest moments were obscured by some glossy-
haired glamourpuss in sunglasses.

Still, at the time, cricket was not supposed to be turning into
my *raison d'être* (though I can quite understand how the fever
strikes some) and with a struggle I tore myself away and sat down
in the lobby to look at the map. Jhansi (in the state of Madyar
Pradesh) was roughly two hundred miles south of Delhi as the
crow flies. Bangalore, the 'Garden City' of the south, in Karnataka,
lies roughly 1700 miles (as the crow flies) below Jhansi. My
grandmother never took much notice of Maharashta and Andrha
Pradesh, the two states which fill the gap between M.P. and
Karnataka, and waved out of the window of her train at Nagpur,
Chandrapur, Solapur and Hyderabad. She always made a bee line
for Bangalore.

It took too much will power for her to resist a stop at Sanchi,
though. For there, in the middle of the desert plain, two hours
south of Jhansi on the railway line and near the ancient city of
Vidisa, capital of the Sunga King Agnimitra, sits a group of
Buddhist *stupas*, looking like giant anthills from miles around,
which are thought to be perfect examples of Buddhist architecture.
By coincidence, the majority of the monuments had been excavated
between 1912 and 1919 by Sir John Marshall, Penelope's first love.

When my grandmother had taken me to Sanchi, the talk had
been not of love but of stirrups. She had a theory at the time about
the origins of the stirrup, and the relief sculpture on the *stupas* at
Sanchi went some way towards proving her point. We spent two
days in the one-horse town (just a railway station lined with a
collection of tented restaurants to service the travellers) photographing the horse sculptures from varying angles in varying
lights. Yet even after we had examined the stone domes in the kind

of pedantic way which is an invitation to boredom, each time you looked again, their massiveness and their symmetry and their proud domination of the flat landscape around them was entirely moving. I was looking forward to having a second glimpse, so I folded my map and went to the station.

Motivated by *stupas* was not how one could best describe the bulk of the female passengers waiting in the Ladies' Railway Retiring Room at Jhansi station. More likely they were stupefied by my unannounced entrance into the musky-scented glorified changing room which most of them regarded as their sacred boudoir. At the receiving end of sixty-odd intrusive brown-eyed stares, I crept into a corner and sat down, pretending to read the biography of Tagore.

The misty room was heaving with bosomy, amply-fleshed begums moving slowly about like sleepy elephant seals. They shuffled in turn into the washroom to sponge their plump thighs and flabby arms and to smooth down their already glistening hair with oil. Bewitched, I neglected Rabindranath and stared openly at a lady with bottom spreading beneath her like an overstuffed armchair, as she unplaited and then replaited her hair which grew to four feet. She did not need to look at her fingers moving rhythmically down the plait, but stared into the distance and smiled as enigmatically as the Mona Lisa. Then she caught me staring at her and winked.

Exchanging this womanly comfort for a 'II seater 3 tier' carriage of the Dadar Express via Sanchi was not easy. I perched on a wooden slatted seat at the front end of the only carriage I could fit into and smiled encouragingly at the young mother of five (or perhaps even six, for was that a tiny baby she held wrapped in the end of her sari?) against whose bursting baggage I was leaning. The young mother wore jewellery at her ears, nose and throat, as well as in her hair and all the way up her slender arms. Most poor Indian women wear their only wealth about their body, perceiving it to be the safest place, and most of the women in the carriage were jingling with gold and silver bangles, for most of them were indeed poor.

But poverty had not made them gloomy and even as the train lurched and baggage fell from the racks and a child whined or bejewelled toe was stepped upon, the women laughed amongst themselves and their eyes flashed with defiance. They offered me chapattis from their picnic meals wrapped in old soiled cotton and held the tin pot of potato curry steady for each other and for me as we scooped up the vegetables with the unleavened bread.

A thin man with a distinguishing white moustache which turned down at the ends wore a Nehru cap and a white lunghi and shirt, and adroitly hoisted himself onto the upper luggage rack opposite me and the young mother-of-five or six. He untied a bundle wrapped in a blue-and-white check handkerchief with long, spidery fingers and pulled back the four corners to reveal a sticky lump of *gur* (unrefined sugar) and a chapatti. For the remainder of the two-hour journey he sat with his back straight and his head held high and nibbled with delicate restraint alternately at the chapatti and the *gur*.

Occasionally he emitted a gurgled chuckle and smiled to himself; his bony feet at the end of his crossed legs were encased in black plastic galoshes several times too big. Four of the young mother's five children and I could not help but steal glances at him from time to time to check and see whether he hadn't lost his composure, but he retained his dignified position until the train stopped at Sanchi and never once shifted his legs, stiff as they must have become on the rock-hard wooden luggage rack.

The desert landscape around Sanchi offers nothing but acre after acre of dun-coloured plain relieved only by a patch or two of shrub-type scrub. In the light of such an undemanding view, distractions within the carriage were welcome. After the cross-legged galoshes wearer, the most distracting amusement was the pair of ticket inspectors, alike as Thomson and Thompson in the Tintin books, with matching navy blazers and pressed white trousers held up by red and blue snake-buckle belts. They sported identical clipped moustaches and each had a badge on his wide lapel, neatly proclaiming his position on the railways. They stepped in unison down the train and stopped together to request tickets from the passengers. The children loved this matching twosome more than the man with the galoshes, and when the train stopped we all followed them off the carriage and watched them walk in time down the platform.

I walked the other way to the Railway Retiring Rooms where my grandmother and I had stayed before. The very same No. 1 'set' was free, and the same caretaker in khaki with a crooked head and a withered left leg limped up to me with the heavy key to the huge medieval padlock fastening the door. He did not remember me, but I recalled the room immediately, as soon as I rested my rucksack against the door.

Quite a few stations in India offered this facility – a room for the night at a cheap price for rail users – and while most Indian travellers would prefer to sleep on the platform than pay forty rupees for a locked door, a bathroom and a mosquito net, not to mention a bed, the facility was ideal for foreign travellers passing through, and in fact, in places as small and remote as Sanchi (population not above 300) the railway station was the best, most convenient and most likely the safest place to stay.

Before, we had met an Australian boy called David at the Retiring Rooms, or rather my grandmother had met him on the platform and she had brought him in to meet me. This was the fifth young man we had met along the way whom my grandmother had invited to join us. As always, she would end up talking to them long after I had sloped off, and the point of the exercise – to introduce me to agreeable partners – was seldom achieved.

One time, when we were in Goa, the former Portuguese colony which lines a coastal stretch on the west coast of India below Bombay, I was approached on the beach by two English brothers – Stephen and Paul. I even shared with them the fairly adventurous experience of being put in gaol for an afternoon for riding a motor bike without a helmet.

Apparently in Goa the police are in cahoots with the motorcycle shops, and the whole business of hiring the bike without a helmet, being stopped after ten minutes, being fined, gaol and the return of the bike by the police to the owner half an hour later (so that he can hire it out again and if he's lucky ten more times so that he pockets ten days' hire fees in a single day) is a daily money-making scam. We discovered all this from talking to the twenty or so other Westerners lined up in the police station, similarly duped.

Anyway, the following day, long after I had waved goodbye to Stephen and Paul, I was recounting the tale to my grandmother in the bar of the Mandovi Hotel in Panjim, Goa's capital city, when in walked Paul (or perhaps Stephen) in a dark blue blazer and a cravat and with his mousy hair combed to one side. Penelope thought he was charming (and so well dressed, darling), and he ordered a gin and tonic. An hour later I excused myself and left them to it, not that either of them noticed me going, and when my grandmother came up to our room several hours later, she said, 'I simply can't think why you didn't like him, he had such charming manners.'

Much the same sequence of events made up Australian David's fate at Sanchi. We had all enjoyed a nice rice meal in the street stall after which he and my grandmother walked up to the *stupas* together talking about archaeology. I had not been able to squeeze a word in at lunch and went off quietly to sit under a tree.

They returned, he boarded the train, my grandmother waved him off, and as the train snaked out of view across the plains, she said: 'But what on earth were you thinking of? I can't begin to understand why you didn't like him. I've never met anyone so polite and intelligent in all my life!' It pleased me but annoyed my grandmother to find that the intelligent David had left his Alistair Maclean novel behind, on purpose, for me to read (and as a result her first glowing report was modified considerably).

Years later, when I walked into my assigned Railway Retiring Room, each detail of the blue and cream room with its reclining chairs and its two wooden beds with wooden frames to hold up the mosquito nets served a memory. My grandmother had paced the room for most of the night, swatting mosquitoes with my flip-flop. 'Bloody hell, bloody hell, the wretched things!' She had covered her arms and face and legs with citronella and she kept her bath cap on her head.

Alone, I walked around on the stone floor and opened all the wooden cupboards and drawers (which I always did to check for interlopers, animal, human or insect) and went to bed unbitten, trying in vain to picture blond Australian David's face. However, proving that good memories do remain while bad ones fade away, I had failed to recall just how impossible it is to sleep on a railway station.

The Retiring Rooms were situated on Platform 1 and every time a train passed through the station, the floor moved, my bed rattled and I sat up sharply, thinking another earthquake was occurring; the trains blew their horns as if they were ships coming into port, and a stationmaster rang a bell vigorously to herald each arrival. By my reckoning two trains passed in every hour, and the stationmaster stood right outside my door. With sleep impossible, I turned to history. At Sanchi, my grandmother had taught me all I knew about Buddhism.

Buddha (or Gautama Siddhartha as he was known then) was born in 624 BC in northern India, now Uttar Pradesh. Later called 'The Enlightened', Buddha, who was a member of the Kshatriya or warrior caste and was the son of Suddhodana, ruler of the Sakya Clan, was also known as the sage of the Sakyas, for at the age of twenty-nine he made 'the great renunciation' of the world and its pleasures.

He cut off his long hair, left his home, his wife and his son to search for mental peace, but under the instruction of two Brahmin sages he found, when practising their extreme self-mortification, only that he earned a weak body, and he became unconvinced of the usefulness of their teaching.

So then he went off on his own, and sat under a bo-tree, the 'tree of knowledge', at Bodha Gaya, where he was tempted by Mara, the personification of carnal desire, to return to the world; but he resisted, and became the Buddha – the Enlightened. Thereafter he travelled the length and breadth of India with an increasing circle of followers or disciples, preaching what he had learnt, until he died, aged nearly eighty, at Kusinagara, modern Kasia, in Gorakhpur district.

Buddhism is all about Buddha, the teacher, himself. There is no central god prevailing, and he, as the teacher of the truth, is the central object of faith and devotion. His teachings aim to lead men to a higher life, and a main tenet is to keep to the 'middle path' between worldliness and asceticism. You have to depend upon yourself in your efforts towards intellectual and spiritual clearness, and your ultimate goal is to reach 'Nirvana', the sinless state of mind after which you have no other lives. Before you reach Nirvana you must carry your existing 'karma' or 'action' (as opposed to the 'soul' which is carried through reincarnation in Hinduism) through from one life to the next until you have become enlightened by meditation completely.

For the lay Buddhist (everyone except a monk), there are six principal virtues to stick by – charity, compassion, truthfulness, chastity, respect for the Sangha (the monastic organization surrounding and perpetuating Buddhism) and self-restraint in regard to the ambitions and pleasures to be had in life. The monks have to follow these first six tenets as well as keep five other, even more difficult, promises, including not eating at forbidden hours and not lying on beds.

One of Buddhism's greatest and most famous devotees in India was Asoka, a Mauryan king ruling in central India in the third century BC, who was converted to Buddhism in 262 BC. His reign is much muddled by legend, and most of the information provided on him comes in semi-historical form collected in Buddhist sources. Most of this material disappeared from India after the decline of Buddhism there in the thirteenth century, but it has been preserved elsewhere, in Buddhist strongholds outside India, like Ceylon, China and Central Asia.

The muddle probably arose because while Asoka issued proclamations all over the sub-continent engraved on pillars and rocks, the Brahmin script in which these edicts were written had, unfortunately, become archaic and the inscriptions could not be read. So nobody knew whether Asoka had indeed propagated Buddhism as the state religion or whether he was just a fervent Buddhist himself. (Later however, in 1837, the Orientalist James Prinsep deciphered the script, though now it was impossible to assign the writings to Asoka with any surety for the inscriptions were always signed by 'Devanampiya Piyadassi' or the Beloved of the Gods. The telling edicts were only attributed to Asoka himself in 1915, when another archaeologist discovered an inscription which tallied with the rest, signed 'Devanampiya Asoka'.)

It was likely that it was Asoka's interest in Sanchi which brought the site into such Buddhist prominence. One of his queens, Devi, was born near by, and it is on the Sanchi hill that a monastery is said to have been built for his son (or brother) Mahendra, the apostle of Sri Lanka. Now on the same hill, you find *stupas*, which were built either to enshrine relics of the Buddha or one of his saints, or to commemorate some holy spot, as well as pillars set up by Asoka and later devotees, then *chaitya* or shrines and lastly monasteries or convents in which the monks or nuns lived.

The *stupas* were the most fascinating edifices, the ones at Sanchi being perfectly spherical domes, like half oranges set in stone. Some have gateways, others have railings around them, all in stone and elaborately carved with animal friezes and scenes from Buddhist history and legend. But solution of the stirrup theory evaded me too and after a satisfying length of *stupa* contemplation, I spent my second night in the station.

After Sanchi, on a southward journey, Bhopal is the next stop.

Famous now after the horrendous chemical disaster which killed thousands of Bhopalis, the city was also a giant railway depot, from where trains left in all directions. The train my grandmother always rode south was the Karnataka Express, so I went to Bhopal to catch it.

The factory from which the lethal gas leaked was placed right bang in the middle of the shanty-town district, where no one had even a window or a door to close against poisonous air, so it was the poor of Bhopal who suffered worst after the disaster. There were still people dying from exposure to the gas now, and a new generation of deformed children were growing up in the shanty towns with their sick parents. As if that were not depressing enough, Bhopal was a big, ugly industrial town, poorly planned, overcrowded and filthy.

I needed to stay a night in town to catch the Express in the early morning and I inhaled my first dank whiff of Bhopal at the station, where we arrived four hours later than expected. Beside me on the train was a man with no nose. It may have been bitten off by a dog, or it may have fallen off as a result of leprosy, but more likely chemicals in the air had brought about its disintegration. However it happened, he seemed not to mind any more, and sat for the whole journey smoking and blowing the smoke out through the two triangular holes in his face where his nose had once been.

I asked for a room in four dim-looking hotels before I found one, and sank into it. I could not think what to do in this gloomy city. When my grandmother first came to Bhopal in 1931, she had experienced an altogether different reception. In her diary she wrote:

July 23rd. Bhopal. We arrived an hour late at our destination after an extremely hot and sticky journey from Simla. We were driven straight to the palace where we were received by the Begum in a charming and very simply furnished room. We then drove on to the guest house . . .

With no begum to greet me I felt totally alone. But my grand-mother had not often had begums waiting in the wings either. She had spent a lot of her life alone, and she had been the last person to dwell upon herself or to magnify minor grievances out of all proportion. She would never have whittled away hours worrying about nothing when instead she might have been writing or riding or collecting wood or making soda bread.

One of her secrets was never to lose sight of the future, whether it was tomorrow or next week or next year. Her second secret was to take delight in the ordinary. Her third secret was not to lose interest in either the known or the unknown – to keep up your will to learn.

She wrote once to the father of one of the two eighteen-year-old boys with whom she was driving about India:

> I am so sympathetic with both boys who are late developers – as
> I was – but now that thro' seeing things of profound interest,
> their imagination has been stirred, they have THE WILL TO
> LEARN and I hope will never look back, as once one has
> developed an inquiring mind, then one will find things of interest
> wherever one goes and one will NEVER BE BORED, which is
> surely one of the secrets of happiness?

With her words in mind, I ventured out into Bhopal, to find the beauty in the detail. I walked up Hamidia Road, grease-lined with mechanics' workshops, and discovered what the engine of a Morris Oxford looks like. I was drawn by the pink-and-white marzipan cake of a mosque at the top of the hill called the Jaj-al-Mujid, and found thirty little Muslim boys inside the large stone square, pressed and neat in white suits with white caps on their heads. They had finished with Allah for the day and were throwing stones at the angry-looking bees' nests which hung from the eaves like fungus.

One hundred-odd real worshippers knelt on their prayer mats in the echoing silent hall of the mosque and they turned not a hair on seeing me sidle in and sit down against the wall. The quiet hum of the kneelers reciting their Koran was soothing. Turning in the street outside, feeling refreshed and positive and calm, a fashionable young woman on a moped stopped and offered me a lift. Her name was Sita and she was a nurse at the Bhopal hospital and she was keen to talk to someone British, so that she might try out her textbook English.

'And you are liking our Bhopal?' she asked as we spluttered, helmetless, up the hill. 'Now I am liking it very much,' I replied, my arms clasped around her waist. She was late for the hospital and could not stop for a cup of tea, so she set me down and disappeared as magically as she had arrived outside the fairy-tale mosque.

In New Bhopal now, which was higher on the hill than the rest of the city and where it felt easier to breathe, I noticed Pia's Beauty Salon, and, attracted by the unlikeliness of it, wandered in. Pia was of Chinese–Canadian extraction but she had lived in the city for twenty years on account of her husband being Bhopal-born. After she had welcomed me with such profuseness and I had noticed that there were no other customers in the salon, I asked her whether she might give me a manicure – the only beauty treatment I could think of at the time.

She sat me down and switched on the television which was showing a Tamil movie in black-and-white, and one of her salon girls brought me a cup of milky coffee. Then the other girl, surly-looking, sloped in and we all sat in front of the film while Pia buffed my nails. She told me that she wanted to move back to Canada but that the Indian government forbade anybody taking more than $500 out of the country. She and her husband had made money in the beauty business and were rich in India, but they could not foresee how long it might be before they would accumulate enough illegal dollars to make it possible for them to set up a new life in Canada. 'The government is happy that the people emigrate from India,' she explained. 'But only as long as the people leave their rupees in India.'

After my hands were completely remodelled, Pia took me to her flat above the salon where we savoured a rice curry lunch served in stainless steel tureens by one of her slant-eyed children, and once we had eaten we made a deal. I gave her $100 and she gave me the equivalent in rupees and then she burst into tears and said that I had brought her Canadian dream one step closer. She would not hear of me paying for my manicure.

My grandmother's first day in Bhopal with the Begum had begun quite differently:

> July 24th. Bhopal. The view from my verandah is lovely: an expanse of twisted trees and vivid green undergrowth leads down to a large lake with low wooded hills on the opposite bank. We went out sailing in the morning. There was a good breeze blowing and we seemed to go a terrific pace. On the whole however I don't enjoy sailing unless I can work everything myself which I didn't because I had forgotten how to. The boat was of the 'tom-tit variety', it was amusing at first but the sun came out and beat down upon my back until I felt quite sick.

Her lunch was of an altogether more formal variety as well:

> At lunch I sat next to Mr Sen whom I met in 1929 at Alwar. He is a great friend of Tagore's and talked a lot about him. He was delighted to hear that I was acting in a play written by that gentleman in September. On the whole he is rather difficult to talk to because he jumps from one subject to another in a very disconnected way. His sister, the Maharani of Mayurburj also does this.
>
> After lunch I read Coomaraswamy's *History of Indian and Indonesian Art* until five o'clock when I went out riding. I rode a fat English polo pony of the Nawab's which shied all the time. We (Major Lucas, Beryl and I) cantered to the top of a hill from where there was a wonderful view around the surrounding

country: vast lakes, the Nerbudda river winding through a grassy
plain, rolling hills covered with leafy trees. India is a revelation
of beauty at this time of year: in place of the bare brown jungle
and burnt up grass of cold weather, everything is a vivid almost
unnatural green.

The lakes were polluted and littered with industrial vessels now,
and the nearest I came to riding was the jerky tonga ride I took
back to the hotel. No Nawab awaited me with sundowners on the
veranda, but instead I met a girl called Lata.

Voluptuous, Hindu and twenty-two, Lata had a Muslim
husband who was working in Dubai. It was a love marriage, she
told me, and she showed me a photograph of the bearded Mussul-
man, and asked whether I thought he was good-looking.

Lata had come to Bhopal to visit her mother (who was in fact
her aunt because her mother and father were killed in a car crash
when Lata was eight), but she always stayed in a hotel when
visiting because her 'mother' lived in a hovel on the lower side of
town. 'I hate Bhopal,' she said. 'I don't like to go out because the
town is bad.' And she sat all day on her bed being tended upon by
her relations. Her mother/aunt was four feet high and as thin as a
child, and grey and toothless and bent. She looked like a village
woman, but she was proud of her well-covered daughter in her
new *salwar kameez*, and watched Lata talking English with pride.
She was more proud though of Lata's proficient poker-playing,
and we played cards all evening while Lata painted her nails (and
complimented me on mine) and talked without stopping about
Bombay films and boys.

Buoyed up the next morning by my day in Bhopal, I boarded
the Karnataka Express which would take thirty-six hours to reach
Bangalore. I was determined to be social, not solitary. And I was
not obliged to try hard at all, for my reservation placed me in a
six-berth cabin with a family of friendly Sikhs, the Bakhshis,
namely Priti Bakhshi (the mother), Gurmeet Bakhshi (the father

who served in the Air Force and was currently stationed in Bangalore, though the family moved barracks every three years) and their two round-eyed children, Gurjot and Japna.

Priti said that she noticed that foreign journalists always came to India and noticed the obvious things – the elephant, the snake charmer, the sun and the bullocks in the road. And the poverty. She said they chose to ignore the people who live quite well and are not greedy or flash, but who are at least contented though they have not travelled abroad, and work hard, speak English and are well informed.

I said that the foreign journalists often found it difficult to feel happy about a prosperous middle class living alongside such obvious and outrageous poverty.

'That is a stupid way to think,' said Priti. 'Everybody helps in their own way.' She said that she had two maids living with her, each of whom had families. She housed them, fed them, paid their electricity bills and paid them a wage. She had told them about family planning, and she made sure their children were educated. In this way, she said, she hoped that she was saving two families from the street, and distributing her wealth.

At the root of the poverty was lack of education, she said. 'Education should be the birthright of all human beings,' she said, 'and only then would people learn about family planning and to avoid being "sold" for a dowry and only then will they have the wherewithal to choose a path in life.'

Priti was a good and wise woman and a first-class cook as well, for I shared their chapattis and various curries which appeared, hot, from round steel containers in her picnic basket. I told the children that in England it would not be possible to stay on one train for as long as our Bhopal–Bangalore journey, because England was not long enough and you would end up going round and round in circles, but they laughed at that and said how ridiculous.

Gurmeet looked statuesque and handsome in his navy blue pyjamas, and went to bed with his yellow turban on. Gurmeet had never cut his hair in all of his life, and Priti said that now he is beginning to go bald and that some of the great long tresses are falling out. Gurjot, their son, had his three feet of hair tied up in a *jurda* or topknot on his head. All Sikh men have a *jurda* because their original guru, Gurunanak, had one, and also because all Sikhs were warriors a long time ago when there were no helmets, so they wore turbans (or *pagdri*) to protect their heads and also to separate them from the rest and give them some sort of identity. Sikhism is all about having God near you, at your shoulder, watching everything you do, and we said prayers together in our blue-and-white-curtained section of the rocking carriage, hoping that God was indeed sitting on top of the train, watching out for the sick girl along the corridor.

She had eaten a boiled egg from the picnic packed for her by her mother-in-law, and had started vomiting four hours later. Now she was weak and lay as if on her deathbed – pale and sweating but also fragile and beautiful, just like dying people are supposed to look in fiction. Her new husband fretted and wrung his hands, and beseeched me to mend her. He thought I would have some miracle of modern medicine in my Western style medical bag, but all I had was Arret, for diarrhoea, or paracetamol. We administered one of each, for good measure, and each held one of her hands. The train swayed and the other passengers slept, and tossed or murmured or shuddered suddenly in their sleep, and it seemed like the night would go on for ever.

At dawn, the girl gave out an almost imperceptible sigh and smiled weakly; her husband hugged me and thanked me profusely for my vigil and said that I had saved her. A party spirit spread along the carriage as the morning wore on, and by lunchtime the four young Indian subalterns sharing a compartment at the other end brought their whisky to the scene of the sickbed, and we merrily partook of a capful or two. Sudhir, the handsomest one, was astounded by my admission that I was the great-granddaughter of 'great Chetwode', and led his fellow men in a resounding recital of my great-grandfather's Credo, which they all knew by heart. They had studied at the Indian Military Academy in Dehra

Dun, and thought much of my forebears, which made me feel quite proud.

I never wanted to get off the Karnataka Express, so sociable had my companions been, but Bangalore beckoned, and for the last part of the ride I stood at the open door at the end of the carriage and inhaled the wet air of the south.

It was wetter than I had hoped, indeed, for the late monsoon rains were still sweeping the state in a violent, sideways manner, and the guard had told us of a cyclone, which had torn through Karnataka the night before while our train had rocked blindly on. The land was green, suddenly, and the trees looked tropical. The bullocks looked fat and the women looked darker. The station signs were now written in Kannada, in the rounded, wholesome script of the state which is different from Hindi.

Kannada is derived not from ancient Sanskrit as the Devanagiri script of Hindi is, but from the separate southern, Dravidian tradition, so I bought myself a new grammar book at the station and determined to master recognition of the consonants at least, so that I might be able to work out (by phonetic intuition and ample guess work) the place names I could expect to encounter. English was still used in the south as a barrier-crossing tongue, especially in the bigger cities like Bangalore, but in the rural areas it is far less known than in the north, so a scant knowledge of the local script is desirable if you want to know where you are.

After the peopled party atmosphere prevalent on the train, I now sought peace and solitude. Following my grandmother's initiative, I knew where to find it. When Penelope first ventured south, she sought out definitive examples of architecture and sculpture representative of the most impressive Dravidian empires: she went to Ajanta and Ellora for the cave temples and soft sculptural lines of the Gupta period (AD 319–606); to Badami for the red-stone architecture of the Chalukyan kings (AD 550–753); to Thanjavur to discover the Cholas (c. AD 850–1100); to Belur and Halebid and Somnathpur for the animated and detailed Hindu sculpture of the Hoysalas (AD 1000–1300); but in none of these places did she stay longer than was necessary to make comparative notes and photograph details in the early morning light, for to her mind, one and all of these places had been 'ruined' by their respective Tourist Development Corporations.

From morning till night the sites were teeming with coachloads of Indian and foreign tourists and it was only when she reached the fourteenth, fifteenth and sixteenth centuries in her studies, that she chanced upon the Vijayanagar kings' ancient empire at Hampi, where ruin upon hidden ruin lies scattered, waiting to be explored, across a lunar-style landscape over an area of some twenty-four square miles.

Vijayanagar sat on the southern end of the great raised plain of the Deccan, one of the oldest parts of the earth's surface. The central southern plain stretched for one thousand miles from north to south and for the same distance from east to west where it is hemmed in on either side by two mountain ranges, the Eastern and Western Ghats.

The twenty-four square miles were spread on two sides of the roaring Tunghabadra river, in among an endless repetition of stony hills, never more than three to four hundred feet high, composed of colossal granite boulders piled precariously one above the other. Some were black, some were honey-coloured and, where man has split them himself for building material, pale silver. My grandmother wrote in a letter home: 'I always get the impression that were a giant to prod one of these hills with his finger it would topple over like a house of cards.'

'Maurice Bowra wrote in his *memories* that I thought India belonged to me,' Penelope's unfinished and hence never published article on 'Vijayanagar: The Ruined Capital of a Forgotten Empire' begins. She went on:

Well I certainly think Vijayanagar does [belong to me] and it is very nice of me to tell other people about it. . . . Selfish as one is inclined to be about places one would like to keep to oneself, I think Vijayanagar can deal with an onslaught of tourists without being spoilt. . . . There is room for all of us: the loners and the coachloads of Indian students who go there on day trips from their colleges, the pilgrims who attend the frequent religious festivals at the great temple of Virupaksha, the hippies who are beginning to discover it and the future members of foreign package tours.

But Penelope kept well away from 'the others' she welcomed so magnanimously in her article, and always slept, when visiting the ruins, in her very own deserted temple 'with prancing horse pillars all along the front'. She slept on a straw mat on the floor and used the *yoni* (the symbolic representation in stone of the vulva) as her dressing-table. In the same article she described her routine:

> Every morning I walk about half a mile through yellow flowering Cassia auriculata shrubs down to the Tunghabadra river to bathe in my private pool. . . . Here too I wash my clothes in Lux which does not pollute the water and spread them out to dry on the surrounding boulders. I have my meals two miles upstream in Hampi with its cracked amplifiers blaring music across the broad 'car street' (the car being the huge wooden temple chariot) from rival restaurants where for the princely sum of 15p you can get an assortment of curried vegetables and rice served on a banana palm leaf, delicious little bowls of curds (I always have three in succession) and a glass of excellent South Indian coffee. The rest of the day I spend wandering about the ruins and climbing the hills, and during the hot afternoons I lie down to sleep on the floor of a pillared hall or under a neem tree. It is an idyllic existence and whenever I am there I want it to go on for ever.

Life was not always so quiet at Vijayanagar. Before the city comes into recorded history, it existed in legend as the mythical site of Kishkinda, the monkey kingdom described in the ancient Hindu epic, the *Ramayana*. When Sita, the heroine, was abducted by

Ravana, the demon king of Sri Lanka, she was carried off to his kingdom in an airborne chariot drawn by a pair of flying asses. As they flew over the Tunghabadra, Sita dropped her jewels on the southern bank, hoping that Rama, her husband, might one day pass that way in search of her. But it was Sugriva, the exiled monkey-king, who found them, and he hid them in a cave nearby which is a venerated shrine today.

Rama, searching for Sita, came to Kishkinda eventually with his brother Lakshmana, and Sugriva showed them the jewels. With the jewels as a clue, Hanuman, the monkey-general, was sent in search of Sita (and traced her, finally, to Sri Lanka) while Rama stayed behind to help the exiled monkey-king Sugriva retain his kingdom from his monkey-brother Vali who has usurped it. The mission was successful. Sugriva was set back upon the throne and in a remote corner of Vijayanagar you can still find a large heap of solidified ash believed to be the remains of the funeral pyre of Vali, who died a gruesome and operatic death which is stretched out over several pages in the *Ramayana*.

'Pious pilgrims,' wrote my grandmother, '(including myself as I have long had a great devotion to Vali), come here to break off pieces of ash as a memento . . .' My grandmother's pious devotion to peace was her excuse for an annual pilgrimage to Vijayanagar. The Viking obsession lasted little longer than it took her to work out that there was not enough connecting the buildings she had thought were connected for there to be substantial grounds for a revolutionary new archaeological theory, and instead she would bicycle about discovering hidden temple after hidden temple in the undergrowth, and bathe contentedly in the Tunghabadra.

India never lets you forget her, however. My grandmother had assumed she was alone one afternoon, when she climbed a steep rock path among giant boulders to near the top of the temple-crowned Matanga Parvatum Hill.

I lay down to rest in the shade of a boulder until the sun got right for certain wide-angle photographs that I planned to take, [she wrote in a letter to all of us at home]. After half an hour I got up and walked about 10 paces in my bare feet up a slippery boulder (bare feet much safer than sandals) to look over the edge of a precipice down at the temple below.

She decided to wait for another half an hour, as the sun was still not quite right for her photography and returned to lie down again and, she continued,

To my HORROR, my camera bag had disappeared: my sandals were there, my hat was there but NO BAG! It was a wild and lonely place and I had not met a soul on my way up, nor was I aware of anyone following me . . . to be cont . . .

At this point the aerogramme ran out and we had to wait, holding our breath, for two days, looking out each morning for the arrival of aerogramme No. 2, which would continue the tale. We strained across the table at breakfast. '. . . but a professional camera thief must have been doing just this for the past two days, WAITING for an opportunity to pinch my cameras.'

She 'rushed down the precipitous path in pursuit,' but, on finding no one, moved into the Hospet Convent, '(God knows what I would do without nuns in India)' she added in an aside, and spent the next two days in and out of the police station, 'with a good interpreter (Mr Charuchandra, who spent eight years in London at the Guildhall School of music, married an English girl, had two children, and was then ordered home by his parents as his elder brother had been murdered. His wife refused to come, so he has now married an Indian girl from Hospet)'. Spare us the interpreter's love life, we thought, we cannot endure the suspense. 'The red tape of the police was unbelievable,' we read on, thankfully, 'and after two days wrangling the Chief of Police arrived from Bellary and invited me to drive out in a jeep to show him the site of the theft. I told him I had twice driven out to India so he said "You may drive the jeep". We all got in: the Chief, his deputy Supt. from Hospet, me at the wheel and two Anglo-Indian girls, Hyacinth and Georgina and their mother to all of whom I was giving a Sunday outing in Vijayanagar.'

About two miles out of Hospet there was an accident: '. . . a bullock cart lurched into our projecting spare wheel and the poor bullock was thrown off his feet. The chief said, "Drive on, drive on" it is no matter!"' [We booed]. 'But I said, "I won't drive on. I must help the bullock up!"' [We cheered]. 'So we all went and assisted the poor beast who was so overloaded that the weight of the yoke kept him flat . . . Then we went to the bottom of the Matanga P. Hill and I hopped up the precipitous path like a young goat, followed by Hyacinth and Georgina and the Supt. 100 yards behind. The Chief – a huge overweight man – got about a quarter of the way up and refused to come any further so his Supt. had to come to the top to make the report. It really was a PANTOMIME. Of course the thief has placed all my equipment (over £400 worth) with some agent in Bombay by now but I had to go through the police ordeal to satisfy the insurers. Back Dec 17th. Love Gr. Elope.'

She returned in time for Christmas that year, bearing, as always, strange things brought from India. One year we were given papier mâché animals – a monkey, a tiger and an elephant – with detached nodding heads – and another year she brought printed smocks from Gujarat.

There was a period when she wanted to bring us three girls a Rajhastani skirt each, embroidered with mirrors and stones, but because of their weight, she could only ever bring one at a time. So we each had to wait until it was our turn for a skirt, hoping that the colour would be nice, and as it was such a big present it had to do for your birthday and Christmas combined. She brought braided Kulu caps for the boys and scarves and shawls for the grown-ups, and on Christmas Eve she would wear her one evening outfit – an Indian silk skirt (in a purply-green swirly pattern) and short-sleeved collarless shirt (green silk).

She was not always home for Christmas though, and once,

albeit by mistake, she spent Christmas at Vijayanagar. She had been touring in her Morris van with the artist John Nankivell, and the pair of them had planned to spend Christmas in Mysore where there is a Catholic cathedral, which was completed in the early thirties and designed by a Belgian bishop who claimed inspiration from Cologne, Notre Dame and St Patrick's, New York. My grandmother deemed the result successful and was looking forward to as many Masses as the cathedral might offer over the festive season.

The unlikely couple (who were best of friends) were staying in a small temple converted into a rest-house by a former British Collector in Kamlapura on the outskirts of Vijayanagar, and planned to drive on south to Mysore on 23 December when disaster struck and their jaunty yellow Morris J4 van developed serious engine trouble. With the aid of Sebastian, secretary to the Fatima Convent High School in Hospet, Penelope placed the van in the competent hands of the Sree Venkateswara garage, and though the competent garage mechanic cured the van of all ills by Christmas Eve, it became clear to the travellers that they would never make Mysore for Mass.

Fate, my grandmother decided, led her towards Father Joachim OFM, whom she met while the van was in for repair. The friendly Father was actually a native of Hampstead, but was stationed at the time in a small Harijan rural Catholic community near Maski. He had come to Hospet for a fortnight to take over the duties of the Keralan parish priest, who had returned to his home town of Ernakulam to celebrate the silver jubilee of his priesthood.

A series of 'lovely theological gossips' later took place between my grandmother and Father Joachim on the veranda of the priest's bungalow, and through the Father my grandmother met the Standens, an Anglo-Indian Catholic family living in Kamalapura. Taking in the predicament, Mr Standen, manager of the local cinema, kindly invited Penelope and Nankivell to lunch on Christmas Day.

'We had no presents to give to our hosts and all the shops in Hospet were shut on Christmas Eve owing to border dispute riots,' wrote my grandmother in her diary. 'So I decided to make them some fudge out of a tin of condensed milk, ghi (clarified butter) and jaggery (unrefined raw sugar). But as I had no scales I got the weights wrong and it never set properly in spite of putting it on the roof of the van in the cool of the evening.'

Exhausted from beating the fudge mixture, Penelope drove into Hospet that evening for Mass, and on arriving at the church at 10.30 p.m., found the compound crowded with families who had come in from the rural areas and who were camping there for the night. The place was hung with fairy lights and every single woman was wearing a new sari – new Christmas clothes being a feature of the festivities in south India, and one man even proudly told her that his wife's sari had cost him all of twenty-five rupees.

Four or five hundred people crowded into the church at midnight and a volley of fireworks was set off in the compound which terrified my grandmother as she thought rioters had come to sack the church. 'The Mass was all in Kannada, the principal language of Mysore state,' she wrote, 'and I'm told the Father preached a very good sermon.'

At intervals, apparently, a group of nuns sang carols in a mixture of Kannada and Latin, though they ended with 'Silent Night' in English, and when the worshippers went up to receive Communion, they had to step over the bodies of hundreds of children who were fast asleep all the way up the aisle.

On Christmas morning I gave John a tin of chocolates, allowed him to eat two, then took the tin back and wrapped it up again for the Standens which we later gave them together with the unset fudge and a copy of the Jesus Psalter,' she wrote. 'We ate mountains of Buffalo pilau with separate dishes of curried vegetables, followed by delicious slabs of home-made jelly cake, a real feast day meal and much more digestible than turkey and plum pudding.

Towards 4 p.m., John and Penelope motored towards Hampi (the tiny village at the centre of the Vijayanagar ruins) where John drew a 'small and perfectly preserved temple' and Penelope dozed – only to be awoken by a powerful amplifier blaring out Indian film music from the village below. They were both amused when the film music then gave way to a four-part choir singing 'Hark, the Herald Angels sing', followed by further old favourites. She wrote:

> Later I wandered among the ruins enjoying the glorious sunset. And I was lured to a temple by the sound of drumming. It came from the pillared hall attached to the shrine of Virabhadra where two teen-age boys were beating two huge drums for all they were worth. This was the evening *puja* when any devotees who care to take part are given *darshan* (a glimpse, or vision) of the God.
>
> A curtain was accordingly drawn aside to revel a tall black standing figure, 12 feet high, of Virabhadra (a form of Shiva) with silver eyes and a silver mouth. The young priest – a lingayat priest wearing a miniature lingum (phallic symbol) – performed the Arati ceremony by waving a brass lamp with a naked flame round and round in front of the image, after which he came forward and distributed blessed water and pieces of coconut to six young men – immaculately dressed in western style – who received these sacraments with the same expression of deep devotion as I had seen on the faces of the Indians returning from the altar at midnight mass. Indisputably God gives grace in a variety of ways to those who sincerely seek him.

My grandmother slept that night on the floor of her secret pillared hall, guarded by the horses prancing in stone:

> As I lay down a large white owl flew out into the night and the bats squeaked a good bit and the crickets sang unceasingly. On the Feast of St Stephen I woke up at dawn to the sound of the black-faced langur monkeys chattering amongst the nearby

granite boulders. Soon after sunrise a fat mongoose with a bushy tail – twice the length of a fox's brush – walked unconcernedly by. Whom should he fear? For he is not only the slayer of serpents but the proud vehicle of the Goddess Uma, who rides him about the celestial places. There was a large light brown one on a pillar close by me; a miniature dragon with a jagged back. He was motionless in deep early morning meditation and appeared, from the seraphic expression on his little face, to be filled with all the completion that God has to give.

CHAPTER XIV

Udupi

'Hindus and Muslims were equally mad about God and their madness was infectious.'

AT NEW YEAR my grandmother was sometimes to be found in the buffalo land of South Kanara. 'Buffles', as she called the buffaloes, were used to till the paddy-fields all over India, but only in South Kanara did you come across buffalo racing, or 'Kambala'.

The district of South Kanara forms a narrow strip of tropical land on the West Coast, wedged in by Goa to the north and Kerala to the south. It is part of Karnataka state. My grandmother thought it one of the loveliest (and it was one of the least visited) districts of India, with hills of red laterite rolling down to the Arabian sea, groves of cashew nut trees, charming little towns with a pleasing vernacular architecture, innumerable temples, churches every few miles, and the misty blue mountains of the Western Ghats as a continuous backdrop along its eastern border.

In the valleys between the red hills there is wetland where three crops of rice can be grown in a year 'as long as the three-hundred-odd devils of Tulu Nadu [the old name for Kanara] are regularly propitiated and the buffalo bulls are raced in the mud to ensure the fertility of the fields.' She wrote 'An Introduction to South Kanara' which she copied and handed out to friends, saying:

It is best visited between late October and early March. But JANUARY is the most agreeable month of all not only because its climate is at its coolest then, but because of the EXCITING NIGHT LIFE: nearly every night in some village or other there is a temple car procession with fireworks, bands, elephants etc and frequent devil dances occur, ie. the BHUTANACH, when a man dresses up and wears elaborate head dresses, dances, gets possessed by the Bhuta, and answers questions in a trance. These dances go on all night, as do the performances of YAKSHA GHANA, the Kanarese version of Katha Kali – dance drama.

We had gone to South Kanara together supposedly to look at the Jain temples prevalent there, but within moments of our arrival in the district we had been bound up in a temple procession. After nine hours on a bus from Goa, we had reached the pilgrimage centre of Udupi, on the coastal side of South Kanara, to find preparations for the procession just beginning.

An elephant, standing calmly amid the fuss, was being dressed up in purple and red, and the silver temple car (twice as high as the elephant and just as heavy) was being polished up by earnest-looking boys with rags in their busy hands. When it was dark, the gleaming temple car was lit by a series of neon bars strapped all around it and electrified by a loud and shuddering generator.

When the elephant led the procession proudly forward, one hundred pilgrims lifted the ropes to pull the temple car (after the image of Lord Krishna had been carefully seated in his throne) while four boys followed panting with exertion as they pushed the mobile generator (attached by an extended flex) along behind it. Then came the *nageshwarans* and the musicians playing drums and pipes, and fireworks lit the route.

The whole town turned out to cheer the procession on, disrupting their evenings at home, leaving their jobs, their meals, their radio programmes. Each window in every building round the square framed at least three bobbing heads, and swagged ropes of frangipani flowers hung from the eaves of every roof. The religious fervour was of a volume one would expect perhaps once annually on the most important feast day, yet there was just such a procession in Udupi almost every night of the year.

Local Brahmins paid for the processions, and there were enough conscience-stricken Brahmins in the vicinity to pay for nearly three hundred and sixty-five processions annually. They donated sums of money to the Krishna temple, and processions were arranged according to their individual generosity. For example, a procession with the wooden temple car commands only 3,500 rupees, whereas the silver car and all the trimmings (elephant, band and players) adds up to the princely sum of 5,000 rupees, and since each donor is keen to propitiate the gods more lavishly than the last, the processions nearly always include the silver temple car (with its implications of generosity) and the firework displays become longer and the band becomes larger as the season wears on.

We had stayed in the Sri Pejavar *mutt*, where many thousands of big black ants and shiny-backed black beetles wandered in and out of our beds and rucksacks at random and our lavatory was a hole in the corner of the tile-floored, windowless room.

The *mutts* in Udupi were the normal stamping-ground of pilgrims who paid ten rupees a night and often remain ensconced for extended periods while they offered their prayers to Lord Krishna. We and the resident pilgrims were looked after by a laconic team of 'sweepers' who swept ineffectually about the place with brushwood brooms and gossiped. There were eight original *mutts* around the square housing worshippers, each one headed by an elected *swamiyar*, who was exchanged for another every two years. The most important *swamiyar* was the head of the Sri Krishna *mutt* (the most important *mutt*) who was known as the Swamiji.

Each *mutt* was connected to its own temple, and the Sri Krishna complex was the most holy and most important temple complex of all. The Udupi 'official information and guide book for pilgrims', translated into English and currently in its sixth edition, was on sale outside the *mutt* for Rs. 3.50.

The book explained: 'Udupi is famous for its Sri Krishna *mutt* which though small is quite beautiful. There is no front door for this temple. Instead there is a window through which one could always get a *darshana* of the idol from outside the *mutt*.' As well as housing the idol, the temple complex provided bed and board for five hundred Brahmin students and over forty temple cows (who used to wander freely – like those insects – in and out of the rooms and chambers and kitchens, but who are now cordoned off into one particular section and only allowed free for an hour in the evening). To the right of the entrance passage there was a hundred-foot-square 'tank' where the Brahmins and the cows and the students (and visitors if they like) could bathe and wash and purify themselves.

Rarely in the day was it possible to find a quiet moment in the Krishna *mutt*, for every hour seemed to be the appointed hour for a certain temple rite which was performed ceremoniously with attendant bell-ringing and incense-burning and idol-worshipping. In the Udupi pilgrim's guide, there were twelve pages devoted to describing the 'Daily Puja System of Udupi Sri Krishna':

> The day's activity commences exactly at 4 a.m. with the blowing of the conch and the beating of the '*Nagari*' in the *gopuram* outside the *mutt* premises.
>
> With this the *swamiyars* and other employees of the *mutt* wake up, attend to their ablutions and take their bath. With the ringing of the bells outside, they open the door of the *garbhagriha*. Then they open the door of the inner room to the beating of *Jaghante*. The assistants get things ready for the early morning *puja* and take the Utsava Murthi to the Madhwasarovara and give it a bath by pouring water over it. Cooks start on the preparation of Rice, Payasam and Dosais for Naivdya. Other assistants start on the grinding of sandal paste for the *puja*. (The Mysore Government sends a little more than 4 tons of sandal wood every year for this purpose.)

Following this ritual reveille, there were eighteen *pujas* to carry out, ending with the Paryayam swami honouring the other swamis present with sandalwood oil, sandal paste and flowers, 'and thus completes the day's work. The blowing of the conch indicates that all the daily rituals have been completed.'

Next in the book came a comprehensive explanation of the

twenty-one annual festivals held at Udupi, and it was on page fifty-three that I found the paragraph I needed. For when I arrived alone in Udupi in the early days of November, I alighted from the bus into the flower-bedecked streets which denote *Deepawali* (pronounced diwali), one of the largest festivals in the Hindu calendar. Page fifty-three revealed the exact programme of celebratory ritual due to take place in the Sri Krishna temple.

Udupi looked as you might have imagined it would if Hindus celebrated Christmas. Glittering streamers hung from shop to shop, drawing customers in to buy dressily wrapped packages of sweetmeats, and sentimental family tableaux smiled inanely on greetings cards declaring Happy Deepawali! The auto-rickshaw drivers had hung flowered ropes around and across their windscreens, which meant that they were obliged to lean their heads outside their vehicles if they intended to see the road.

There was one main street along which the buses came, and the general stores on either side, selling everything from watering cans and hair spray to deck-chairs and chestnuts, had lined up their wares in symmetric patterns, attending to detail so closely that even the biscuits in jars were layered in alternate colours.

The bliss of shopping in India lies in the right of the customer to buy just one of anything he fancies – and this applies to biscuits and sweets as well as Biros and cigarettes – so it is not embarrassing to ask to 'try' one biscuit before buying twenty, because the one biscuit is for sale (for a quarter of a rupee or less).

Even the chemist in his shop had ordered the alternate rows of Colgate and SR toothpaste into satisfying patterns of green, red, green, red, but best of all were the copperware and steelware shops which spilt over into the way of passing cyclists. Graters and ladles and pots (some small to keep your garlic in and others, like cauldrons, large enough to hold broth for forty) gleamed from their hooks all wrapped in gold and silver tinsel, and buckets lined the roadside like short tubby soldiers.

More lavish than anywhere else were the decorations adorning the *mutts*. You walked from the main street down GPO road to the

Car Street square, lured by the heady scent of jasmine, flower after tiny flower of which had been carefully twined with cotton into streamers, necklaces, anklets, neckstraps for horses, headbands, and hair ties worn by every man, woman, child and pony mingling in the square. A greasy-skinned grandmother in a dirty white cotton sari sat on the street corner buried in white jasmine and orange frangipani, her head bent over her hardened hands which bound yet more flower heads together. It was her son perhaps who broadcast her work and invited worshippers to adorn themselves at 5 rupees a time.

Udupi was alive with excitement as I had been led to expect, and as the day wore on and darkness descended, the children began to light their firecrackers which go rat-a-tat-tat like machine-guns, and leave behind them no sparks, but a smoky smell of gunpowder. It was like November the Fifth and Guy Fawkes and England and bonfires, and it seemed as though Deepawali (being as it was at the beginning of November too) must have had something to do with the Houses of Parliament as well.

But Deepawali had deep-rooted origins in Hindu tradition, not seventeenth-century British treachery. For while Deepawali too celebrated good over evil, this ancient 'Festival of Lights' was particularly bound up with the memory of the death of Naraka Asura ('asura' denoting a demon) at the hands of Lord Krishna. For the business community, Deepawali marked the beginning of the financial year. Businessmen settled old transactions, kept the record books and bill books on a pedestal, performed *puja* and opened new account books. They assigned particularly fervent worship to the deities Lakshmi and Saraswathi (Lakshmi for wealth, and Saraswathi for the cash register).

The rural communities made their own *puja* to the Pandava brothers (heroes of the epic *Mahabharata*) by moulding images of them in cow dung and decorating these with flowers. At Deepawali, farmers began again to store their yearly quota of dried cow dung cakes, and always at that time in the south, crops like jowar were ripening in the fields and the grass everywhere was green, the plantain trees, jackfruit trees and tamarind trees were in full blossom, so Deepawali brings with it a feeling of fecundity and plenty.

Traditionally, a game of *pagade* (dice) was played during the festival period. Wily storekeepers played on their front steps on upturned packing cases, and the children pretended to play the same game in the street with pebbles, reiterating a ritual derived from the *Mahabharata*, in which the Pandavas lost their kingdom in a game of dice to the Kauravas.

At the heart of celebrations, though, Deepawali was a time of gifts and donations, of thanksgiving for the past year and of optimism for the coming one. Behind the gaudy front of every shop there was a shrine set up, with candles and flowers and an image of the Goddess Lakshmi of wealth, or sometimes of Ganesh, the elephant-headed and pot-bellied god of success.

These gods were propitiated with serious prayer and offerings of sweets, and on a particular day in the festivities, you could follow a Brahmin, bare but for his white lunghi and his sacred priestly string over one shoulder, as he moved from shop to shop, blessing each one and scattering holy water and murmuring prayers, servicing each business.

For children, fireworks promised the most fun of the festival. The *Indian Express* issued a list of guidelines for junior pyrotechnicians: 'Never wear loose, flowing garments while lighting fireworks,' the newspaper warned. 'Keep a bucket of water handy whilst lighting fireworks. Light rockets pointing them straight upwards. Never light flying fireworks when there is a heavy wind. Show concern for the aged and the sick; never light fireworks next door to them.' And finally, 'Never take unnecessary risks while lighting fireworks just to show off to your friends!'

But the religious side of things amused them too. Instead of having to sit fidgeting in a church pew for an hour, praying not so often for Jesus as for the sermon to end, Hindu children dressed up in new clothes and, in Udupi, visited the Sri Krishna temple.

At Deepawali time, visiting the temple was like wandering into Santa's grotto – an experience of dark passages and twinkling lights and flowers and sweets and secret silver icons in secret alcoves.

When I visited the temple there was a candle ceremony taking place accompanied by a lot of chanting and bell-ringing and mystical swathes of sandalwood smoke. The bullocks had their horns painted and walked freely about with tinsel tied to their tails and flower-clad monkeys sat on the ledges, eating nuts thrown to them by the overexcited children.

There were a lot of families bowing about the place, and kneeling and walking three times round a certain lingum and four times clockwise round a certain holy tree, and it was all so much more interesting and fun than singing old hymns to an altar and listening to some self-righteous vicar telling you on Christmas morning to think less about the presents you will soon open (as if it is ever possible to think about anything else) and more about 'others'.

After 'church', I treated myself at Diane's Café, which, despite its name, was more Indian than any restaurant named more appropriately Ashiana or Poppadum. But a banana split on your own is never half as delicious as a couple of chocolate éclairs with a friend, or (to be more precise) with your grandmother (if she happens to be inclined towards éclairs).

Penelope pronounced éclairs 'ayclairs' with stress on the first syllable, in the same way as she pronounced profile 'profeel', so as to make you realize the word came from the French, as well as to make you comment on her pronunciation either with mild annoyance (if you were her granddaughter) or with admiration (if you were an American).

So I held back on the pistachio ice-cream with tutti-frutti sauce and plumped for a banana milk shake instead, and wallowed not so much in gluttony as in memories of my grandmother's predeliction for sticky buns. On glancing through my old diary, I found a reference to our shared coffee-house treats on every page, the most frequent items on my grandmother's menu including kulfi ice-cream sodas and sugared doughnuts.

My grandmother had so enjoyed Café Life (though she pronounced it 'cuffay') that she once opened her own in an oblong one-storey brick and timbered building which used to be P. B. and D. Martin's Bookshop in the town square in Wantage.

It was while she was living at The Mead that a plan had been hatched to merge the bookshop with a café serving 'home-made specialities, cakes and preserves', and with the aid of a bank loan, the dual-purpose eating house was opened in 1957. A board of directors was formed for the venture consisting of J. Betjeman, P. B. Martin and D. Martin, and 'King Alfred's Kitchen' or KAK as she wrote it in shorthand, was run almost single-handedly (with only occasional help from likely Women's Institute types living in Wantage) by my grandmother for four years.

The advertisement published regularly in the local paper for King Alfred's Kitchen read as follows: 'Down with the sack! LADIES, KEEP YOUR CURVES! on a diet of our DELICIOUS Ice Cream Sundaes – King Alfred's Burnt Special Hot Chocolate Fudge and Walnuts – Mixed Fruit Sunshine Sundaes. Espresso Coffee – lunches – teas – meringues – liver pâté – home-made cakes and jams.'

The aim had been to make money, as well as to provide my grandmother with a daily excuse to deal with fudge-type delicacies (the likes of which she described in letters to my mother who was boarding at St Mary's School in Wantage at the time, 'I have made some really HEAVENLY rum truffles for the café at 8/- per lb,' or, 'It took no time at all to whip up a HUGE amount of butter toffee and coconut ice at 4/- per lb. We can sell as many sweets as we can make.') But KAK had failed to make commercial sense and it eventually closed in 1961 due to lack of interest (lack of hers in the end being just as much a deciding factor as lack of the customers').

Nevertheless, my grandmother had retained her love of all things sweet and it is nigh on impossible now to sit down with a cup of coffee in a 'cuffay' without having a bun in her memory. All the Indians in Diane's Café were indulging themselves with sundaes and splits, and all the children, once smart in their best new frocks, were covered with ice-cream. Outside, as it grew darker, the rounds of firecracker fire rang out ever more frequent, and though you thought the children might have tired of the amusement, the cracker-din never ceased all night.

My candy-pink-walled en suite room in the comfortable concrete Hotel Keyidoor (newly built since my grandmother and I had come to Udupi together and stayed in the bug-ridden *mutt*) faced away from the heart of the explosive centre of town, but still from the balcony I could see the sky lit up pink and then yellow or green from the fireworks.

Udupi attracted all sorts, but rarely did you meet Westerners there bar the Hare Krishna variety. Shaven and clad in faded orange robes, former accountants and art students and school-teachers wandered weakly about the town in much the same way as they did in Oxford Street in London, muttering Hare, Hare, Hare (hail) Krishna, and begging for alms.

I asked a noticeably morose-looking blond whether he was happy in Udupi, and I had to assume that he was too stoned to notice the thousands of beaming Hindus around him when he answered: 'There is no room for happiness on the eternal path to salvation.'

My grandmother met and befriended two similar aimless souls on her way to Udupi once and recounted the tale in a letter to Alfred Wuerfel:

At the bus stand I had to wait two hours so I ate 2 masala dosas and drank several glasses of good south Indian coffee. There were several hippies around and the ones I chose to sit beside turned out to be Deutsch! Susannah spoke a little English, but

Rein had practically none so for the next two days I spoke a mixture of German and English. They said they were going to Mangalore and on to Kerala but I said Mangalore was an uninteresting large European town and that S. Kanara was much nicer than Kerala and they MUST stay with me at Udupi and see the Krishna temple with 200 cows and calves.

She continued:

5 kils outside Coondapur the BUS BROKE DOWN (clutch trouble) and we all sat in the road in the moonlight with the Arabian Sea to the west and waited for $1\frac{1}{2}$ hours when another bus picked us up, meanwhile I got into conversation with some very dirty English hips who offered me a smoke of their large charas-filled communal cigarette which I declined with thanks; they could not believe I had spent so much of my life in India and never tried their excellent selection of drugs! Then we had a conversation on religion and drug-produced religious experience versus prayer produced ditto, a young Indian listened attentively and turned out to be a Goanese R.C.

Well we got to Udupi at about 9.30 pm and the German couple and I crammed into a scooter rickshaw and got a triple room in the APSARAS Hotel for Rs. 20! We all slept very soundly after that $15\frac{1}{2}$ hour bus journey I can tell you! But I woke up at 5.30 am and went off to morning puja at the Krishna temple. There is 0 much re sculpture there bar lovely repousse silver on some of the doors and grills (latter a great feature of Kanara architecture) and some fascinatingly repulsive life-size oil paintings of the Krishna stories: BUT it is such a live temple that I love it: 0 like such a vast complex as the gt. temples of Tamil Nadu but more compact and they don't mind where you go bar the Garbha Giha itself . . .

She waxed lyrical for several paragraphs about the temple inhabitants, bovine and human, and then continued:

Well after puja and a delicious breakfast of puris, curds and coffee I returned to the Apsaras and fetched my young German friends and took them round the temple and they were interested but completely ignorant. I hardly knew where to begin; THEY HAD NEVER HEARD OF GANESH, let alone Nandi or Garud or ANY of the devas and devis. I showed them a lingum and said it was the phallic emblem of Shiva and Rein said 'Was ist das?' after some attempt at explanation, Susannah cottoned on to it and said 'Es ist der phallus,' but R. still said 'Der phallus? aber was ist das?' So I had to give up.

They have both been two months in India, 6 wks of this being spent on the dreadfully depressing hippie beaches N & S of Panjim, the HIPPIE MECCA. I visited two of them when I was going round in my van in 1973 and there were crowds of dirty hippies of several nationalities, some in the last stages of drug addiction, some walking about stark naked and all of them doing 0. They rent rooms for 10–15 rupees a week where they do their macro-biotic cooking and otherwise have to KILL BOREDOM by taking trips with a variety of drugs. I could not believe that anyone could spend two months in India and never come across Ganesh! Anyway I HOPE I have started S & R off on the right path and they became so interested that they planned to stay an extra two nights at Udupi. . . .

My second and third nights in Udupi were tormented by uninter-rupted fire-cracker din, so on the fourth day I forsook the festivities and made for the open country where the buffaloes roamed.

'*Kambala?*' I asked the bus conductor.

'Mmm, yes *kambala* we have,' he replied.

'Where?' I asked.

'Not here,' he said.

'Then where?' he said.

'Not now,' he answered.

'Then when?' I persisted.

'After,' he said, nodding energetically.

'After what?' I dared to ask.

'Before the rains,' he replied, smiling now.

'Never mind.' I gave in. 'Ticket for Karkala please.'

As he sorted my change from the ten-rupee note I had given him, and then handed me the pink ticket, he looked up, grinned at three long-armed youths who had turned in their seats to witness our enigmatic exchange and said, with perfect enunciation:

> If you are purposefully wishing to attend our speciality South Kanaran races between the noble sons of the buffalo-demon Mahisha, you must be re-entering our district in the month that is in English January my name is Sunil de Sousa from Mangalore where I am attending Catholic Christian churches always on Sunday.

I then moved up along my seat to make room for Mr de Sousa from Mangalore and he offered me a *bidi* from his packet before divulging further wisdom concerning the 'kambala'.

The Indian village cow gives perhaps a cream-jug full of milk a day, yet she is sacred and may never be killed. The water-buffalo gives up to three gallons a day, but this beast is regarded as evil in Hindu mythology and may be slaughtered legitimately. In temples up and down the states of India from the Himalayas to Cape Comrin, Mahisha the buffalo-demon can be seen carved in wood and stone in mortal combat with Durga, the St Michael figure of Indian mythology who triumphs over the devil.

The finest living specimens of Mahisha's progeny are found in South Kanara, and the strongest bull buffaloes there are raced in the *kambala*. So called after Kamblasura, the brother of Mahish-asura (asura meaning demon), the races are patronized by the Bunts, the people who make up the chief farming community of Tulu-Nadu.

These agriculturalists speak Tulu and live in houses of considerable size on their estates, which are usually built round a courtyard with a stone pot in the middle containing the sacred

Tulasi plant (balsam). The verandas of these houses are often supported by pillars of wild jackwood, and the jambs and lintels of the doors are often richly carved.

The manor houses are set in emerald green valleys with groves of coconut, banana and areca nut palms between the rice cultivations, and when you arrive at 'the races', you must sometimes walk through the groves for a mile or two before reaching the *gadde* or racecourse. This consists of a narrow flooded paddy-field about 170 yards long with a steep bank at one end to slow down the beasts at the finish of a race.

When my grandmother first announced her intention of attending a *kambala* at a town called Parari in South Kanara, she was told that women never went buffalo racing. She wrote in a letter to me:

> I insisted, however, and ended up being so well received that I was asked to make a speech (which was translated into Tulu sentence by sentence) and to give away the rosettes and certificates when the races were over!

By the time I had arrived at a *kambala* in South Kanara with my grandmother, she had become a local celebrity and a regular prize-giver at various race meetings across the state – it was not much different from presenting the rosettes at the local Pony Club gymkhana, she said – and we were ushered through the deep mud into prize seats at the top of the makeshift grandstand.

Penelope had been wearing one of her Marks & Sparks useful cotton frocks (blue-and-white-striped sleeveless) and was sitting quietly conversing in pidgin Tulu to a group of local notables, when suddenly, on impulse it seemed, she almost fell down from the wooden stand, hastily clipped her camera onto its strap around her waist, hoicked the skirt almost up to her neck, and waded across the 'racetrack' (literally a flooded paddy-field at least two and a half feet in water) with her ancient woollen bloomers bared for all the Bunts to see.

Her shameless flight across the water was all in aid of a more spectacular angle for a photograph, she later explained to the officiating Bunt, expecting to be dismissed from her prize-giving duties. But the genial Bunt was quite used to seeing his grandmother and his wife and all his aunts with their saris up about their hips as they bent over the paddy at harvest time, and he made it clear that her exhibition in front of the whole crowd in the stand could have only raised her credibility with the local farming community.

If her enthusiasm for the *kambala* extended so far as to take her wading into the murky mud-filled water, then, he felt, by her bravery and dash she had only increased her eligibility for the bestowing of the rosettes. So she went back and sat down in her place again and said she would be sure to send the Bunt and his friends several copies of the particular photograph she had tried so publicly to take.

Only pairs of buffalo bulls are used for the *kambala* and they are not bred for it so success depends entirely on selection and training. The beasts are not ridden in the races, but driven by athletic-looking men who either run behind them or are pulled on a small plank. In the old days, the sons and nephews of farmers did the driving, but now, with the land ceiling (of fifty acres per person) cutting down the acreage on each farm, such boys have mostly gone to work away from home and professionals are hired, who travel to each meeting with one particular 'stable', like racehorse jockeys.

My grandmother described the technical side of *kambala* in an article she wrote:

There are four types of races, the most spectacular for the uninitiated being the 'kane halige'. This is not really a race, but a competition to see who can make the highest and widest splash, and the teams run one at a time. All over India a levelling plank, drawn by a pair of beasts, is used in agriculture in place of a roller, and in the 'kane halige' this is cut down from the customary five feet to about fifteen inches in length. An extra piece of wood is fixed to the centre and hollowed out to receive the driver's left foot. The right foot rests on a pole which joins the 'chariot' to the yoke. The driver holds the near-side buffalo's tail in his left hand and his stick in his right. On either side of the little plank, holes are drilled to let the muddy water through and when the charioteer presses on the pole with his right foot an extra high spray springs up.

It impressed the horsewoman in my grandmother to watch the 'charioteers' driving their beasts without reins. 'He guides his team entirely by voice and stick,' she wrote, 'and the art of training lies in teaching the bulls to run in a straight line.' They are not always as well trained as they might be: 'Sometimes a pair runs off the course into the surrounding fields and scatters the spectators and for this reason photographing the *kambala* is an exciting affair.' At one meeting she had removed her sandals and stood for the duration in water up to her knees right next to the course. 'On two occasions,' she wrote, 'I had to leap nimbly to one side with my camera to let rebel pairs – whose drivers had fallen flat on their faces – dash by me and charge the crowd . . .'

But most thrilling was the start. Besides the driver standing ready with his team there are four attendants – two at the rear to stop the buffaloes from swinging out their quarters and two at the heads to hold the bridles until the starter's red flag goes down. Sometimes all four attendants have quite a job to stop the animals lying down and wallowing in the water, which it is their nature to do. Sometimes the animals get out of control and floor all the men before the off, but if they are lucky and still have hold of the demon beasts then there is the thrill of watching the footwork of the men at the head. For at the 'They're off!' moment they have to step aside to a set pattern like a matador which is not easy in more than a foot of water.

For our *kambala* at Karkala the buffaloes were grandly decked in ribbons with plumes between their horns, and three 'charioteers' were sent flying through the air before us which meant that six wild buffaloes careered dangerously off the track and towards the crowd before the day was out. With my grandmother's celebrity enhanced by her 'bloomerdash', we were photographed more than six times standing proud with various officials about the course, and all the spectators roared with approval as Penelope handed the winning rosettes to an eager line-up of wet athletes, their rippling muscles glistening wth coconut oil and their smiles broad across their faces.

That night, back in our bug-ridden *mutt* in Udupi, my grandmother wrote a five-page eulogy of the *kambala* of South Kanara in a letter to Alfred Wuerfel, with whom we had stayed earlier in Delhi. On the last page she added:

P.S. I forgot to say that what brings me to South Kanara is the remarkable similarity of its architecture to that of Nepal and the Western Himalaya. It was that great man James Fergusson who brought my attention to it with an engraving of the Jain tombs at Moodbidri which I came to see last year . . .

CHAPTER XV

Pineapples and Protestants

'A fundamental discovery which every Englishman must make is that God made people differently.'

On a walk in the vicinity of Moodbidri, the Kashi of the Jains, I went into a farmyard as I wanted to photograph the thatched buildings. The two brothers who owned it were delighted and posed in front of their buffalo shed. Then one of them shinned up a tall coconut tree and I thought to myself: 'How kind! He knows what a nice photograph he will make,' and accordingly I clicked away. But it was not that at all. It was simply the traditional form of hospitality to the stranger within your gates: I was invited to sit down on the wooden bench on the veranda of the very nice red laterite farmhouse, the top of the coconut was lopped off and the bulk of the fruit handed to me to drink. As I am very unskilled without the help of a straw I poured lots of it down my front whereupon a metal mug was produced. The shell was then opened up and I was given the delicious slippery flesh to eat. I cannot speak a word of Tulu so all I could say was 'Daniawad! bahut daniawd!' hoping that my hosts would have learnt that much Hindi from All India Radio. I walked out of the yard so deeply touched that tears welled up in my eyes and I thought: 'This is international friendship! This is the sort of act which will stop war and make the whole world one.'

SUCH A WARM reception as my grandmother was given by the Tulu coconut farmers is common in India, and, familiar as she was to the spontaneous generosity of the Indian nature, she was delighted to accept an invitation to take pineapple juice and cake with the intriguingly named Dr Livingstone Soans, just twenty minutes after meeting him at a South Kanaran roadside *kambala* in 1973. She might never have guessed that afternoon tea and pineapple would lead to a fifteen-year association rich with shared interests and trust and affection that truly lived up to the title of international friendship.

At the *kambala* she was putting questions in Kannada (the Karnatakan state language) to the local villagers, but no one understood a word of what she was saying. In stepped Dr Soans, fluent in English, to rescue the floundering English lady. He interpreted for her and issued the invitation to tea. It was when they were sitting on his veranda at his farmhouse north of Moodbidri that they discovered their mutual interest in botany, and religion.

For Livy's family were Protestant converts, and one convert is always fascinated by another. My grandmother learnt that her host's grandfather was converted from Hinduism by German missionaries in the 1890s, and that the farm where she was taking tea had been purchased by the Basel Mission (a Swiss-German missionary society with headquarters in Basel, Switzerland) in 1910. The Basel Missionaries came to Mangalore from their homeland in 1834 and founded one of the best printing presses in India and started the great tile industry which flourishes now up and down the coastal strip.

The Basel Mission Farm originally consisted of forty-six acres of dry land used only for grazing, and to the farmers then it was unthinkable to imagine the land could ever support a crop like pineapples. But Livingstone's father – whom my grandmother described as 'an Evangelical God-soaked saint venerated all over Kanara as an apostle of anti-waste' – said that if Indians were not so wasteful and destructive they could support themselves. Every monsoon 600 million tons of top soil are washed into the Arabian sea and the Indian Ocean because of bad farming, especially cutting down trees. Mr Soans was brought in as manager of the Basel Mission Farm in 1928. Being a progressive and adventurous agriculturist, he took a gamble (and a loan of Rs 36,000 which he later repaid) and obtained fifty pineapple suckers of the Kew variety from a Mr Barton Wright, Port Officer of Cochin, in Kerala.

Against all odds, thirty-five of the original fifty survived and from this small lot he produced several million suckers and bought adjoining lands to extend the farm to 109 acres. He ended up buying the whole farm, and Livy and his brother Irwin now run the farm themselves, producing 10,000 pineapples per acre per year which are renowned nationwide for their quality and juiciness. They built their own canning factory and a fibre factory for making mats out of the leaves so as not to waste a single by-product of the succulent fruits.

I had been heading towards Basel Mission Farm on the Karakala bus when my Mangalore friend Mr de Sousa divulged all his knowledge of Kanaran *kambala*. But he regretted that the bus could not take me on to my destination and that it would be necessary for me to seek alternative transport to continue my journey on from Karkala. Karkala was a bustling south Indian market town halfway (that is about fifteen miles from each) between Udupi and Moodbidri. I reckoned on the Basel Mission Farm being well enough known in the area for me simply to ask a rickshaw driver to take me there.

The driver of the first rickshaw I happened upon at the bus station nodded knowingly at my request and took me out into the rural wilderness to an ashram. When I said no, this isn't it, he took me to a petrol station, and again I said no, this isn't it, and then he took me back to Karakala bus station and shrugged his shoulders. He demanded fifteen rupees for the ride and then motored off down the market place.

A taxi driver offered his services next and arrived at the same petrol station, a quarter of an hour later. The taxi driver filled the taxi with petrol and asked me for the money and then asked the pump attendant for directions, whereupon the pump attendant alighted into the front seat of the white Morris Ambassador, asked me for a cigarette (which he smoked without fear while the taxi was still parked on the garage forecourt) and started up a friendly conversation with the taxi driver which did not appear to be about pineapples at all. I gave in, lit a cigarette and leant back on the worn brown leather of the back seat, closed my eyes and prayed in private to St Anthony, for illumination of the whereabouts of the pineapple farm.

Two further Morris Ambassadors drew up at the petrol station bearing two persons each who joined our now somewhat muddled discussion (with my hopeless Kannada not helping much) which now centred on a tourist map of South Kanara that I had pulled from the depths of my rucksack.

Every Indian taxi driver wants to prove to his fellow taxi drivers (as well as to his often bemused passengers) that he knows exactly where he is going. He just doesn't need to go yet, he will imply, give me a minute, he will say, while he racks his brains for a route.

It took the wife of the petrol attendant to break up the party, complaining (as far as I could gather from her menacing tone) that we were blocking the forecourt and discouraging passing custom and that if we did not beat it swiftly, she would a) call the police and b) start denting the gathered cars with the wooden stake she held in her raised right arm. Her husband, the pump attendant, slipped sheepishly from our taxi and asked her, as a last resort, whether she knew about this pineapple farm.

With a dismissive glare at the rest of us she dropped the stake, raised both her hands in despair and said words to the effect of (as far as I could gather from her dismissive tone) you silly bunch of fools, is that what all the fuss is about, and proceeded to give a speeded-up run-down of directions to the farm which were received gratefully by the shamefaced driver of my taxi. He dropped me off at Basel Mission Farm ten minutes afterwards.

There was a big, obvious board with a pineapple painted on it, like a pub sign, which stood out on the verge along the road to Moodbidri. You turned in through white gates up a straight metalled drive bordered by lush palms and bougainvillaea bushes which leads up to the wide bungalow in which the Soans family lived.

Benita, Livy's wife, was standing on the steps as our car drew up, but she was shy and spoke little English and when I jumped out she lowered her head and gestured right along the veranda to where I could see Livy on the telephone. He grinned jovially at me over the mouthpiece, wound up the conversation in speedy Kannada, placed the receiver back on its black cradle and said, in perfect English, 'But we were expecting you yesterday!'

Sustenance in the form of pineapple juice buoyed me up sufficiently to respond to Livy's chirpy requests for news of the family, as he reintroduced me to his brood. For I had come to the pineapple farm with my grandmother in 1985, long after it had become a regular stopping point on her many south Indian tours, and I had already met Vinodh, the eldest, now faintly mustachioed and studious, Sunil, the second, also quiet and studious, Sonia, pretty and occasionally vivacious, who was taking commerce exams in Mangalore in the week of my visit – so disappeared to revise all the time – and Sahana, who had grown from a chubby, mischievous imp of a six-year-old into a leggy teenager who was accomplished at the piano.

Livy and Benita's two sons and two daughters had welcomed my grandmother as a surrogate aunt. Her visits had become annual landmarks in their childhoods, when she would arrive with chocolates made by Cadbury and books of English nursery rhymes. She stayed at Basel Mission Farm for Christmas one year and sang German hymns for them and crawled about on all fours with the littlest ones on her back, pretending to be a horse, and bucking them off on to the living-room floor.

All the children learned English at their convent school in Moodbidri – (Livy told me with pride: 'Sahana you see, is trilingual. She learns Tulu from our farmworkers and her local .riends, she speaks Kannada at home and she learns her lessons in English') – and so they would practise their latest sentences on Penelope.

The sight of her waving from her bicycle became less of an oddity to local villagers after it became a regular sight every January. My grandmother would cycle all round the district along the flat lanes, visiting temples. 'Here [in South Kanara] there is beautiful walking country with red laterite lanes leading into the interior,' she wrote in a letter to Alfred Wuerfel when she was seventy-one, 'were I a bit younger, I would plan a cycle tour in the district.' She expanded:

> When people are horrified by the congestion and dirt and poverty in India SEND THEM TO KANARA, it is not at all highly populated, there is less traffic than elsewhere, the towns and villages are much cleaner and the houses, proper houses built of red laterite with Mangalorean tiles, not the usual shanty bazaars of North India, but really nice pretty and solid towns and villages, and quite a lot of farmhouses built right out in the country as in Europe. I bicycle out on a huge gent's bike every morning for two hours exercise: I take great delight in exploring the lanes, and this farm is about 5 miles as the crow flies from the base of the Western Ghats, so the scenery is quite beautiful with hills covered with cashew trees, colossal outcrops of granite boulders with sadhus living in caves, emerald green paddy-fields in all the valleys, framed in the tall slender areca nut palm groves and coconut, and always the beautiful blue Ghats as a back cloth, from which Parasuram threw his axe into the sea, about 20 miles! And the sea became dry land and that is North and South Kanara!

When she was tired from bicycling my grandmother would sit with Livy on the veranda, both of them sipping pineapple juice noisily through straws, and discussing botany, or God. Livy learnt his excellent English while studying for a master's degree in botany at the Jesuit College in Mangalore, and then won various grants to study in America, ending up with a doctorate in microbiology from the University of Montana.

When he led me round the farm he was able to show me the herbs and spices he grew – the cinnamon and cloves, the peppercorns, cocoa beans (which grow on a creeper) and allspice, which is not a mixture of spices like mixed herbs, but one fruit of the allspice shrub. He was then experimenting with various Amazonian varieties like the egg fruit tree, and a strange one called the diesel tree, from which some Brazilian tribe extracts oil for healing purposes but which Livy intends to develop as engine fuel.

Notorious for his pineapples, Livy had also achieved public recognition through his dowsing abilities and was called upon regularly to find water on other people's farms. He was very encouraging to dowsers like myself who possess little in the way of even a sense of direction above ground, and he spent a patient morning with me wandering about the farm with a stick between my hands trying to find a spring he already knew about. Even with considerable guidance I missed the source entirely; put the stick in Livy's capable hands and it takes a nose dive for the earth the minute he walks over so much as a trickle of an underground stream.

His other interests included pyramid power (and he has erected his own pyramid for meditation in the palm grove) and natural energy. He has sectioned off an eco-friendly acre of forest in which he has built a house forty feet up a tree. This has grown abnormally high due to its position on an energy spot where ley lines cross. He found the spot by dowsing, of course, and he plucked a V-shaped branch from a tree to show me where the ley lines lay.

He was most excited by my knowledge of the corn circles which reappear each year at Alton Barnes in Wiltshire, and entered fervently into a discussion of their cause. I argued for inter-galatic communication while he plumped (with much more authority and relevant data) for natural energy. Penelope had got him enrolled as a life member of the International Dowsing Society and sent him any dowsing books and articles she came across by surface mail, though her own personal dowsing talents never achieved much more success than mine.

Not only did Livy offer my grandmother his wealth of knowledge of water-divining and plant nurture, but his information on the local Jain temples pleased her even more. Moodbidri contains eighteen Jain temples, including the 'Tribhuvana Tilaka Chudamani' (popularly known as the 'thousand pillared temple', though I've tried to count a thousand and have never got that far) and not far away are the monolithic Gomateshwara statues at Karkala and Venur.

Jainism had held a steady fascination over my grandmother, and she made much use of Moodbidri's Jain Swami's willingness to receive Western visitors and had countless discussions with him. Also at Moodbidri there is a little explored library of palm leaf books for scholars of Jainism to which she often bicycled for extracurricular studies.

Jainism became popular in South Kanara in the twelfth century AD but its origins are buried further south. The religion is contemporaneous with Buddhism and was founded in 500 BC by Mahavira, the twenty-fourth and last of the Jain prophets, known as *tirthankars* our 'finders of the path'.

The three and a half million Jains in India believe that the universe is infinite and was not created by a deity. They also believe in reincarnation and eventual spiritual salvation, or *moksha*, through following the path of the *tirthankars*. The strictly following of such a path requires the practice of *ahimsa* or reverence of all life and avoidance of injury to living things. This belief makes devout Jains strict vegetarians who will even avoid certain root vegetables such as parsnips or turnips which are believed to be living.

Some Jain monks all of the time, and other less devout Jains at festival time, will only eat meals within the daylight hours between dawn and dusk, so as to minimize the possibility of attracting insects to a lamp or candle, thereby luring them to their likely death. Jains wear masks to avoid accidentally swallowing insects and brush the ground before them so as to avoid stepping on one by mistake.

The keenest Jain I ever met was His Holiness Swastishree

Karmayogi Charukeerty Bhattarak Swamiji who lives at Sravana-belgola. 'Sravanabelgola is popular, especially from Jains from all over India,' I read in my locally printed guide booklet as I sat in the bus which sped towards the isolated town which lies in the plain on the way to Mysore from Moodbidri. I had taken Livy's leave for a weekend at the Jain centre and continued reading:

> 'Few places in the country are so replete with romantic memories of devout monarchs and valiant ascetics, pious generals and heroic women. Nowhere else in the world are to be found as many as 573 inscriptions in a single site, all important and interesting. The present celebrity of the place is no doubt due to the magnificent monolith of the early Jaina saint Gommata to be found there. The statue is reputed to be the tallest in the world. Even if the claim is disputed, it is undoubtedly unrivalled in the excellence of its execution. Its artistic merit is obviously supreme . . .

And so it went on.

The guide book also told me that His Holiness Swastishree Karmayogi Charukeerty Bhattarak Swamiji presided over a community of Digambaras Jains. For there are two types of Jains – the Shvetambaras and the Digambaras, the latter being the more austere kind whose name means, literally, 'sky-clad', since as a sign of their contempt for all material possessions they are not supposed to wear clothes. His Holiness Charukeerty Bhattarak was wearing clothes when I met him, however, and had also been modestly clothed in orange robes when my grandmother had met him years before.

He received me in his 'state room' within the monastery enclave, where he sat cross-legged on a throne which rises only about four inches above the floor. He was a well-covered, fleshy man with three or four podgy chins and the kind of smooth skin which comes from abstinence from alcohol and cigarettes, coupled with a nutritious vegetarian diet. He was quite young, only in his early thirties, yet he had been chosen from the community of Jain monks to be the head of them all when he was just nineteen.

He came from an orthodox family who have always been engaged in the temple practice, and he said he felt it was his destiny to become the Swamiji. However, he was already searching for a successor, because he wanted to devote himself to writing. His Holiness saw his task as providing new thought and new direction to the up-and-coming Jain generations, who were ever more easily tempted to desert the path of Jainism. He promoted agriculture and industry and business as worthy professions for the Jain laity, as long as they abided by the Jain practices of non-violence and vegetarianism. If they were non-violent in their thinking too then these three things were enough, he said.

Jains are not interested in propagating their ideas, and His Holiness was pleased to inform anyone interested that the Jains have never taken measures to convert people by military or other means. It is all right to be a soldier, he says, but only in order to protect your country, and not to occupy the territory of others. The fact that there are 25,000 Jains in Leicester, in England where a new temple has been built, is not to do with evangelism, he said, more a spreading realization of the worth of Mahavira's philosophy.

There is a Department of Jainology at Mysore University, and in south India the Jains have earned a reputation for hard work, diligence and success in business. Their austere way of life seems to equip them well for managing their professional and personal lives. Fifty Jain monks at a time at Sravanabelgola are trained to go out and serve the community, spearheaded by the generous Swamiji himself.

He was delighted to receive a foreign visitor in the middle of the afternoon's 'durbar' when local people come to the monastery to discuss their problems, business ones or otherwise. 'Sit,' he said regally as I was escorted through the door by two humble white-clothed servants, who bowed their heads in his presence. 'Happy Diwali and Season's Greetings,' he said in a friendly manner, and offered me fruit from a basket beside his throne. I was not sure whether to sit cross-legged, to kneel or to squat on the orange carpet, so in the end I compromised by half-kneeling and half-sitting in a sort of starting position for a race.

I had enjoyed a short audience with the same Holiness with my grandmother, and I remembered we had talked about Shakespeare, for His Holiness had expressed a strong interest in English literature. So I reminded him of our visit. He looked thoughtful for a moment, and then lifted his head again:

'She was married to the poet, is that it?' Then he slipped back into engrossing thought. 'She lived at Hereford – See! My memory is not all so terrible!'

By coincidence, the Swamiji himself had been to Hereford once. 'I was lucky to be in London on the return journey from a religious conference in Nairobi, you see,' he revealed. 'And I asked my disciples to take me to the villages, whereupon we went in a bus to Hereford.' He liked the River Wye and the red mud of the Black Mountains which was like the red laterite earth at Sravanabelgola, but he didn't think Jainism was likely to catch hold there, because of it being so cold (which would, he thought, make it difficult to discard clothing willingly) and on account of the meat-eating tendencies of the border sheep farmers.

'I was interested to discuss with Western people our custom of *sallekhana*,' he said. On the left-hand hill at Sravanabelgola there are carved out of the rock 200 pairs of footprints in memory of the 200 Jains who commited *sallekhana* there; this is the holy custom of self-purification by way of declining food and drink gradually therefore killing oneself slowly. It is the ultimate act of devotion to Jainism for a Jain.

His Holiness was at the time trying to reconcile the Western world to the idea of *sallekhana* which has been seen by other nations as a form of suicide or at best euthanasia, which should not be encouraged. His Holiness chose me as a missive, to send back to England convinced of the validity of this fatal form of religious devotion. I shifted my kneeling position so that I might transfer the cramp from one leg to the other and was served with lemon tea by a tiny man who walked out of the room backwards, bowing, before His Holiness began on his favourite subject.

'We want to teach the people how to die,' he said. 'In certain circumstances people can die in a religious and non-violent way – by a conscious conversion of the mind. It is practised here and it is accepted by religion. I will certainly commit *sallekhana*,' he finished, and I did not doubt him.

'This way gives a lot of happiness. I know that this body,' and he pointed down at his voluminous orange caftan garment, 'is different from my soul. I want to die with no anger or hatred or fear, but with a clear understanding – a clarity of thought – and therefore I must separate the soul from the body.'

To commit *sallekhana*, you have to accept the concept twelve years before and sign a contract. He does not advise the young and fit to take it upon themselves to do it, but in the Jain community in India, it is accepted by the religious body and the law, for people to do it in three circumstances: when they are terminally ill, when they are aged, or when they have no means otherwise to live, for example, they suffer extreme poverty. He is not sure whether the Mayor of Leicester is happy about the prospect of his 25,000 citizens threatening *sallekhana*, and so he is keen to spread the idea of the worthiness of this ultimate self-purification.

At the same time as conversing quite readily about his proposed method of death, His Holiness was keen to talk about 'This Major fellow', and to discuss the relative merits of *Middlemarch* as a novel. I said that John Mortimer had once said that any potential novelist should read *Middlemarch* before they started writing, for it was the best-constructed role model any novelist could look to, and His Holiness said, 'His Rumpole is an ordinary man if you ask me, but this Titmuss, he is worth thinking over.'

His Holiness liked English politics and yoghurt-covered raisins and carried a soft brush of peacock feathers to sweep the ground before him (although the ground before him was already scrutinized carefully by his disciples anyway). He telephoned me three times at the Jain rest-house where I retired later that night, and had a basket of fresh fruit and nuts brought to my room by one of his junior monks. The keepers of the rest-house were so impressed by my exalted position as telephone co-respondent of the Swamiji's, that they too brought gifts to the bare room, until there were touching posies of flowers and bowls of almonds decorating every high window ledge.

I ate my dinner in one of the town's Jain refectories (known as the Hotel Mahaveer) where thirty or so green-Formica-topped tables support a constantly moving passing trade from six in the morning until ten at night. There is an open kitchen running down one side of the hall, so you can see the swarthy bare-chested cooks in their *lunghis* stirring the curry in the cauldron. For six rupees only, you are served with a *thali* (plate) piled high as you like with rice and marrow curry, bean curry, pea curry and curds and mango chutney. A lone diner is not uncommon, for people come here to eat, not to talk, and when faced with such a steaming delicious mountain of perfectly spiced vegetarian fare it is task enough to eat it with your fingers without having to make conversation at the same time.

An army of thin men in filthy shirts with smiling faces and dirty dishcloths over their right arms (as proudly borne as white napkins by their smooth counterparts in Italian restaurants) replenish your plate with rice as soon as the mountain looks to be receding at all, and weave nimbly through the tables ladling curries from dripping pots. When satisfied you take your 'bill' (a smidgeon of smudgy paper no bigger than a bus ticket) to the fatter, oilier Jain at the cash desk, who sits in his seat unsmiling all day, counting out the money from the customers, and piercing the 'bills' on to a metal spike, set before him for the purpose.

Afterwards I sauntered down Sravanabelgola high street, feeling safe even though it was after dark, for there is a certain security to be felt amongst the Jains. They make you feel entirely welcome and safe and part of their community. One particular stallholder was anxious that I join him and his son for a cup of milky south Indian coffee, so I introduced myself and sat on a blue metal chair

at the blue metal table at the open side of the three-sided, lop-
sided wooden shack. The son, who was shy, and his father sat
down as well, and drank their coffee, and we didn't say anything,
but simply smiled at each other every so often.

A glamorous couple of young Indians entered the shack soon
after, she, willowy and tall in her green chiffon sari edged with
gold, and he proud in a maroon close-fitting shirt and white
trousers. They both wore wedding rings and they told me they had
been married just one month before, and that they both came from
orthodox Jain families with business interests in the silk trade in
Mysore.

They were called Jakakumar and Indira Jaina, and they were
vegetarian and alcohol free and they told me they believed in
the Jain philosophy absolutely and that they were proud of their
hard-working commmunity. Jakakumar, who was twenty-four
and well muscled to the point of looking beefy, worked in the
Sravanabelgola museum and played cricket on the Sravanabelgola
side. He also played football in a local Karnatakan league every
Sunday.

We had a brief discussion on the recent Sharjah series, and
then Indira told me about their honeymoon by the sea south of
Madras on the east coast. She had not swum in the sea, but
Jakakumar had and she had taken some playful photographs of
her new husband frolicking in the surf with the camera which they
had received from her uncle for their wedding present.

Then they put me right on a few Jainisms that I had muddled
myself with: 'No, you see, we are not eating the root vegetables not
because we think they are living, but because they grow underground and they do not receive much light and then there are
more bacteria present in them and in the cooking you are killing
the bacteria and in the eating you are killing more of these
organisms, so it is best that they are avoided.' I quite saw, and I
remarked upon their evident glowing health despite their restricted
diet, and Indira said that she was thinking of writing a Jain
cookbook, to inspire Jain cooks to vary their cooking practices, and

I said that might go down particularly well in Leicester where I imagined 25,000 Jains were probably having a hard time of it trying to stick to their prescribed diet, what with the temptations on offer in England.

The next morning I returned to the pineapple farm of Livy Soans, a man who was always experimenting with various diets.

'Another area of my work these days is experimenting with a raw diet (on myself),' he wrote in a letter to my grandmother. 'It is my realization that in addition to using a lot of energy in producing food on the farm, we again use a considerable amount of energy (fuel) to degrade that food before consuming it. I have found that with a little scientific thought to nutrition, a small amount of food can go a long way in improving health and reducing costs while effecting energy conservation as well . . .'

When I was there, Livy ate his own preparation at the evening meal while the rest of us feasted on fresh fish from the Arabian Sea – fried sardines most often, chick peas, chapattis, mulched brown rice from a steel tureen, piles of chapattis, curd, chutney and, of course, pineapple.

The whole family would gather for dinner, regular as the sun, at 8.35 p.m. every evening, even Benita's mother and father who live in their son-in-law's house. The dining-room was a dark room in the back of the house with net at the windows and piles of magazines and books on the sideboard.

Livy's house was neat and clean and practical – perhaps even puritan. Some might say minimalist, but it is a pragmatic consideration which determines the interior – in the tropical heat of the summer, the fewer cushions and curtains and colours the better. In the heat, you want cool stone floors and empty, airy rooms.

So the dining-room walls were nondescript and pale and the plates and glasses were plain ones. Despite the variety of foodstuffs, the dishes even seemed to take on a uniform tone – a sort of watery, yellowy beige – and in the dark gloom of the poorly lit room, it was difficult to discern between cabbage and cucumber.

Livy and Benita, Vinodh, Sunil, Sonia, Sahana and the grandparents too lowered their heads in unison as near their plates as was possible and noiselessly conveyed mixed, pressed balls of rice and fish and vegetables into their mouths with four fingers and the thumb by the shortest possible route. Eyes were lowered, and sparks of conversation were as scarce as colour in the food.

My attempts at mealtime chat fell on deaf ears or were answered in monosyllables followed by a muffled 'Pass the butter, please.' Livy tried to break the silence once or twice, but his family's lack of support in the endeavour made his one or two jokes or questions seem like lone ships set sail on a vast windless calm sea.

After the first night Livy told me that his family were shy with their English visitor and that it had taken them two years to become accustomed to Penelope. Normally, he said, mealtimes were full of arguments between the children, but after the first night I gave up speaking at dinner and settled in with the family observance of silence, and only when I made individual friends with Benita and each of the children (except for Vinodh who boarded a bus back to his college and whom I did not see again) did I find out that they laughed and got cross and were clever and funny and argued as much as the next family.

Sahana was especially full of beans and since she was at day school just down the road in Moodbidri, I saw her often. After school we bicycled together up and down the red laterite lanes and she giggled when I nearly fell off the gent's bike and then lent me her girl's one. But any giggles were set aside at precisely 8.20 p.m. every evening, when we were summoned to prayers. I longed to have a giggling partner to catch my eye during the Prayer sessions, for the Soans family were so properly serious about it.

We would start by singing a hymn in Kannada which I hummed along to, then either Sahana or Sunil (the best two readers in the family) would read from the Bible and then from the psalter. In my honour the readings were often in English, which Sahana read beautifully, followed by prayers and finally the Lord's Prayer in English. The Soans children had attended a home service like this every night of their conscious lives and after church on Sunday they went all afternoon to Sunday school.

My grandmother had held up Livy and his family as exemplary Christians, and when she was with them she would become suddenly more devout. She had often tried in vain to encourage my mother to say prayers with us each night at our bedsides, but regular evening prayer had not noticeably become a part of our daily lives. So taking her grandchildren to Livy's was like the next best thing and she hoped that the sincere Christianity to be found within the Basel Mission Farm would leave its impression on us.

'Your grandmother fitted into our family ways with the minimum of fuss,' said Livy as I wriggled with uneasy guilt after the third prayer meeting of my visit. 'She was so good at communing with all sorts of people, and she made me, at least, more openminded.' He was grateful to her for widening his vista by introducing him to so many English people – her family and other friends to whom she had given Livy's address if they were passing through Karnataka.

He hoped that she had been impressed with the wholesome Christianity she had found within his children. I said she had, and gaped at Sonia who, after five days of taxing accounting exams, started reading a book called *Who is God?* for relaxation purposes. I thought even my grandmother might have thought that was taking it a bit too far.

On Sunday I attended church with the family, remembering my first time at the Moodbidri Protestant Church, when an angry vicar had almost spat out his guilt-giving sermon for over forty-five minutes in a stream of flowing Kannada and I had got cramp. My grandmother would always bicycle off for Mass early on Sunday morning, and by the time we were perching on the edge of our wooden pews, she would have done with the day's public worship and be sitting back at the farm on the veranda sipping pineapple juice, looking forward to Sunday lunch.

Sahana spent most of the service muttering under her breath and testing herself from her Bible in preparation for the two-hour exam on the scriptures that she was obliged to endure that afternoon. I had tried my hardest to look neat (for my grandmother's sake) and was wearing my only dress, a supposedly crumple-free floral number, which had not lived up to its label and hung not only crumpled but uneven, for the last dhobi-wallah who handled it had somehow tampered with the hem. Still, from the waist up I looked presentable, I suspected, and that part of me was all the vicar could see from his pulpit. Still he thought it necessary to rain down upon us in a torrent of emotive Kannada at sermon-time but I did not understand a word.

So I prayed instead for my two grandmothers and for my grandfather and for various others and for the 50,000 dead from the Uttarkarshi earthquake and their families and for the 5,000 killed by a typhoon in the Philippines the day before, and for the 250 Indians killed when the Karnataka Express from Bhopal to Bangalore was derailed the day before that, after a monsoon-provoked landslide blocked the line only ten hours after the Sikhs and the soldiers and the sick lady and I had travelled along the same route and docked in at Bangalore safely. I thought I owed some thanks for our lucky escape.

I walked back from church with Sonia, feeling rather like one of Jane Austen's Bennet sisters, walking arm in arm after Sunday worship discussing marriage. Benita would be most upset if Sonia did not marry a Christian, but Livy says that if she did meet a non-Christian and both sets of parents approved the union, then he would consent to his daughter's own choice. Sonia professed herself destined for an arranged Christian marriage and said that if two people married and one was a devout Hindu and the other a devout Christian then who would the children worship? She had no one particular in mind but felt that she was of about marriage-able age.

Needing release from the Christian confines of the farmhouse, I walked across the field to Livy's brother Irwin's house, a bright and sunny bungalow on the edge of the Soans estate. The walls are candy pink and bougainvillaea grows up the veranda bannister.

Irwin's wife, Maureen, is as modern a girl in a sari as I have ever met, and their two children Lavi (short for Lavinia) and Nita, who are thirteen and eleven, abound with energy and an unstoppable stream of questions. 'Who's your favourite film star? Madonna?' 'What's your favourite colour?' 'Is your boyfriend good-looking?' 'What lipstick should I wear?' 'Do you think Robert Redford's better looking than Paul Newman?' and more of the same things of proper importance to the growing girl. They had a Labrador-type dog called Bimbo, which barked at me with vicious teeth bared but settled into a lap-dog at a word from Maureen, and the girls grabbed both my hands and dragged me up the stairs into the living-room.

It was clean and bright and full of lovely plastic objects and a huge wall painting of a mountain and a lake. They take pictures of each other in front of it so it looks as if they are in the mountains. There's a goldfish tank and the tall blue fridge takes pride of place in the living-room, next to the colour television. We ate Maureen's 'Chicken 65' for lunch (the girl's favourite dish of fried chicken with barbecue sauce), and afterwards Lavi played 'The Entertainer' on the piano and then we watched a classic John Wayne film with Ava Gardner, called *Hitari!*, on the video, which Lavi and Nita had seen twenty-odd times before, so they knew all the lines and chimed in with Wayne's macho dialogue.

After the film I was introduced to their pet turtles called Jack and Jill, and Lavi asked me about make-up and told me how she was worried about the size of her lips and her dark eyebrows. I told her she looked like Gabriela Sabatini (which she did and she was very pleased about that) and then she told me with my white eyebrows I reminded her of Boris Becker and I was less than happy about that. So we watched some re-runs of Wimbledon on the video to make sure (and she retracted her comparison, thank goodness) and then we flicked through some Bombay film magazines with Lavi and Nita saying which actress they would like to be.

In fact they were more likely to run businesses or teach than to fall into the glamour world, for both girls were bright and eager and full of hopes of going away to university. Maureen encouraged them in their ambitions, and I rather felt that while their cousin Sonia might be married quietly by Aunt Benita's arrangement, these girls had their mother's approval to use their education to reach for more distant horizons where they might find freedom and choice.

Leaving the perfect pink and white microcosm of modern life in the middle of a pineapple field was hard to do, and I promised to return the next day for more videos and girls' chat. I was due to go on an outing the next day, with Livy, to Sringeri, a temple town high in the Western Ghats where there are sacred fish in the river, and we were going to have lunch at my grandmother's favourite restaurant.

It took two hours to climb through the thickly forested foothills in Livy's small red Fiat. The woods were wet with tropical foliage, and live with panther and wild pig and possibly tigers. Livy said it wasn't a good time to go trekking (it was November) then, because of the forest leeches. They creep on to your skin, under your clothes and spurt an enzyme into the wound which they make with their teeth, to make the blood flow fast and free. They sit there sucking silently and then they drop off when they've had their fill. 'And you never know they've been there until you see the blood pouring through your clothes and the enzyme prevents it from clotting, so it bleeds and bleeds,' he said, relishing the information as he drove speedily through the forest.

At Sringeri, which is the southern seat of the orthodox Hindu hierarchy, it was cooler than it had been on the plain, but the sky was clear of rain clouds, and the view stretched for miles and miles. First cultural stop was the Vidyashankar temple, which is built like a stone ship sitting in a paved courtyard. Dedicated to Vishnu, the temple is adorned with stone carvings of the nine incarnations of the great god, and wishing to prove to Livy that I had learnt something from my grandmother, I led him round identifying Matsya, the fish, and Kurma, the tortoise, Varaha, the boar, Narsingh, the man lion, Vamana, the dwarf, Parasu Rama, Rama and the axe, Rama, just Rama, hero of the *Ramayana*, Krishna, and finally Buddha. Livy was quietly impressed.

Then we fed puffed rice to the sacred fish, who jostled for attention and jumped out of the water snatching at the offerings like greedy piranha fish. No man must kill or eat these fish whose territory in the Tunga river is guarded by the gods of the temple. Livy bravely rolled up his trousers and ventured down the stone steps into the river, so that the large grey and black shiny invertebrates clustered round his ankles, but I did not dare follow him.

Fish fed, we decided it was time to feed ourselves, and so we walked from the temple courtyard into the village itself, which is built in neat straight lines of wooden stalls and stone and wooden houses, not tall, but neat and short and even. Every street looked the same as the last one and it took Livy some time to find my grandmother's favourite restaurant. We kept on going into an eating house, sitting down at a narrow wooden table, and then Livy would think for a minute and then say, 'I don't think this is it,' until we must have visited all the restaurants in town. The Mallika Mandira, in which we finally stayed put, looked exactly the same as all the others, I thought, but Livy was convinced of its being the right one.

I was the only woman in the dark, low-ceilinged room, which was not much bigger than a garage for two cars. 'Penelope, she loved the ceremony of the banana leaf meal,' said Livy, as we washed out individual banana leaves with the cup of water provided and then made the trek through the cramped tables to the enamel sink in the corner to wash our hands. An efficient service system was in operation with one boy handing out three vegetable curries, curd, salt and pickle, while another boy doled out huge ladlefuls of rice, dahl, soup, different curd, and then buttermilk. All the different little piles formed a row across the top of the leaf, while the rice stood like a sugar mountain between you and your condiments.

Livy dived in with his right hand, left hand tucked on his lap, and I followed suit. Livy became quite bossy, informing me what I was supposed to be doing with the lime pickle and in which order I should be sampling each brown pile. He ate at an alarming rate and polished off half my rice before beckoning the boy over for more of everything. I think he was rather pleased to have an excuse to come off his raw vegetable experiment for a day, and he ate as if he hadn't eaten properly for a week.

I traipsed after him to the sink again, where he rinsed out his mouth, burped, washed his fingers, patted his tummy and then held the hose-pipe attachment on the end of the tap out for me. 'No, no, no, you must let me pay for this,' he said, handing the teller at the door nine rupees for both meals, and out we marched into the sunny street again.

'Your grandmother, she used to bring her tour parties to this restaurant,' he said. 'To give them a true banana leaf experience. And you should see some of their faces, especially Americans!'

My grandmother always tried to prepare her tourists with a sheet of advice: 'A FEW TIPS FOR MEMBERS OF LADY BETJEMAN'S TOUR OF INDIA' had five points to it, No. 1 being the most important. 'TUMMY TROUBLE IS LARGELY PSYCHOLOGICAL,' she wrote in emphatic capitals. 'It is in the mind and if you are DETERMINED TO GET IT then you WILL.' She advised them to bring out whichever pills their doctor recommended and to have Arret on stand-by if they felt the need. Of course it was fine for her, because as she wrote in an article about tourism: 'I HAVE NEVER SUFFERED FROM GIPPY TUMMY. I am always drinking water from everywhere: from taps, wells, spring and *jheels* (when there are plenty of frogs I know it is pure).'

Indeed, though, she may have been right about it all being in the mind, for when we were together in India, we ate unwashed grapes at stations and curd from urns on the roadside. We drank water from the village pump like the rest of the village and neither of us had any cause to bring out the Arret. Perhaps our good health, which was envied by all the stricken travellers we met, was a state of mind, but it probably had something to do as well with my inheritance of my grandmother's 'marvellous constitution'. She used to revel in drinking ostentatiously from a public tap with a coachload of thirsty Americans watching, horror-struck, frozen in their seats.

Livy had been astounded by Penelope's capacity for random consumption of Indian food. He warned her away from certain hot south Indian curries on a menu, only to find her savouring a hotter dish five minutes later. Curds were the secret of her diet in India. When you have curds at hand to cool you off, she reasoned, no curry is unmanageable.

We filled our afternoon by wandering about the town, looking for a friend of Livy's, who had moved away to another town as it turned out. Sringeri sits in a basin like a volcanic crater in the middle of the mountains surrounded on all sides by peaks. It feels like a sanctuary, not only due to its geographical perch, but because of Sringeri being so remote in the mountains and somewhere you would make a specific journey to get to. It is not a thoroughfare for buses as Indian towns more often are. There are many Brahmins there, wandering about aimlessly (a bit like we were) looking contented and chubby, as I've discovered most Indian priests do, because they have not much else to do all day but sit guarding their temples and consuming the offerings of food brought by devotees.

The drive home was spectacular: the tops of the mountains (which reach up to 6,000 feet) were bare of trees, and we drove round them and in and out of the mountain mists. Livy let me drive for a bit, and not having taken a wheel for more than a few months by then I was quite enthusiastic and pressed on speedily along the mountain roads, causing my passenger to clutch his seat more than once. He had no real cause for alarm, though, until my foot in its flip-flop mistook the accelerator for the brake as I meant to slow down in the face of an oncoming lorry, and we nearly swerved into the forest. Livy took charge after that, and eased the

Fiat smoothly into Kudremukh, a mining town in an even deeper basin than Sringeri's, right in the middle of the mountains. It had the air of a James Bond style secret weapons armoury, looking as if someone had pressed a button causing a fake lake to slide away to reveal the new and pristine buildings.

Livy said it was so picturesque that it was often used as a backing location for films, and even as he said it, we noticed an excited crowd held back by uniformed police and straining over a rope to watch the making of a Tamil movie. The policemen in fact were just as eager as the crowd they were supposed to be restraining, to catch a glimpse of the stars. We wheedled our way through the crowd to the front line, just as overexcited, and managed to achieve prime positions behind the rope.

A slim little director with yellowy white hair, who wore denim shorts and a T-shirt with Hollywood written on it, had a megaphone slung round his neck, through which he issued directions to the actors. She was voluminous in pink, with a make-up girl fussing around her, and he was tall and bulging, stuffed into a Western-style dinner suit, with blackened eyebrows and moustache, and as much make-up caking his face as his co-star. There is only a 'he' and a 'she', for these locally made movies never have a more complicated plot than a him/her relationship which is thwarted several times by character actors (evil stepmothers/wicked landlords/roguish gypsy lovers) and finally comes to fruition at the end of the film, when the scenics are cut to make way for footage of ocean waves crashing rhythmically against the sand, simulating sexual ecstasy.

Livy found the whole flashy film set quite distasteful and wondered how it could possibly interest me, but I was glued to the scene, where, at that point, the heroine was doing a dance number that she seemed to get wrong time after time. There was a lot of ostentatious 'CUT!' type language coming from the director until he said, loudly and for the benefit of the mining audience, 'Cool, that's it. It's a wrap!' in American-accented English, impressing me and the rest of the onlookers hugely.

I took lots of photographs of the stars and stood in a queue to get the hero's autograph, until Livy stamped his foot and said, 'Oh, so this is the sort of thing you are interested in!' To which I replied, to annoy him, 'Yes, this is much more fascinating than temples!' and he went off to sit in the car.

We made our peace on the way home, however, and I explained how I was unable to prevent myself being impressed by movie stars, and he laughed and motored back to Moodbidri in a jovial mood. He told me about the birds we saw – the jungle bush quail, which is like a European quail with a more colourful plumage, and the crow pheasant, which, as its name gives away, looks just as if God got muddled making it and put the tail and body shape of a pheasant on the head and shoulders of a crow. It is called a coupal locally and sings 'coup-coup-coup' in the woods.

We saw neither panthers nor tigers, but the next morning, when we rose at 5.30 a.m. to climb the twin-peaked Connage Hill in the dawn, we met a Hindu sadhu on the path who said a tiger had been calling in the night. The sadhu led us to his cave, which was fully equipped with cooking utensils, and fronted with a white-washed stone wall with windows and a door. The sadhu was playing host to two women from Bombay who had come to the forest for a weekend's retreat and religious contemplation. We met the women on their way back from the stream where they had been washing their hair. One was an architect and the other worked in advertising and they both spoke English.

'We have come to pray and meditate in peace, away from the rat race,' the younger one, Sita, admitted. 'Sometimes the city becomes overwhelming and you need time and space for thought.' Lucky for them there was a wooded hill and a bearded sadhu with a yen for hospitality within a day's journey of their city, I thought, as we had a breakfast of chapatti and curds together on the rock in front of the cave, watched by a scavenging family of brown monkeys.

It appeared that people's needs were the same the world over, 'And that is why', said Livy that night after prayers, 'it is desirable and not difficult to reach across the time zones and the border control and the language problems, to make friends. Penelope chose to make the effort to do that and because of her effort, I became her friend, and because of her, now we are friends.'

CHAPTER XVI

The Deeper South
and the Fifth John

*'I am a born schoolmarm. Had I been able to have a career in
my youth, it would have been as a teacher.'*

Ladies and Gentlemen, as I have rather a lot of slides to get
thro' in an hour, I will dispense with the usual elaborate
introduction and get straight down to business. We will start
with the map . . .

The part of India I am going to talk about tonight is this S.E.
slice formerly known as the Dravida Desa after the Dravidians
who inhabit it . . . Those of you who are perhaps unfamiliar with
this part of the world will however be interested in it as being the
traditional country to which St Thomas the Apostle journeyed
after the death of Our Lord and where, here, somewhere on the
coast of Coromandel, he was martyred. To readers of Edward
Lear also, there will be an added interest in that it is the land of
the Yonghi Bonghi Bo . . .

A PENELOPE CHETWODE lecture raised laughs from the most
unlikely audiences, such as the Finchley Public Library Lecture
Group and the Leominster Round Table. 'I always write and
lecture under my maiden name, thank you,' she would state in no
uncertain terms to withering WI secretaries and presidents of
sorority groups who had hoped that Lady Betjeman might agree
to give a little insight into 'Life with the Laureate', perhaps?
One keen request came from the Mother's Union at Preston-on-
Wye:

'Dear madam,' the letter began. 'We were pleased to hear you
were willing to come to our M. Union meeting on February 6th.

You will choose your subject. Possibly on your husband's interesting life as a poet. Or your travels. We have a member who was born in India. Her father was a colonel. Have you transport? The husbands occasionally come. Yours faithfully, etc etc.'

My grandmother was launched on to the lecturing circuit in 1969 by the Maurice Frost Lecture Agency, who managed an eclectic book of some 175 public speakers. Their varied lecture subjects were advertised under enticing titles like 'Garden Fallacies Exploded' by W.E. Shewell-Cooper, or 'Honeymoon behind the Iron Curtain' by Tony Smythe, an RAF jet pilot. The lecturing agency secured bookings for my grandmother in far-off venues for obscure organizations such as the Maidenhead Lecture Society and West Bromwich Institute in Birmingham, but it was the requests from groups closer to home that filled her lecture diary to the brim.

The local Women's Institutes adored her 'Village Life in the Himalayas' lecture, and the Soroptimist International of Hereford keenly applauded her 'Position of Women in India'. She lectured to the local horticultural society on 'Flowers of the Himalaya', and to the Mid-Wales Harness Club on 'The Use of the Horse as a Means of Transport', but given an unconditional choice, the lecture would invariably be titled 'Temple Architecture of the Western Himalaya', toned up or down architecturally according to the intellectual capacity of the audience.

Before the lecture could take place, a great deal of correspondence was necessary. Often my grandmother would have disappeared to India in say, November, just as the WI were trying to type up leaflets to advertise the January evening in question, and were obliged to wait for her return before going ahead with details. My grandmother would then bombard them with apologies for her absence, which were followed closely by inquiries about the projector facilities.

For example, her letter to the secretary to the Greathouse Cheshire Home Appeal in Chippenham, who had asked my grandmother to give an illustrated talk about temples began:

I am sorry I have not answered your letter dated Feb 1st sooner but I am ALWAYS AT LEAST FIFTY LETTERS IN ARREARS.

One needs as large a screen as you can borrow (from a local school??). I prefer a MANUALLY OPERATED PROJECTOR at least 500 watt (preferably 1000 for a largish hall) but VERY few people have them nowadays. I have a v.g. Aldis manually op proj but as I no longer have a car I cannot cart it about as it is very heavy. So you will just have to get what you can, but as some of my slides are framed in cardboard and some in glass, an automatic proj often chews up the slides it doesn't like and SPITS THEM OUT. Also it means taking them out of my box and putting them into a special slide I mean Proj box.

The lecture will take about an hour and I will answer questions IF ANY afterwards . . .

Members of the Hay-on-Wye WI, and the Radnor Round Table, and the Arrowvale Wine Club all recall the jokes which Penelope delivered in her talks, and the unfailing way in which several of her slides would always appear upside down or in the wrong order. She became professionally adept at appearing inept on the platform, so giving an impression of amateurism which always endeared her to the audience. And they always invited her back to talk again next year, or to preside as guest of honour over an annual banquet at the Green Dragon in Llandrindod, or the Bull Ring in Hay.

However, her timetable took some juggling to set in order. To the Ireland and India Cultural Society who had offered her an Apex fare to Dublin, she wrote:

I was very interested to hear about your cultural society and would love to show you some of my slides but the question is WHEN? On November 3rd I am taking a party of 16 people to South India and as soon as they have gone home I am taking two Americans on a private tour around Gujurat and Rajhastan.

323

In April 1980 I am taking a party of trekkers to the Western Himalaya to see Temples and Rhododendrons! The following winter I am planning to spend the whole six months in India beginning and ending with conducting Tours so that I get free flights both ways!

For by 1979, when this letter was written, conducting tours had become my grandmother's passage to India. Her career as a tour guide had grown in harness with her renown as a lecturer, and after conducting several groups of tourists round the temples in the Western Himalaya for Christina Noble and her Manali-based West Himalayan Holidays, my grandmother was approached by Mr Swan of Swan Tours.

At first she declined to lead any tours for Mr Swan, on account of his chosen methods of transport. When the style of the Indian tours were changed, she relented.

Dear Mr Swan,

As I said in a former letter, I cannot stand the PACE of your thirty-two strong tours, travelling by Indian Airlines mostly. BUT now that you have started an AIR-CONDITIONED COACH TOUR, I would like to conduct one of these. No. 119 would suit me best. I can honestly say that I know all the places on this tour bar Ujjain. I wish we could stay at MANDU instead of just going there for a SINGLE AFTERNOON. I never go there for less than a week, it is so beautiful and romantic. JBP once took me there in his white ambulance and we stayed in the Jahaz Mahal Stable RH and all my candles and soap were eaten by RATS. But they have built a small hotel there but I presume there would not be room for big parties? I can also never understand why you send people to that very ugely mis-sahpen [sic] bogus Taj at Aurangabad when there are 36 caves at ELLORA and we only go there for a SINGLE AFTERNOON. It is CRAZY: one should go there to Ellora I mean first thing in the morning and have lunch and a rest in the nice resthouse above the caves in the afternoon, CUT OUT S/S IN AURAN-GABAD ALTOGETHER, for there is 0 there to equal the Ellora Caves . . .

Accordingly, Penelope was booked as Guest Lecturer for tour No. 119, 'The Art Treasures Tour of Palaces of Rajasthan' leaving 17 February 1979, returning March 9, but she did not set foot out of England without having some considerable say in the tour arrangements.

She asked Mr Swan in a letter dated 22 November 1978:

How is the Rajasthan Tour No. 119 filling up? With regard to the list of lectures I have made one up which I enclose but I don't expect I will keep strictly to it. I find that there is always a party on these tours who is devoted to bar life in the grand hotels and usually the members prefer to drink rather than to listen to me waffling away! However, I am always very conscientious to talk to the faithful few whenever the opportunity arises, and I encourage them to ask questions and try to help them with their individual difficulties in understanding Indian culture. But with regard to the subject of each lecture I usually play it as it comes, so to speak, and quite often one gets very behind trying to catch up on the different religions etc that one is coming into contact with.

I told you in a previous letter that Rajasthan is not my subject and I had actually signed on for your coach tour of Northern India which you are not now putting into operation, as you said the distances involved are too great. However, I do know a good bit about Rajput architecture, and can only say I will do my best.

Having admitted her shortcomings, she dictated terms:

AHMEDABAD. It is essential for us to see the Calico Museum which is one of the finest museums of textiles in the world. We must also see the Rani Sipri Mosque and Tomb and the Stepped Well of Dad Hari. These stepped wells are one of the most notable features of Gujurati architecture, and the above one is one of the finest examples in existence.

Finally, she advised:

> As our time is LIMITED to one day in this architecturally rich city I personally would cut out Gandhi's Sabarmati Ashram which is just a collection of old photographs! Also the completely modern and HIDEOUS Gita Temple which the local guides so love to take one to.
>
> Yours sincerely,
>
> Penelope Betjeman.

Twenty-four people duly followed my grandmother around Rajasthan, and were astounded by their Guest Lecturer's stamina. A thank you letter from one of the tourists, Margaret Hortin Smith, spoke for the whole of the party: 'We had a truly wonderful time which was truly made even more enjoyable by your knowledge, patience with our questions – foolish or otherwise – and intriguing sense of humour! I think we all realised we were privileged to have your company ... I'm getting back to normal, but still feel somewhat dazed and crazed and "out of this world". I send good wishes for any other tour you have plans for: the people on the tour are lucky to have you ...'

Little did they know of their leader's misgivings prior to the tour. Penelope had written to Alfred Wuerfel, her German friend in Delhi, confessing things which she had not dared include in her letters to Mr Swan:

> .... then I have to travel down to Bombay to meet a large party of SWAN TOURISTS which will be a nightmare tour, 24 of them, PALACES OF RAJASTHAN which I am not at all conversant with as I have never been to half of them, I shall just give background lectures on history and religion and on Rajput architecture which I know a bit about. YOU should be conduct-

ing such a tour! The point is I signed on for quite another one
but they cancelled and then substituted this one but as the fee is
good I must do it somehow!

Halfway through the tour, she wrote to him from the Rambagh
Palace Hotel in Jaipur:

> ... This tour is so pressurizing that we are all in a state of
> collapse. In future I shall only conduct tours which I PLAN
> MYSELF. Too tired to write any more. Much love, immer deine
> Penelope.

In fact she was already planning an experimental tour for Cox &
Kings which would enable her to lead a smaller party of tourists
through her own favourite district of South Kanara. With Livy
Soans, the pineapple farmer, she arranged an itinerary which was
to include an afternoon at the *kambala* (buffalo races), a week at
the Basel Mission rest-house in Karkala, and a picnic lunch at the
pineapple farm. She named the tour 'Lady Betjeman's Special
Interest Adventure Tour', and via a three-way correspondence
among herself, Livy Soans and Ken Lister at Cox & Kings (which
continued for a year leading up to the departure date of 3
November 1979) an itinerary was published, and the tour was
booked out immediately by twelve keen tourists – ten Britons, one
American and a New Zealander.

In the spring before the great adventure tour was to depart,
my grandmother was interviewed by a journalist to whom she said
that had she been able to have a career in her youth, it would have
been as a teacher. She explained:

> I love to project my enthusiasm about places to other people.
> There are a lot of tourists now who like to be allowed time to
> absorb what they see. I like to guide them around a site, then
> give them a good kick in the pants and say: 'You're intelligent,
> go and look at the ruins and think about them for yourself.'

Penelope was determined to organize the tour in the kind of way in which she found it most rewarding to travel; that is, she refused to parcel up her tourists in air-conditioned hotels. 'I'm not a five-star girl, it's just not my income level and I get claustrophobic in those hotels,' she told the journalist. 'They bring a veil down between you and the country you've come to see.'

To make up to her tourists for their lack of comfort she would organize unusual excursions. A highlight of the adventure tour was to be luncheon at the Madras Club at Adhyar, a private members' club founded in British days, which my grandmother had visited last in 1931 when she accompanied her father to a Christmas shoot in Madras as guest of the local Maharajah.

> I feel I should mention the matter of weather, which will be, in November, pretty chancy, [wrote Cyril Cayley, the English acting secretary of the club, to my grandmother, prior to the tour.] This part of South India does not get the South West monsoon with rains from June to September as over the rest of India, but the North East monsoon starting 15th Oct. up to end of December. There are USUALLY plenty of breaks in the rains, but November is the main period of Depressions and Cyclonic storms, so I feel I should warn you.
>
> Another word of warning – Prohibition is very strong in Madras, despite the recent fall of Morarji Desai, and while non-Indians, over 21, can get permits, it is illegal for them to drink without a permit. Perhaps you might obtain permits from the Indian Tourist Office in Bond Street? Anyway we will be delighted to see you for luncheon, which we can provide at Rs 17.50 per head. Perhaps we can escort the party to visit the Theosophical Society in the afternoon for tea?

Cyril Cayley welcomed the party of thirteen (my grandmother, as tour leader, included) when they arrived, equipped with their permits, in time for gin and tonics on the Madras Club lawn. 'This was one of the highlights of the tour for everyone,' wrote my grandmother in her report for Cox & Kings, which she delivered to their offices after the safe return of the whole party to England on 25 November.

She headed the report, 'Confidential Note for Their Excellencies the Directors of Messrs Cox & Kings Travel Service' and filled eight pages of foolscap paper with daily accounts of the proceedings annotated with detailed accounts of savouries consumed at various points of the journey.

> On the whole, the tour went very well, apart from the unfortunate breakdown of the bus on its way to Panaji, so that we missed our drive to the Jog Falls. However, Thank God, the bus broke down BEFORE it picked us up. After that the engine gave us no trouble and as I had so many friends in South Kanara they were able to get us plenty of diesel.
>
> ... The only unpleasant incident on the Adventure tour was when Mr Kossow announced he was going to sue Cox & Kings as Mrs Kossow's tummy upset was later diagnosed as Amoebic dysentery. However, Thank God Mr Kossow has cooled down – his wife really was not very ill and was able to bathe in the Taj swimming bath in Bombay! Since my return I have learnt that Mrs Kossow's dysentery tests (at the Hospital for Tropical Diseases) have proved negative.

The sole flirtation with five-star luxury allowed by Lady Betjeman for her Adventure Tourists, was a buffet lunch at the famous five star Fort Aguada Hotel on the beach at Goa. In her report to Cox & Kings, she was determined to do it down. 'We had a buffet lunch by the swimming pool,' she wrote. 'Fair choice for first course,' she admitted, 'but REVOLTING puddings worthy of a low-class English boarding house: so-called "lemon soufflé" with very little lemon juice and far too much gelatine in it, the custard tart with leaden pastry and a stiff cornflour filling, UGH!!'

Eulogy was reserved for the three nights spent with Sister Hannah of the Basel Mission at the Christa Sevaki ashram at

Karkala. 'I was apprehensive as to how the tour members would take to the living conditions, with Indian style washing arrangements and several people to a room,' wrote Penelope, 'but to my relief, there were no complaints at all. The food was consistently good, and several members of the tour voted our stay in the primitive but clean surroundings of the ashram the highlight of the tour.'

Next, they rode on the Brindhavan Express train to Madras and checked in at the Connemara Hotel, an accommodation choice which was justified by my grandmother in the report: 'Though the interior decoration at the Taj Coromandel (a five-star establishment) is more exciting and there is a choice of three restaurants, the old Connemara is much more central and next to Spencer's Stores [an old-fashioned department store which my grandmother could not resist when in Madras].'

The following morning, they left the hotel at 8.30 a.m.

'We planned to leave at 8am but the bus was delayed by the dreadful diesel queues. I asked Mr Samuel (our very pleasant guide) why the driver had not filled up the night before and he said that the bus had been out with tourists till after closing time at the garages. Mr Samuel belongs to the Methodist church. He said that out of 60 trained guides on the Madras ITDC Panel, 8 are Christians of various denominations.

The tour report ended on a high note in Bombay, where my grandmother celebrated on the final evening by taking most of the tour members (bar those who had decamped to the Taj Mahal Hotel for respite from 'adventure') to the King Edward VIII 'Juicy Nook' café on Colaba Causeway for toasted cheese sandwiches and kulfi ice-cream milk shakes. 'On the final morning I got up early and had breakfast with the party before they departed to the airport at 7.30 a.m.' she wrote. 'The Kossows were picked up first at the Taj and then the bus came on to the Ambassador

Hotel and that was the end of an unusual and HIGHLY ENJOY-ABLE tour.'

MY GRANDMOTHER never stopped leading groups around India even after her seventieth birthday, though some of her later tours were admittedly more sedate than previous trips. However, this did not necessarily make them more enjoyable for her: the 1984 Linblad cruise tour, for example, was certainly easy on the legs but my grandmother, who held the position of ship's lecturer, was afterwards to deem it 'HELL ON EARTH (OR RATHER AT SEA)'.

Tony Pugh, a bank manager in Bristol and a good friend of Penelope's after he had experienced one of her South Indian tours, had recommended my grandmother's lecturing abilities to Mr Linblad, the enterprising Swede who ran a cruise line catering for rich Americans. Linblad asked Lady Betjeman to lecture on the MS *Linblad Polaris* on her inaugural voyage along the Malabar coast of India (the west coast) and round Cape Comorin to the island of Sri Lanka, and she replied: 'I should very much like to act as guest lecturer for your first two cruises up and down the west coast of India, parts of which I know well, others less well. I have not been to Sri Lanka since 1929 or 1930, I cannot exactly recollect which, but I saw the chief archaeological sights then and I know a certain amount about Buddhism.'

Later, while on board ship and steaming towards Sri Lanka, my grandmother was to write in a letter to my sister Lucy:

OH GOD, we are now in Ceylon, Sri Lanka, and I haven't been here for fifty years and am bluffing all the time. Never had a moment to do my homework before leaving the Hereford Himalaya because of having to write that intro to Travels with a Donkey by RLS, did I tell you? I knew 0 about him and had to read two biographies (and unlike your Pa I am the slowest reader in the world), the Travels twice through and various other chores but as I am being paid £250 for 2000 words, I couldn't turn it down and the generator went up in flames before I left so I couldn't use the slide sorter till the last 2 days and had to throw 6 lectures together willy nilly (where IN THE HELL does that expression come from??) and 0 on Sri Lanka as I ph. it all in black and white circa 1930 and only have huge slides which a modern projector won't take. I gave quite a good lecture on Buddhism before leaving the ship but left out half of what I meant to say including STUPAS which play a very big part in Ceylonese Buddhism as they have been mad on relics ever since they were converted in 3rd century BC by one of Ashoka's monk's sons.

The stupa omissions would have worried few of the passengers, though, for it was about their stomachs that the Americans were most concerned. Penelope wrote to Lucy: 'The passengers are of course all incredibly rich with a high proportion of Jewish couples who are mostly very intelligent but the men are monstrously FAT with hairy chests like gorillas and they eat such ENORMOUS quantities of food that I can't think how they survive.'

Breakfast was served between 7.30 and 9 a.m. and Penelope reckoned most of the passengers needed that long to do justice to the spread before them.

Breakfast consists of several kinds of cheese and ditto sliced cold meat, plus cereal, yoghurt, stewed fruit, fruit juices, toast, rolls, bacon and eggs and fresh fruit, and, I nearly forgot, PANCAKES which they eat with JAM! Most of the Americans, including the women, have fruit juices, cereal, bacon and eggs and 4 pancakes each!'

Penelope, meanwhile, was a paragon of virtue: 'I never feel very hungry at breakfast and have stewed prunes, and one bit of toast and tea with fresh lime juice.' However, she found herself unable to hold back so admirably at all times; the cocktail parties (which she hated) were her downfall. There was one on board ship to celebrate someone's birthday: 'It took place in their de luxe cabin and everyone shouted so loud I nearly went mad but I was given iced orange juice and there was an inexplicable saucer full of TOBLERONE among the snacks and I ate the lot and felt rather sick.'

Intermittently, as they ate their way down the Malabar coast, my grandmother gave lectures, usually after the sumptuous buffet lunch aboard ship, 'when most of the people are asleep,' she wrote. By the time the 2000-ton MS *Linblad Polaris* reached Cochin, Kerala, she was more transfixed by her fellow passengers than they would ever be about the cultural history of India. She wrote from the harbour at Cochin:

'I am more amazed by day at these rich Americans.' They are a FASCINATING study: a RACE APART. Yesterday I took a local bus to the Santa Cruz Cathedral on Cochin island and from there I went circa 15 kms on another bus to St Teresa's College at Ernakulam on the mainland to see a nun friend of mine, and then I got an auto-rickshaw back to the ship. The people I talked to that evening just couldn't understand how I could go by local transport. One neurotic woman said she would rather die as she was so afraid of 'CATCHING SOMETHING'! Most of the passengers went off to the Periyar wildlife sanctuary (5 kms in luxury buses) but 23 stayed behind, 16 of whom are ill.

As the ship rounded Cape Comorin and turned to glide up the eastern coast of Coromandel, my grandmother became desperate to break free of shipboard constraints. She wrote to me:

When we stay on shore for 2 or 3 nights we go to 5 star hotels only but the food is seldom so good as on the ship and I get satiated with luxury and sometimes I feel I want to smash everything up as it is all so BOGUS and all the tourists agents who deal with us are so SMOOTH and pretend to be so sophisticated which they are NOT.

Her chance for escape came when she accompanied four of the keener sightseers on an individual trip ashore to photograph the early Hindu sculptures and the romantic shore temples at Mahabalipuram, which lies about an hour south of Madras in Tamil Nadu. 'The photographers clicked away and were delighted they had plenty of time and a guide (ie ME) whom they could understand. They were so keen they went without lunch but Dr Sussman (a medico from New Jersey) had brought some fruit from breakfast.' Her time came:

> I suddenly felt a STRONG DESIRE to go native so I sent them off to the Shore Temple in the taxis and went myself to a restaurant (a proper south Indian eating house with formica-topped tables) and had rice and curds and veg on a banana leaf which I ate with my right hand. I normally prefer to have a spoon but I just felt I MUST get away from the incredible cleanliness of everything to do with the ship and the precautions that are taken to avoid contamination ... After lunch I bought 250 grams of those delicious little black grapes and, spitting out the pips in all directions on the way, I walked to the Catholic church of the Holy Family and en route I inspected a Vijayanagar period pavilion I had never noticed before where some fishwives were selling little silver scaled fish and oranges and I bought several of those loose skinned oranges which we ate on the way back in the taxis.

Restored by her afternoon's bathe in reality, my grandmother managed to stay on board at Madras while the first sixty-four passengers left and the next sixty-four passengers embarked. They were now to retrace the route back down from Madras, around Sri Lanka (docking at the northern port of Trincomalee), down around

Cape Comorin, back up to Cochin, and thence to Goa and finally back to Bombay.

> We steamed out of Madras harbour after dark and there was great excitement as the *QE2* had come in that day and looked BEAUTIFUL with her portholes lit up.
>
> She is on her way around the world and I am told some elderly American millionairesses more or less make their homes on her as they feel so lonely in their own houses and are so frightened of being robbed. Each one takes a suite on the top deck and has her own steward to wait on her and gets to know the ship's doctor and other personnel. It is terribly sad and one can THANK GOD one isn't in that sort of income bracket.

Apparently six or seven passengers die on every QE2 round the world cruise and are deep frozen in the mortuary.

But my grandmother did not cruise for long enough to expire en route and following the second sailing she bade farewell to the MS *Linblad Polaris* at Bombay, one month after she had first embarked ship. Three thousand dollars richer and 8lb heavier she took a south-bound bus immediately, in search of the simple life and her senses.

Penelope's other great South Indian friend – after Livy Soans – was the fifth John in her life (following on as he did from Johnnie Churchill, Sir John Marshall, John Betjeman and John Nankivell), who was a former miner from Kettering called John Foster. The fifth John founded and ran a network of orphanages in South India called Goodwill Children's Villages, of which my grandmother became Patron. For a quiet life and rest and time for reading and writing and reflection my grandmother would repair to Thandi-gudi, the tiny village high in the wooded Palni Hills of Tamil Nadu where John Foster presides over the original Goodwill Children's Village, overseeing the lives and education of some two hundred South Indian girls and boys.

*

I LEFT THE buffalo land of South Kanara where the pineapples grow to seek out John Foster. Livy drove me into the Catholic coastal town of Mangalore (I did not stop long there; my grandmother had always said it was uninteresting) where I boarded a train to Madurai. The train ride was entirely pleasurable. I slept well in my own cabin until 5 a.m., when the train stopped at Coimbatore, an industrial town just inside Kerala, and everyone had to bail out on to the platform for two dark hours until our connection was due to leave at 7 a.m. I found a *Learn Malayalam Through English* handbook in the bookstall, and I sat in the Railway Refreshment Room until I had learnt all the vowels.

Fourteen major languages are spoken in India and probably over two hundred minor languages and dialects, which is probably why English is so widely spoken all over India so long after the British have left. Cross a state border and you find the script has changed: in the north, Hindi looks upright and spiky, Urdu (derived from Persian and therefore the Arabic script) looks more elegant and elongated and sloping, but as soon as you get to Karnataka, you find the rounded, podgy letters of Kannada, and when you cross the border into Kerala, the letters are even rounder and smaller and bubble-like.

In a short time, the best one can do to make headway in understanding the language is by learning the letters and transliterating the sign posts. The odd words, like coffee and thank you, come phonetically, but it is muddling because as soon as 'coffee' in Hindi is mastered, a state border crops up and soon no one knows what you are talking about because they all speak Kannada or Telegu or Tamil.

The Tamils are particularly protective of their own language and despise Hindi. This is because there is a movement in India to make Hindi into the national language, and the Southern Tamils from Tamil Nadu, a fiery people by nature, are strongly against the idea. English is not so widely spoken in the south as it is in the north either, for the same reason, and also because there are some places in the south which the British just did not bother with.

Communication problems aside, it is quite nice to be switching language all the time because it makes you realize how different all the separate Indian states are – like separate countries almost.

Anyway, I was sitting there in the dingy gloom of the Railway Refreshment Room, using up page after page of my notebook copying out the curling, bubble-like consonants, and the waiter (a bent little man with no teeth and a filthy shirt smeared with grease stains who ambled between the small wooden tables and served whom he liked when he liked) tapped me on the shoulder. He smiled brightly when I showed him my letters, and beckoned over his friend the cook and his other friend the cashier, and by then I was just about ready to write my name. For the consonants in Malayalam come with vowels attached by signs, so to write IMO I needed to find the 'M' and attach the signs for 'I' and 'O' before and after it. This I did and the three men of the Railway Refreshment Room went off dancing about saying 'Imo', 'Imo', to themselves and pointing to me and laughing until all the other breakfasting gentlemen knew exactly who I was. They gave me a free *masala dosa* (the spiced pancake which is ubiquitous in the south and takes over as a breakfast dish from chapattis and the 'jam, butter, tost' which you can find in north and central India), and the waiter came to sit at my table over coffee. Still, I had to get to Thandigudi, so I caught my train and sat for five and a half hours on a hard wooden slatted seat opposite a whale of a woman munching greasy *samosas* which she pulled out one by one from her string bag with slippery fingers. I counted that she ate twenty-four, making it almost five per hour.

Madurai is a seething city of a million people, bristling with rickshaws and tonga carts, businessmen, buffaloes, beggars and pilgrims, tailors and flowersellers and Brahmins and dust. Life for the city's population revolves round the huge Sree Meenakshi temple in the heart of the old town, which receives 10,000 visitors every day. Like a marquee the four square walls which surrounded the inner sanctums and chambers and the images and pillars are striped vertically in red and white, and the sculptures inside – the carved doors and prancing horses and the lathed pillars and monkeys and elephants and pot and foliage friezes – are painted with childish abandon in a spectrum of clashing colours.

The Hindus who worship there buy jasmine strings and frangipani from squat chubby women who line the streets around the temple and leave their sandals at one of the four great doors, before entering with their children and children's children and their sons-in-law and their grandmothers. Inside, on the cool stone paving, sit quiet pilgrims, skinny in white or orange sarongs, heads bowed, hands moving silently over their beads. But the raucous Hindu families chatter and smirk and flit from image to image, bestowing their gifts on the various gods and goddesses – Ganesh, Shiva, Parvati – with unrestrained gaiety.

The temple, which has twelve towers each between forty-five and fifty metres high, as well as the four nine-storey towers rising above each of the four gateways on the outer wall, is named after the daughter of a Pandyan king who was born with three breasts. At the time of her birth the king was told the extra mammary would disappear when she met the man she was to marry, and it duly disappeared when she met Lord Shiva on Mount Kailas. Shiva said, 'Go back to Madurai,' and eight days later he arrived there himself, in the form of Lord Sundareshwara, and married her.

Shiva was a man of his word, and so was the driver of my rickshaw who took me from the station straight to a room he knew of. (It is often difficult to find a room in Madurai because there are always so many pilgrims visiting the city who fill up the hotels.) The room was a windowless cube but a room at least in the heart of the bustle, and I lay down to rest in the heat of the day, as my grandmother would have done. Come evening, I did my *puja* at the temple and afterwards went to watch the *son-et-lumière* at the Tirumalai Palace, where there was a touch more *lumière* than *son* as the loudspeakers appeared to be faulty.

The noise outside my room No. 502 (of men guffawing and Tamil film music) did not die down until after 2 a.m., and began again with a studied clanking of pots accompanied by shouting at 6 a.m., so I was woken well in time for my bus to Vatallagundu. There, twenty miles from Madurai, I waited for a bus to Thandighudi and ate a breakfast of bananas and coconut juice while reading *The Mayor of Casterbridge* by Thomas Hardy. Racked with guilt I had succumbed to the shelf of English classics in the Madurai bookshop, and was now revelling in rural Wessex, while all around me a typical south Indian small town began its day.

The swarthy cook in the bus stand eating-house turned *dosas* over on his blackened hod with his right hand and steamed *idlis* (rice cakes) in his pressure cooker whilst he stirred a huge tureen of *dahl* with his left hand. His sons, or somebody's sons, cantered to and fro from the kitchen to the wonky tables balancing loaded plates along their arms and collected coffee glasses to swill under the rusty tap in the corner of the smoky room.

Sour-faced travellers, droopy with the weight of bundles tied up with string and suitcases bursting with clothes and bedding, hunched themselves over their belongings drawing on *bidis* with sulky mouths. Their exhausted wives argued with their whining children and bargained with the bawdy female fruitseller who was angrily swatting the flies which swarmed over her black grapes.

The magazine stall dripped with bangles and anklets and glitzy pink shiny beads, and the young stallholder smoked and bantered with his friends as they came to buy cigarettes. Every so often a sneaky child would lunge at a string of beads, taunting the stallholder with the threat of robbery, and then gallop off back to his giggling friends who would wait round the corner of a standing bus.

An occasional pitiful sadhu passed, emaciated and barely able to hold up his begging bowl, and the children taunted him too. There were women, mad-looking and deranged with matted hair and loose saris worn with no underskirt so that you could see one sagging breast flapping against their scarcely skin-covered breast bone. One of these women had hoops in her ears which pulled her lobes to her shoulders with their weight. I was the only person in Vatallagundu wearing shoes.

Six different men came up to ask me where I was going and each one told me a different version of the bus timetable, giving me less idea of the time the Thandighudi bus was due to leave than I already had. I adopted the method of asking every driver where he was headed as soon as his bus stopped at the stand, and I prepared myself to wait all day.

But my preparation was unnecessary and we (myself and thirty or so men, women and children, chickens and goats) trundled out of the station in a twenty-seater old metal bus with wooden seats and no panes in the windows at 11 a.m. or thereabouts. The road surface was uneven – at times just a rough track – and the pace was slow for the only other vehicles along the road were bullock carts, behind which we often became stuck. It was the time of the harvesting of the first paddy crop, and once the farmworkers (predominantly female) have separated the rice from the stalks, they lay all the straw on the road for drying, making a soft and inviting golden carpet off which their children spend all day chasing dogs and donkeys.

Once the straw is dry enough, the women weave it into rope. They stand, two of them fifty yards apart, and one pulls and twists and the other one channels the loose straw through a narrow opening made by her two hands and, as if by a miracle, the straw becomes rope. What with the bullock carts and the buffalo-drawn ploughs, the scene from my bus seat appeared positively medieval. The sole reminders of modern appliances were the wailing amplifiers we passed, which reverberated with Indian film music.

My grandmother had developed an antipathy for the ubiquitous use of Indian amplifiers (for the apparent pleasure of the populace) about which she ranted in an article published in an Indian weekly, about tourism in India:

AMPLIFIERS! The scourge of modern India! But if you like them who are we tourists to interfere with your pleasure? An Indian friend of mine once asked a donkey-wala why his leading donkey had a blaring transistor hung around his neck? 'Sir he will not move without it,' was the reply. Transistors are bad enough but you can usually get away from them (except in a bus); but amplifiers, if there happens to be a wedding in the vicinity of your hotel, may plague you through the night. All my life I have wanted to see the famous Sun Temple at Konorak but I was never allowed to go there as a girl because of the curious nature of some of the carving: 'People might talk,' my mother said. My ambition was at last realised four years ago [she was writing in 1976] when I was touring India in a Morris van. We camped on the shores of the Indian ocean, we bought fish from the fishermen and grilled them on the ashes of our camp fire, we bathed by moonlight in the divinely warm sea. We were in the right mood for a great aesthetic experience and at sunrise the following day we drove the mile or so to the temple and had it all to ourselves for two glorious hours. Then three busloads of Indian University students drove up and – I could hardly believe my eyes – there was a huge loudspeaker strapped onto the roof of the middle bus. But I had to believe my ears when it began to blare out film songs from the latest movie at the top of its crackling voice. The magic spell was rudely broken and I felt only anger that educated people could be so insensitive as to want that noise when looking at some of the most marvellous sculpture in the world.

My amplifier was not interrupting an exactly aesthetic experience (considering the stench and the filth our bus was bidden to plough its way through at times) though the figures of the women, with brass pots balanced on their heads, shoulders back and ramrod straight backs, walking with untaught grace along the roadside were sculptures in themselves, and the shimmering views through the rice-dust-filled air across the yellowing straw in the fields and the red mud, could not have been painted finer.

The towns we passed through had phonetically satisfying names like Allayampallayam and Mangalagombu and I sang the names to the baby I was now holding on my lap. The wriggling, chubby boy belonged to the girl sitting next to me who had a two-year-old yelling on her other knee so she was relieved when I offered to be *ayah* for the ride, and she put a towel on my lap before handing me her son (I do not think nappies exist in India). An annoying young man in a leather jacket (which he kept taking off and showing off and putting on again like a peacock displaying its feathers) who grinned inanely, spent the whole ride trying to attract my attention almost to the point of harassment, and the mother of the boy and I were able to communicate in the inter-national language of women by exchanging despairing looks and rolling our eyes to the ceiling and smiling at each other knowingly.

As the bus began to climb into the Palni hills, the foliage at the roadside became darker and darker until the palms and the deciduous scrub of the plain were overtaken by evergreen forest and creepers. The paddy-fields disappeared to be replaced, in the clearings in the forest, by banana and coffee plantations. In the forests there are leopards and panthers and wild boar and deer, but we saw none of these animals. There have been tigers reported in the area, but very few, and we did not see one. We did see monkeys, and as the bus climbed up and around the hairpin bends the air became thick with jungle sounds of tropical birds (though we could only hear those when the bus driver stopped for a tea break which he did quite often).

The peacock bloke with the leather jacket got out finally, at one of the tea stops, though it was only another ten minutes up the road in the bus before I alighted at Goodwill Children's Village, one stop before Thandigudi itself. I was looking forward with glee to seeing John Foster. My grandmother and I had come to visit him together in 1985, and though I remembered he had talked about his piles quite a lot and had roasted rabbit most nights, I also recalled him being the friendliest, kindest of men, and so English. Though I was loath to admit it to myself, I was quite keen to talk to another English person.

He hugged me like a long lost daughter and he looked exactly the same: he is sixty-six now and his white beard had just been trimmed (for Christmas, he said, he was going home to Kettering on 29 November for a month) and his belly protruded no more or less than it had done in 1985.

Goodwill is laid out on a slope like a neat, whitewashed Greek village, with stone pathways between the various bungalow buildings and door jambs painted blue and green. It was quiet at midday, for all the children were out at their local schools, and John showed me to Peace Cottage, the same tiny house which I had shared with my grandmother. It had a red tiled floor and was jam-packed with furniture; there was a railing on which to hang my clothes and lots of nice plastic flowers stuck in vases round the room.

'Stay as long as you like,' said John. He said that Penelope always said she would come just for two days and then she would stay for two weeks or more. He reckoned I would be the same, although I assured him I had to be off and away by the end of the week.

After rice and a delicious spiced vegetable omelette for lunch (which I ate with my right hand sitting on a mat on the stone floor of the children's dining hall), I walked up behind Goodwill on to the saddle between two Palni peaks, where there are large flat grey rocks spread out like resting elephants to see a full 360 degree panorama across the neatly forested hills. The air up there is fresh and cool and reminds one of England.

My grandmother and I had come up on to that saddle every morning to breathe the air at dawn when we had stayed at Goodwill together. Daily Penelope had insisted upon her lung-expanding exercises – a series of extravagant arm-swinging movements – in public (watched, if at all, only ever by a couple of shepherds or woodmen whom we could leave stunned in our wake, crooks and axes petrified in mid-air and mouths gaping at the very sight of the two English ladies at their 6 a.m. limb-swinging). Her exercises completed, she would exhort me like a gym mistress into a rigorous toe-touching routine and after I had reached my toes several times she would say, 'Gosh, you ARE athletic!' and then we would amble back down the hill to the dining hall for breakfast.

John told me that night that I was a friend of Goodwill and could stay for ever. He cooked me the famous rabbit stew for dinner, which I might well have savoured had not I come across one of the orphans selecting one of the fluffiest bunnies from the rabbit house only two hours before dinner and making away with it towards the kitchen. John left the head of the rabbit in the stew and I found myself unable to look at the pot. But I was keen not to offend him on day one, so I picked passably at the white flesh and feasted instead on the cabbage and roast potatoes and, of all treats, mint sauce.

We shared a bottle of beer ('I never drink alone, but I'll bring it out for guests,' says John) and he told me about when he went to stay with my grandmother at Hay-on-Wye, and they drove down to town with Ben, my grandmother's beloved border terrier, and went to browse in the Oxford Bookshop. Penelope tied Ben to a table leg in the bookshop and said that they could leave him there while they went shopping; so they did and a couple of hours later they climbed back into the car with their stuffed string shopping bags and when they had climbed the hill and driven the mile to New House, they got out of the car and went into the house. Penelope unpacked the provisions and John put on the kettle and then Penelope started shouting, 'Be-en, Be-en, oh, the maddening dog, where has he gone?'

John then remembered and said, 'Penelope, I think we've forgotten something,' but my grandmother said, 'What? No, we haven't, I've everything here,' as she cast an eye over the unpacked groceries. But what about Ben, said John, and Penelope remembered finally, and they had a good laugh at her expense and raced back down the hill in the car to find Ben still tied to the table leg, waiting patiently for his mistress.

'Typical!' said John as he cleared our plates and wiped a splash of gravy off his beard, and then he suggested we might take the minibus down to the chai shop in Mangalamgombu for a nightcap. His number two in command, Paneer Silvam (P.S.), a former Goodwill orphan who had joined the staff, ate with us and drove the bus down the lane.

At Mangalamgombu the chai shop was crowded, but nobody took any notice of John and P.S. and me. They had long got used to the white-bearded Englishman and his friends. The yellow-stained room was wallpapered with old newspapers and magazines: 'Penelope used to sit there always,' said John as I went automatically to a corner seat which looked in on the small, dim room. 'She used quite often to slink off down here for a *masala dosa* or an *idli* off a banana leaf,' he said. 'They became quite familiar with the sight of her.'

All the children lined up to greet us later. 'Good evening, sister,' they chorused. 'Good evening, brother,' they said to John. John left the pits in Northamptonshire to teach, and imagined that his life's work would be in education, but after visiting India in 1965, he says he realized he had a calling, and brought his wife and two sons to south India. 'We came out to work for an organization which was fairly disorganized and there was no job when we reached Kodaikanal. But we could not turn back, so we scrimped and saved and bought three acres here. We built two cottages and looked after a handful of children and we were so poor I walked the two miles to Thandigudi every day to save the 50 paise bus fare.' Slowly Goodwill became established, by which time John did not feel he could leave. After two years they had thirty children with a house-mother to watch over them and they became a registered charity. 'So Pam went back with the boys to Northants and Goodwill grew and grew. It's been a miracle,' he said. 'It's no credit to me, though. All the credit goes to the people – our helpers and friends. I ask them, why do you want to help Goodwill? and they say, "Because we trust you." Never will I belie that trust.'

John chanced upon my grandmother when she came to visit a boy sponsored from Wantage, who was living nearby at Tiraman-golam. She dropped in on John at Goodwill and ended up staying a week. That was in 1979, and every year afterwards she dropped in on Goodwill, bringing boiled sweets for the children and Marmite and English newspapers for John. She always said she had to be getting along, but each time she stayed at Peace Cottage in the Palni hills for longer and longer, roused each morning by the voices of 200 children and sent to sleep each night by the whispering of the animals in the forest.

'I wrote and asked if she would become patron,' says John. 'She didn't reply for a long time of course. She never does! But when eventually she did, she just wrote of course I will as if we were silly to have asked – and that she almost was already!'

Every week, John spends a day visiting the other Goodwill homes he has set up. We went on Wednesday, when the rain did not stop. We drove over the mountains to Oddamchatram where John bought a house off a doctor. He has installed a young Christian couple there and so far there are seven children for them to look after. Monsoon chaos drenched Oddamchatram, where the mud ran in rivers, not just rivulets, along the street and over dead dogs that had drowned. But children played with the empty upturned coconut shells, pretending they were boats, and clerical workers still steered their bicycles to their offices through the mud and Oddamchatram was not defeated by the rain.

We went to Pattiveeranpatti (which means village inside a village) where there are two Goodwill homes knocked together, overseen by a tyrant of a warden with whom John was uneasy. The children looked unhappy and John wanted to sack the warden but was biding time until he found someone to take over.

Our final call was at the girls' home in Dindigul where forty-one neatly dressed and smartly plaited orphans welcomed us royally. We had our fourth or perhaps fifth cup of tea of the day pressed upon us, and were bidden to our seats for a 'performance'. The girls had been practising their songs for a week and ended the recital with a dance followed by an English hymn. 'Sing, sister,' they then cried at me. 'Please sister, sing,' they pleaded. In front of an unfamiliar audience I had to stand up and sing the only song which came into my head which turned out to be 'I could have danced all night, I could have danced all night and still have begged for more . . .' from *My Fair Lady* while my cheeks burned hot and red and sweat prickled under my arms. They roared with approval as I collapsed in a sweat and a dither into my cane chair again, and we managed to slip off before they squeezed another toneless ditty from me.

The next day we went on an outing to Kodaikanal, the former British hill station which the British called 'Kody'. A minister was coming to the district, and though nobody knew who the minister was or from which government department he came, all the villagers had erected bunting all along the lanes and strip-lighting and banners and loudspeakers, and we drove along this avenue of festive decoration – John, number three in command, Shivalingum, and three orphan boys and two girls – all the way there. Kody perches on another Palni hillside about forty-nine miles and 2,000 feet up from Thandigudi (which sits at 505 feet).

John wore a nicely gaudy embroidered shirt in honour of our outing, and with strength and skill he steered the minibus along the mountain road avoiding lorries, buses, donkeys, ponies, calves, dogs, goats, bundle-laden women, school-going children and boulders, past banana groves and coffee fields and forest glades. The vivid blue Morning Glory creeper which my grandmother loved, wrapped itself round every second tree, and as we climbed we came across firs and Scots pines and apple trees with the leaves about to turn gold.

Kodaikanal bazaar consisted of an uphill street lined with vegetable stalls and hotels (what the Indians call hotels are actually eating-houses) and a couple of 'gift' shops. It was freezing cold and drizzling as it might on a November morning in England and it was obvious why the British had chosen the site as a refuge, a home from home. We enjoyed a cup of tea with the Chief of Police, John's friend, and then went to the English grocer's shop where Shivalingum, under John's direction, spent over 500 rupees on familiar things like fruit and nut chocolate and tinned bacon and crisps and ice-cream wafers and plum jam and cornflakes. 'I know

I shouldn't have chocolate, as I must watch my figure,' said John, patting his ample belly. 'But one deprives oneself of so much out here that one needs a few treats.' (Where had I heard that before? My grandmother's like mind must have led to a multitude of treats shared with John at Goodwill.)

We walked up the hill in the rain, through the bazaar and across town to the lake, on the British side of Kody, where the cream-painted Victorian bungalows peep up from behind box hedges and rose bushes border the road. There are ponies for hire at the hundred-year-old Boating Club, where I saw a thin, upright lady leaning against the wall. She had bluish-white hair set in a permanent wave, crowning a powdered, cracked face – a blur but for her vivid pink lipstick. She wore a neat blue suit and a smart patent leather hand bag, of the snapping shut variety, hung from the crook of her elbow; and she stared out across the misty lake, across to the pseudo-Scottish glen on the farther side with a look of such sadness and longing that I knew she must be English. She had the nostalgic yearning in her eyes of someone who had 'stayed on'. John said she was the last Englishwoman in Kodaikanal and that she visited the Christian cemetery every day and spoke to no one at all.

John told me that his own father had been cremated in Kodaikanal; he had come to stay at Goodwill and died when John was visiting England for a month. It was John's wife who made the decision to bury his ashes at Kody, along with the hundreds of other Englishmen who had died there before him. I sat on a low wall by the lake and the children went off to buy candy floss. A village woman came and sat down next to me, and surprised me by bursting out in perfect English: 'My name is Pushpa,' she said. 'I used to cook at the Kody school where the English boys went. Even I can cook pizza and plum pudding! But now there are no English boys.'

My spirits had soared as we had driven up and up into the Scottish landscape shrouded in drizzle and mist, towards the romantic old English outpost of Kody. But it was not Kody any more, it was Kodaikanal again and there seemed little point in trying to summon up again an image of young subalterns boating fresh blondes on the lake or ladies' bridge clubs meeting on the rose-embroidered verandas. There was little point in the pink-lipsticked English lady lingering over her past and her dead relatives, and quite suddenly I was overcome by an urge to get back to England. There comes a moment when there isn't any point in looking back any more and it is time to go home.

The next day, on my last day, an assembly was held to announce the plan which John and I had hatched to commission a stone horse's head in Penelope's name for the courtyard. John gave a short talk about my grandmother and introduced me; however, I was so moved by what he said about her, that when I stood up from my chair to speak I was struck dumb. Two hundred shining, expectant faces looked up at me, but all I could think about was the assembly we had attended back in 1985, a gathering called for the occasion of my grandmother's seventy-fifth birthday.

We had walked up on to the hill on 14 February, the same as any other day. I had picked lantana and ageratum and at breakfast I gave my grandmother a bunch of flowers, a copy of *The Vendor of Sweets* by R. K. Narayan and a bag of acid drops. We had walked into Thandigudi on the sunniest mornings and munched our way through two iced buns apiece with milky coffee at one of the tea stalls. John had cooked us roast beef (a rare commodity in Hindu India) with roast potatoes and cabbage and mint sauce in the evening and then the children had performed a dance and dressed up to sing songs at the assembly. My grandmother had stood up and thanked them and she had almost cried, so moved had she been by their performance rehearsed especially for her birthday. 'I will continue coming here to see all of you every year for as long as I live,' she told them. And they had cheered and looked forward to it, but she never came again.

Yet I was not moved to tears of sadness by John's speech, but to tears of joy, and that is what I finally told the children. 'Think of all the things she gave us,' I said, looking at all those upturned faces. 'Think of the goodness and kindness and open-heartedness she taught us. Think of her optimism and her enthusiasm and her generosity and let's build this stone horse not in memory of her but in celebration of her life.'

CHAPTER XVII
The Last Climb

'I don't mind how many panthers share my lunch as long as I can walk in the blessed shade of their forest.'

ON HER RETURN from India after our trip in 1985, my grandmother decided to sell her house above Hay-on-Wye. She was thinking for the second time about the cash she could release for Paul (who had three children by now) but she was also beginning to find running the house too much; the 'Pahari' style woodcollecting, the snow-clearing in winter, the remoteness, the ponies to look after – all these tasks were taking up so much of her time and energy that there was little time left for writing.

After much deliberation (about perhaps moving nearer my mother, or going to live in India, which would be cheaper, or building a bungalow somewhere) Penelope made up her mind to move into a convent. She chose a convent at Llandrindod Wells where she had been in retreat several times before, and where she made arrangements to move into one of the cottages in the grounds. In that way, she could attend meals and services with the nuns, but still retain a degree of privacy. She also made it quite clear that all her grandchildren were welcome to stay and she even said that one of the reasons she wanted to move there in particular was because of the convent's proximity to the River Wye on which she could take my brothers white-water rafting, so they wouldn't be bored. There was a pleasant gabled Victorian hotel in the town too where any friends could come to stay.

Slowly as the year progressed and New House went on the market officially, my grandmother packed up her belongings. She divided her furniture and pictures and started to hand them on to my mother and to us. She said that she was pre-empting death duties but that also she had no use any more for chattels. I remember visiting in the spring and there being brown paper labels with PAUL written on them tied to particular lamps and chairs, and some of her crockery was already in boxes. Yet she was nowhere near selling the house.

For everyone who came round to view her mini-estate as she called it, was vetted by Penelope herself first. She would ask them pertinent questions as they rounded the landing and if she felt they were insincere or were unlikely to be happy in the house or incapable of coping with the winters in the foothills of the mountains, she would point out the damp patches and tell them that sometimes the electricity was cut off for weeks and that the water from the spring often dried up in summer and that it was unbearably cold in February. She put off a high tally of prospective buyers in this manner and the estate agents who were managing the sale began to despair.

However, buyers' unsuitability was not the only cause of her doing New House down, for though she had chosen to sell and was not under pressure to do so at all, there was an element of reluctance in her going. For she had made a garden there out of nothing and wild though it was it bloomed on the hillside with crocuses and primroses and later daffodils, and in the early summer, her rambler roses were a triumph. She had built a new wing on to the tiny original cottage, in which she always hoped my grandfather would come and stay. She had even sound-proofed the walls of his bedroom so that he could work in silence and not be disturbed by the cars or tractors which sometimes sped along the lane past the house. He had indeed come to stay, but never for very long, and though there was reason in her selling now that he had died, she was also loath to part with the place she had made for him.

At the convent she intended to write the books she had been meaning to write (the horse one and the Raj one) and to be free to travel to India whenever she felt like it. Without a house to worry about she would be able to rush off to Delhi at a moment's notice and leave her books in the good care of the nuns. When she told all her friends of her decision and her family, there was some dissent, especially among the friends who were worried that she might go off into retreat and never be seen again. But she reassured them that she would use the convent only as her base and with the money she was saving and the lack of responsibilities to shoulder, she would in fact be much freer in the future to take buses and trains across England to see them, much more often than they all had been used to. She would keep Bracken, her beloved chestnut Welsh Section C pony which she had reared and broken in, and lodge him with farmers near the convent so that she could ride regularly, and she had no intention of giving up hunting with the Golden Valley Hounds.

It appeared she was taking stock of her life suddenly. She began to order her papers, to slip all her letters into alphabetical box files, and to catalogue her research notes. She arranged to donate her collection of over 10,000 architectural slides to an institute for Asian studies at Cambridge, and she gathered all her loose notes and photographs into labelled envelopes. Towards the end of the year it looked as if a retired colonel (of whom she approved thoroughly) was interested in making an offer on New House and she began to make plans for her next trip to India.

She said she did not feel energetic enough to lead a tour in the spring – it had been a busy year at home, after all – and she planned to go to Simla to work at the Secretariat library on her book about the days of the Raj. As her plans for India came into focus, the deal with the colonel was clinched and New House was sold, subject to contract. They would exchange once and for all after her return from India.

It was in the New Year that Penelope bumped into Christina Noble in London who asked her whether she might possibly manage to lead a Himalayan temple trek in April. The original leader had fallen out and Christina was unable to accompany the tour, which was already booked by fourteen eager clients. Penelope dithered for a while but finally agreed when she saw what little harm there was in the prospect, and that travelling out with the party meant that her return fare would be paid, which made financial sense at least. It was to be a trek over a favourite and familiar route of hers as well, and now that the house was sold she was feeling less encumbered and more energetic; she began to look forward to the expedition. It had been too long since her last trip to India.

It was 1 April 1986, therefore, that Penelope took the train from Hereford station to London, on her way to Heathrow and to India. By chance, she met her good friend Thomas Dunne on the train. They sat together in a second-class carriage for the remainder of the journey.

She said to him, just as they drew into Paddington: 'I think I might never come back from this trip. The funny thing is, if I die on the mountains, I know that everyone will say what a wonderful death I have had. They'll say, what a wonderful way to go, it is just as she would have liked! But I don't want to die now at all, I've so much to do.'

Thomas Dunne thought nothing of it and Penelope departed from London on 5 April as planned, with the West Himalayan Tour party.

On their first night in Simla, the fourteen of them and their leader stayed at Chapslee House with Reggie and Mrs Singh, where Penelope asked them all to stand up after dinner and introduce themselves. There was a doctor on the expedition (who kept having to administer antibiotics to several members of the party who had arrived in India with flu), one American gentleman, two German ladies, two Queen Alexandra Nurses retired from the Royal Navy, a pair of sisters, five more English single people (three men and two women) and a couple in their late sixties from Berkshire, who had been trekking in the Himalayas once already. None of these people had ever encountered my grandmother before meeting her at Heathrow, but after the first evening they all said they felt they could put their trust in her completely.

The following day in Simla, the travellers pottered about on the Mall, acclimatizing, and Penelope disappeared off to see her old friend Mr O. C. Sud at Maria Brothers Bookshop. She had not said a proper goodbye to her family or to any of her friends in England – as usual she had slipped off to India before they noticed – but she went to say goodbye to Mr Sud in Simla, just before the party was to leave the hill station for the mountains: 'I may never come back,' she said to him, but he thought nothing of it at the time.

On the first day of the trek, when the touring party was packed into a stuffy bus with narrow seats, Penelope told them it was not the bus that mattered, but the driver and that he was the best in all India (and the tour members were grateful for the information as the road became increasingly treacherous through the day). After a picnic lunch of hard-boiled eggs and rissoles and oranges at Narkanda, the bus driver turned on to the old Hindustan/Tibet road (the narrowest road in the region with a 1,000-foot drop to the left), and when somebody remarked upon how narrow it was, Penelope apparently told them just to wait until they got to the next stage which was even more terrifying, and that she'd only ever seen the road from the other side of the river and that she'd always hoped she'd never have to go along it. 'So it is just as exciting for me as for you,' she finished. Someone else said she was lucky to be sitting on that side of the bus (the mountain side, as opposed to the drop side), and she replied, 'Not lucky – I chose to sit here deliberately.' To which she added: 'If we do tip over the edge we must all go limp as if we're drunk.'

After eight hours they had covered seventy miles and crossed the Sutlej River to get to Dalash, a village at 6,000 feet in Outer Saraj where the porters awaited them. The porters beamed when they saw Penelope, whom they had not expected, and after an extensive welcome, they hurried to pitch the tents and get supper started in the cookhouse. Bihari, with whom she had trekked many times before, was especially pleased to see Penelope and gave her several hugs. When they were settled and washed after their day in the bus, the tour members ate round the camp fire on that first night out in the mountains and afterwards Penelope talked about Hindu religion and unravelled the mysteries of the Hindu pantheon for them.

The following day after bed tea at 6 a.m. the party addressed a fortifying breakfast of cereal, dried fruit, eggs, chapattis, butter, jam and tea or coffee before starting to walk at eight o'clock. Penelope rode along this first leg, through the forest, past small hamlets and farms and little village schools where the children always came out to wave the party on, and late in the day they came to Shila, where there is a rest-house in part of a Forestry Commission village. Again that night, though sleepy after their first day at altitude, the travellers listened to Penelope's tales of Vishnu and his nine incarnations until they crept into their tents by ten o'clock.

Their destination on the third day of the trek was 1,000 feet higher and Judith Watson (one half of the couple from Berkshire) rode up to Margi rest-house through the woods with Penelope. There were carpets of violets and clumps of primulas spread alongside the track and the day was warm. By this time many of the party members had already formed relationships with Penelope. She found time to talk to them all individually and talked as she rode about her love of India and her adventures and past, and she answered all their questions, however ignorant. Judith Watson says that she seemed to find something in everyone which was what made her an exceptional leader.

Christina Noble had assigned Paddy Singh to the tour, to act as Penelope's support and to assist in organizing the porters and ponies, and often Paddy would take the more energetic members of the team on a more difficult and sometimes a circuitous route, to include a farther temple or a spectacular view. Penelope would bring up the rear on horseback, with anyone else who wished to ride on one of the two extra ponies apart from hers. At Margi, the whole group slept in tents and as they were in possible bear country, Penelope insisted on having her tent pitched as near the fence as possible in the hopes of seeing one. There were no bears in the night, however, although some of the travellers did discover that they had been sleeping on scorpions.

On the fourth day, there was a steep climb to contend with – up to Taralla at 9,000 feet and everyone managed it at their own pace, stopping every hour or so for a rest. Again Penelope rode, but as soon as they reached the rest-house, which was perched some way above the village, she assembled a party of temple enthusiasts and had them follow her down to a temple she wanted to show them in the village. She opened the holy shrine to show her group the god inside and when someone asked her whether they were allowed to do that, she said, 'No, we aren't, but I shall give a tip to Shiva so he won't mind.' They climbed back at dusk, up to the rest-house (where the Watsons had one room, and Penelope the second, with everyone else camping on the lawn) and then washed themselves and their hair in cold water before tucking into the *dahl* and rice and soup and cabbage that the porters had prepared. Edith Schmidt, one of the German ladies on the tour, wrote later in her diary; 'That night we all sat together in the rest-house. There was no light except the burning log fire, and there was the old white-haired lady, sitting in an armchair, her eyes half closed, telling the ancient myths of the land, talking about the gods and the goddesses, their meanings, their attributes, their deeds and adventures. What she gave us was no lecture on history or art, neither chronological nor systematic. It was like painting a picture in many colours, soft colours and strong bright ones as well. Sometimes there was a hidden awe in her voice, giving room to mocking irony in the next (those Indian devis and devas showing somewhat strange behaviour from time to time).'

On the morning of 11 April, Penelope rose exceptionally early and was packed and waiting, sitting on her rucksack outside her room at 5.30 a.m. when Ronnie Watson emerged from his room opposite.

'You're up terribly early,' he said to Penelope.

Somewhat distracted apparently, Penelope replied: 'I know, I feel as though I might be on my way to Heaven.'

The day for all the others began as all the other mornings on trek had begun, with tea and washing followed by breakfast. Spirits were up as everyone was feeling fitter as each day progressed, and this particular morning had dawned sunny and clear. They were climbing higher each day, and learning more about the flora of the country and its legends and history and architecture; the whole party had fallen for my grandmother's charm, and counted themselves extraordinarily lucky to have chanced upon this original, knowledgeable, funny and energetic leader. They anticipated six more days of the pleasure of her company on trek.

After breakfast the party was to begin a long walk and steep climb up to 9,500 feet. Because of landslides and fallen trees, the usual track was blocked, however, and the porters told Paddy and Penelope that the ponies would have to go a much longer way round, about which arrangement Penelope was not at all happy as she had particularly wished to visit a temple at the tiny hamlet of Mutisher which had beautiful bronze door knockers. Mutisher was along the original route and Penelope, determined to get there, said that she would ride as far as she could go along the route and that she was sure the ponies would get through somehow.

There was some confusion about arrangements then, and while Paddy and the doctor, Moira, led the fittest on up the trail to Khanag, where they would stop for the night, several others followed on at a slower pace, and the remaining two said they would stop halfway at Mutisher and wait for Penelope, riding at the rear, to arrive and show them the temple.

Three hours later, with the larger parties way ahead, Penelope reached Mutisher on her pony where the two tour members (one of whom was a nurse) and a couple of the porters were waiting. The temple *pujari* was pleased and overexcited to see Lady Penelope, whom he knew from many former treks and he rushed out to greet and bless her. Then he performed a service of *puja* in her honour, and rang the temple bells.

Penelope got down off her pony and climbed three high steps

up towards the temple. She sat down on the third and she rested her head against the stone wall. She shut her eyes for a moment.

The nurse turned round: 'Come on, Penelope, we've got to make Khanag – let's get going.'

Penelope didn't move. The nurse walked up the steps to her. She shook her, she shouted at her, but there was no movement.

The nurse tried artificial respiration, the temple priest began to wail. Prem, one of the porters, turned on his tail and leapt up the mountain to where Paddy and the other members were waiting on the hillside.

'Come quick, come quick, Lady Penelope, oh, Lady Penelope,' he wailed. Paddy and Moira, the tour doctor, leapt down the sheer face of the mountain, leaving the others confused and worried on the plateau they had reached.

In twelve minutes Paddy and the doctor had reached Penelope, and they pushed through the crowd which had gathered around her. Moira tried again to revive her by mouth to mouth resuscitation, but to no avail. Everyone stood back in shock and the porters began wailing again, but Paddy, taking control, organized some of the villagers to carry her down to Ani, which was thought to be the nearest village. The others, high on the opposite hill, could see to the village with binoculars, but could not understand what was going on. Shortly afterwards they caught sight of a porter, Chem, coming up the hill. He had been sent by Paddy to tell them that Penelope had died at the foot of the temple and that they were to walk on up to Khanag and wait for Paddy there, and that one of the bearers should carry Penelope's belongings back down to Ani.

They still had three and a half hours' walk before them, so after an attempt at lunch, though none of them could eat much, they moved off feeling stunned and bewildered. Meanwhile, Paddy and Moira had found it impossible to contact the outside world from Ani because all the wires were down due to storm damage, so they sent a runner back to Manali (three days' journey at least, by foot) to tell Kranti Singh what had happened, and they began to make their way, with Penelope on the shoulders of the villagers, up the mountain to Khanag.

The others were sitting up at four o'clock in the morning when the cortege arrived at the rest-house. That night they prayed and by dawn they had come to a group decision to cremate my grandmother on a funeral pyre in the Hindu fashion. They improvised a Christian service, using Penelope's Bible as their guide; there were no Catholics among them, and several different nationalities, and they had no prayer book, so they made up the service with things that were familiar to each of them.

The women of the party bathed and dressed her, and the men and the villagers of Khanag gathered wood to make the fire. Paddy told them that the bearers would expect to walk in procession behind the litter but it was not easy as there was no track down the steep mountain to the place they had chosen by the stream. There was a long wait while the pyre was being built by the villagers and porters and the members of the tour party looked for flowers or sat beside the stream in numbed silence. When the pyre was built they were all given small twigs and asked by Kama, one of the porters, to dip them into bowl of water he was holding and to throw them on to the pyre. Then Ronnie Watson took the service.

After saying a few words in tribute to Penelope he read a passage from St Paul to the Corinthians II that they thought she must have been reading, as it was found marked in her Bible. They then said, 'I will lift my eyes up to the hills . . .' and afterwards the Lord's Prayer. They sang the 23rd Psalm and ended with a Hail Mary which Paddy had remembered from the days of his youth at a Jesuit College and which the rest of the party repeated after him.

Being the oldest man present, Ronnie was offered the honour of lighting the pyre, but he waived it in favour of the eldest porter and Paddy who had known her for so long. The trekkers sat by the burning pyre for fifteen minutes in silence before rising to make their way back up the hill to the rest-house, leaving her in the care of the porters and bearers who had loved her and known her. The porters and the villagers then held their own mountain service for Penelope, the Hindus and the Buddhists among them coming together in prayer. They sat in vigil for the remainder of the day and gathered the ashes in the evening.

The party moved on the next day, trekking slowly on towards Manali in daily stages. Kranti (summoned by the messenger) met them en route, and when he came he told them he had in his possession a note which Penelope had left with the British High Commission which stated that were she ever to die in the mountains she wanted to be cremated and have her ashes spread in the Kulu valley.

On Saturday, Bruce Chatwin (who had been travelling in the Mussourie Hills when he read of Penelope's death in the *Times of India*) arrived and he joined with Kranti Singh to scatter her ashes with flowers into the raging Beas River at the bottom of the Kulu valley.

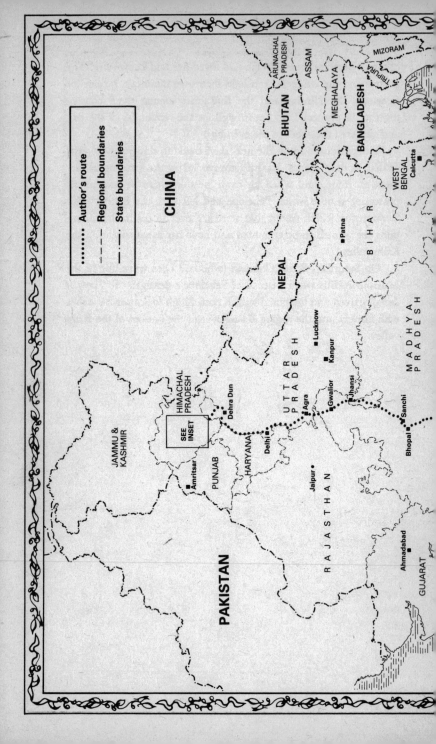

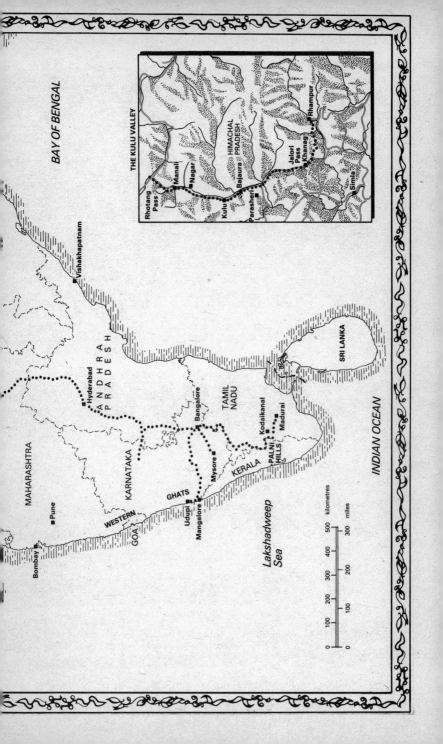

Sara Henderson
From Strength to Strength £9.99

'God, how I loved you, you son-of-a-bitch, Yankee bastard . . .'

In 1959 Sara Henderson was swept off her feet by American war hero and shipping magnate Charles Henderson III, and so began what she calls the world's most demanding, humiliating and challenging obstacle course any human could be expected to endure.

Three years of a luxury expatriate life in Manila and Hong Kong could not have prepared Sara for what was to come. Neither could it have prepared her for her new home at Bullo River – a tin shack in a million acres of red dust.

After twenty years of backbreaking work on this remote Northern Australian cattle station, Charlie's death revealed that Sara had not only been left with a floundering business, but also with a terrifying mountain of debt. With very little to lose, Sara took up the challenge of rebuilding Bullo River. Through sheer strength and determination, she transformed the debt-ridden million acres into a working property worth millions. As a tribute to her resilience she was named the 1991 Bulletin/Qantas Businesswoman of the Year.

Tough, spirited, warm and funny, *From Strength to Strength* is an uplifting story of extraordinary courage and determination.

Le Ly Hayslip with James Hayslip
Heaven and Earth £4.99

The triumphant sequel to *When Heaven and Earth Changed Places*.

Imprisoned and tortured by the South Vietnamese soldiers, sentenced to death by the Viet Cong, Le Ly Hayslip quickly learnt how to survive in war-torn Vietnam. Escaping to the United States, she thought she was swapping hell for heaven.

What she found was a bewildering country of fast food and mod cons where she was still seen as the 'enemy'. Her attempts to fit in only made her seem further apart. Adrift in an alien culture and still haunted by the past, it took all her courage and determination to overcome set-backs and personal tragedy and find in this strange land a home for herself and her children.

Child of War, Woman of Peace is a moving story of reconciliation and hope and an unforgettable tribute to one woman's indomitable spirit.

'. . . bears witness to a traumatic past of both East and West, that cannot be known through formal histories alone' NEW YORK TIMES

'. . . one of the greatest sagas of the '90s' SAN FRANCISCO CHRONICLE

Rebecca Stephens
On Top of the World £5.99

'Pass me a hot toddy! By page nine I had vertigo, by page 36 I had the shakes, and when I came to the colour photographs I just curled up and made pathetic whimpering noises . . . an extraordinary account' VAL HENNESSY, DAILY MAIL

In May 1993, Rebecca Stephens became the first British woman to climb Everest and was awarded an MBE for her achievement. *On Top of the World* tells the story of that historic climb, the courage and determination it took to scale the world's highest peak.

Rebecca Stephens's interest in climbing came surprisingly late, considering her unprecedented Himalayan triumph, when, as a journalist, she accompanied an Anglo-American expedition on Everest's North East Ridge in 1989. Her passion for mountains grew at an astounding rate – in only four years of climbing she scaled some of the world's major peaks: Mont Blanc, Mount Kilimanjaro, Mount Kenya and Mount McKinley. Here, she gives a step-by-step account of the preparation – physical and psychological – for her celebrated feat on Everest, telling of difficulties and fears during the climb, as well as the elation she felt on the summit of the world's highest mountain.

More than a single mountaineering book, *On Top of the World* is an inspirational story of how a woman – and an amateur – faced an extraordinary challenge that changed her life.

'Rebecca Stephens has a fascinating story to tell' FINANCIAL TIMES

'Rebecca Stephens is living proof of how far a head for heights and a taste for adventure can take you' THE LADY

'Gripping stuff' TODAY

All Pan Books are available at your local bookshop or newsagent, or can be ordered direct from the publisher. Indicate the number of copies required and fill in the form below.

Send to: Macmillan General Books C.S.
              Book Service By Post
              PO Box 29, Douglas I-O-M
              IM99 1BQ

or phone: 01624 675137, quoting title, author and credit card number.

or fax: 01624 670923, quoting title, author, and credit card number.

Please enclose a remittance* to the value of the cover price plus 75 pence per book for post and packing. Overseas customers please allow £1.00 per copy for post and packing.

*Payment may be made in sterling by UK personal cheque, Eurocheque, postal order, sterling draft or international money order, made payable to Book Service By Post.

Alternatively by Access/Visa/MasterCard

Card No.   □□□□□□□□□□□□□□□□□□□□

Expiry Date □□□□□□□□□□□□□□□□□□□□

Signature   _____

Applicable only in the UK and BFPO addresses.

While every effort is made to keep prices low, it is sometimes necessary to increase prices at short notice. Pan Books reserve the right to show on covers and charge new retail prices which may differ from those advertised in the text or elsewhere.

NAME AND ADDRESS IN BLOCK CAPITAL LETTERS PLEASE

Name _____

Address _____

_____

_____

_____

3/95

Please allow days 28 for delivery.
Please tick box if you do not wish to receive any additional information. □